Fundamental Moral Theology

Franz Böckle

Fundamental
Moral
Theology

Translated by N. D. Smith

Pueblo Publishing Company

New York

Originally published in German as *Fundamentalmoral*
© 1977, Kösel-Verlag GmbH & Co., München.
Translation © 1980, Pueblo Publishing Co., Inc.,
and Gill and Macmillan Ltd. All rights reserved.

Printed in the United States of America.

ISBN: 0-916134-42-3

Contents

Foreword

There is clearly no end in sight to the task of renewing the structure of moral theology. It should not be forgotten, however, that the builders' hut was not first set up on the site just at the conclusion of the Second World War. Work was already going on even during the Middle Ages, when new elements of style were being introduced in quite large numbers. We should therefore not be anxious if the present generation of architects and builders are trying out their art and skill. We are bound to experiment, to see whether the building can be safely erected and sustained and at the same time to find out whether it can be given a successful contemporary expression. One of the preconditions of such an experiment, however, is that we should from time to time look critically at the building as a whole. This has admittedly been difficult to do over the past ten years or so. Various plans have been submitted and there has been intensive work on certain parts of the building. Anyone who was not an architect or a member of the building trade would, however, not understand much of what had been going on. He would have the impression that whole walls and roofs had been taken away and well-known parts of the structure had been removed and he would inevitably have asked himself whether anything of equal value was ready to take their place. In the meantime, the work of many of the builders has succeeded so well that it is possible to go on a tour of inspection and at least gain some idea of the basic structure of the renewed form of moral theology.

It is chiefly the fundamental problems of moral theology that have been discussed in an international dialogue of specialists over the past fifteen years or so. This discussion has, moreover, not been the exclusive concern of churchmen. Theologians have been encouraged by the Second Vatican Council to enter into dialogue with everyone who is in any way preoccupied with the need to improve social order. The questions — including those asked critically of theology and the Church — are heard. Consideration has been given to the specific contribution that can be made by Christian ethics and to the possibility of a wider social consensus of opinion about fundamental questions of moral norms. In fundamental moral theology as it is at present, we try to introduce important aspects of philosophical, sociological, and theological knowledge into a comprehensive presentation of moral theological principles. These insights should help us to find a well-founded answer to concrete moral questions, an answer that will both be universally valid and also give the individual the latitude and the certainty that he needs in his own decisions. The reader will probably notice that there is no chapter specifically devoted to conscience. This is because I feel bound to leave the psychology of the human conscience to others who are more competent than I am. On the other hand, the whole of the book has to do with moral judgment and its foundation.

I am indebted to many people in the writing of this book. First of all to my colleagues, who will undoubtedly find many of their own ideas assimilated into my writing. I also have to thank many of my students at different levels for their questions and researches, many of which have been very stimulating. My assistant, Gerd Höver, who has been preparing a work on experience and insight into values, has always been available with his specialized knowledge of the social sciences and his constant readiness to check and complete the text of this book. His wife, Ingeborg Höver-Johag, has been particularly valuable in criticizing and improving the Old Testament part. Claire Reiter has been a constant help, not only in typing the whole manuscript, but also in stimulating me and encouraging us all to bring the work to a successful conclusion.

Franz Böckle

Introduction

§ 1 The Concept and Task of Fundamental Moral Theology

A.The Concept of Fundamental Moral Theology

The subject that concerns us here was usually in the past known as general moral theology or the doctrine of moral theological principles. The term "fundamental" has, however, become more and more widely used and is no longer simply applied to theology in the strict sense of the word. We also speak of fundamental catechetics, for example, and fundamental moral teaching or fundamental moral theology. Is it just a fashionable word? I think it is more than this. The change that has taken place in our terminology points to a change in the problem itself. This is in turn connected with the general historical, intellectual, and cultural situation in society. The process of emancipation by which the contemporary sciences have struggled to free themselves from subservience to theology and philosophy was completed some time ago and the process of breaking up into individual scientific disciplines which are autonomous in their methods is continuing apace. Functional thinking predominates in science today. Philosophy is looking for a new identity in the theory of science. Questions of value and meaning are relegated to the prescientific sphere or else only accepted as objects of science insofar as they are hypotheses that can be tested. Nonhypothetical knowledge is not thought to be compatible with a free and open society. In this situation, theology, as a science, is confronted with serious problems. Can it justify itself?

The discussion about the scientific character of theology is therefore of great importance today.[1] In this debate, two questions predominate. The first is concerned with the theory of science and the second is more concerned with methodology. The first question is preoccupied with the relationship between theology and the other sciences. Is theology a science at all? The answer to this question depends, of course, on what we mean by a science. If the object of science is confined to the sphere of hypotheses that can be tested, then theology cannot logically be said to be a science. This radical reduction of the concept of science is based on a position that contradicts the wider concept of human experience. The exact sciences have limited the original, wider meaning of *empeiria* and

1

experientia by referring it one-sidedly to the methods and knowledge pertaining to empirical control.[2] The original meaning of both the Greek and the Latin words points not only to the process of experience, but also to experience as such as the result of many processes of experience. The different levels and aspects of experience have been pointed out by phenomenological studies. There is, for example, at the cognitive and theoretical level, experience that we measure (empirical experience in the narrow sense of the word). There are also the experiences that we have and live at the pragmatical level, and finally, at the level of the understanding of meaning, there is experience that we form and interpret.[3] We are therefore right to oppose any establishment of the concept of science on the exclusive basis of one method. Science as such simply does not exist. There are various sciences and each one of them can, subject to clearly defined conditions, investigate its object with its own precise methods, and the knowledge acquired can be systematically ordered and communicated. The question of the scientific character of theology therefore leads almost automatically to the question of its method. In my opinion, theology should not spend too much time considering the preliminary question as to whether it is one of the noble sciences or not and, if so, what position it occupies within that sphere. It has above all to confront its object — God's revelation in history — and from this determine the methods with which it will be able to communicate its knowledge in a convincing way to modern man with all his questions. But since modern man is inevitably deeply influenced by scientific expectations, theology must take these expectations sufficiently into account. We are therefore bound to try to satisfy this demand, not by a discussion of the part played by the theory of science, but by clearly defining our point of departure, the problems that confront us and the methodological stages that should lead to results.

As far as these questions of method and legitimation concern theology in general, they belong to the classic sphere of fundamental theology. The answer to these questions serves as a basis for moral theology too, since the latter is obviously a theological discipline. It is also an ethical theory and, as such, is concerned with a number of additional problems of legitimation. These problems arise, on the one hand, from the above-mentioned understanding of science which, because of the implied value judgments, either relegates all ethics to the purely subjective sphere or else insists on their being treated only as a hypothesis to be tested. On the other hand, they arise from a distinctive tradition in moral theology that has reached an impasse because it has made certain moral judgments absolute. The objections raised to these and other presuppositions of moral theology, and certain reservations felt with regard to them, do not allow us to confine ourselves to a systematic exposition of the principles that are inherent in the system. On the contrary, we are bound to attempt once again to justify the foundations of a theological and ethical theory against the background of the new historical and intellectual situation today. In order to give expression to this comprehensive intention, I would prefer to speak, not of a teaching about principles, but rather of a fundamental moral theology.

B. The Task of Fundamental Moral Theology

The task of fundamental moral theology is to justify an ethical theory for the establishment of values and norms in the present social, intellectual, and cultural situation and, in this task, to draw special attention to the function of Christian faith.

There may possibly be objections to this definition of the task. The statement of it would seem to suggest that a universally valid ethical theory should be elaborated into which the special insights arising from faith are to be incorporated as complementary and corrective elements. This is not what is expected of moral theologians, who are required to produce a theory of action firmly based on faith and constantly informed by it. Just before the opening of the Second Vatican Council, the demand was made that moral theology should be "an organic structure centered on the revelation of Christ, with a firmer elaboration of the sacramental and ontological basis in the moral subject and a methodically more powerful and more textually critical use of the positive historical sources of Christianity."[4] There was at that time a lively debate among theologians on the principles of salvation history on which this kind of moral theology could be built up.[5] It soon became clear, however, that it would not be possible to formulate a universally valid normative theory on the basis of such slogans as the "imitation of Christ," the "kingdom of God," or "sacramental conformity with Christ." It also emerged quite soon from Karl Barth's idea of christological concentration[6] that the figure of Christ as the

Universale Concretum had to be in opposition to a normative generalization. It cannot be denied that life is given an entirely new direction when a Christian bases his existence on faith and when a person, in his search for God, lets himself be found by God. This means, moreover, more than a new ethical motivation — it opens new horizons and hitherto hidden possibilities of action. But — and this is of decisive importance — these new possibilities are the fulfillment of man's original vocation and indeed of the vocation of all men. There can therefore be no sectarian restriction of the Christian message, which is a universal message for all men. The Second Vatican Council gave a renewed impetus to this universality of the message by insisting on the co-responsibility of Christians with regard to society as a whole. This led to a change of emphasis in Christian theology. Clear recent examples of this can be found in the "theology of the world," "political theology," and "theology of liberation," in all of which there is a marked opposition to restricting Christian salvation to an individualistic perspective. The message of salvation has always to be seen in reference to its social impact. Theology as a whole (and not simply certain special branches of it) has the task of re-defining the relationship between religion and society, Church and society, and eschatological faith and social praxis.[7]

Faith and action, with special emphasis on the public nature of the Christian message, have therefore become the central theme of moral theology. In this, however, moral theologians cannot remain contented with the universal claim that society should be penetrated and formed by the gospel message of liberation. Nor can they be satisfied with the mere task of formulating individual concrete criticisms of society. It cannot be denied that all Christians must commit themselves fundamentally to such tasks as the abolition of racial discrimination, the fight against world poverty, and the protection of the unborn — and the already born — child, but the task of the moral theologian is more all-embracing. Fundamental claims are sometimes in competition with each other; they have to be recognized and rules of action have to be evolved. Moral theology has correctly been seen, since it was first given scientific form by the scholastic theologians of the High Middle Ages, as a normative theory. In other words, its task is to establish, justify, and present a comprehensive system of moral norms (that is, of universally binding commandments and prohibitions). Insofar as it has continued to appeal to the biblical tradition, it has not been able to discern anything in that tradition that was opposed to universally human norms. It has therefore always continued to emphasize the fact that the morality of revelation is the true morality of reason. It is this that justifies our attempt — and indeed makes it necessary — to ask the basic questions of ethical theory and then to question the meaning of Christian faith for ethics.

Any normative ethics has to answer two (or three) fundamental questions. These are: *why* should we? and *what* should we? The second of these questions can be subdivided into two parts: what goods and values (aims) are already given in our actions? (This is the question of insight into values.) How can human activity be judged morally against the background of these insights into values? (This is the question of the foundation of moral judgments.) Moral philosophy today is deeply concerned with this second question about the possibility of a rational justification of universally binding moral judgments. It is a question that to some extent dominates in ethical debate. It will therefore inevitably be present in our own search for an answer.

1. The Question of the Ultimate Basis of Moral Claim

Instead of asking about the ultimate basis of moral claim, we could well ask about the basis and limits of man's moral autonomy. This is also the special concern of our own enquiry. It is a simple matter of course for theological ethics that the ultimate basis of man's moral obligation is found in God's radical claim imposed on man. But everything depends on the way we understand this divine claim. It can only be understood properly if it is seen as the universal sphere and the ultimate foundation of human freedom. Man's dependence on God and his autonomy are not mutually exclusive. Since Kant, autonomy has meant man's determination to define himself as a rational being by his own doing. This interpretation of man's autonomy to some degree determines his ethics. It is a proclamation of freedom from the restriction of alien authorities. It would seem, however, that this takes the ground away from under the feet of all religious morality. It would be dishonest not to admit that many forms of the mediation and justification of the Church's moral teaching can only with difficulty be united with this theory of autonomy. One can speak of a heteronomous morality based on commandment. Laws — commandments or prohibitions — that are communicated to us by nature or the biblical revelation are regarded as an expression of God's will that is always valid and inviolable. These laws are norms of the divine law that are guaranteed by God himself. On the other hand, however, it can be demonstrated that this is not necessarily the case and that it does not in any sense correspond to the classical pattern of Catholic moral theology. On the basis of faith in God's creation, we ought rather to see man's ethical task in his moral self-determination. Man is certainly not free if he lets himself be determined by mood or arbitrary decision. He has to act according to rational laws and norms. But he would also not be free if these norms were imposed on him from outside. He has to set himself such norms, not arbitrarily, of course, but in freedom. This very freedom reveals itself to him as a task, but it can only do this if it is given to him and he has given himself to it. Moral duty does not arise as a result of a conglomeration of necessity and chance. The moral law, as rational, is ultimately based on the special mode of man's being — that is, finite reason, which finds itself confronted with the task of realizing freedom in the world. We respect the philosophical conviction that nothing more can be said about this. All that we can do is try to demonstrate how our faith in God does not put an end to our duty to realize our freedom in this world, but rather justifies our giving of ourselves as free, rational creatures. We do not need to presuppose God in order to impose commandments or prohibitions, but we are convinced that a recognition of creation and a knowledge of our own state as creatures are the basis of our duty to exercise our freedom rationally. We also fear that without this — and therefore, in the last resort, without God — everything would be the same to the autonomous will. And that would be a threat from within to autonomy.

This basic question of the relationship between theonomy and autonomy will be discussed in chapter 2 of the first section of Part One of this book. But the answer that is elaborated there is of decisive importance for the whole project of fundamental moral theology that is developed in the book.

2. The Question of the Justification and the Claim to Validity of Moral Statements

The question with which we are concerned here is a materially ethical one: How can we know what we should do? And what validity can normative judgments have? Since Max Weber's postulation of the need for value-free research,[8] it has become widely accepted that the ethical question of the justification of moral judgments should be excluded from scientific investigation. Any discussion of the foundation of moral norms is bound to be irrational because it will inevitably be based on subjective evaluations and views that are restricted to certain groups. An evaluative attitude may well have effects on man's actions, but it may also be neither true nor false.[9] In the meantime, analysis of moral language has revealed the special character of prescriptive statements and has also pointed to the conditions that are necessary for subjective justification.[10] In addition, in practical philosophy (within the framework of the constructive theory of science) a search is now being made for a method of rational argument for concrete aims and corresponding modes of action. In other words, more objective or better forms of intersubjective or transsubjective validity in particular value judgments are required. The point of departure in this search is that the person who asks: What should I do? is usually in a situation of decision-making and wants to know which of the possible actions that are open to him "are/is from the transsubjective point of view, the best or, more precisely, which alternative has, again from the transsubjective point of view, the predominant reasons in favor of itself, if indeed there is any question of predominant reasons."[11] Help can, however, only be available to that person if he considers, in open dialogue in a "good reasons approach," the for and against for one and for the other possible action. On the basis of this situation, the conditions that are necessary for a community of communication can be worked out and in this community certain aims and models of action should be presupposed for a universal rational discourse.[12] Potentially all partners who are ready for such a discourse can be included in such a community of argument and communication. In this way, a "justification can be understood as a rational dialogue (or the project of a rational dialogue) which will lead to the consent of all concerned that the orientation in question can become a matter of consent for all those involved in a situation of communication that is not in any way distorted or faked for them".[13]

I mention this project in some detail because it is valuable to our discussion of the justification of norms in moral theology and the aims of fundamental moral theology as such. It ought by now to be clear that what we have in this method of moral argument is a model of a rational way of solving the problem. This is not in any sense a negative qualification. Mankind's apparently almost insoluble problems and conflicts (overpopulation, mass hunger, protection of the environment, problems of minorities and so on) call for a rational organization that is recognized by as many people as possible so that it has at least some chance of success. The obvious presupposition that there must be a community of argument and communication and that the mutual consent achieved among the members of that community is bound to be hypothetical because new and better insights cannot be excluded is not a fundamental objection. Enough examples of a similar way of solving the problem (problems such as self-defense and the right to wage war, religious freedom and minority questions) have been supplied by the Church's traditional moral theology in the course of its long history. Its rules applied until new insights into changed circumstances called for a new form of safeguard or a new definition of the goods and values in question.

We have referred to "goods and values" and this makes it clear that a pure model of argument based on reasons and counter-reasons can never be sufficient for a normative theory. Our insight into goods and values must be clarified before we can achieve a balanced assessment of man's action. We must know what man means to man. This, however, is not possible without recourse to an all-embracing anthropological understanding of man. There are therefore two interrelated tasks included within the one task of justifying norms. On the one hand, we have to develop and justify the goods and values that are relevant to human action and, on the other, we have to develop and justify concrete judgments about actions. We can therefore make a brief and simple distinction between insights into values and moral judgments.

a) What I mean by morally relevant insights[14] is our knowledge and our ascertainment of non-moral values. (These can better be called pre-moral values.) In manuals of moral theology, it was customary to speak of *bonum physicum* in contrast to *bonum morale*. In this context, "physical" means something that is not seen as having its origin in man's free self-determination. "Moral" (*bonum morale*) is always related to action. Strictly speaking, only man's action can be evaluated morally. His action realizes value. In the case of insight into value, we have a knowledge and an assessment of certain data that are significant for man and his behavior, that are taken into account in his action, but that do not immediately produce concrete rules of action.

A judgment by which values are ascertained is therefore not a moral judgment, however significant it may be for the moral act. In this sense, the value that is automatically attributed to every man (human dignity as a so-called symbolic value) is a fundamental and pre-moral value. Human society and its institutions are also such values. Human sexuality and its meaningful aspects, physical integrity and property can be regarded as such values too. I would suggest that these data or realities, which do not exist as qualities of the human will, but are previously given in our action, should be called quite simply "goods," as distinct from certain value concepts that are, as a kind of stereotype, related to a value-realizing act. In this way, the value that we call "faithfulness" is an expression for man's readiness to keep a promise. What we have here is a value that is related to action and therefore moral. It is not only obligatory for human action, but also indispensable. "Justice" therefore means a firm will to give to each man his own. I would suggest that the concept "values" should be used for this.[15] These moral values do not, however, point to any concrete moral judgment or concrete rule of action. Seen from the normative point of view, the question that is of most interest to us is when a promise must be kept and when it will not incur the criticism of lack of faithfulness if it is not kept. In a moral judgment, this has to be clarified. An ethical theory has to be concerned, in logical priority, with the knowledge and ascertainment of these goods and values that underlie action. No ethical theory can do this entirely on its own. The different humane sciences can provide it with a great deal of help. It must not, for example, begin at zero with the justification and development of morally relevant insight. The task with which it is confronted has a long historical background, in which practical experience, revelation, and faith all play an important part. We shall give our attention to the development of insights into values together with the factors of development that we have mentioned.

b) The justification of concrete moral judgments is nowadays of central concern in moral theology. Traditional moral theology claimed absolute validity for certain moral judgments. It was taught, for instance, that to tell a falsehood could never be permitted, even if that falsehood meant saving the life of an unjustly persecuted man. A false statement or a sexual act that did not have procreation as its aim were regarded as absolutely wrong in themselves (*intrinsece absolute inhonestum*). There could never be any reason under any circumstances for justifying such actions. This absolute validity of a judgment about a human action, whatever the case, the circumstances, or the consequences, is disputed by many moral theologians today. What is not disputed is the fact that the objective moral quality (the transsubjective justification) of an action depends on the good to be realized. The present-day moral theologian does not question the basic teaching that *actus specificatur a suo objecto*, but he believes that a conditioned, contingent good cannot determine the action absolutely. The justification and validity of moral judgments has, however, to be analyzed exactly. The debate taking place at present about this question has striking parallels with the discussion that was conducted in America about utilitarianism and the question of "deontological" or "teleological" ways of justifying normative judgments. Our task will be to point to relationships and distinctions in these propositions and to clarify the independent position of a theologically based morality. With regard to method, I am bound to point out that the two parts of the question "what should we do?" — that is, the question of the genesis of insights into values and the question of the justification of moral judgments, will not be dealt with strictly within certain chapters. These two questions are continually related to each other and yet have to be again and again distinguished from each other. I shall be constantly alert to this reciprocal relationship between the two questions especially when I am dealing with the sources of our

10

material norms (Scripture, human experience, and the teaching of the Church).

Part One

Man between Claim and Fulfillment

Section One: Claim

My aim in this first section is to discuss the question of the ultimate ground of the moral claim made on man. This is, of course, the same as the question of the ground of man's responsibility, freedom, and autonomy. As theologians, we believe that we know that ultimate ground. We believe in God as the ultimate ground of our freedom. As theologians, we also want to speak about God and, what is more, not simply as a synonym for rationally based human praxis. In calling God the absolute ground of our freedom, we mean more than simply a life trusting the sufficient good will of others to collaborate in the shared attempt that is necessary if rational life is to be achieved. God is, for us, not simply the interpretation of the "objectively rational life." [1] An unconditional claim of the kind that is made in the sphere of morality calls for an absolute point of reference as a ground. In my opinion, there is no such point of reference in this world. I do not, however, conclude from this that the only possible claim is hypothetical. This may be consistent in a world without God and it cannot be denied that we live in an increasingly hypothetical civilization, [2] which is the result of a (hypothetical?) decision to limit reality to what is accessible to hypotheses that can be tested. It seems to me that a meaningful and human way of life presupposes nonhypothetical approaches to reality. [3]

We should not, however, begin this section with assertions and counter-assertions. We know how easy it is to misuse the name of God in an attempt to claim divine authority for human laws. Theological ethics are always suspected of heteronomy. Many of our contemporaries outside the Church (and in it) can conceive of a theologically based morality only as a morality of commandments and prohibitions with a directly divine justification, in other words, as a collection of divine commandments. The attempt to explain theological ethics theonomously and to some extent autonomously is usually not taken seriously.

For this reason, I shall proceed cautiously. I shall begin with an analysis of the phenomenon. Everyday life is full of expectations and obligatory claims. There are many different kinds of sentences containing the word "should." This is a fact that is beyond dispute.

The validity of prescriptive statements can be bracketed together in an attempt to create a theoretical distance, but, as we shall see in the first chapter of this section, the factual existence of claims to the validity that is expressed in them cannot be disputed. One question at least must be asked of this fact: Should that which is regarded as something that should be, be, and why? I shall also try to explain how the consciousness that something should be done is constituted and whether the absolute nature of the moral claim can be satisfactorily justified. (This will be done in the second chapter.)

CHAPTER 1: OBLIGATION AS A PHENOMENON

The phenomenon that we shall be considering in this chapter is so widely recognized as a fact that it can be quite satisfactorily discussed in a few carefully chosen comments. We are not exclusively concerned with the fact alone, however, but also with the distinctive and many-sided character of the phenomenon itself (§ 2) and with its necessary prerequisite, man's consciousness of action and his ability to decide (§ 3).

§ 2 The Distinctive Character of Normative Reality

A. The Existence of Many Forms of Obligatory Claims

The empirical evidence of everyday experience points to the existence of many different kinds of obligatory claims as a constant and universal fact. Human life bears the normative imprint of verbal and written rules, table manners and ways in which people associate with each other, moral commandments and prohibitions and many other human precepts and regulations. Since we rely to a very great extent on social institutions we follow these rules almost without question.

I propose to call the whole complex of cultural, economic, legal, political, and religious structures together with our personal relationships, in which our attitude is deeply involved, the "reality of action." This reality of action is that aspect of the real that is marked by man's will and also refers decisively back to his will. This reality of action is, generally speaking, the object of the social sciences, which are in this way objectively separated from the natural sciences. The natural sciences are concerned with physical reality and try to grasp that aspect of reality that does not in fact belong to man's will itself and make it available to man's will. Research into the many different aspects of the reality of action by sociologists and cultural anthropologists has shown that man's life with his fellow-men in all societies is deeply impressed with norms and that there is also a necessary structure of human praxis. Human society requires a normative orientation, in other words, human action has to be guided and stabilized by valid standards and obligatory claims which act as a guarantee for human behavior. According to philosophical anthropology, this need is based on the fact that man is impelled to take up a position with regard to himself and fashion his life.[4] Because of his instincts, he is not fixed and immovable. He moves by his action in a sphere of possibility and actuality. This raises him above the level of a purely natural attitude and makes him a civilized being. At the same time, however, because of the same instincts and impulses, which he has to excess; he is subject to considerable stress. Symbolically (verbally) mediated rules of behavior and models of decision-making are therefore a necessary condition of his practical pattern of life because they relieve the pressure and set him free.

On the other hand, however, this anthropological view of man is too individualistic and has to be extended to include man's constitutive sociality.[5] Human praxis is, as interaction, essentially sociopolitically mediated. This has resulted in the need for a universally obligatory structure of modes of behavior and their trans-subjective justification. This in turn requires a reconciliation between conflicting interests and needs in the motivation of action. The mediation between praxis and norm takes place above all in the language of morality. An analysis of that language, which follows, will give us an insight into the formal meaning of obligatory claims.

B. The Meaning of "Should" in Moral Language

Attention has been drawn in recent years by linguistic analysis to the diversity of expectations and claims made in everyday language. It has even been said that a moral language is contained within everyday language. This language includes "those words, sentences and links between sentences that prescribe human actions."[6] Obligatory claims are not only found in sentences that show themselves, by their grammatical form, to be prescriptions or commands. They are even more frequently encountered in a concealed form in statements expressing a value-loaded comment or a value judgment. When someone says, for example; "It is good to tell the truth," this value judgment usually means; "It is good for one to tell the truth," or, "One should tell the truth."

What is the meaning of this "should"? An answer to this question is sought by linguistics. By taking language as the place of knowledge, the study of linguistics is concerned on the one hand with the question of the meaning of sentences containing value words such as "good" or "should" insofar as an obligation is expressed in one form or another; and on the other hand with the question of where the obligatory ground of claims expressed in this way can be found.

1. The Content of Moral Language

As far as the content of this moral language is concerned, the initial assumption that these sentences have an irrational character and are therefore "theoretically meaningless" can be regarded as invalid.[7] Is the meaning simply to be found in the fact that emotional attitudes can be expressed by those using language in the various elements of moral language — without any linguistically verifiable circumstance?[8] Or do commandments, prohibitions and promises, for example, belong to the sphere of "what one is doing in saying something"?[9] This would mean that there would, strictly speaking, be no moral communications. According to J. L. Austin, these are "illocutionary actions" that bring about, in connection with locutions, certain obligations.[10] We have therefore to question the validity and justification of moral statements. The only decisive elements, then, are the conventions and the context of verbal actions. "According to Austin, the case has already been decided. There are no moral statements. There are no moral communications, either in intention or on the basis of the content of statements. . . . The search made by the logician for ideal unambiguous language, clear criteria and — ultimately — moral principles is futile."[11] The obvious conclusion, then, is to cease worrying about moral language.

R. M. Hare, who was himself a student of Austin's, has, however, disputed his teacher's view, showing that the distinction between descriptive and prescriptive sentences that was almost abolished by Austin has a legitimate existence. Words like promise, obligation and so on (the so-called illocutions) also occur in negative and interrogative sentences or are used in the past tense (Mr. A. promised yesterday . . .). It is therefore impossible to say that the speaker of the sentence quoted is carrying out a promise. The expressions in this way acquire a constant meaning (they have "sense and reference"), with the result that sentences in which such words occur can be interpreted and analyzed as sentences of prescriptive language.[12] According to Hare, prescriptions express evaluations, in which things, people, or modes of action are judged as capable of being preferred or disregarded in any process of choice. The person making the evaluation refers to implicit or explicit standards of value or maxims of action and expresses, with such value predicates as "good" or "correct," or quite generally with "should," what the person who wants to act correctly must choose. The meaning of "should," then, which is prescriptive, is to be found in the fact that something is recommended to someone as preferable in a possible choice.

2. The Possible Ground of Obligation

It is important for us to recognize the prescriptive meaning of the word "should," because it provides the clue to the linguistic analysis of the phenomenon of obligatory claims and their mediation. This, however, also raises the question as to which binding force is peculiar to such claims and how this binding force is attributed to them. It is, in other words, a question of the ground of the obligation mediated in these claims. It is one of the fundamental insights of moral philosophy that an obligation as such (regarded in the formal sense: "that I should" and not "what I should") cannot be inferred from a mere description of facts. In other words, expressed in a more modern way, prescriptive sentences cannot be deduced from exclusively descriptive premises. This is a statement with which Hare would agree completely. For him, the ground of obligation is to be found in an obligation carried out by the speaker or by the one who hears a prescription and consents to it. For Hare, this is to some extent an act giving meaning that determines the meaning of the prescription itself.[13]

There can be no doubt that the unconditioned nature and the sincerity of the carrying out of the obligation is a necessary condition, but it is not a sufficient one, since the possibility of making the maxims universal and the universal equality of all men can also be included in this process of carrying out an obligation. The very demand that it should be made universal is in itself a moral rule. "There must be universal moral principles if the subjective justification and the logical deduction of any individual prescription are to be complete. It is extremely probable that the principle of universalization and that of the equality (of all persons) are such universal moral principles. Both principles play a very important part in Hare's theoretical argument and we obviously have to recognize them."[14]

It would, however, seem that these moral principles cannot be demonstrated as being universally valid obligations simply by applying the methods of linguistic analysis. This does not, on the other hand, entitle us to regard the question of the justification of obligation as irrelevant and to turn simply to an attempt to justify concrete suggestions for action and rules intersubjectively.[15] As we have already pointed out, this cannot go beyond hypothetical statements. Once again, then, we see here that the objective justification of a concrete rule in a similarly objective process of justification (by considering the reasons, for instance) is one thing and a search for a universally valid, unconditioned moral principle that forms the basis of obligation is another. This is ultimately the question of our insight into the categorical situation of being commanded in a universal commandment. What has therefore to be elucidated is how our consciousness that something should unconditionally be done is constituted and this will be done in detail in the next chapter. In the meantime, however, the concept of "norm" and the psychological presupposition of freedom will be explained.

C. The Concept of "Norm"

As we have already seen, the reality of action is the object of the social sciences. In methodical self-limitation, they concentrate on the task of defining and analyzing normative reality. They try to separate the normative element and define it conceptually. They also try to understand connections and interpret developments. The social, psychological, and economic conditions of human action are investigated with these aims in mind. In this way, a universal definition of the concept of norm can be reached and used in ethics.

1. In a Sociological Definition

Sociologically norms are called "concrete rules of action or behavior" which "claim validity" in a particular society and "have the opportunity to be accepted." This is known as the process of internalization.[16] In this very universal form, the concept of norm is understood as a kind of generic concept in which various types of norm are subsumed.[17] Examples of these are custom, laws, directives, conventions, and fashion, as well as the criteria of decision-making. The free behavior of persons as members of a society is regulated in a special and universal way by all these forms. It is, for example, clear that the behavior of the members of a closed society, in which moral claims are based on traditional values, is regulated mainly by custom and conventions. "Custom" is a collective conviction based on traditional experience and traditional norms.[18] Experience and tradition act as unquestioned principles fashioning the details of everyday life. Custom is to some extent, as Max Weber pointed out, lived and therefore bears its own justification in itself. Morality takes place by a process of adaptation to custom.

In an open society of the kind in which most people live in the West today, the situation is very different. Our understanding of ourselves is determined by our openness toward a constant supply of new information and a corresponding change in our attitude. We cannot simply take what is commanded in the concrete from "mores." We are invited to judge concrete human action morally. This is evident from the fact that our insights and our opportunities to shape our own lives and our environment have become much more abundant. Even more important than the many complications is the fact that a new kind of normative guidance from outside has taken the place of custom in the form of fashion. A praxis of social behavior which can no longer be determined by traditional contents, but incorporates "the value of new, convincingly modern and creative stimuli in an extremely plural way"[19] has come about with the claim to validity of fashion. In contrast to custom, fashion provides much wider scope for personal differentiation. It also creates in the individual the idea of self-determination, but at the same time frequently puts an end to this by its value as a stimulus. The individual lives to some extent as though he were in a self-service shop where free self-determination allows him to choose anything in the range of his imagination, but in fact in making his decisions in this way he is being obviously influenced.

2. A Systematic Classification and Interpretation

A systematic classification and interpretation has been attempted by various scholars, who have developed various theories about these phenomena and processes.[20] Such efforts try to clarify the influence of different social factors on the validity and development of values and norms. It is, however, not possible to justify the evaluations themselves. The simple fact that certain social norms are valid or that they are subject to change when they are influenced in certain ways tells us nothing about whether they are legitimate or binding. If knowledge of these aspects is required, we have to look critically — and that means, in this case, evaluatively — at the reasons for their validity. In view of our aims, as outlined above, we have the task of laying the foundations for such evaluation in this work of fundamental moral theology.

3. The Connection between the Reality of Action and Moral Reality

The social phenomenon is clearly directly related to the moral reality. Because it is related in this way to man's free will, the reality of action is at the same time a moral reality. There is, in other words, a fundamental interdependence between sociality and morality. This reality of action, understood as an already given reality, can be seen as a model of action on the basis of which moral possibilities — what can be — can be formulated and made present. The same reality, understood as something that has again and again to be brought about, also continues to be a plan of action on the basis of which moral obligations — what should be — must be confirmed or substantiated. Whereas the social reality, seen as an already given model of action, provides a point of departure for empirical and analytical sociological study, the problem of social ethics in the widest sense arises in the concept of this social reality as a plan of action that has to be carried out.

The separation of these two spheres is based on the difference between empirical and normative knowledge. In the empirical mode, it is not the content of truth or the ethical obligation of the reality of action that is in question, but only the empirical phenomenon and the empirical presuppositions of the factual reality. In the normative mode of knowledge, on the other hand, an evaluative standpoint has to be taken up. Man's rational will is repelled by, corresponds to, or identifies itself with the will that is always present in that reality. If, however, the reality of action is not only a firm model, but also a plan of action that must, within the sphere of what should be, be substantiated or developed further, this cannot be done without the use of an evaluative judgment. It is therefore not disputed that evaluations are involved in social structures. What is disputed about social structures is whether the limit of what can be expressed scientifically is reached with what can be expressed empirically. In this conflict, it is ultimately a question of the scientific character of social ethics and the checking of the nonempirical aspect of the social phenomenon. The adherents of a purely empirical concept of science relegate the process of making value judgments to the prescientific, subjective sphere that lies beyond the reach of reason.[21]

§ 3 Freedom of Choice as a Precondition

Man's ability to make free, responsible decisions forms the precondition for the possibility of his moral behavior. The earlier philosophical dispute between the determinists and the indeterminists has been outstripped by the contemporary discussion about the problem of freedom. Modern man, who has been educated in the natural sciences, is, on the one hand, aware of the fact that he can only think as long as his brain is functioning. On the other hand, however, he also knows that he is in the position to think about this materially conditioned aspect of his thinking and to know about that aspect. He can therefore behave in accordance with that knowledge. It is on this basis that he is able to guide and correct the biological conditions governing his physical life. Man is a thinking being who is conscious of his distance from the "how" that makes him dependent on the apparatus governing his thinking. He is therefore able to try to solve the problem of freedom neither by defending an indeterminate freedom nor by supporting a total determinism. Insufficient justice is also done to man as a real, concrete being by Kant's distinction between a noumenal freedom of the acting will on the one hand and man who is marked by natural causality on the other. Modern man no longer regards determinism and freedom as mutually exclusive opposites. He is less interested in philosophical arguments than in finding an explanation for his own consciousness of human life. Helped by the different humane studies in which such advances have been made in recent years, he is conscious of the many ways in which man, who is one, is determined. He is, however also aware of the possibility of manipulation and that he is responsible for what he makes of himself. In view of this situation, W. Schulz regarded it as meaningless "to try to help modern man's consciousness by pointing to his freedom or his being determined in the abstract. . . . We have rather to recognize the legitimate claim of the open dialectics of freedom and the lack of freedom, which cannot be closed in an abstract, theoretical way, and regard it as the anthropological sphere of ethics that can help man to greater freedom."[1]

A. Consciousness of Action in the Dynamic Relationship of the Experience of Activity and Passivity

Human experience is determined by two apparently opposing phenomena — activity and passivity — and we are bound to ask how we are able to experience ourselves as active and passive at the same time in the one person.[2] In the first place, this experience is the result of spontaneous, willingly active self-expression. This does not take place simply in the sphere of the subconscious. It is a knowing activity that includes acts of knowing and enquiring. It is also accompanied by an experience of causality and judgment. Man experiences directly that, in connection with his action, something else is made of something, so that he can dismiss his own action. It is here that the experience of causality takes place most strikingly. In all that we do in life, we experience prototypically what causality really means. An element of spontaneity forms part of our activity, so that the man who acts experiences his action in connection with a judgment. In other words, he believes that it is good to act in a certain way and not in another way. This "good" has an explicitly or implicitly comparative character.[3] "Good" then becomes "better than." The explicit nature of this judgment differs according to the situation of the action. In one case, it can take place in a relatively long process of coming to judgment. In another case, this judgment comes down to a single reaction. What is essential is that spontaneity and judgment come together in the unity of personal activity that forms a constitutive element in personal freedom of choice. It therefore appears in the first experience as the "power of self-achievement in a sphere of changing possibilities."[4] On the other hand, there is also the opposite experience of the limitation of our possibilities, the experience of passive suffering. No choice is a choice made on the basis of a beginning without any presuppositions. We bear the imprint of our birth, constitution and environment and the society in which we live has a constant effect on us. No act pointing to a complete freedom of choice has a pure beginning without any preconditioning. Our choices are made on the basis of presuppositions and previously made decisions, which themselves determine the decisions that are made later. Every act that is felt to be free is involved in a mesh of previously experienced decisions, actions, omissions and so on and every apparently free act similarly determines and limits the freedom of every subsequent act.

The correct distinction and orientation of our experience of activity and passivity is the key to our understanding of our freedom of choice. In the first place, passivity can be seen as a limitation of freedom. Where activity is discontinued by passivity, all choice is made impossible and freedom is therefore discontinued. Passivity, however, belongs to our understanding of the freedom of the creature. Only an act of divine freedom — a *creatio ex nihilo* — has to be understood as a pure activity that is not in need of resistance. In the human sphere, an understanding of freedom that provides a choice of unlimited possibilities would appear to be an imitation and a perversion of divine omnipotence. In human experience, then, activity has always to be balanced by passivity. Passivity is not so much a limitation as a condition of the possibility of activity. A readiness that is determined by our environment underlies the impulse and the judgment of our will. This environment is not simply calculable. It is a fragment of history, from which the individual is always receiving both unexpected and expected experience. "Readiness is tense. The tension is released when something new occurs in a given situation and changes it. It is then that the activity that is latent in the readiness is set free." Freedom is therefore an "answer to a concrete challenge, the solution to a problem which admits not of one solution, but, because of its very nature, of several solutions."[5] The human person must develop in such a way as to be able to deal with what is encountered in the world. The activity of choice is balanced only by the stimulus of passivity. In this way, it retains its creative impulse by discovering new possibilities of choice, by which the other acts that are performed in life are determined. The effects that are opposed to the activity of self-achievement are therefore not simply limitations to human freedom. On the contrary, they provide an opportunity and even a condition for the possibility of that freedom.

B. The Anthropological Basis

The dialectical experience of activity and passivity that determines our freedom has its basis in the distinctive character of human subjectivity.[6] Man experiences himself in and through his intersubjective conditioning that is revealed in corporeality. As a unity of soul and body, the "one, real man can be understood as completely soul and completely body. Both stand, as completely human definitions, for the one, complete man himself."[7] The body is an original aspect of man into which he is always admitted whenever he determines himself in his actions. Body and soul are not physical parts of man, but metaphysical principles interpenetrating each other in the constitution of man's being. The relationship of the unity and the difference of body and soul in the one human being is dialectical. The non-identity of soul and body is based on the unity of spirit and matter in man. Man is a person only in this unity and wholeness. According to scholastic philosophy, in which this unity is stressed, these two metaphysical principles (spirit and matter) are essentially different. How can this essential difference in being be understood without falling into an absolute anthropological dualism in which spirit and matter are seen as disparate realities and the unity of man that has hitherto been so strongly emphasized is once again radically questioned?

If we are to answer this question, we must combine the dialectical relationship to which we referred above and the scholastic ontology together with its idea of participation, according to which a being is all the more present here and now, the more fully it participates in being. A participation in being and the act of being are parallel. A difference in degree in the participation in being therefore also constitutes a difference in being — the difference between act and potential. The relationship between spirit and matter has therefore to be developed and understood on the basis of this difference. A pure spirituality without reference to materiality then appears to be impossible for a created spirit, insofar as this spirit is determined by the potentiality in its distance as a creature from absolute being. "This means that the human spirit finds the completion of its spirituality in its unity with the body, with the result that the human spirit as such does not simply become more and more spirit, the more it becomes separated from the body, but rather the more it embodies itself."[8]

We are able to understand the inner dynamic tension that is present in our experience of freedom more easily in the light of what is said above about the structure of human corporeality. On the one hand, it is clear that passivity is not a limitation, but a condition for the possibility of freedom. The more we recognize the determining factors and influences, the more the sphere of freedom is able to grow. On the other hand, however, we also know how much our freedom is threatened from within and from without. The human body is not only the constitutive medium for man's being. It is also the medium for other, alien influences. When man is in his body, he is with himself and at the same time in alien territory. The experience of being and having body is a clear expression of this situation. "On the basis of his corporeality, man's understanding of himself is in a constant constitutive interaction with the world as the quintessence of what is previously given as a natural or supernaturally conditioned situation for his self-expression and of what is imposed on him. Man's corporeal being is therefore again and again threatened constitutionally from without and his freedom cannot be preserved by autonomously excluding or suppressing this uncontrolled exposure to danger; it can only be maintained by obedience, by inwardly consenting to what is inevitably imposed from outside and, in a word, by accepting suffering."[9] This situation of being threatened becomes more acute when we remember that the world situation is not neutral, but is deeply marked in advance by alien decisions made in freedom. This situation "therefore always affects man's subjectivity, which is ecstatically inherent in the world, with definite tendencies and impulses."[10]

C. The Consequence for Human Action

Human actions performed in freedom, man's moral act (*actus humanus*), have therefore to be judged accordingly by moral theology. If it is regarded as a purely spiritual act, accidentally confined by the body, that moral act would be fundamentally misunderstood. Both the inner human act (*actus internus*) and the outward act (*actus externus*) are essentially corporealized acts. If these acts were not corporeal they would not be human. In an attempt to clarify the distinctive aspect of corporealized human will, a distinction has been made between an originally intelligible act of freedom as such and its corporealization.[11] On the one hand, it should be noted that these two aspects of the one act are not separable. "Man's act of freedom is never absolutely creative in the sense of a pure existentialism. It is always essentially also a subjection to the laws of matter of free action (man's nature, his corporeality in a metaphysical sense, the nature of the world)."[12] On the other hand, however, the intelligible act and its corporealization cannot be identified, insofar as the spirit-soul is not simply a form of the body. "This means that there is a real and distinctive dialectical tension between what is freely willed as such and what is done in freedom, in other words, what is expressed by the human person into the dimension of nature . . . is an expression and revelation of this decision made in freedom in man's spatio-temporal materiality, his 'visibility.' It is at the same time also a concealment of this original act of freedom itself because it is different from the original freedom."[13]

In other words, the moral act takes place at the point of intersection of activity and passivity, of what is done and what is imposed and of what belongs to the subject and what is alien to him. The usual battery of concepts used in moral theology and law (compulsion, error, ignorance, etc.) is clearly insufficient to explain the diminished responsibility that emerges from this deep anthropological insight into human acts of freedom. There is a fundamentally ineradicable ambiguity in human activity and this applies to the one who acts and to the one who is outside. We can also see in the corporealization of human will the reason why man (in contrast to the power of decision that is assumed in the case of the pure created spirit) always has the possibility of venial sin. This can ultimately be traced back to the limitation of moral decision (*imperfectio actus*) that is made possible by corporealization.[14]

28

D. The Claim of Freedom of Choice

Man himself is involved personally in this freedom of choice. Choice is not meaningful in itself and free will is not a mere turntable on which man can move as he likes or arbitrarily say yes or no to God and the world. Freedom of choice is aimed at man. It does not take place in a choice between objects, but is fulfilled as the self-expression of man who chooses objectively (as *reditio completa subiecti in se ipsum*). In his freedom, man is confronted with a task. He has to decide freely. This necessity of choice means that freedom forms part of its definition. As a person, man always has a relationship with himself. He is able to make a distance between everything and himself and between himself and everything. He can even make a distance between himself and himself.[15] Because he is in this way raised out of himself and is not simply available as things are, he has "to be." He has "to gain a new closeness to himself from the distance from himself and to give himself the concrete form of himself."[16] He is therefore unable not to decide, since not deciding corresponds to not wanting to decide and therefore to a decisiveness of freedom. The necessity to have to decide is not opposed to freedom. It is rather its essential characteristic (essential freedom).

There is no necessity in the question as to how one should decide. Man has the possibility of deciding in one way or in another. If he wanted, for example, to leave the "how" of his decision to the arbitrary fortune of pure chance, he would cancel out his freedom in self-contradiction. He would submit himself to an alien determination and in this way negate freedom itself. Arbitrary choice is clearly not a mode of freedom.[17] The only meaningful course of action is to choose freedom. In drawing attention to a connection in meaning and to the consequence of meaning, we bring into play that special form of necessity that we may characterize by the concept of "obligation" or what should be done as distinct from what must be done.[18] Obligation is directed toward freedom and aims to lead the freedom of indecisiveness to the freedom of decisiveness. The obligatory claim presupposes in every case the psychological freedom of being able to decide differently, but it does not permit the (moral) freedom of being permitted to decide differently. Obligation evokes the freedom to decide for a certain possibility and against other possibilities. Freedom to decide presupposes the freedom to plan different possibilities.[19] The possibility that is distinguished by obligation, however, seems to be the only possibility of freedom. The acquisition of freedom is therefore the secret motivating force of free decision. Man is essentially free so that he may become existentially more and more free through his decisions. (This is existential freedom.)

What, then, is this ultimate form of freedom that calls on man unconditionally to obligation? Is it simply his autarchy? Or is it the freedom of the individual or a freedom that is made real for society in history? We shall later have to discuss this question at some length, concerned as it is with the ground and the limitations of moral autonomy. Here, however, we can say this with certainty: "The choice of actions and of beings to whom those actions refer is preceded by a basic choice that can only in the strict sense be called decision — the choice of what we really want to be, the plan of our own essential form." [20] This includes a distinctive interpretation of the world, our position in the cosmos, our relations with our fellow-men, and our understanding of society and its institution. It is a decision to accept a hierarchy of values, an order of preference in which we perceive a guarantee of more freedom. Our own personal freedom is to be found in our freedom to make this decision. It is within the freedom to decide in this way that the values that determine individual actions acquire their motivating force. [21]

CHAPTER 2: THE GROUND OF OBLIGATION

We are able to say here, as a result of our considerations so far, that both our everyday experience and our reflective consciousness of action are aware of the phenomenon of obligation and claim. This claim is mediated in moral language. Sentences containing the word should usually give prominence to a statement about how a right choice should be made in a situation involving decision. We should not overlook the fact that, in such statements, there is also an obligation to choose and decide, at least in the background. The ability to decide involves man himself whenever he expresses obligations to himself and others. It would seem that an act of self-obligation or a fundamental decision of freedom is the indispensable presupposition for our understanding of the phenomenon of obligation.

We are therefore bound to ask such questions as: what is the nature of this fundamental decision? Clearly, what is at issue here is a fundamental act of moral self-determination on man's part. But what is this self-determination or autonomy that is demanded on so many sides? Is it a question of the self-constitution of man's self as a free subject of morality? Or has it to do with the claim of the empirical subject to the free and independent satisfaction of his needs? In this chapter, we shall examine critically the various ways in which these claims to autonomy are expressed (§ 4) and then we shall pay special attention to the problem of the extent to which our contemporary understanding of autonomy can be justified with theological ethics (§ 5). To summarize the contents of this whole chapter, we can say that in it we are looking for the ground and the limitations of moral autonomy. In other words, we have to deal with the ultimate ground of the obligation of man's moral claim.

§ 4 The Claim to Autonomy

Modern thinking is above all characterized by its emphasis on autonomy. The concept of autonomy as such is not new. In Greece, where it originated, it pointed, since the middle of the fifth century b.c., to the aim of the city-states to be able to determine their own affairs independently of another power.[1] During the period of the religious wars in Europe, the concept of autonomy also came to mean a claim to confessional self-determination.[2] Kant later used the concept in his philosophy, thus raising it above the level of institutional self-determination (independence, sovereignty) to that of a fundamental human claim.

Now, autonomy means man's possibility and task, as a rational being, of determining himself and of being in harmony with a law that he has given himself. The greatest common denominator in this modern claim to autonomy is the rejection of every kind of alien determination or heteronomy. Why should heteronomy be so feared today? This question evokes different answers, some of them mutually contradictory. Is it because there are so many different desires which have an effect on man and threaten the autonomy of his pure rational will? Is heteronomy to be found in dependence and being, determined by needs and society? Or should we not look precisely at those human and social needs for the point of departure for man's liberation from heteronomy? Does the flight into subjectivity and abstraction not lead to man's alienation from himself and society? Does man acquire his freedom as free self-determination by transcending his needs or by developing and satisfying them?

These are all questions arising from the claim to autonomy. It is also clear from a study of history that the "constitution of the self as a free, self-conscious subject, which regards itself as worthy of notice, insofar as it is the originator of the law to which it submits itself," is subject to a process "which is always unthinkable to itself in its origin and its end."[3] The main aspects of this historical development will now be outlined in order to clarify the claim to autonomy.

A. The Autonomous Subject

In a process of Copernican change, Kant and the philosophers of idealism who followed him turned their attention to the human subject. Man was no longer regarded as a whole being, but rather as an object of finite subjectivity. Subjectivity became the central interest of philosophy. In the first place, attention was devoted to knowledge and will. The Kantian critique of reason proposed a differentiation between appearance and the thing in itself. There was also a corresponding distinction made between the "empirical" subject, accessible to contemplation, and the "intelligible" subject, accessible only to a specific type of reflection. In this "transcendental" reflection, attention was given to the conditions of subjectivity and its knowledge and this made it possible to think about the reality of the consciousness and reason as freedom. In this context, autonomy was seen as a fundamental condition of the intelligible subject. As moral autonomy, it meant the binding of the subject to the law of rational self-determination.

1. Immanuel Kant

Kant is the originator of this approach in which the autonomy of nature, in the sense in which this was understood by such philosophers as Leibniz and Wolff, was abandoned in favor of the autonomy of the subject.[4] It was Kant, then, who brought about this anthropological change in thinking. His point of departure was not the claim that man, acting, fitted into the peaceful harmony and perfection of the universe, but the question of the self-justification of knowledge and the binding of the will. The distinction between nature and reason[5] and between the empirical and the intelligible subject was for him of decisive importance. In man both were present: he was at the same time nature and reason. Kant believed that man himself was a world of the senses and because of this exposed to the natural mechanism of desire and inclination. At the same time, however, he was also a member of a world whose being was determined by absolute freedom and reason in its universality and necessity.[6] As a rational natural being, man was able to "overcome the impressions made on his capacity for sensual desire by ideas of a more remote kind of what may be useful or harmful."[7] According to Kant, then, man was able to determine himself by his intelligence in the choice of his actions. In this way, he could break through the immediacy of sensual compulsion, although he still remained in a comprehensive way within the circle of natural things. This kind of freedom — which Kant called *arbitrium liberum* or "free arbitrary choice" or "practical freedom" — was, he taught, revealed in man's daily experience.[8] It did not, however, form the basis of man's real dignity as a rational being. As such, he remained therefore necessarily subjected to alien purposes. As a rational being, Kant insisted, man had to be understood as a purpose in itself. This raised the question as to whether (and how) human will, striving and acting, could be determined by reason alone. Kant concluded that this was only possible if the will, in identity with the reason, gave itself, independently of all objects of the will, the law. Moral autonomy was to be found in this self-determination of the will that, by the universal law of reason, was free of all puposes. Seen in this light, autonomy was not the arbitrary choice of the individual subject, but the binding of oneself to the law of reason. "Kant's problem of autonomy as the law of reason with regard to desire is not concerned with man's possibility of choice with regard to various objects of desire. It is also not concerned with the rejection of or the preference for certain aims in action with reference to whether those aims can be achieved, whether they are useful or whether they are harmful, however much that rejection or preference may be guided by reason. . . . It is also not concerned with practical instructions for action in order to achieve an aim. . . . On the contrary, Kant's problem of autonomy in the practical sense is concerned above all with the possibility of a will or a pure practical reason."[9]

The highest principle of morality could be found, for Kant, in this process whereby reason, as will, gave itself a law. Man was in this way raised above all determination by nature. Autonomy, as the transcendental idea of freedom, also raised man above himself (as part of the world of the senses). Kant saw autonomy as the determination of the transcendental (intelligible) subject, binding him to an order which could only be considered by intelligence. For the theoretical use of reason, then, the idea of freedom was simply a possibility open to thought, whereas for the practical use of reason freedom was clearly necessary, so that pure morality might be possible as the self-determination of the will.

In this way, Kant was able to connect the moral law with the idea of the will of a rational being. It thus has the dignity of the necessary and universal validity of reason. If, however, we are concerned, in the case of this rational being, with a subject whose will is not as such in accordance with the essence of reason (this is so in the case of man, who always continues to be a sensual being), then the principle of morality acquires the character of an unconditioned claim. In other words, it is expressed as a categorical imperative: "Act only in accordance with those maxims through which you can at the same time wish that they were a universal law."[10] According to Kant, this imperative, in which an obligation was originally expressed, is a "practically synthetic sentence *a priori.*" This *a priori* aspect is the result of the direct connection with the rational will itself. The synthetic character "results hypothetically from the concept of a will which does not automatically realize the law of reason, but experiences it as a commandment of identification of subjective maxims with the objective principles of reason factually on the basis of the idea of man who knows himself to be the point of intersection of two realms."[11]

In this analysis of reason as the basis of the moral law, Kant completely neglected empirical sentences, which could never claim universal validity. The only sentences that might be universally valid were those that were in a relationship with the transcendental level. Kant, however, went far beyond this transcendental level and stated a material principle by declaring explicitly that "man and every rational being exists as a purpose in itself."[12]

In his foundation text, he took as his point of departure the contact with the substantial being (the "I in itself") which was given in the spontaneous consciousness and from which the idea of morality and that of the moral law resulted. In his later writings, however, Kant tended to use another approach, according to which the categorical demand of the moral law was regarded as a fact of human reason which was theoretically not deducible, but which, in order to be meaningful, presupposed the autonomous law. Kant in this way made freedom and autonomy postulates raised by the moral law.[13] Not the theoretical I, but only the moral self was thus able to understand itself as freedom and mediate a real access to the intelligible ground of its being.

In speaking about the fact of the moral law, Kant was not referring to an empirical fact. For him, it was a fact of pure reason, a direct consciousness, simply given to finite reason, not as something alien, but rather as the product of that reason. Its ground had to be sought in the special mode of being characteristic of human reason itself. "Whereas the theoretical I . . . persists in complete uncertainty about its origin, the form and content of the moral law provide the practical I with a certain indication of the absolute autonomy of its intelligible being, without in fact opening this to a theoretical insight. However paradoxical this may seem, human reason is a factually previously existing possibility and a factually previously existing claim that can only prove that it is real through the act that calls for the ground of its possibility to be deduced from itself, but cannot in fact infer it."[14] Kant cannot give a metaphysically satisfactory answer to the question about the ground of the obligatory character of noumenal being for man.

2. J. G. Fichte

Fichte was not satisfied with Kant's conclusion that the autonomy of intelligible being should remain an unfathomable postulate for theoretical insight. The moral law, as a fact of reason, had also to be considered and justified theoretically. The whole sphere of freedom and interpersonality had to be revealed to knowledge. Fichte's point of departure was the expression of moral existence in man's moral consciousness, within which, he believed, the moral will could be experienced directly and the knowledge of pure reason could become capable of knowing itself. This was an important step in the development of the philosophy of subjectivity. What

Fichte tried above all to do in his scientific teaching was to interpret man's being as a whole from the point of view of his subjectivity. The world had to be understood as the product of an absolute I. Man's intelligence, his I and his reason were, for Fichte, as the absolute, "pure activity"[15] or "action" which "presuppose no object, but produce it."[16] If, however, the I assumes the world, it can fashion the world within the laws imposed on it by the I in an *a priori* assumption. Because of this, scientific teaching led, in Fichte's case, directly to moral teaching. The moral world that is obliged to be had, in fashioning the world, to be applied to the given world.[17] The content of the moral law was therefore what was to become eternal through us and our freedom from the spirit.[18] Nature was, in Fichte's teaching, related to this as "suffering matter without any inducement to be so."[19] In his moral doctrine (published in 1812), he linked together the realization of the common moral consciousness and the historical human race,[20] maintaining that the fulfillment of morality was the aim of history. In this, it was possible to know where the human race, that had until then been educated by God, itself took over "its own education with freedom and unmistakable art."[21] The human race, raising itself to the morality of the whole, is to some extent the "great universal I." The morality of the individual I is therefore to be found in the fact "that it becomes, as a subject, the organ and the expression of the absolute life that is orientated toward the whole and also toward the fulfillment of mankind in its aspiration and that this absolute life is moving, in the element of the moral aspiration of the individuals, toward its ultimate aim."[22] This allusion to the "absolute life," the organ of which the moral subject was to be, means that Fichte was considering here the ground of unconditioned obligation. The concepts of light and life mediate theoretical and practical reason to the unity of knowing activity as a subject. They also function as a unifying force among the multiplicity of rational beings, each of which is an I and free.[23] Light and life have an absolute character in their mediating function. Fichte defined the relationship between this absolute character and reason dialectically, saying that it was both immanent in reason and at the same that it absolutely transcended it. Insofar as life was immanent in reason, it was subject to the conditions of interpersonal difference in freedom, in other words, it could only be realized subject to the difference between a free call and a free response, both of which leave the person free. As an absolute, however, it functions constitutively for the state in which the self is recognized and wanted. "This absolute that makes absolute mediation possible was called God by Fichte and was also identified by him not with the God of metaphysics, but with the God of the fourth gospel and therefore with the understanding of God in the Judaeo-Christian tradition."[24] This God did not, according to Fichte, have an influence on men and human history from outside. On the contrary, he realized himself subject to the intersubjective conditions of reason and freedom, the ground of which he was himself.

3. G. W. Hegel

The moral teaching of Fichte that was based on the theory of science was intended to overcome the distance between ethics and reality. Insofar as this speculative theory of science is not determined by history, the moral law cannot attain reality with the applicative concepts of the transcendental system. The ideal structure is indeed opposed to the historical and social reality and there is no mediation between them.

Hegel attempted to do away with this opposition and to provide mediation by giving serious consideration to the relationship between subject and object or between the consciousness and its object.[25] Experience of the human consciousness shows that, whenever it confronts an object, it only encounters itself and that it can only know of itself what it finds in another. In any other object, then, the subject understands itself in its own self. Subject and object are in this way so interwoven that the definition of the one is at the same time also the definition of the other. An encounter in thought, involving reflection about the subject and the object, can therefore do away with the opposition between the two. In accordance with the basic structure of dialectical tension, the self can be unified with itself in another. The perfect mediation between the consciousness and its object is attained only at the highest level of absolute knowledge. Absolute knowledge and knowledge of the absolute are identical. The absolute — the spirit — is always already with us in the process of thinking. According to Hegel, then, the relationship between subject and object had to be seen within the all-embracing context of the spirit. The spirit is the quintessence of all reality as such.

Because of this approach to the question, Hegel was critical of Kant's and Fichte's insistence on the absolute autonomy of the subject as developed in their philosophies based on reflection about the nature of subjectivity.[26] According to their teaching, reason appeared to some extent to set itself free from the better aspect of itself and posit this "as a beyond in a faith outside and above itself."[27] Instead of including experience of the negativity of the absolute in their thought and trying to do away with the subjectivity of the absolute idea, they made this subjectivity absolute. This fixation on subjectivity isolated it and inevitably led to an abstraction from the reality of history. A neglect of the infinite also led to a loss of the finite. In Kant's philosophy, Hegel found "a formalism of jurisprudence and morality without vitality and without truth."[28] In the philosophy of Fichte, through "the absolute subjectivity of reason and its opposition to reality . . . the world of reason is opposed absolutely, thereby absolute finiteness without reason."[29] As a consequence of this system, the legal structure and the state were bound to be a "being for itself and absolutely opposed to vitality and individuality."[30] In contrast to this dualism of legalism and morality, Hegel developed a doctrine of the state, according to which man, in his morality, became the subject and ground of legal and state order. In so doing, he was able to go beyond the opposition between subjectivity and nature and the individual "by understanding the family, middle-class society and the state under the heading of morality as the historical institutions in which morality and man's attitude toward his actions are realized and achieve reality in the unity of the object and the subject."[31]

In criticizing the autonomy of pure subjectivity, Hegel did not intend to abolish the autonomy of reason. On the contrary, his aim was to save it. He therefore opposed the exclusion of the absolute as something unthinkable. He recognized the autonomy of the subject (the subjective spirit) "as the form in which the divinely realized freedom of man from the world appears in history." He denied it, however, "insofar as it aims to make itself absolute independently of its being concretely mediated."[32] If it did this, it would be self-contradictory. In connection with his criticism of this attempt to make autonomy absolute, Hegel also criticized the abstract nature of pure subjectivity and the loss of reality associated with this. He claimed that concrete reality should be understood as a process in which the subjective spirit and the objective spirit functioned as mutual mediation. By the subjective spirit, Hegel meant the individual I or man as an individual; by the objective spirit, he meant the entire good of a given culture (its languages, customs, laws and so on). The subjective and the objective spirits presupposed each other. "The individual can only come to himself if he is mediated with the goods of his culture and if this happens in such a way that he penetrates fully into what has been handed down in the tradition of that culture and thus becomes an integral part of the transcendent aspect of that tradition. These cultural goods, however, do not exist in themselves and in isolation from man. They are only real because of man and only live in his knowledge and activity."[33]

In this way, Hegel directed his followers' attention emphatically toward history and at the same time involved history closely in the process of subjectivity. He recognized the autonomy of the historical subject (man) and at the same time relativized it. The degree to which it continues to exist alongside the idea of the absolute spirit, which, as the world spirit, is the real actor of history, is the same as the question as to whether finite man is able to accomplish the infinite event of the spirit.

B. The Autonomous Reality

Hegel contrasted abstract and formal autonomy with the reality of history and society. He rediscovered man in his historical mode of being. An individual separated from history and society was, for Hegel, alienated from himself. According to Hegel's idealistic view, history was the development of a single absolute idea. World history was, for him, the history of freedom that had realized itself. It was this aspect of his teaching that was so criticized. Karl Marx and others went much further.

1. The Autonomous Social Process

Karl Marx criticized Hegel for the abstract nature of his philosophy, despite his criticism of the philosophy of reflection. He insisted that "Hegel's view of history presupposes an abstract and absolute spirit which develops in such a way that mankind is only a mass bearing it up consciously or unconsciously. Within empirical, concrete history, he therefore allows a speculative, esoteric history to continue. In this way, the history of mankind becomes a history of the abstract spirit of mankind existing on the far side of man as a reality."[34]

Marx therefore re-examined the real subject and the aim of history. Only man could, in his opinion, be that real subject and he could not be it simply as an organ of the world spirit.[35] Real man had to pass through real history and in it his self-consciousness would be set free. A mediation of opposites in a purely spiritual process was not enough. This mediation had to take place in history — in other words, it had to be brought about in the concrete by society. Marx did not aim simply to interpret history — he believed that "it was essential to change history."[36] Man had to come to terms with his natural and social environment. This process was determined by his needs. For Marx, the primary historical act was the production of means for the satisfaction of the basic needs of life and the production of new needs connected with that satisfaction.[37] The real motivating force of history was, in his view, to be found in the satisfaction of needs and the production of new needs. In view of this, work was not only a means to life — it was also the primary need of life.[38] This called for the free development of needs in a social order in which it was possible to achieve a balance between the various needs and their satisfaction. This development had been, Marx believed, fundamentally distorted by the capitalist system of production and its aim to produce illusory needs. In this effort, capitalism had been helped by the needs favored by religion and the promise that they would be satisfied in the hereafter.

Marx's solution to this problem was to correct the balance by an intervention into the historical process. This could not be done by any individual. An appeal had to be made to the proletariat or working class as the real historical subject. The proletariat had become totally alienated by the capitalist process of purchasing the labor force. It had therefore to be set free by an opposite process in which it would regain consciousness of itself. It would only be as a class that had once again become conscious of itself that it would be able to regain control of the history that it had in fact made. "In socialist society, in which the aim and condition of production is greater satisfaction of the growing needs of all employees, the tendency toward an increasing complexity and universality of needs can only be brought about as an organized process supported by careful planning. This is the case not only with individual needs, but also with the whole system of needs, from the carrying through of a socialist idea of consumption to the development of work or labor to the primary need of an fully evolved socialist personality that is, however, also rich in needs."[39]

According to Marxist theory, need provides the necessity for human activity and is therefore the constant condition of the objective laws governing the evolution of society. It is in a state of dialectical unity with the demands of society. Because of his need, man is embedded in this evolution of the system of needs.[40] He is both the subject and the object of an autonomous social process. The claim of obligation therefore arises from the inner logic of this process.

2. The Autonomy of Values

M. Scheler and N. Hartmann were primarily opposed, in their "material ethics of values," to formalism in ethics. They also did a great deal to change our understanding of the nature of autonomy. They contrasted the autonomy of ethics, that is, a world of material *a priori* values, with the ethics of autonomy, that is, the pure morality of an autonomous subject. In this world of values, ethics have their own sphere of autonomous objects. We may attribute a value quality to someone bearing a value when we make a value judgment (for example, we may say that Jack is brave). We can only do this on the basis of an insight into the value content of that particular value quality. According to Scheler, that value content determines the value predicate (or value concept) and this is not dependent on whether it is attributed or not to a bearer of value. A "material apriority" lies behind the value concept.[41] This material aspect of the value is given intuitively and is also quite translucent in its givenness. Insofar as the value is known as a value, it belongs to the sphere of what ideally should be. The obligatory claim therefore communicates itself directly and clearly with the insight into the value itself. And insofar as the insight "only follows the immanent law of the emotional acts of insight themselves,"[42] the act of insight mediates an autonomous claim. The autonomy of the person can therefore only be a consequence of the act that reveals itself to the *a priori* value. On analysis, however, we are bound to ask whether the identification of what is meant by the value predicate with a value quality in itself does not underlie the problem of

41

the normative claim of expressions of value.[43] "Why what is regarded as 'what should be' in fact should be and even should be in
itself cannot be explained on this basis. . . . It ought, however, to
be possible to explain how a thinking or regarding acceptance of a
content as a consciousness that something should be done can be
constituted."[44]

C. Autonomous Praxis

It would seem that it is not possible to do justice to man's desire
to be responsible for himself and the world either by referring back
to pure subjectivity or by exposing him to autonomous processes.
Modern man, who is conscious of the limits of what can be done
and of the compulsions exerted by contemporary social structures,
inevitably asks whether moral autonomy is not bound to remain no
more than a dream. Theodor Adorno believed that this was a myth
or a fragment left over from the Enlightenment that was not fully
understood. Is modern man's claim to autonomy only "an attempt
to replace the original feudal form of government by his own rational control communicating itself through the market"?[45] Is it
enough simply to take man out of the rational sphere of aims and
the domination of social compulsions and guide him toward a free
and independent satisfaction of his needs? We are bound to conclude that the problems raised by our technical civilization cannot
be solved in this way and that we must look for a rational solution
to those problems.

1. The Autonomy of Praxis

The debate that has taken place in recent years about the theory
of science has shown that scientific rationality cannot be based
either on a formalization of linguistic operations or on an empirical
verification of the theoretical armory used. On the one hand, K.
Gödel and A. Tarski have demonstrated that "no formal system
can be closed in itself and that we must always go back to the
linguistic activity in the communicative praxis of subjects if we are
to justify the formal system at all."[46] On the other hand, it is possible to object to the thesis of physicalism of the Vienna circle[47]
because of its insistence "that concepts must be used in science
that can be traced back, not directly, but only partly to an empirical
basis."[48] The knowledge that the closed circle of an empirically verifiable and formalized, ideal single language must be opened again

and again at the level of metalinguistic communication if we are to justify its rationality at all presents us with a fundamental difficulty in positivistic thinking. This difficulty was brought out by Wittgenstein who, in his later philosophical writings, opposed "the ideal of a single unified language copying the world"[49] and went back to the "praxis of the use of language"[50] as the ultimate basis. Among those who took part in the discussion about the theory of science in relation to the pragmatics of language — that is, the relationship between language or linguistic action and the subject using language[51] — there was sufficient agreement about J. L. Austin's theory of the linguistic act, according to which "all speaking, even representative and affirmative language, has a permanently intersubjective character as an action"[52] for it to be regarded as providing the necessary point of departure for an intersubjectively verifiable rationality.[53] The communicative action of the subjects thus becomes the ultimate ground of reflective and rational activity, in other words, the autonomous ground of that activity. Expressed in a more precise form, this means that autonomy is based on the socially mediated praxis of subjects acting communicatively. However important this reference back to praxis may be for the constitution of theoretical systems, we can only become aware of the full extent of this measure when we include the normative implications of communicative praxis as well. If we consider the structure of everyday linguistic communication, we recognize that, in every interaction, "valid claims for truth, correctness and truthfulness are made and are understood as such,"[54] even if they are not made explicitly. The question then arises as to how these claims can be justified and this leads at once to the question about the normative element of communicative praxis. If normative claims are to be justified rationally at all, "the only way that this can be done is to derive the criteria for the legitimation of those claims from the structure of reciprocal and reflective communication itself. And this means, at least in this case, showing that, in the elementary process of communicative activity, mutually normative presuppositions are made and accepted, on the basis of which the communicating partners commit themselves as soon as they have entered into communication."[55] This in turn means that the question of the justification of normative claims presupposes the transcendental philosophical question of the structure of obligation of communicative praxis and its justification. In other words, the jus-

43

tification of normative linguistic praxis presupposes the justification of that praxis itself.

2. The Justification of Praxis

If the basic structure of communicative activity is analyzed, it becomes apparent that a community of communication is only possible when the participants accept each other as having equal rights, recognize the claims made by others at various times, and are prepared to justify their own valid claims. These basic rules of argumentation form what are known as the normative element of the community of communication or the "pragmatic universal norms." [56] If this basic norm is constitutive for the development of an argument or for the conditions governing its critical possibility, then the valid claims (for example, the concrete moral norms) can only be justified argumentatively provided that the basic norm can be justified as a necessary condition.

It should therefore be clear that we are concerned in this section not with the question as to the methodical means by which norms can be justified, but rather with the question of the status of the basic norm of all argumentation. It is precisely this status that is challenged in the present debate. The representatives of value-free empirical pragmatics maintain that this normative element can be regarded as a quasi-institutional fact and can therefore be justified by its pure expression in praxis. [57] Others have tried to exclude this question and to limit themselves to a practical and rational solution of the problem in communication that is free of control. [58] A failure to attempt to justify the pragmatic universal norms, however, does not solve the problem of justification, but, on the contrary, makes the recognition of these basic rules of argumentation an arbitrary act. On the other hand, the representatives of a transcendental and normative conception try to demonstrate that this normative basic structure is the *a priori* condition of all meaningful argumentation. According to K.-O. Apel, for example, at the beginning of all ethics — that is, of all argument about moral claims to validity — there is the "evidence that every possible partner in discussion (that is, everyone who is able to raise the question of a possible justification of the intersubjective validity of norms) has already recognized the pragmatic universal norms of ethics (as conditions governing the possibility of meaningful argumentation)." [59] Apel was of the opinion that only a transcendental reconstruction of the subject and his reason by himself could provide evidence of this type. Only a transcendental pragmatic reflection about the *a priori* intersubjectively valid ethical norms, in other words, a reference back to a transcendental justification of the universal ethical norms that are necessary for the bringing about of all communication, can justify the claim to recognize the basic rules of communication. The question about the ground of obligation is therefore posed in the case of the theory of communication as a question about the ground of the recognition of the pragmatic universal norms of ethics. For Apel, this recognition was a principle of reason that is implied as a basic norm of the ethics of the unlimited community of communication in all argumentation. It is the necessary "obligation of all who argue to the idea of the 'discursive redeemability' of all normative claims to validity according to whether it is possible to universalize intersubjectively the interests represented by those claims."[60] This principle, which includes the free obligation of all subjects to recognize all their partners in communication and justify their own claims rationally and argumentatively in the discourse, in other words, the will to "continue the action of consensus,"[61] has, for Apel, "not the character of a fact in the sense in which this term was used by Hume, but rather the character of a fact of reason, in the sense in which Kant used the phrase."[62] Since the recognition of the basic moral norm is constitutive for the meaningfulness of all communication and also for man's understanding of himself, Apel has concluded that "the acceptance of the basic moral norm has the character of an obligation, at least on condition that the questions in a fundamental philosophical discussion — and indeed any questions at all — should be asked meaningfully. This presupposition, however, is not the condition of a hypothetical imperative, because it cannot be meaningfully negated if the discussion itself is not to be discontinued."[63] If, then, this acceptance of the basic moral norm as a fact of reason is in every case an obligation, then the human subject has to be understood, for the purpose of constituting human communication, as a claimed being, a being who is already claimed again and again.

What is the basis of this obligation? For Apel, its ultimate ground is a fact of reason. It is questionable, however, whether it is possible for this basic moral norm to be made compellingly clear in the intersubjective sense to every person on this basis. For Apel himself, it was subject to the condition that questions should be asked meaningfully. This presupposition is certainly not that hypothetical imperative, since what is involved here is the possibility of meaning as such. But is the claim that questions should be asked meaningfully not in its ultimate necessity unfounded, if an absolute meaning is not positively presupposed, a meaning that conditions the possibility of every constitution of meaning? Does the self-reconstruction of reason not make the acceptance of an absolute necessary, an absolute that is the ultimate ground of its being already claimed again and again and that is able to justify in a compelling way recognition of the basic moral norm? Was it really a "metaphysical dogmatic remnant"[64] when Fichte, in his attempt to reconstruct reason via the "action of the I" arrived at the "absolute I" of God, which was, as an absolute, the ground of the human I which created meaning and was at the same time hidden? I shall attempt to answer this question in the next section.

§ 5 The Theological Justification of Moral Autonomy

Modern man has made himself the subject of history by claiming autonomy. He is conscious of no longer being embedded in a static world order. He feels that he is responsible for himself and is ready to accept his historical and social destiny. In this Copernican revolution, is there still a place for God? There is certainly no place for a superpower intervening arbitrarily in the course of events in the world. There is also no place for a supreme moral authority acting as the author and guarantor of the moral law. And yet the idea of God still preoccupies every thinker concerned to lead man to a recognition of himself as a self-conscious, autonomous subject. Almost all such philosophers find that there is no end to the question of finite freedom and ultimately acknowledge that the claim made by this freedom and its fulfillment call for a basis in the absolute and infinite.

It cannot, however, be denied that religious faith was quickly recognized as an obstacle by man in his drive toward unrestricted freedom and the formation of himself and the world around him. God seemed to be a relic from the past that could be dispensed with quite easily in the task of shaping the world. It is quite likely that this brusque self-assertion on man's part has contributed a great deal to the fact that his claim to autonomy has often been regarded as a myth of the middle-class period that has not yet been completely overcome by the Enlightenment. Is God perhaps seen as the guarantor of real moral autonomy? We shall attempt to answer this question in two stages. In the first place, we shall ask whether it is possible to think of God in the philosophical perspective and in connection with man's claim to autonomy. In the same context, we shall investigate the part played by faith in God in transcendental philosophy. (This will be found in section A: "The God of the Philosophers.") Secondly, we shall ask whether it is possible to think of an all-embracing moral autonomy in connection with faith in God (section B: "The God of Faith").

It is not my aim to provide a proof of the existence of God in this section. I am concerned in this attempt to show that it is possible to think of certain ideas. My aim is not to prove those ideas to be real. My first question is whether faith in God has to be excluded when man claims autonomy or whether it can be combined meaningfully with that claim. Even if a particular form of autonomy were unthinkable without God, this would not prove the existence of God. On the contrary, the existence of that form of autonomy could be seriously called into question. I deal with this type of problem in the first section (A). In the second section (B), I take faith in God as my point of departure, assume this faith in the God of creation and ask whether full moral autonomy on the part of man can be combined with that faith and what such an autonomy may therefore mean in its concrete expression. If it can in fact be combined with faith in God, it may well find a deeper foundation in that faith and be more fully justified, but this still does not mean that the existence of God has been proved. All that would be established is that faith in God (not God himself) and moral autonomy are not in conflict with each other. And this is really quite a considerable achievement, in view of the suspicion of heteronomy that is so often associated with theologically based ethics.

A. The God of the Philosophers

The title of this section should not be misunderstood. My intention is not to provide philosophical teaching about God. As I have pointed out above in the introduction to this section and the following one (B), I shall ask a number of questions about the teaching of those philosophers whose claim to autonomy was examined in the previous long section (§ 4). That section showed the great divergence in the understanding of autonomy by those thinkers and these differences are also reflected in their ideas of God.

1. In Autonomous Praxis

The representatives of an autonomy of praxis confine themselves mainly to a discussion of the conditions governing a dialogue that is free of repression. In a community of argument and communication, the participants are aware of the autonomy that is due to them. The problem of the justification of values or that of the ultimate ground of the subject's obligation are relegated either to the sphere of the history of civilizations or else, as scientifically insoluble, to that of speculation. Positivistic and critical rationalism regards itself as incompetent to pass judgment in this case.[1] It confines scientific competence to that sphere of reality that is open to verifiable hypotheses. It deals with the question of God in the same way.[2] The question as to whether a human, meaningful way of life presupposes a nonhypothetical access to reality is left open. A complete hypothesization of civilization — in other words, a transformation of all convictions into hypotheses — would in fact lead to a disintegration of free society. "The aim of a complete hypothesization of human existence — that is, the process by which it is made completely scientific — is meaningless because it does not take into consideration the fact that the subject of science is infinite but fictitious, whereas real man is finite."[3] It is simply not possible to test all thinkable hypotheses. Obligation and self-determination in the context of moral freedom cannot be treated in this way.

2. In the Autonomous Process

A basic condition for the undisturbed course of the process of the satisfaction of needs is a limitation to pure this-worldliness. As Marx, for example, insisted, "the end of religion as an illusory happiness of the people is the demand of that people's real happiness. The demand to give up the illusion about the state of the people is a demand to give up a state that is in need of illusions. The criticism of religion is therefore embryonically a criticism of the vale of tears whose halo is religion."[4] Marx was convinced that

Ludwig Feuerbach had dealt with the theme of God when he destroyed faith in God as a theme. He regarded the criticism of religion as essentially over in Germany. It was "the task of history to establish the truth of this world, now that the next world of truth has disappeared."[5] Man had to be placed firmly in the center of human thought. "The criticism of religion ends with the doctrine that man is the highest being for man. It therefore ends with the categorical imperative to overthrow all relationships in which man is a humiliated, an enslaved, an abandoned, a despised being."[6] It is no longer possible to ask about the strange being existing outside man. Atheism has no further meaning for socialist man, "since atheism is a negation of God and by this negation assumes man's existence. But socialism as socialism no longer needs this mediation. It takes as its point of departure the theoretical and practically sensual consciousness of man and nature as being."[7] Marxists always, however, suspect religion, as an illusory reflection of basic structures that should not be, of being an ideology.[8] According to the Marxist criticism of religion, God is in an insuperable relationship of competition. Any counter-criticism must therefore take the supposed image of God as its point of departure and attempt to show how it is possible to think at the same time and in the same context of faith in God's creation and the shaping of the world on the one hand and the idea of God and freedom on the other.

3. In the Philosophy of Subjectivity

The discovery of autonomous subjectivity was from the very beginning overshadowed by the discussion about the traditional metaphysical concept of God. The metaphysical attempt to think about God had been based on knowledge of natural objects. (This was the *via eminentiae*.) By extrapolating a content to a formal principle (*primum movens, prima causa, finis ultimus, ens necessarium, summum ens, actus purus* and so on), a concept was developed which was not only factual (like the "highest mountain"), but was also in its conceptual form in principle (like "first cause") unique.[9]

When philosophers returned to man and a criticism of his knowledge, they were unable to approach God from the departure point of natural objects. This does not mean that the question of God no longer existed for them. It was simply that it had to be asked differently. With the discovery of human subjectivity, the

question that was asked was whether that subjectivity could be justified in the power of thought itself. The question has to be denied,
since every new and deeper insight into subjectivity leads to a
deeper insight into finiteness. Reflection about subjectivity shows
"a twofold orientation. With regard to man's being in the world,
human subjectivity understands itself in its whole power. Nicholas
of Cusa, Descartes and Kant all stressed subjectivity as the real
condition of knowledge of man's being in the world and in this
way provided a new impetus for scientific research into that being.
But, on the basis of the insight into human subjectivity, these
philosophers all recognized the impotence of that subjectivity with
regard to itself and for this reason posited a power that could not
in any way be thought to be over and against that subjectivity, a
power which they recognized as finite, as the ground of its being." [10] In this way, the whole problem was extended by the question as to how being oneself and the relationship with God could
be thought of at the same time. How, in other words, could being a
free person be justified despite and in its justification of itself?

Kant regarded both the transcendental justification of the consciousness as self-consciousness and also freedom and autonomy
as the necessary presuppositions of the moral law without having
recourse to God. "Theoretical knowledge has failed in the attempt
to understand God as the first cause and absolute substance. God
is also not known, but simply thought of, as the unconditioned one
with regard to everything that is conditioned and as the most real
being (*omnitudo realitatis*)." [11] In contrast to the knowledge of God,
the idea of God, then, was not excluded from Kant's philosophy.
In the sphere of theoretical reason, God was, for Kant, a transcendental idea, a principle that was thought of, but not knowable.
It was therefore the task of reflective thought to raise the conditions of objective knowledge. The idea of an absolute unity "of all
the objects of thinking as such" was present, Kant believed, in the
movement of this thought. There was, as it were, a theoretical
need for a regulative idea, according to which everything that was
real or possible was seen as though it was the result of a principle
that was necessary in itself. This idea or principle of unity was
called by Kant the "ideal of pure reason." The idea was transcendental and at the same time peculiar to finite reason, and was
removed from objective knowledge because it lacked vision. [12]

50

In the sphere of practical reason, there is also a similar longing for a state of perfection, in which man finds happiness (as a natural being) in radical morality (as a rational being). Since, however, moral reason is capable of everything via the will, but of nothing via nature, the finite rational being is not able to bring about the unity of morality and happiness. If morality is not to be meaningless, a principle must be thought of which is able to justify the orientation of nature toward moral order. Kant called this postulated principle, this moral cause of the world, God. It was "the idea of an intelligence in which the most morally perfect will combined with the highest state of blessedness is the cause of all happiness in the world, insofar as it is closely related to morality (as the dignity of being happy)."[13] Kant's acceptance of God's existence as that of the highest moral being and author of the world was not a theoretical, but a practical necessity.[14]

Fichte's understanding of God I have already discussed above in the latter part of section A 2 of § 4 ("The Claim to Autonomy"), but it is necessary to add a little more here in this context. His idea of God is to be found above all in the mediation of interpersonal and historical freedom. Being oneself and being justified, immanence and transcendence and finally reason and the absolute are all mutually mediated. With regard to history, he, like Kant, was conscious of a factual discrepancy between morality and happiness. Unlike Kant, however, Fichte did not postulate a God who brought about this mediation of the quasi-metaphysical contrast between reason and nature, morality and happiness as it were from outside and subsequently. Fichte's God was the ordering order of the origin. There was not, according to Fichte, a mediation of morality and a happiness that was appropriate to it. The order of the origin was related — and in this Fichte took Kant's approach to a more radical level — to the unity of morality with itself.[15] Similarly, reason and freedom were held responsible for the cancelling out of this discrepancy. This involvement of reason was, however, to be understood "not in the sense of a performance by individual human reason alone, but in the medial sense of an interaction (not at the same level) between reason as the reason of God and the reason of men and freedom as the freedom of God and the freedom of men."[16]

As we have already seen in the section on Hegel above, this thinker criticized Kant and Fichte for their limitation of autonomy

51

to pure subjectivity. Hegel thought that the autonomy of finite subjectivity could only be saved if it was seen to be in a state of inseparable unity with the infinite. The finite was an essential aspect of the infinite, in such a way that the infinite mediated itself by its opposites.[17] This mediation took place in the real conditions of history. "The question of God therefore came to be seen, not as a problem of freedom and reason subject to ideal conditions, but as the task of thinking of freedom and reason, in and despite their unconditioned character, subject to the conditions of their own historical state of division."[18]

In consideration of this, our point of departure was whether it was in any way possible to think meaningfully of God in the context of our contemporary understanding of autonomy. We can now provide, with Walter Schulz, an answer to this question. Schulz says: "Contemporary metaphysics are limited to God, but this God is only present for the one who has experienced the power and the impotence of thought in thinking. As long as God is approached as a definite and understandable being, only the power of thought will be experienced, the power of thought that has power over the definite divine being as thought, because it is the being of thought, transcending in thought all definite and understandable being. Only the person who thinks of the power of thought beyond this being and to the end will be in a position to experience the impotence of thought, the impotence that could not be thought itself and thought as such if it were not conditioned by being itself and made possible by being. The person who ventures to take this ultimate step will find the God of the philosophers who can no longer be disintegrated into thought."[19]

B. The God of Faith

God who reveals himself also continues to be hidden in the concealment of his being from the believer. The whole of the Bible bears witness to God and his power, praises him as the creator of the world and proclaims his wonderful deeds, performed for his people. At the same time, however, this God of the Bible continues to be nameless and incomprehensible. It is impossible for the biblical authors to express his reality or to define him in ideas or images, because he anticipates all their definitions.

This mysterious character of God determines not only the biblical presentation of God, but also all theology as theo-logy or the right way of speaking about God. How are we to address the God who is nameless? How can we proclaim the God who is inexpressible? Our words and concepts cannot, because of their inevitable orientation toward concrete, objective experience, grasp God in his nonobjectivity and unlimited nature. This is why the theme of the hidden God (*Deus absconditus*) has, since the time of the Greek Fathers of the Church, preoccupied those who have considered God and his revelation of himself — Augustine, Meister Eckhart, Nicholas of Cusa, Luther, Pascal, and Newman all gave their attention to it. In order to testify to the God who is hidden and who also reveals himself, the concept of the dissimilar similarity or analogy has been used. The analogy as a mode of thinking and speaking about God is based on the presupposition that human knowledge is orientated toward the absolute mystery. The possibility of an analogous relationship is based on the openness of human thinking. God is given to our thinking as the nonobjective and mysterious direction of all spiritual movement. This original relationship, in which we are confronted with the aim of our transcendence, is "what we call analogy. . . . We exist analogously by being grounded in the sacred mystery that is always removing itself from us by constituting us through merging into and initiating us into the concrete individual realities of a categorial nature in our own experience, realities that also mediate and at the same time provide the point of departure for our knowledge of God."[20]

Analogous thinking about God is always misunderstood whenever it is regarded as a seizing hold of God through the medium of objective human knowledge. Any knowing orientation toward any being at all always presupposes God as the invisible and nonobjective ground of all knowledge. Even when God is called, and objectivized as, the Absolute in metaphysical terms, he is not the object, but rather the ground of our knowledge and understanding. Transcendence is therefore more original than the univocal individual concepts of metaphysics. It is the condition, the sphere and the ground enabling us to compare individual objects in our experience with each other and to classify them.[21] Touched by the infinite and constantly orientated toward it, we are also able to understand, because of this orientation, the finite in its finiteness. It is also from the same transcendental experience that we gain access to the creatural state as a fundamental theological concept of revelation. We are not able to understand what it means to be created in the light of the empirical phenomenon of causal connections. If we were to think of the creatural state as the extrapolation of a functional connection between two categorial realities or as an exalted form of application of that relationship, the way would be blocked in advance to any true understanding of the state. The creation of man and the world is a continuous process of being "constantly sent to itself from the free initiative of the personal God."[22] This, of course, brings us to the decisive question as to how man's autonomy can be justified against the background of this interpretation of creation and man's state as a creature. We can take as our basis for discussion of this question two factors: God as the ground of man's freedom and the autonomous formation of the world as a task given by God.

1. God as the Ground of Autonomous Freedom

According to this understanding of theology as a creative process, God and man are not in competition with each other in the same sphere of activity. God's creative activity transcendentally embraces the whole categorial evolution of the world, and man and the world are borne up by the sovereign and creative freedom of God in such a way that God himself is in no sense dependent on the world. On the other hand, the world cannot hold anything that is independent of God, but this is because he founds the world and man on their being themselves and on their own activity. It is on this foundation that man is able fully to affirm his existence as an autonomous, moral rational being. In this section, I will provide a brief transcendental analysis of human freedom in order to clarify this statement.[23]

When I was discussing man's freedom of choice above (in § 3 D), I pointed out that freedom was not expressed in a choice between objects. It was rather man's expression of himself as someone who chooses objectively. In its fundamental being, freedom aims at the subject as such and as a whole without losing itself in the subject. Subjectivity cannot, however, be understood as closed. It is always open to other subjects. It is fundamentally incapable of "determining itself in itself and through itself. The circle presented by concentrated subjectivity has therefore to be broken. This, however, only happens when subjectivity is restricted in such a way that it truly fulfills itself."[24]

This is the background to the transformation of the philosophy of the subject into a transcendental and pragmatic theory of communication. It would seem that it is only in this context that a recognition of another freedom can be contained within the expression of transcendental freedom. H. Krings's analysis of freedom must be understood against this background, especially his extension of Kant's and Fichte's concept of freedom as an original act of self-determination on man's part. According to this act, man's will becomes a definite and determining will. This does not, however, take place by the will looking for a content that has not yet been grasped and by giving this to itself. Viewed transcendentally, the determining content of this fundamental act of self-determination is not an empirical object of the will, but the material of the desire — that is, the relationship of the will to the content as such. This giving of oneself is, moreover, not an "objective giving or producing, but an original opening of oneself to content, as a primary decision of the will to one's own materiality."[25] The expression of freedom as an original act of self-determination therefore implies an opening of one's will "to oneself as material desire."[26] This original opening of oneself, this consent of original desire, is what is meant by the concept of transcendental freedom. It is the foundation of empirical freedom (or freedom of choice), because the transcendental decision preserves for the will the character of transcendental self-determination, even when its act of choosing is materially determined by objects.

If transcendental freedom is thus able to reveal different objects to the will, we are bound to ask what content corresponds to the dignity of freedom. The fulfilling content of freedom can only be freedom itself. It is only then that the content is not inferior in dignity to desiring oneself. This, however, means that "freedom gives itself both in the first and in the last place a content by consenting to another freedom. It is only in accepting another freedom that freedom does not make itself inferior to its full form."[27] This does not provide any answer to questions concerning empirical decisions, but it does point to a fundamental aspect of all self-determination. Self-determination is therefore seen as the "concept of the transcendental affirmation of another freedom."[28]

This "other freedom," then, can be regarded as the adequate content of transcendental freedom. It cannot be regarded as the fulfilling content of that freedom. It can place no limits to freedom as the transcendental act of opening itself. It cannot, as it were, make that act succumb. Finite freedom is therefore related to unconditioned freedom for the sake of the unconditioned nature of this act of opening itself. This cannot and should not mean that it is subject to the demand of an infinite but unattainable approach to absolute freedom. It means, on the contrary, that freedom as the unconditioned act of opening itself is subject to an unconditioned claim. Transcendental freedom therefore anticipates, by virtue of its own form, unconditioned freedom.[29] It "realizes its unconditioned character, which formally belongs to it, in its original opening of itself, that is, in its consent to another freedom and in its anticipatory opening of itself to unconditioned and perfect freedom. . . . Human morality, the essence of which consists of the realization of freedom, therefore has, as a condition of its possibility, to consent to another freedom and to anticipate perfect freedom."[30]

An analysis of the conditions of finite freedom has therefore clearly led us to think about perfect freedom as the fulfilling content of transcendental freedom as such. Perfect freedom is the ultimate orientation of the state of being open of finite freedom. That perfect freedom is not the limit, but the fulfillment of finite freedom. Perfect freedom, as the idea of the unity of the unconditioned form of the opening of itself of freedom and the unmediated fullness of the content of freedom, provides us with the possibility of thinking about God.[31] God is conceived as freedom providing "another" freedom and at the same time as unconditioned and directly fulfilled freedom that is conditioned by nothing. This way of thinking about God on the model of freedom is closely in accordance with the idea of God that emerges from the Old and New Testaments. In this way too, the attempt "to think of God in the context of a transcendental philosophy of freedom . . ." overcomes the "opposition between the God of the philosophers and the God of Abraham, Isaac and Jacob invoked by Pascal."[32]

Finite freedom can only be understood if it is considered within the situation of dynamic tension between perfect freedom and other freedom, between the absolute and the limited state. This has become very clear to us as a result of the speculations conducted by the philosophers of idealism, who became lost in the infinite in

56

their attempts to justify pure subjectivity, too concerned with the infinite and went back again and again to an essential practical link with the world in connection with the constitution of the I. If the I is to be thought of as unconditioned, it must of necessity be undetermined. The idea of an absolute self-projection of freedom becomes lost in the unlimited aspect of the divine state[33] and, at the precise point where the I is expressed, reaches the limits of the finite. It is true to say that the problem of freedom has its deepest roots in the finite aspect of man. Freedom abolishes finiteness and is also surrounded and delimited by finiteness. In his freedom, man is always tempted to understand himself through himself, in other words, either by making the I absolute in idealism or by choosing existence in existentialism. Self-projection, however, by raising the I to the level of an absolute I ends in an undetermined, empty state. As unconditioned, the I is undetermined, purely negatively determined or a non-thing. Determination and limitation are very closely related. It was as a result of this knowledge as well as bitter experience of the world that made the existentialist philosophers include limitation and annihilation in self-choice as decisive aspects. This limit is required by human freedom, so that it can concentrate itself and achieve sufficient determination to act.

This is completely in accordance with the idea of the freedom of the creature. In the light of faith in God's creation, the unconditioned obligatory claim is simply the dependence of a personally free self, over which a total claim is made, in this freedom, to be in control of itself, also in freedom. Existence subject to this obligatory claim can be seen theologically to be the necessary state of man who is not indebted to himself for himself, but who knows that he is constituted as a creature. The origin itself is perhaps only anonymously present to his consciousness as a duty or as a prompting of his conscience. It is only insofar as he is able to comply with this fundamental claim (which is, after all, the claim of perfect freedom) that he can, as a moral being, gain possession of himself in free self-determination. Every one of the aims which we set ourselves and to which we commit ourselves completely is bound to limit our freedom. However valuable it may be, every aim that we make absolute is bound to compel us to make an object of everything that exists as a stage or a means on the way to realizing that aim. Only being bound to the freedom that makes free is able to avoid limiting finite freedom and to bring it to fulfillment. "Only an ultimately obligatory orientation toward the unconditioned and infinite God is neither humiliating nor harmful to anyone, is not in competition with anything and does not exclude any worldly value, any valid possibility or any way in which man is able to realize himself. On the contrary, it allows men and things, events and plans to take their proper places in the scheme of things and provides correct perspectives."[34] In interpreting man as a creature, theological reflection "only" includes the philosophical insight into man's finite nature. It positively affirms the anthropological assumption that man may not make an absolute of himself, either as an individual or collectively. He has to realize his own freedom within the framework of this experience of contingency. This means that there is no change in the structure of his moral reason. There can therefore be no question of making categorial moral judgments absolute on the basis of the theological justification of obligation.[35] This statement about the unconditioned claim of moral life as a whole includes, on the contrary, a reservation with regard to any attempt to make the categorial absolute. It is, of course, undeniable that any assumption of contingency in our acceptance in faith of man's state as a creature has an inevitable effect on value judgments, but these are really no more than consequences that seem at least to be meaningful in the light of our anthropological experience of contingency. We shall be discussing this question more fully in the second part.

2. The Autonomous Formation of the World as a Task Given by God

We have not completely solved the problem of moral autonomy by demonstrating that faith in creation does not do away with man's personal responsibility, but, on the contrary, that it forms the basis of that responsibility and evokes it. Autonomy is not simply transcendental freedom with its possibility of positing an original act of opening itself to God (or closing itself). The man who is in accordance with maxims of action that he has given to himself is autonomous man. It is of no importance whether he recognizes the moral law as a given fact of reason or whether he devises valid forms of action intersubjectively. What is important is that these originate in him. This, of course, inevitably gives rise to the suspicion of heteronomy with regard to any form of ethics in which God is regarded as the author of the moral law.

The evolution and justification of moral norms and of the necessary insight into goods and values will be discussed fully in the second part of this book, where I shall try to demonstrate, within the context of the Bible and the doctrine of natural law, how — bearing in mind man's connection in faith with God — the formation of norms takes place and has always taken place as an independent process in the history of human civilization. Religious experience and theological reflection have played an important part in influencing this development, but, as we shall see, this influence has been strongly marked by man's practical reason.

In this section, I shall investigate the ground and the limits of autonomy and shall also try to show that man's submission to God's transcendental claim does not do away with his legislative autonomy, but that, on the contrary, it bears it up transcendentally in accordance with the relationship of creation. This is in no sense a theological justification that has been developed at a recent stage in Christian history in order to deal with the contemporary emphasis on autonomy. In order to establish this fact, I shall briefly outline, in the rest of this section, the way Thomas Aquinas argued in favor of moral autonomy in his treatise on law in the *Summa Theologiae*.[36]

In his ethical teaching, Thomas followed the Aristotelian model and took human experience as his point of departure. In its external structure, his *Lex* treatise is presented as a deduction from higher principles. The inner structure of thought, however, moves from experience via reflection to the foundations. Thomas did not, in other words, work deductively, but inductively and reflectively.[37] His concept of law was therefore derived from experience.

According to Thomas, law had its place in man's communal existence. It is experienced there as the rule and measure of activity. It is determined by the relationship between the legislator and those who are subject to the law. It therefore has the character of an "external principle," through which we are "instructed" to right action. Thomas used the general concept of law in an analogous sense, that is, in a way that transcends different spheres, but at the same time binds them together. This means that the various laws with which he dealt in his treatise (*lex aeterna, naturalis, humana* and

59

divina) should not be seen as species, but rather as aspects of the one sphere of the legal regulation of human activity. This orientation, as developed by Thomas, was connected with his attempt to provide a basis for the whole complex of laws by way of reduction and reflection.[38] He reasoned from what had been founded to the founder and the relationship between the various species or kinds of law is therefore one of reductive foundation. This is an important precondition for our understanding of the different laws. It will also help us to "make the unconditioned, nonarbitrary and at the same time dynamic essence of normative action . . . clear."[39]

The key concept in this treatise and above all in Thomas's search for an ultimate justification of moral norms is *ratio*, reason. Thomas ' for example calls law itself *ordinatio rationis* (I–II, 90, 4 c). It is this *ratio* that regulates law. It is the regulating factor in law because it directs action toward its aim (as its first principle).[40] Human action is human only because it is determined by reason. It is therefore a self-determining action, because it determines itself toward its aim and indeed sets that aim itself.[41] The ultimate, all-embracing aim, however, is not at man's disposal. That aim is given *a natura*. (Thomas, of course, understood this in the light of the theology of creation.) The means to this end are the object of human *ratio*.[42]

Action should not be regarded as purely instrumental in this case, nor should human decision be seen as technically rational. A consideration of *ratio* mediates the universal aim through whatever situation prevails at the time and thus gives it its concrete form. Following Aristotle, Thomas regarded the "setting of aims *a natura* as a way of giving a framework to the situation that at the same time included the finding both of means and of concrete aims without setting them *a priori*."[43] End or aim in this context (*finis*) is not primarily material in meaning, but formal. The real aim of the human will is the idea of what is good, the *bonum universale*. Man is bound to this *a natura*, by his nature.[44] Human will strives, in all goods, to achieve the good.

In his commentary on the Nicomachean Ethics (I, 1. 2, n. 11), Thomas pointed out that this good was God himself. A *summum bonum*, thought of as in itself infinite, may have an objective character. The real orientation of the will toward the unconditioned good transcends all categorial thought. In the perspective of the ultimate, all-embracing and absolute aim, all other goods have a relative value and are regulated by human reason as objects of the will and belonging to the sphere of determination. This regulation by *ratio*, discussed by Thomas in his definition of law and his analysis of human action, should "not be understood simply as a regulation or setting in order."[45] *Ordinare* in this context has the meaning of *imperare*, to command or govern. This applies to man as an individual and to the legal structure governing the communal existence of man. Thomas insisted on the primary function of *ratio*, as a legislative structure. Obligatory legal enactments are basically "dependent upon reason as the factor forming the foundation of a meaningful interrelationship and, insofar as the latter owes its existence to a free attitude, the factor creating that relationship. In this way, *ratio* is the *regula* and the *mensura* of human actions."[46] It is, in other words, the normative factor in morality. It can also be demonstrated that the morality of human activity is not based on a claim asserted by man's nature or essential being, "but on reason as a principle of action, that is, as a specific ability that is founded on man's being, but is not identical with it."[47] Thomas took it as a matter of course that *ratio* was not subject in this process to individual arbitrary choice. The ability of reason to organize action was, in his view, determined by man's orientation toward good as such, and reason is able to discern a similar order in certain goods that man naturally finds it valuable to strive to achieve. At the same time, however, *ratio* has to regulate these goods in the light of an ultimate and meaningful formation of the world. Man's legislative activity is in a special way orientated toward the common good for which man, as a social being, is responsible.

We shall not consider the justification of this question here, but shall discuss in detail the development of value insights in the second part of this book (§ 20 ff.). (There we shall show how value insights are developed through "natural inclinations.") For the present, however, it is important to point out that Thomas believed that the creative activity of human reason formed the basis of man's insight both into his task as a legislator and into the importance of goods in a well-regulated society. Man, according to Thomas, participated in divine reason because he was made in the image of God.

Thomas took the idea of the participation of man's reason in God's reason from the Graeco-Roman tradition stretching from

Plato through Cicero to Augustine, but he certainly transformed it radically. What is new in Thomas's presentation is his emphasis of man's state as a subject. Man's particular dignity was, according to Thomas, to be found in his active participation in God's guidance of the world.[48] Within the framework of his reason as a creature, man is burdened with himself. He has a share in God's providence by being destined (and being conscious of this destiny) to be rationally responsible for himself and for others (I–II, 91, 2). Thomas was, in other words, convinced that man was not a creature without reason, driven to his aims simply by his natural inclinations and urges. He was completely at one with tradition in this. Unlike Augustine, however, he did not believe that man was irradiated or illuminated directly by divine ideas. He did speak of an *impressio* or an *irradiatio* of divine light or wisdom, but this *irradiatio* only took place "via man's knowledge of creation as the *effectus* of divine effectiveness, by which Thomas re-interpreted the neo-Platonic concept of the Aristotelian theory of knowledge and in this way renewed his understanding of earthly realities."[49] The natural moral law was not, therefore, in Thomas's view, to be found in man's reason being guided by divine reason by means of an innate principle. Even the first moral principle (*bonum faciendum, malum vitandum*) was, Thomas believed, acquired by man through the activity of his reason. In this, human experience was not the source of the principle, but the means by which it was grasped. As soon as it reached man's consciousness via his experience, it became immediately clear to him. His participation in God's providence (in the eternal law) is to be found, then, specifically in his natural inclination, experienced in practical reason, to create norms with regard to his ultimate fulfillment. It is this type of participation — and only this type — that Thomas regarded as the natural moral law (I–II, 91, 2). Thomas recognized that man was a moral being who was given to himself and he traced this characteristic in man back to God. It was, in his opinion, only through man's rational nature, which can only in a relative sense be said to participate in God's providence,[50] that man could be thought of as giving laws to himself or closely united to his legislation.[51] The legislative character of the natural moral law is therefore to be found in the natural activity of practical reason (*ordinatio rationis*). It is by means of this that reason is able to understand that good is what is to be done and evil is what should not be done.[52] The structure of human reason itself is not changed by the attempt to trace reason back to its ultimate transcendental ground. What does in fact happen is that the claim to rational self-realization acquires an unconditioned character by being founded on the *lex aeterna*.[53]

The contradiction that an unconditioned subject is unconditionally claimed by itself or by other conditioned subjects ceases to exist when the moral claim is theonomously justified. The paradox of finite freedom, on the other hand, continues to exist. The obligatory claim is understood as a total dependence (the creatural state) in the independence of self-determination (the personal state). On the one hand, freedom implies total dependence, insofar as man is offered the possibility of deciding in favor of freedom as a gift (creation as grace). On the other hand, however, it is also total independence, insofar as man finds himself confronted with a choice with regard to the only possibility of freedom. The paradox of finite freedom therefore consists of man's being confronted with the absolute self as a self-centered being. He can only gain himself when he is left to himself. He can only have power over himself when he is responsible for himself. This antinomy is not a real contradiction so long as God's and man's personalities are not placed on the same level.[54] It is, however, the source of radical temptation and the ground of the possibility of self-alienation, self-contradiction and sin.

Section Two: Contradiction

There is greatness, but also danger, in man's moral autonomy. The tendency to make it absolute has led to a contradiction. Every human being is confronted with this contradiction if he thinks, as a limited being, that he is in possession of the absolute. According to the history of salvation and revelation as narrated in the Bible, this is precisely the sin committed by everyone who turns to idols that he has made himself instead of turning to God to give him honor. It is the possibility and the many forms of this contradiction that I shall be discussing in this second section. In the first chapter, I shall outline the phenomenon of guilt as a suitable point of departure. In the second chapter, I shall provide a theological interpretation of it.

CHAPTER 1: GUILT AS A PHENOMENON

The question about the origin of evil affects us at every period of history. It has in recent years been taken up in depth by ethologists, psychologists and sociologists[1] and their findings have aroused considerable interest. The myth of man as naturally good has been dispelled by the experience of two world wars and the threat of destruction by mass means. We are profoundly aware today of the fact that man himself is the greatest danger to man.

In the same way, evil is also seen to be closely connected with a form of human behavior that endangers the foundations of human society. Evil, in other words, is not attributed to anonymous powers, but to man himself. It is, however, not simply the individual in his individual acts of freedom who has to be taken into account in this. Many different factors and relationships have to be considered and brought to light. Human behavior has to be viewed not only as a case of individual self-expression, but also within the framework of the individual, social, and historical influences and conditions that have affected man and society and that underlie all human attitudes. All these are, moreover, themselves continuing objectivizations of good or bad acts of human freedom. The latter have therefore to be seen as "contrary to our better judgment and reason

. . . an objectivized and bad form of freedom that has been co-determined by guilt and sin as these have become effective."[2]

It is therefore impossible to ignore the phenomena of evil and guilt today. They have been traced in the conscious and unconscious depths of the human psyche and attempts have been made to strip off the layers of their disguise. Not only psychologists have been active in this sphere — dramatists also have thrown a clear light on human morality in many modern plays. Yet, despite this, contemporary man has been less ready to allow himself to be examined by theologians in the name of God. This may at least partly be attributable to the fact that the authentically Christian teaching about sin has not always been widely known. It is more probable that a certain morality underlies our catalogue of sins that we would like to reject. Moral theologians are criticized for having an external, legalistic concept of sin and are regarded as persons who make fine moral distinctions and tend to use terms appropriate to a morally unobjectionable form of behavior in cases in which deep guilt can hardly be denied. The view is also put forward that an act cannot be justified simply by fulfilling the law and that a mere transgression of the law does not make a man guilty. Anyone who understands the Christian doctrine of sin is bound to be surprised by misunderstandings of this kind, but he is also bound to ask what mistakes have been made in the proclamation of the Christian message and in Christian praxis to enable this very wrong type of impression to arise.

In order to avoid solving the problem of evil without reference to the problems of the modern age, I shall try to show, by means of examples drawn from modern literature, the concrete phenomena of guilt and evil that preoccupy modern man (§ 6). I will then look again at the basic historical and cultural forms of man's experience of guilt (§ 7) in the Old and New Testaments.

§ 6 Reflected Experience of Guilt

In their different interpretations of human experience, poets, dramatists and novelists provide an important source of insights into the experience of guilt in any given period. Their aim is to provoke, disconcert or otherwise affect us in some way. They draw

attention to conflicts, contradictions, discords and insoluble en-
tanglements. They uncover hidden guilt. For this reason, they
may be valuable to the theologian in communicating to him a renewed sensibility to reality. There is a constant danger in theology
— and philosophy — that reality may be lost in theological (and
philosophical) distinctions. God and the world are reduced in
theology to a system and human tensions are sometimes obscured
or ignored in this process. Literature points to these tensions, often
in a very dramatic way.

It is possible to discern a historical development which makes it
clear that the cause of evil is situated in social relationships. "The
individual or a certain number of individuals were accused in
classical drama. Society as a whole emerged unscathed. The order
of society was accepted as a basis or as a meaningful, guiding criterion. In any case of conflict, the individual was always guilty with
regard to society. Society was never regarded as guilty with regard
to the individual. By the nineteenth century, realism had increased
and the problem arose of knowledge, perception and lack of freedom in the case of the individual with regard to the 'it' in him and
the environment and relationships around him."[3] (An example of
this is the figure of Danton in Georg Büchner's *Dantons Tod*.)
"From the middle of the nineteenth century onwards, authors such
as Flaubert, Dostoievski, Proust, Musil, Kafka and Joyce were increasingly concerned with the problem of the destruction of the
unity of motivation in the subject . . . with doubts about previous
moral ideas, with the urgency of the problem of meaning and with
the ideology of authority overlaid with morality."[4]

A. Guilt and the Guilty

In this section, we will consider a number of works of literature
written since 1945 and look especially for the accusations of guilt
that are made in them, the way in which the guilty characters
themselves behave and how others behave toward them.

1. Accusations of Guilt

These accusations refer to typical phenomena found in interpersonal relationships. One of the constant underlying themes is that
of the real significance of man for man. The terrifying contempt of
man for human dignity that was revealed in the persecution of the

Jews in Germany and in other war crimes was a prominent theme at that time and still is. Memories of these crimes prevented men from making hostile images and stereotypes. What we condemned on a large scale was possibly happening every day and unnoticed in our midst. If men were forbidden to make images of God, they were also forbidden to make images of men. As Max Frisch wrote in 1946 in his diary: "We are told that God said: You shall not make any image of God. This ought also to mean any image of God as the one living in every man, as what cannot be grasped in every man. It is an offence that we do to others what they do to us — again and again, unless we love."[5]

He also showed clearly in his play *Andorra* how this sin had its effect in middle-class society.[6] The people of Andorra have branded Andri as Jew. He accepts the burden of being different and in this way reinforces the prejudice of the people. When they look for a guilty man when a murder has been committed, they all agree that only the Jew can be the murderer. In the same way, the commandment not to make images is also found as a theme in Frisch's novel *Stiller*.[7] When Stiller visits his wife Julika for the last time in Davos, she reproaches him:

"You have made an image of me. I know that — a finished, perfected image and there's an end to it! It is not just empty words when the first commandment tells us: You shall not make any image! Every image is a sin. . . . If you love someone, you leave every possibility open for him and despite all your memories you are always ready to be amazed . . . at how different he is and that he is not just like that, a finished image of the kind that you have made of me."

Sybille, the public prosecutor's wife, also accuses Stiller of making an image of his wife, when she discovers in his workshop a sculpture in the shape of a vase and he tells her that it represents his wife: "Isn't that terrible for your wife? I would think it was terrible if you were to transform me into art."

Stiller himself writes about himself: "After his attitude had become closed, Stiller knew that he was only married to a beautiful, rare, dead vase." He reveals a tendency to objectivize Julika immediately after her first visit to the prison: "I regard her as an object. Quite soberly — as a woman, a strange woman, any woman . . ."

Even Stiller's final remark about the dead woman, "She is beautiful," takes the aspect of personal relationship away from the previous confession "I love her." The difference in the relationship between subject and object is also reflected in the explanation that Rolf finds for Stiller's marriage. It also corresponds to the relationship between God and man that is again and again mentioned by him: "This woman never made you a task in life. Only you made her a task and I think you did that from the very beginning. You were her redeemer and . . . she was your creature."

Other contemporary authors do not aim their accusations directly at the individual. They tend rather to accuse the system or modern society in which achievement is so highly valued. The modern world of commerce and the competitive struggle for achievement makes man into a wolf in his attitude to his fellowmen. "If you cannot be a wolf or if you refuse to serve wolves and their system, you do not count in this society. Man is trained here to be a wolf. Without noticing it, he behaves like a wolf in concrete situations."[8]

In Dürrenmatt's radio play, Die Panne, Alfredo Traps is accused of murder because he "uses a knife on his competitor, Gygax's, neck" at least psychologically and with cunning calculation. Traps does not kill with a devilish intention, but "because it is the most natural thing for him to do to press someone against the wall and to go ahead unthinkingly, whatever happens."

In Böll's Gruppenbild mit Dame, the managers of the building company, who have Leni and her foreign workers evacuated forcibly in order to obtain higher profits, do not think that they are behaving immorally. They are only, they believe, exercising their middle-class rights.

In so many modern works of literature, guilt is described as sleepwalking, indifference or simply as guilt by association. The individual is not alert to the reality of the situation. He is incapable of acting critically. He cannot come to any judgment about the relationships and makes platitudinous pronouncements (War is war"; "Business is business"). He wants only to survive, to get through, and so he passes untouched, like a sleepwalker, through immorality. He is fundamentally indifferent toward his fellow-men.

It is often social relationships that, as it were, almost compel the individual to be guilty. (Peachum sings about the "uncertainty of human relationships" in Bertolt Brecht's *Threepenny Opera*: man would like to be good, but the relationships will not let him.) An individual or a group of individuals is held to be guilty, for example, for not trying energetically enough to change these relationships.[9] The intellectual is accused of guilt because he theorizes instead of doing. Günter Grass makes the director of the Berlin Theatre (Bertolt Brecht perhaps?) reflect about the revolt of the plebeians in ancient times, yet hesitate to help the workers to formulate a declaration for their own revolt in the present (*Die Plebejer proben den Aufstand*). In the same way, Dürrenmatt's *Die Physiker* and Kipphardt's *In der Sache J. Robert Oppenheimer* show how a scientist can incur guilt by failing to perceive the responsibility that his own specialized knowledge gives him.

2. The Accused

Modern authors have written in various ways about the attitude of the "guilty" toward their guilt. J. Kopperschmidt has headed his analysis of the subject "guilty guiltlessness" and this title goes right to the heart of the matter.[10] On the one hand, there are no guilty people any more, either because everyone is to some extent guilty or because they are able to exonerate themselves from the burden of guilt placed on them. The people of Andorra, for example, all declare in public in court: "I am not guilty." And the author of the play has himself declared in his book on the problems of the theatre:[11]

"In the mess of the present century, in the rubbish that is left of the white race, there are no more guilty and no more responsible people. No one can do anything about it and no one wants it. It has just happened without our doing anything . . .

"We are all collectively guilty, too collectively embedded in the sin of our father and forefathers. We are still only children and grandchildren. That is our bad luck, not our guilt."

This universal guiltlessness, however, is not simply exonerated. It is, on the contrary, exposed again and again in modern writing and made the object of accusations. Siegfried Lenz, for example, entitled his first drama *Zeit der Schuldlosen* ("Time of the Guiltless Ones"). By this title, he meant that "guiltlessness as a profession or as a presentation of a clean conscience in the absence of a conscience is a guiltlessness that we cause ourselves, by our own guilt, in other words, a guilty guiltlessness." [12] In Martin Walser's play *Der Schwarze Schwan*, the concentration camp doctor, Dr. F., ritualizes his confession of guilt and integrates it so completely into his life that it does not prevent him in any way from deriving scientific advantages after 1945 from the medical experiments that he conducted during the war on prisoners in the concentration camp. [13]

Whenever guilt is admitted in postwar literature, it is not usually admitted in public. The priest in *Andorra*, for example, accuses himself, not in public, but in prayer. This private confession of guilt is even more pointed in the case of Professor Liberé in Walser's *Der Schwarze Schwan*. He is also an ex-concentration camp doctor and has been living since 1945 in a remote mental hospital. He voluntarily surrounds himself with signs of prison life. He sleeps in a room like a prison cell, eats from a tin plate and makes brooms as a self-inflicted punishment. In the garden he has planted a seven-branched tree of life and he has adopted a mentally retarded child. He does not want to forget his guilt, but he cannot bring himself to make a public confession, because he believes that the judge and the members of the public present would, in their ignorance of guilt, rejoice in their own decency. [14] So he lives with a false name and has invented a past in India for his daughter.

There are many clear examples of the indestructible entanglement of people in the phenomenon of guilt in contemporary literature. Let us consider Frisch's novel *Stiller*, however, once more. [15] On the one hand, Stiller feels guilty with regard to his wife Julika: "We cannot run away. I ran away in order not to murder and found that my attempt to run away was murder. There is only one thing to do — to accept this knowledge, even if no one can share with me the knowledge that I have been murdering throughout my whole life."

These feelings of guilt accompany almost all the statements that are made about Stiller's relationship with his wife: "Of course it is not your fault that you have to go to the sanatorium, Julika. It is all my fault . . . I am the guilty one."

Stiller's guilty feelings, which crystallize in the imaginary idea that he is a murderer, conceal his dislike of Julika. His generalized reflections about murder make it easier to see that he has also regarded himself as sacrificed for Julika's benefit: "There are many different ways of murdering a man or at least of destroying his soul, all of them unknown to the police. A word spoken at the right moment — that is all that is needed. . . . All these murders, of course, take place slowly. Has it never occurred to you why people are so interested in a real murder? . . . Surely it is because we usually do not see our daily murders. It is really a relief when the bullet finds its mark, when the blood flows or when someone dies of poisoning and not just because his wife will not speak to him."

At the end, however, Stiller does not know what his guilt is. He asks the public prosecutor: "What is my guilt? Tell me. I don't know. What have I done?" The public prosecutor points to the deeper foundations of the phenomenon of guilt: "Guilt as the sum total of the mistakes that you should have avoided — is that what you mean? I think that guilt is something quite different. We ourselves are guilt."

Albert Camus also had a very complex view of the phenomenon of guilt. In his novel *The Fall (La Chute)*, he confronts his readers with hell — the hell in which man finds himself and from which he cannot escape. The narrator lives in Amsterdam and we have to follow him there: "Don't you think that the concentric canals of Amsterdam are like the circles of hell? Middle-class hell, of course, populated by nightmares. Coming from the outside, the more circles you cross, the more impenetrable and the darker life becomes and, with it, its crimes. We are in the last circle here. The circle of . . . Ah, you know! In any case the lechers and newspaper readers can go no further."

The heart of the novel is the experience that the respectable Paris lawyer Jean-Baptiste Clamence has one night on the Seine, when he watches a young woman commit suicide. He hears her cries, but he does not help her in any way. He goes away and tells no one. But the event continues to have an effect on him, even though he did not let himself be summoned as a witness. "From that time on, when I was summoned — and I had really been summoned — I had to answer or at least I had to look for an answer. It was not easy and for a long time I went astray."

Now, however, he has discovered the "deep twofold being of man" and the whole novel becomes a "breathtaking confession" made to an anonymous guest at the Mexico City, a café in the port of Amsterdam. The aim is to make us all recognize our own guilt. Clamence freely chooses his only practical course, that of "making a public confession." He also chooses to play the part of a prophet in the desert, but, as he himself admits, in the knowledge that he is "a hollow prophet for lamentable times — an Elijah without a Messiah." He puts on the guise of a penitent judge and, as often as the opportunity occurs, preaches in his church, the Mexico City: "Since it was impossible to condemn others without at the same time judging himself as well, he had to cover himself with accusations, in order to have the right to judge others. Since every judge one day must become a penitent, he had simply to go the other way and act like a penitent, in order to become a judge one day."

Clamence also makes every effort to present "contemporary man" as he is, a "nuisance" to himself and to others. However rich and varied the range of errors may be, only one crime is really decisive and it hardly deserves to be called a crime, because it is a purely negative omission and as such calls the possibility of crime into question and ultimately makes even morality impossible. This "crime" is innocent-guilty indecisiveness, spiritual indolence.

This, then, is the essence of the experience that Clamence had that night. "It is the classical fall through a sin of omission, as opposed to a sin of action or a crime carried out. . . . The real fall of man (*la chute*) is to be found in his omission, in his passing by, casually, unnoticed and unpunishable by any court." [16] Indifference, to which no one can appeal and which is never prepared to go beyond what is required by society, is the real sin and it hides its true nature under the cloak of morality. It is clear from the description of Clamence's past that "the direct social role can be mastered and played perfectly, even according to a traditionally Christian code of morals, and yet the person playing that part need not necessarily be inwardly involved." [17] His outwardly virtuous appearance is not matched by an edifying interior. "I lived among men without really sharing their interests and therefore did not succeed in believing in the obligations into which I had entered. I was polite and indolent enough to fulfill the expectations that had been placed in me with regard to my profession, family and life as a citizen. But I did it absentmindedly and in the end this spoiled everything. My whole life was under a double sign and I often did not participate inwardly in even my most significant actions."

Clamence's penitential sermon does not, however, lead him out of "hell." He cries in the wilderness, but refuses to leave it. He does penance, but only in order to be able to judge: "I have not begun a new life. I continue to love myself and to serve others. The only difference is that the confession of my faults enables me to give myself up with even less concern to them and to enjoy the double pleasure that my own being and the stimulus of remorse give me."

From this time onward, he gives himself up without scruple to everything that is offered to him — "women, vainglory, satiety, resentment and even fever." He is deeply convinced that nothing has changed in his situation. Even when a second opportunity is offered to him, so that he can make a decision as he did not on the bridge over the Seine, he does not risk his life. So the novel ends with the words: "A second time! How frivolous! Just imagine, my dear colleague, if we were taken at our word! We would have to jump! Brr — the water is so cold! But never fear! It is too late now. It will always be too late. Luckily!"

B. Open Questions

It is, of course, obvious that only a partial view can be gained from the few examples of the phenomenon of guilt that I have provided from contemporary German and French literature. All the same, the theologian can recognize several important questions that arise from them.

1. Personal Decision

No one will deny that the traditional morality was concerned to call sins by their name. The code of morals was clear and detailed. The basis of this traditional code was the ten commandments and these have not in any way been superseded. Literary criticism does not therefore direct its attention to the code of morals as such. It is critically concerned with what we have made of that code and how we have used it to make sure that our lives are moral. What is pointed out again and again in works of literature is how easily we can take shelter behind conventionally moral behavior without being morally committed. Theology has also been criticized for having concentrated too much on legal casuistry and the description of possible faults in its teaching about sin. In this system, neither God nor one's fellow-men are encountered in personal responsibility. A repressive morality leads to a purely negative defence against possible losses in social and individual integrity. The I, as the factor mediating between the vital impulses and forces and a necessary adaptation to the world outside, is dominated and suppressed by the superego, as the factor inwardly representing the concrete moral norms of behavior. The situation of accusation that results[18] may therefore prevent man from accepting himself and others as being responsible. It may prevent him also from giving love, and security to others in the community. It is a fairly widespread conviction that the Church's moral teaching is to a considerable extent responsible for this proto-ethical, mechanical form of morality.

On the other hand, however, as I shall show, man has not, according to the ethical teaching of the New Testament, reached the form of moral being that it is possible for him to reach either subject to the law or through the law. In the same way, I shall also try to demonstrate that the biblical idea of sin is primarily directed toward man's fundamental decision in life.[19] What is decisive for the biblical authors is man's response to the personal appeal, his answer — yes or no — to God's call. This answer determines man's concrete actions. From it come the fruits of the Spirit or the works of the flesh. Our concern, then, will not be with a struggle against acts that are contrary to the norm ("sins"). We shall rather direct our attention toward the call from slavery to freedom.

2. The Power of Evil

One of the most striking themes in late nineteenth and twentieth century literature is that of the social involvement of evil. "From Ibsen and Strindberg, Wedekind, Sternheim, Musil and Brecht to Böll, Dürrenmatt, Frisch, Grass, Enzensberger, Walser, Lenz and Peter Handke, a literary connection can be distinguished, despite great differences in form, expression and tendency, with a common critical purpose — that of exposure. The individual is exposed, society is exposed and the individual is exposed as a representative of society. The idealistic view of the world was exposed at the end of the nineteenth century and the Christian and middle-class ideology was also exposed at much the same time."[20] Ideology has now become a dangerous word, pointing to the power and influence of those holding certain ideas and the passivity of the subjects. The collectivity is hidden in the ideology, anonymity is

74

hidden in the collectivity and "the mass is a hiding-place, representing the impossibility of grasping the person, and the situation in which no one is responsible."[21]

One is reminded again and again of the biblical account of the fall of man. There is also frequent reference to the guilt of society, in which society is regarded as more than simply a casual complex of relationships between individuals acting independently of each other. In its essence, society is an institutionally structured multiplicity of individuals, with the result that responsibility for many phenomena of evil cannot be explained without a critical examination of the institutions and norms of society. Guilt, then, is not simply a question of individual morality. It is also a collective political problem. It is to be found in the contradictions into which men enter in the process of socialization, technological development and authority. Our task in the following sections will therefore be to throw constant light on the social aspects of sin. The Bible speaks of the power of sin and stresses that all men are subject to it and are mysteriously involved in it. We are therefore bound to consider this question in our struggle against evil in the concrete.

3. Redemption

The modern word for freedom is liberation. The hidden background of this passionate search for liberation is clearly to be found in a deep experience of the lack of freedom. The phenomena and causes of the exterior and interior compulsions and their interrelationships have been analyzed and various theories have been developed to enable them to be overcome. Since the Enlightenment, prominence has been given to a "false consciousness" (ideologies, prejudices, deceptions about the true state of affairs and so on), in which people go astray and which prevents them from becoming truly human. It was first thought that mankind would come to autonomous freedom by the power of human reason, but later more confidence was placed in the will to change society by revolutionary praxis. Both of these approaches are found in the literature of exposure discussed in the preceding paragraphs. Quite often, however, a deep resignation is encountered. If there is no God, no forgiveness and no grace, then man himself has to justify his guilty existence. Clamence went the way of a penitent judge and knew that man's fate was slavery. Camus confronted us in his novel with the question as to how guilty man can justify himself within the context of atheism, without forgiveness and absolution. What is really interesting in the case of *The Fall* is that "the old Pauline and Protestant problem of justification is presented in a new situation and with completely new aspects as a fundamental question for modern man. Its deep human significance is re-examined in a new way. Camus considers it not as an academic question, but as a serious practical question about the justification of a guilty existence and man's re-acquisition of innocence. In this context, the question of the absolute inevitably arises."[22] For Christians, the mystery of sin is always presented together with the anticipatory offer of redemption.

§ 7 Symbolism and Concepts

It is clear from our brief consideration of man's reflected experience of evil in contemporary literature that man is directly and deeply affected by the experience of guilt. He speaks of this experience in images and metaphors. He has developed a special mythological language to express it ("late middle-class hell" and "on the edge of the continent"). He feels a need to confess, judge and evaluate the experience. This confession corresponds to a deeply felt human need. He speaks spontaneously about evil in his confession of it. His experience of sin is expressed originally and spontaneously in the mythological narratives of primitive peoples. The way leads from the mythos to the Logos, from spontaneous expression to the reflected concept. In this section, we shall first consider mythological texts and then, against this background, examine the reflected concepts of the Bible.

A. The Symbolism of Evil[1]

The phenomenon of failure can be empirically represented, but the central problem of the transition from innocence to guilt resists the empirical method. Paul Ricoeur has tried, in his research into old myths, to throw light on this problem of the transition.[2] He has provided a number of texts of confessions in which believing communities have expressed an admission of sinfulness. He is himself of the opinion that the philosopher can, by a sympathetic and imaginative approach, learn something from these texts about the motivation of man's consciousness. In the background to these confessions, mythical interpretations of reality are often expressed. These form the ground of the language of ritual actions. In the language of confession, an "experience fraught with emotion, fear and anxiety is often raised to the level of intellectual penetration."[3] We will now consider this symbolic content under two aspects. On the one hand, symbolical language makes it possible for us to understand the experience of guilt. On the other hand, seen in the light of the experience of guilt, this symbolical language is the language in which this experience can be expressed originally and spontaneously.

1. The Images of the Language of Confession

The language of confession contains a number of characteristic images that recur again and again. There is, for example, the image of the spot or stain. Other images are those of losing one's way, of the crooked path, of trespassing and wandering around and of a heavy burden or pressure.[4] Even a rudimentary semantic analysis of these images reveals different meanings and enables us to reduce these images to a number of categories.

The image of the spot or stain can be placed within the category of exteriority or outward contact. That is, it points in the first place to something material that makes man outwardly unclean. The images of going astray, of the crooked path, of trespassing and of wandering around can be classified under the heading of deviation. That is, they point primarily to a reality that is not in order or to a relationship that is disturbed. The image of pressure or of a heavy weight or burden belongs to the category of interiority. That is, it refers above all to something that is subjectively experienced.

If these images are regarded as symbols of the experience of guilt, it soon becomes apparent that a complex world of experience underlies them and that various levels of experience are also expressed in the individual categories. Subjective feelings of guilt are, for example, clarified by the images expressing a burden or weight or pressure. Images belonging to the category of deviation express this feeling of guilt less forcibly, but do express "a deep experience of sin surrounding all men and describing the real situation of all men in the presence of God, whether men know it or not."[5] Finally, in the images of exteriority, the experience of evil is clarified and the "how" of something material that surprises man and makes him externally unclean is expressed.

2. Relationships between Symbols

This phenomenology does not end with an analysis of the meanings of symbolic expressions and a classification of those images in various categories. The various symbols have to be seen as elements of the unity of the language of confession, just as the different levels of man's experience of guilt, sin and external stain can only be regarded as various levels of the one experience. If this essential unity is borne in mind, it is possible to follow Ricoeur and distinguish certain relationships between the symbols of the spot or stain, sin and guilt and between the corresponding levels of experience. These relationships should not be understood simply in the sense of a historical development. We should rather bear in mind that "the mythos is on the way to the Logos."[6] The more clearly linguistic expression is recognized as symbolic, the more it can gain strength to survive. The different symbols therefore have continued to exist up to the present time in a more or less allegorical form.

In the first place, it is possible to discern a movement from exteriority to interiority. This movement is accompanied by a change in the sphere of religious experience. The symbol of the spot or stain originally belonged to the archaic sphere of religious experience, the sphere of magic and tabu. The experience of guilt is externally connected to religious experience, but is not firmly attached to it. A stain or spot in this sense is not a precise point, nor is uncleanness literally dirt. These concepts are rather to be found "in the *chiaroscuro* of a quasi-physical infection or a quasi-moral unworthiness."[7]

This archaic mode of experience is replaced by the experience of sin. Instead of the image of unclean contact, we have the symbol of a disturbed or damaged relationship. The symbols of the missed target also belong to this category and that of going the wrong way. Even more closely related to the person are the images of obstinacy, faithlessness (adultery) and deafness. The images may also be related to a disturbed relationship between God and man or between men or even between man and his own self. This very strongly personalized symbolism is also in the background "of a new category of religious experience, the experience of being in the presence of God, to which the Jewish covenant, or *berith*, bears witness."[8] This mode of religious experience is in turn replaced by the experience of guilt in the narrower sense, a mode of experience that would seem to be completely subjective and interiorized. This penetration to the existential level is expressed by such metaphors as that of a burden or the prick of conscience. It is the experience of man reflecting alone on his failures and faults. For this reason, a typical symbol of guilt is also the image of judgment or the court of justice.

In the second place, according to Ricoeur, this movement from exteriority to interiority is also accompanied by a kind of iconoclasm. One image destroys the other — the religious symbol of sin destroys the magic symbol of the stain. The ethical symbol of guilt destroys the religious symbol of sin. This "iconoclastic movement proceeds . . . from symbolism itself."[9] This destruction of symbols, however, that takes place at the same time as the breaking down of the related sphere of religious experience, is not simply negative in its effects. The symbol that destroys another symbol at the same time transforms the symbolism of the destroyed symbol and includes it within its own symbolism. The symbol of sin, for example, whose symbolism is based on the specifically religious experience of the covenant, destroys the archaic and magic conception of evil as a spot or a stain. At the same time, however, the symbol of sin includes within itself the symbolism of the stain — in other words, the category of exteriority. This is then retained in the category of deviation in a transformed manner. In this category of deviation, however, evil no longer appears as something material that makes man outwardly unclean, but as a "broken relationship" and thus as a "nothing." The transformation of the category of exteriority into the symbolism of sin can be recognized in the category of deviation by the fact that evil is contained in the latter as a positive reality that is expressed, for example, in the images of power and captivity.[10]

The symbol of sin, on the other hand, is destroyed by the ethical symbol of guilt. The category of interiority replaces the image of deviation and going astray. But even in the category of interiority, the category of exteriority is still preserved and, what is more, it is retained in a repeated transformation of the image of captivity, which is in itself a transformation of the category of exteriority into that of deviation. "The conscience, which is crushed by the law that it will never be able to fulfill, knows that it is caught in its own injustice and, what is worse, in the lie of its claim to its own justice."[11]

B. The Concept of Sin in the Old Testament[12]

There are many different concepts of sin in the Old Testament,[13] but three can be regarded as fundamental in any Old Testament hamartiology. These are the concepts of *ḥaṭṭā' th (ḥṭ')*, *peša' (pš')* and *'āwōn ('wh)*. These three terms are partly interchangeable and are to some extent used, not as synonyms, but as pseudonyms. The relationship to each other is determined less by semasiological differences than by the period when they were used, the place where they originated and the position that they occupy in each case in the context and in historical understanding.

1) The root *ḥṭ'* (to miss the mark, to miss one's way, to fail, to offend) is the most commonly used term for sin.[14] It came from the secular sphere and continued to be a concept in general use, although it was increasingly employed in the Old Testament, especially in the substantival form *ḥaṭṭā'th*, in the theological sphere.

The basic meaning of *ḥṭ'* points to a concrete action — that of going astray or missing the mark or failing. It is also objectively a purposeful action that points to an existing social relationship.[15] This purposeful activity is especially clear in 1 Sam. 2.25: "If a man sins against a man, God will mediate for him; but if a man sins against the Lord, who can intercede for him?" It is precisely the existence of a social relationship that makes this failure possible and this relationship exists not only between men, but also between God and man. "The basic meaning of *ḥṭ'* is a failure to reach one's target or aim or a going astray from that aim because of the existing relationship between the one acting and his aim."[16]

We may say, then, that *ḥṭ'* is a formal concept undetermined as to content, and which cannot be restricted to concrete, definite failures, but has to be understood as a general term. It is a leading concept "which designates every failure as a failure to observe the commandment of Yahweh from the theological point of view and therefore as a sin. . . . The root is not simply a leading concept that formally includes all the contents of a failed act. It is also, in connection with this, a qualifying concept that evaluates these concepts critically."[17] This means, in other words, that *ḥṭ'* does not really point to the fact itself, but evaluates it.

The official confession of guilt (*ḥāṭā' ti*, I have failed; *ḥāṭā' nû*, we have failed), made by the individual or the people, originated as sacral legal action and was connected with a plea for forgiveness, a prophetic announcement of punishment, expiation, another confession, an interruption of affliction, the setting up of an altar and the offering of a sacrifice.[18] The confession of sin made by the people (*ḥāṭā' nû*, we have sinned) took place in every case in the Old Testament in a situation of oppression and distress. This confession "forms the essential *word* part of the penitential act in which the people submit to the fact that their sin has been made public in a situation of distress and ask Yahweh to change the situation."[19] The two formulas function as formally qualifying statements of fact and they form the essential and constitutive part of the confession of sin in Israel.

Although it cannot be restricted in its content, *ḥṭ'* is not an abstract concept, but is always related to concrete action: "*ḥṭ'* says, this act is a failure and this failure is an act."[20] The offence is an inescapable reality: "When a man or woman commits any of the sins that men commit . . ." (Num. 5.6). This passage refers to the connection between "objective failure" and "subjective responsibility," both of which form part of the concept. The root *ḥṭ'* is always used for conscious and unconscious sins, but the aspect of subjective guilt predominates.[21] It is worth bearing in mind, however, that the concepts of guilt and failing or missing should not be separated from each other. They point to the same thing. Guilt is the "constant reality that is objectively alive and active and is directed toward the one who has acted sinfully. It is, by virtue of a failure, the reality and sphere of that sinful action."[22] This means, then, that a man is subjectively held responsible even for an offence that he has committed unknowingly. This is very clear evidence of the existence in Israel of radical personal responsibility which transcended the ability of the actions themselves to function as a check[23] and which did not take into account the differences in human attitudes underlying consciously or unconsciously committed offences.

It was not until later that the subjective principle of guilt came, without loss of the objective principle, into the foreground and this took place on the basis of anthropological and psychological conditions.

2) The root *pš'* occurs forty-one times as a verb and ninety-three times as a noun in the Old Testament. Unlike *ḥṭ'*, this concept was derived from legal terminology, in which it was used to denote a crime or an offence against the community. The translation suggested by L. Köhler[24] and at one time almost universally accepted — protest, rebellion or conflict — is no longer tenable.[25] A more acceptable translation is undoubtedly "outrage," since this points to a concrete action, but not to a psychological attitude. The concept *pešaʿ* applies to property offences such as robbery or theft or for bodily injury or the carrying away of a body (see Gen. 50.12; Amos 1.3–2.16). It points to a violation of relationships within the community and is always used in the sense of a deliberate, conscious action. The person committing *pešaʿ* is "personally and entirely identical, with the whole of his humanity, with his action."[26] This means that only the psychical and social aspects of *pešaʿ* are visible; its content is not. As with *ḥṭ'*, it is a formal qualifying concept, in which it is always a question of taking someone or something away. Fahlgren[27] has therefore correctly translated the verb *pš'* as "to break with." The basic meaning of the root, then, is "the breaking away of a person or a thing from an owner; the breaking away of oneself from a community."[28]

If this idea is transferred to the theological sphere, it clearly indicates an attempt to make the action underlying the concept of *pešaʿ* more concrete and more radical. To commit *pešaʿ*, in other words, means breaking with God, withdrawing completely from his presence. The relationship between Israel and Yahweh was laid down in legal categories and since Yahweh was Lord of the law, a *pešaʿ* was always committed against Yahweh. This is why *pešaʿ* is the most clearly outlined and most radical concept used for sin in the Old Testament.[29] It is certainly stronger than *ḥṭ'*. Whereas *ḥṭ'* was used by the Old Testament authors for a crime committed against a presupposed order in the community, an offence which did not, however, harm the community as a whole, *pešaʿ* meant a total break with a community.

3) The verb root *'wh* (to bend, distort, pervert) is used seventeen times in the Old Testament and the noun *ʿāwōn* occurs 231 times.[30] Whereas the verb is to a great extent replaced by *ḥṭ'*, the noun is common in confessions, affirmations of innocence, discussions of

guilt, accusations and exonerations from guilt, petitions for forgiveness and God's self-predication.

Originally a secular term, '*āwōn* became, however, more and more theological in meaning in later texts, where it came to indicate a wrong relationship between God and man. In the theological sphere, then, the concept of divergence, bending, distortion or perversion was used metaphorically to qualify generally theological situations. The seriousness of an '*āwōn* was essentially determined in Israel by the significance of the deliberate subjective offence or the unconscious committing of a crime. In other words, the '*āwōn* was measured according to the degree of the intention underlying the offence and also according to the importance of the consequences brought about by the offence. There is clearly, then, a connection here between the action and its consequences. The action does not simply exist in isolation. It also brings about a process that leads to an end that corresponds to the action and, as well, determines the relationships in the community within which the offence is committed. "The '*āwōn* committed by an individual has an effect on the whole of the community (Lev. 22.16) and the '*āwōn* committed by the whole of the community is also borne by the individual (Lev. 16.22; Ezek. 4.4 ff.; Is. 53.5)."[31] Bearing in mind this sequence of action and consequence, the concept of '*āwōn* must be seen within a total understanding of reality as a unity of "offence–guilt–punishment."[32] In this context, '*āwōn* should not be understood as describing the course of an event. On the contrary, it includes the whole procedure in all its details.

As a concept used in theological language, '*āwōn* "denotes man's attitude toward God within the framework of the relationships between God and man in the community at any given time."[33] This statement, however, says nothing definite either about the content of that relationship or about the content of the offence committed. What is essential is that consciousness of the reality of the '*āwōn* is closely connected with consciousness of the presence of Yahweh, the living God. Whenever the Israelite was confronted by Yahweh, he was conscious of the oppressive burden of '*āwōn*, which then had, as the judgment of Yahweh, the nature of a revelation.[34]

Looking back at what we have said in this section, we can say that there is no scale of values with regard to theological importance in the three terms for sin used in the Old Testament, although it was common to grade them in earlier hamartiologies. "These concepts point less to the gravity and quality of a sin . . . and more to its appearance.[35] They are all equally serious as judgments in the mouth of Yahweh, since Yahweh's reaction to them and his judgment are always the same."[36]

C. Statements about Sin in the New Testament[37]

Jesus did not provide his followers with any doctrine of sin, nor did he ever say what he meant by sin. He did, however, know about the reality of sin and behaved accordingly.[38] He was committed to overcoming sin. (See, for example, Mk. 2.17 par; Lk. 19.10; Mt. 26.28; see also 1 Tim. 1.15; Col. 1.14; Eph. 1.7.) The reality of sin is expressed in the New Testament in many different formulations. In the synoptic gospels, the traditional meaning of sin that was commonly accepted at the time is presupposed. Sin is regarded therefore as a transgression of God's commandments. This is the concept of sin that is always in the background whenever the New Testament speaks of confessing or forgiving sins (see, for example, Mt. 3.6; Mk. 1.5; 3.28; 11.25; Lk. 11.4 etc.), even when the words tax-gatherers and sinners are used. It can also, however, be seen from the synoptic accounts that Jesus aimed to free his contemporaries from a purely juridical and external understanding of sin and to lead them to a more interiorized understanding of the concept. He clearly wanted them to recognize that sin came from the heart of man. In his heart, man was clean or unclean and valid or not valid in the presence of God. (See the Sermon on the Mount and the controversies with the pharisees in Matthew 23.) Against the background of Jesus' radical offer to guide men fundamentally by the love of which he himself was the clear example, a flight into legalism was obviously sinful. Thus, in the theological statement made by the synoptic authors, the real sin that underlies the universal moral concept of sin is that of lack of faith. In this sense, then, the concept of sin found in the writings of John and Paul is deeply theological. It is of special interest that both authors refer frequently not to sins in the plural, but rather to sin in the singular and, what is more, to sin as an attitude that was made objective in individual sinful acts.

Paul saw God, man and the world in the perspective of the salvation that had dawned with the coming of Jesus. Without Christ and before the coming of Christ, man was in darkness (see, for example, Eph. 2.12). This situation is depicted with great clarity by Paul in his letter to the Romans (1.28–3.20): "Both Jews and Greeks are under the power of sin" (Rom. 3.9) and Scripture has been fulfilled: "None is righteous, no, not one . . . no one seeks for God. All have turned aside" (Rom. 3.10-11). This ought not to be so and it is not possible to say that men have always been unable to do anything about it. God's invisible being was revealed, in his creation, to the pagans: his creation has been perceptible to them, "so that they are without excuse" (Rom. 1.20). On the one hand, Paul was clearly taking into account here man's call to know God and at the same time his moral responsibility located in his conscience (Rom. 2.15 ff.).[39] On the other hand, however, he recognized that all men had, without exception, failed.

A disastrous situation, in which even the Jews found themselves despite their law and God's revelation of himself to them, underlay this failure. "Paul was therefore conscious of the fact that, behind the dark backdrop of individual sinful acts committed by all men — pagans as well as Jews — acts which are relatively easy to ascertain, all men were subject to the power of sin. He recognized, reasoning in the light of the revelation of Jesus Christ, that the many sinful acts were symptoms of a more deeply rooted sickness and could be traced back to a fundamental human sinfulness which was inaccessible to man himself and acted as a central focal point of evil from which new sinful acts were again and again emerging."[40] This interrelationship between sin as an act and sin as fate or as a state of inner determination is mentioned by Paul in several places in his epistle to the Romans (8.2; 7.14, 17, etc.).[41] In this, two ideas are always in competition with each other — on the one hand, the conviction that man is able to decide for himself and is responsible for his own decisions and, on the other, that actual sins are an expression of his subjection to the power of sin, thus resulting in a solidarity among sinners, a perceptible connection between guilty men.

This interrelationship can also be found in the Johannine writings. According to John, there was, behind individual acts of sin, a mysterious power that was opposed to God and enslaved men and only the sinless Son of God was able to set men free from this power (Jn. 3.5; 8.46; see also Rom. 7.14-25). Behind sin, which was closed to Christ, the light of the world, was the "prince of this world" (Jn. 12.31). This sin was, as it were, man's primordial choice against God, his lack of faith (Jn. 8.21, 40 etc.). It was, according to John, revealed by the Holy Spirit (Jn. 16.8-11).[42]

There is, then, a twofold concept of sin in the New Testament. Sin is regarded by the New Testament authors as basically a rejection of God, a mysterious power which controls man and is able to make him a sinner. There are also many sins, that is, acts of sin, in which sin understood in this first sense is expressed and revealed.

The distinction between sin and sins, then, makes it possible to understand that the sin committed against the Holy Spirit leads to death and cannot be remitted (Mt. 12.31; 1 Jn. 5.16b). There is also sin as an attitude of opposition to God, in which man in complete control of himself commits himself to death by his deliberate separation from God. This is, of course, the sin of hardness of heart, obstinacy and determination to remain unbelieving in which man does not see himself as God's creature and therefore does not accept his dependence on God, but prefers to see himself as his own redeemer and exclusively responsible for himself.

It is clear, then, that the Old and New Testaments have an important contribution to make to our understanding of the phenomenon of sin and guilt. No answer is provided either by Jesus himself or by the members of the early Christian community to the question about the essence or meaning of sin as such. What Gerhard von Rad said about the Old Testament can be applied to the Bible as a whole: "It is obvious from even a brief glance at the Old Testament that the authors had little theoretical or theological to say about sin. Although the texts are full of references to sins that are committed somewhere, at some time and by somebody, there is very little theological reflection about sin as a religious phenomenon of great complexity. In the psalms, it is true, there are statements tending toward a degree of universal validity, but even they are for the most part based on a personal event, of which the psalmist complains. The Old Testament prefers the form of expression which is really best suited to the phenomenon of sin — that of confession."[43]

CHAPTER 2: THEOLOGICAL REFLECTION ABOUT GUILT AND SIN

It should not surprise us that it is so difficult to find a definition of sin that satisfies all demands. Despite all the differences in the literary genres contained in the various books of the Bible, it is true to say that the Bible as a whole is in no sense a theological manual. It is a confession, a testimony and an account of man's experience of God's dealings with him in the history of the people of Israel and, as far as the New Testament is concerned, especially in and through Jesus of Nazareth. Sin is therefore — as we have already seen above — discussed in the light of the confession of sin. Any theological reflection of the kind that I propose to undertake in this chapter and any attempt to systematize and conceptualize the idea of sin in the Bible must therefore take this fact seriously into account. In confession, a total experience of the reality of sin is revealed and a consciousness of that reality is raised to the level of verbal expression. We can reflect about this experience but we cannot divide it.

In this chapter, then, I shall discuss three aspects of guilt and sin and shall take care throughout to deal with each as an element of a single all-embracing phenomenon and to recognize that each is meaningful only within the context of the whole phenomenon. The three aspects can be distinguished by acknowledging the existence in sin of a decision or act (§ 8), a mysterious power (§ 9) and a sign pointing to a personal reality (§ 10).

§ 8 Sin as an Act

In an attempt to justify his crimes, man has often appealed either to the way he is constituted or to his environment. Adam appealed to his wife and his wife Eve in turn appealed to the serpent, blaming it for the decision. In sin, however, man first finds himself quite alone (*ego sum, qui feci*) in the presence of his God (*coram te domine peccavi*).

A. An Act of Freedom

Sin is only possible as a result of human freedom. In his freedom, man is confronted with a task (see above, § 3 D: "The Claim of the Freedom of Choice"). He is not simply available and present. He has rather simply to be. He has to convert distance from himself into nearness to himself. He has to give the concrete form of himself to himself. As a finite spirit, he is released into that being that can consent to the self and at the same time express actively the movement that allows him to be. The ground and ultimate aim of this process of freely finding himself is perfect freedom, good as such, God. Man is essentially orientated toward this state and is on the way toward it, with the result that, even where he does wrong, he can only do this subjectively because of his restless search for the good, at which he aims under the mask of a temporary pseudogood. In other words, he is always bound in his orientation toward good and his freedom is always inwardly qualified. If, however, within the latitude of freedom that is open to him, man freely decides in favor of what is temporary, finite and purely available, in favor of things, passions or impulses, and completely expends his freedom on such things and thus breaks away from his orientation toward the ultimate good that transcends him, he sins. This wrong decision is the result of premature synthesis and violent totalization. This attitude places man in a situation in which he is in contradiction with himself and his real being, so that he is not the person that he should be. He ought to act as what he really should be — a person on the way toward that to which his essential being is aiming. As long as he is not completely at one with the transcendental ground (and aim) of his being in knowledge, love and self-expression, he is still able to make wrong decisions (and thus break away from himself) by deciding independently of the transcendental ground of his being. He can, at any given time, act as if he does not want what he can never cease to want — that all his actions be rooted in the ground of his being.[1]

This brief outline of the special nature of the freedom of the creature as the prior condition of the possibility of man's sinful state of contradiction with himself[2] does not, of course, throw any light on the mystery of evil as such. All that it does is to draw attention to one fundamental condition in the subject. I shall later on discuss the historical and social conditions of evil, but for the present we

must continue to consider the subject. This outline of the fundamental prior condition does not, moreover, tell us much about sin
as an act of freedom. Man's confession of sin may tell us more
about that, because it has a performative character. If the psalmist,
for example, tells us in a confession of guilt: *iniquitatem meam ego
agnosco*, "I acknowledge my offence," he is combining the past and
the future in the decisive moment of his present. He is also accepting responsibility for his action and its consequences.

1. Acceptance of Responsibility

Moral evil is malign because it is a work of one's own freedom
and as such a work of freedom itself.[3] In the act of confessing, man
in fact, by speaking, applies this freedom to himself. He can only
make this confession in a meaningful way if he reflects about his
action, and he has to tell himself that he might have been able to
act differently. It is possible, of course, for him to make a mistake
in judging his situation at the time of his action, but this is not of
decisive importance. Judges and lawyers may reflect about it. The
personal confession and the conviction expressed in it cannot in
this sense be objects for reflection by others.

The confession has a performative character. The person making
the confession declares himself to be one who might have been
able to act differently. He does not look for an alibi, but accepts full
responsibility for his decision and the resulting action. The significance of the immoral action that can be objectively described in
a confession should therefore not be devalued. It can be expressed
in descriptive sentences and it can be judged within the sphere of
normative ethics. But sin is very much more than behavior contrary
to the norm. Insight is an essential aspect of sin, and confession is
also, in a sense, an element of sin. It is only in confession that sin
becomes fully conscious of itself and of its full reality. It is only
when it is confessed that it is existentially accepted. There is, however, no sin without guilt. Sin and guilt are indissolubly united
according to the evidence of the Bible and it is precisely for this
reason that the Bible clearly prefers to represent sin under the form
of confession. Sin is expressed in the Bible as an all-embracing personal reality and the traditional moral theology of the Church has
tried to do justice to this concept of sin by affirming that knowledge and will were essential aspects of sin. In fact, however, these

two elements have normally been simply presupposed as data, and sin has been equated in practice with action contrary to the norm and as a result have been understood descriptively. In this way, sin has come to be seen as an offence and sins have come to be regarded as actions capable of being described. But it is precisely what distinguishes sin from a moral action — sin, in other words, as an existential self-expression — that can only be described with difficulty. The person who has committed the sin can explain his action only by confronting it with the way he experiences his faith and lack of faith, and he can only do this in the form of a confession. "An understanding of sin that keeps exclusively to ethical or even legal categories bypasses the historical reality, because it does not plumb the meta-ethical depths of the decision that gave rise to the action performed by the Christian [and by Abraham]."[4] The form used to represent sin, then, is confession. But there is also another aspect to this question, which we must consider now.

2. Acceptance of the Consequences

The person confessing declares, when he confesses, that he is ready to be converted. In other words, he turns his gaze from the past to the future. In his confession, his sin is not simply finished by his acceptance of guilt. The condition for its overcoming is also created. David's confession to Nathan is a classical expression of this: "I have sinned against Yahweh." And Nathan said to David, "Yahweh also has put away your sin; you shall not die" (2 Sam. 12.13). This unity of the moral subject of past, present and future, of the action and its consequence, in the act of confession is made clear again and again in the Old Testament.[5] It is above all in the Wisdom literature and the psalms that sin and the consequences of sin are regarded as a single, connected event. In Hebrew thought, there were in fact no stages — the action and its consequences — but only the single, whole event. The dynamic Hebrew view of history resulted in every historical event being seen in its dynamic development and effectiveness. Static being was not meaningful to the Hebrew mind.[6] Suffering in the present therefore always raised questions about the whole disastrous process that was made visible in that suffering and man, in his suffering, always turned from the particular disastrous event in his own life to consider his origins. His view of life was, in this respect, clearly synthetic. In this way, the Israelite resisted an extrinsic idea of retribution, in which punishment and reward were alien to the essential being of one who had sinned and to that of the act itself.

The fact that sins are expressed in the Bible principally in the form of confessions also implies a clear rejection of all forms of dualism. Man declares himself to be the author of evil. He resists any attempt to describe evil as a substance or to give it the status of a thing that can be observed by outsiders. Ideas of this kind are found "in the metaphysical fantasies of the kind attacked by Augustine. These include Manichean representations of evil and all those ontologies according to which evil is a being. In the form of psychological or sociological determinism, these ideas can still be expressed in a positive, highly developed scientific form. To accept full personal responsibility for the origin of evil means that one is ready to dismiss the view that evil is an object, a being or an effect in a world of ascertainable physical, psychological or social realities. I declare: *ego sum qui feci*, 'I am the one who has done it.' There is no object or being known as evil. There is only evil done by me." [7]

This personal decision and personal responsibility, however, form only one aspect of the act of confession, which is only completed by being a confession in the presence of God.

B. *Coram Deo*

Sin is not simply a question of human guilt — it is also guilt in the presence of God. If a man does not believe in God, he does not sin. In that case, each man is guilty only with regard to each man. It may even be that "there are no guilty people and no responsible people any more. No one can do anything about this situation and no one wants it." [8] We have seen from our analysis of the biblical concepts for the phenomenon of sin above (§ 7 B) that sin had an essentially religious aspect in the mind of biblical man. This has two implications. First, to turn away from God is an alienation from oneself and second, it implies a sign of hope.

1. Turning away from God as Self-Alienation

Man becomes alienated from himself when he makes an idol of himself and therefore turns away from God. Sin is always a destruction of the covenant with God and therefore a destruction of self and of community. It may take a cultic, a legal or an ethical form. [9] The Yahwist's account of the fall is a classical example of this. In the foreground, there is the transgression of a cultic commandment or prohibition. At the deeper level, there is the beginning of a self-produced history, in which no limit set to finite beings is respected. "In the Yahwistic account of Genesis 2–3, it is not simply a question of mortality breaking into man's life, although this mortality is in fact presupposed in Genesis 3.19a. What is in fact presented in this story is the end of life as such. . . . Genesis 3.19b should therefore not be understood as the pronouncement of a punishment which corresponds to a certain concrete reality. The punishment pronounced over mankind is to be found above all in the banishment of Adam and Eve from the Garden of Eden as the place where man has community . . . with God (Gen. 3.23 ff.). Man does not become fully conscious of the fact that he has become a victim of death until he is excluded from community with God, since this exclusion deprives him of an essential means of fulfilling his existence. He becomes conscious for the first time of the intrusion into his life of a reality which is hostile to life and which is for Old Testament man always the expression of death." [10]

This had extensive consequences, many of which are indicated in the Yahwistic account of the fall and the subsequent stories. Man became alienated from his fellow-men — this is clear from the references to shame and from the accounts of the conflict between generations. Man also became alienated from his physical constitution — work is shown to be difficult and tiring. He also became alienated from his natural environment — there is enmity between him and the animals and the soil is infertile. Relationships between men became disordered. There was fratricide, an increasing division of labor (Gen. 4.20), intermarriage with the godlike Nephilim (Gen. 6.4), drunkenness and shamelessness, the building of towers and the spread of confusion in languages. These were the immanent consequences of a history of man's attempt to show himself off and of his loss of respect for the finite limits to his existence. The reason for this history and its consequences is his refusal to recognize the limits to his autonomy as a creature and his desire to be God himself.

In the New Testament, man's break with God lies in his refusal to believe. Secret fear causes "the one who is called to avoid the all-embracing challenge of personal encounter that takes place paradigmatically in Jesus Christ." [11] He seeks refuge in legalism and in this way brings about a "change in the fundamental structures of the economy of salvation outlined in the New Testament and at the same time in New Testament anthropology."[12]

In the gospel of John, this turning away from God is represented in the rejection of the Logos: "He came to his own home, and his own people received him not" (Jn. 1.11). God's creatures, men, are self-sufficient. They refuse to open themselves to God's light and to his life. They do not need his revelation of truth. What is truth? If it can be found at all, it can be found in oneself or one's fellow-men. An autarchy prevails.

In Paul's epistles, *hamartia* or sin is also an act of rejection of God. In the context of Paul's doctrine of justification, this rejection is a *kauchesis* or boasting about oneself. Man, in other words, has his own achievements to offer. He has no need of a redeemer. He boasts of his own works. In the extended sense, this boasting is a belief in his own limitless power to fashion himself. It is an indication of his Utopian conviction that he can overcome his own alienation and evil in the world by his own power. In refusing God in this way, man is ceasing to accept the historical nature of his own existence in faith and trust in God's will to save now and in the future. On the contrary, he is anticipating the future in an isolated process of self-determination. In other words, lack of faith is manifesting itself in an exclusive faith in oneself: *aversio a Deo quia conversio ad se solum*. Man's autonomy is distorted into autarchy.

2. A Sign of Hope

The consequences of turning away from God are depicted in a very radical way by the biblical authors, but they make it clear that there is always hope. The essential presupposition for this is the confession of guilt, and sin is always nullified as soon as it is confessed. Nathan was therefore able to say to David: "Yahweh has put away your sin; you shall not die" (2 Sam. 12.13).

When sin is placed before God, it is seen as part of the movement of God's promise. The call is already a renewal of a bond and the beginning of a new creation. With God in view, man's passion for what is possible (for what is possible in God's promise) takes possession of his confession of evil and he recognizes that it is possible to be different. In this way, evil, presenting itself to man's moral consciousness essentially as a transgression of the law, is already qualitatively transformed as soon as it is placed before God as sin.

Paul Ricoeur has paraphrased Romans 5.20 in the following way: "Wherever evil is present 'in fullness,' hope is also present 'in abundance.' We must therefore have the courage to include evil in the epic of hope. Evil functions, in a way that is unknown to us, in the growth of the kingdom of God. Faith sees evil in this way. This vision is not that of the moralist. The moralist contrasts the predicate 'evil' with the predicate 'good.' He condemns evil, attributes it to man's freedom and goes no further when he reaches the limit of what can be investigated, because we do not know how it is possible for freedom to be enslaved. Faith, however, sees the situation quite differently. It is not concerned with the origin of evil, but with the end of evil. Together with the prophets, faith places that end in the category of God's promise. Together with Jesus, it places it in the proclamation of the God who is to come and, together with Paul, it places it in the law of superabundance." [13]

The Synod of Bishops in Germany declared recently that the Christian confession of the forgiveness of sins constituted a very important element of hope at the present time. "In its proclamation of the reality of guilt and sin, Christianity is opposed to the unhealthy illusion of innocence that has become so widespread in contemporary society and to the practice of attributing guilt and failure, if their presence is acknowledged at all, to others and other causes — our enemies and opponents, the past, nature or the environment. The history of man's freedom is one of conflict. It is divided into two. A sinister mechanism for exonerating men from guilt is active within that history. We attribute successes and victories to ourselves, but for the rest, we cultivate the art of denying our human condition or thrusting it into the background. We are always in search of new alibis in view of the dark side, the catastrophic side, the unhappy side of the history that has been made, experienced and written by ourselves." [14]

In his commentary on this text in the bishops' pronouncement, Johann Baptist Metz pointed clearly to the theological and philosophical connections. [15] Since the Enlightenment, Metz has pointed out, attempts have been made to solve the problem of theodicy radically by simply denying the existence of God. God has been dethroned as the subject and lord of history and has lost his central position in that historical process. When, however, man is defined as the one who takes in hand his own fate, in both its historical and its social aspects, we are confronted with the history of man's suffering and see history in a completely new light. This history of suffering has, after all, certainly not ceased to exist as an accusation. "Since God is no longer available as the subject who can be held responsible, all guilt has apparently . . . to be attributed to man as the maker of history." [16] In this situation, theodicy, as the justification of God in view of the suffering of the world, has been replaced by an anthropodicy or an attempt to justify man in view of that suffering.

Various attempts have been made, then, but these do little to "conceal the contradictions and conflicts inherent in a post-theological theory of history and society." [17] Man as a subject who can be held responsible has been to some extent divided into two parts. At one time, he is treated as the quasi-transcendental subject of history and at another he is forcibly enrolled in the historical process or he is held responsible in freedom for a form of anthropomorphism, although his freedom is thought to be no more fully developed than that of a very adaptable animal. An irrational desire to assume innocence in all actions has also been evolved. The unsolved problem of theodicy has also apparently arisen once more, this time in the recent theories aiming to exonerate man from all guilt. Is it possible that God is nowadays regarded as nonexisting because we cannot face the abyss of our experience of guilt and the demand to turn away from it? God calls for our conversion as a consequence of his existence, but this conversion is also dependent on his existence itself. The Synod therefore declared that "the God of our hope is very close to us and is above the abyss of our reasonably recognized and known guilt as the one who directs our decisions and forgives our guilt. Our Christian hope does not, therefore, lead us past our experience of guilt. It rather calls on us to keep realistically to our consciousness of guilt — even in a society which is struggling to achieve more freedom for all men and to make sure that all men will come of age and is therefore sensitive to the abuse that can so easily be caused by speaking about guilt and has in fact been caused in the history of Christianity." [18]

If we look back at the history of moral theology and consider briefly Thomas Aquinas's treatise *De vitiis et peccatis* (*Summa Theologiae* I–II, 71–89), [19] our first impression is not of a radical and existential understanding of sin in the sense outlined above. The understanding of sin developed by Thomas in this treatise is apparently not genuinely theological, but rather an understanding based on "a philosophical form of ethics in which the data pertaining to the Christian revelation were subsequently included."[20]

It is, of course, true that Thomas took over concepts and models from Aristotle's philosophy, but these were changed and adapted by their theological content. A close examination of the text of his treatise reveals a theocentricity as unmistakable as that of the treatise on the law.[21] Thomas first considers sins as morally evil acts of the kind that occur in everyday life. In this sense, sin is understood as *actus humanus malus* (71, 6c). Even while he is outlining this definition of sin as an evil act, however, Thomas moves forward to examine the heart of the matter. The act is evil, he says, because in the first place it is in contradiction to reason. This contradiction to reason is not, however, simply a contradiction of human nature or of the center and the measure of virtue, as it was for Aristotle; it is above all a contradiction of the *lex aeterna* in which God's creative claim is expressed to man.[22] Sin is therefore a contradiction of oneself. It is self-contradictory because it rejects the claim made by God's creation. In various contexts, "Thomas stresses the decisive aspect of sin — that it is an opposition to God."[23] It is directed against God as the objective of love (78, 1c). It is contempt for God and comes about as a result of disordered love of oneself (73, 2, 3, 4, 5; 77, 6 ad 1). Pride is directed against God's right to rule and hatred is directed against God's love.

Thomas defines the essential aspect of sin as an *aversio a Deo* (77, 8c). This turning away from God is not, however, a pure negation of God. It is rather the inner consequence of a turning toward (*conversio*) a substitute objective, a substitute God. "The fact that the *aversio* always goes together with a *conversio* was to be found, for Thomas, in the metaphysical law that all that is bad and consequently all evil is based on a good as its material cause, insofar as this good can only be revealed in evil as a defect."[24]

In this interpretation of evil, Thomas was following Augustine's well known definition of sin: *peccatum est factum vel dictum vel concupitum aliquid contra legem aeternam* (*Contra Faustum* 22, 37). Thomas also used Aristotle's concept of matter and form to distinguish two constitutive elements in sin.[25] The first of these elements is quasi-material — the human act. It is *per se* (directly) caused by the human will. As a positive act it is borne transcendentally by God. The second element is the quasi-formal aspect of the defect

96

that is part of the act itself, the privation of the relationship to the right objective (*debita carentia boni*). The will is the *causa deficiens* for this and has no need of any transcendental ground when it appears in this light. Finally, what makes sin sinful is the breaking of man's relationship with God.

If we look at the whole of Thomas's reasoning about sin in this treatise, we may conclude that "there is in Thomas's teaching a clear movement from thinking about sins to thinking about sin. Sins in the plural can only be understood in the theological sense if we go back to what really makes them sinful, in other words, to sin in the singular. This is turning away from the true God, refusing to be subject to him as the ultimate objective and the dominating orientation in man's life and, instead of this, raising one's own created person to the throne of God as an ultimate objective in itself and as the ultimate norm of one's actions."[26]

§ 9 Sin as a Power

Sin is rooted in man at the deepest personal level of his existence. It cannot simply be equated with an activity that is contrary to normal human behavior, although such behavior is one possible expression of sin. No, sin is above all a personal act. No man, however, is an isolated individual in his historical and social existence. He bears the burden of his origin and is therefore involved in man's total history of guilt and suffering. The task of shaping the future cannot be completed, but this does not mean that the Christian should sink into passive resignation. On the contrary, he is required to fight against evil in the world.

A. Man in Contradiction

The history of man's salvation did not begin with sin, but with man's creation and election. The priestly tradition in the Old Testament reveals man not as in opposition to God (as in the myth of Prometheus), but as God's image and administrator, working with him. Sin, on the other hand, points to a break with what God wants and has ordained. In almost every case in which God's covenanted people in the Old Testament are accused by the prophets of sin, they are reproached for having fallen away from God, for having departed from his way, for having been unfaithful to

God, for having abandoned him, for having broken his covenant or for having turned to strange gods. In the great hamartiology of Genesis 3–11, the Yahwist depicts the intrusion of sin into man's life and its breathtakingly rapid growth from the fall to the flood and the building of the tower of Babel. The ideas that emerged from Israel's reflection on its experiences in faith with Yahweh are recorded in this history of man's origin in the first chapters of Genesis. As a nomadic people, Israel knew God in the events of the people's history and especially their liberation from slavery in Egypt, their passage through the desert and their entry into the promised land. These acts of salvation performed by Yahweh provided the background to the history of salvation that was remembered and recorded in the time that followed their occurrence and it was against that background that sin was seen as faithlessness and rebellion. The break with Israel's origin was thus a break with God's election and saving intention. The significance of this break was first experienced in the negative consequences that led to faithlessness and disobedience with regard to the Torah. On the positive side, God's promise was expressed in what Israel hoped for. For a long time, this hope was for a happy and fulfilled life on earth. Very gradually, however, from the promises made by Yahweh in his covenant with his people, there evolved in Israel the specific hope of the bringer of salvation and the time of salvation, the hope of resurrection and the hope of a new and changed life. This hope was accompanied by a deepening of Israel's consciousness of sin and a realization that only God could and would renew men's hearts, that only he would make the new man capable of obedience (see Jer. 31). The real fulfillment of God's promise, of man's hope, and sin as a break with the promise, is to be found in the teaching of the New Testament.

The New Testament reveals the fullness of God's promise and therefore the full background to man's understanding of sin. In his proclamation of the kingdom of God (see below § 16), Jesus was, of course, above all addressing his own contemporaries. His point of departure was not an abstract image of man, but man in his concrete historical existence. Jesus called on all men to be converted and taught that all men were in need of conversion. God's demand made to man, calling on him to make a decision, reached man in the concrete statement made to him here and now by his neighbor.

When the first Christians looked back in faith at the death and resurrection of Jesus, they were able to interpret man's sinful existence in a much clearer light. The statements made in Paul's epistle to the Romans, to which we referred above (§ 7 C), can be understood in this sense. Paul based his argument on the event of Christ and insisted that all men, both Jews and gentiles, were in need of the redeeming and liberating love of God, as revealed to all men in the crucified Christ. Looking at his fellow-men, Paul saw them entangled in a great historical complex of guilt that no human power could break. The countless faults of men pointed, as symptoms of a much more deeply seated illness, to man's fundamentally sinful state which, as the source of evil, broke out again and again in renewed acts of sin. The apostle did not throw much light on the darkest background to man's fate in this respect, but he did make it clear that, in his opinion, man himself was the cause of sin and the disastrous situation that resulted from it. On the one hand, he stressed the fact that man was master of his own decisions and was therefore responsible for them and, on the other, he was conscious of a mysterious connection between the acts of sin committed by individual men and the sinfulness of all men. On the one hand too, individual man was, in Paul's view, characterized by the burden of being remote from God, but, on the other hand, that distance was increased by every new act of sin committed. Just as sin in the life of the individual creates a situation that conditions further sins, so too does sin create a sphere in the history of mankind in which further sin is bound to flourish. This is the situation, without grace or redemption, in which mankind finds itself, a state which makes it impossible for man, in the presence of each personal sin, to realize the love for which he is longing in the depths of his being.

Are we mistaken in our belief that the literary evidence that we have quoted provides a striking illustration of this situation? Camus' call or summons is always there, but, because of our selfishness, we are always too late to jump. Camus resignedly dismisses the problem by merely wishing us luck and perhaps such an attitude causes us our greatest trouble.

The doctrine of original sin is an attempt made by theologians to provide an etiological explanation for this situation. In recent years, many further attempts have been made to re-interpret this doctrine, the best known of these being the theology of sin developed by Piet Schoonenberg.[1] He regards original sin as the "sin of the world" — in other words, as the sum of all actual sins including the first sin with which history began. Sum in this context should not, of course, be understood as a simply external joining together. In the type of Adam, the Bible sets before us the element that is common to all men in the divine call and in the rejection of that call. The past, the present and the future flow, as it were, together into a single moment from the point of view of God's call. From the very beginning, man wanted to decide for himself. He wanted to be God. The logically first step, God's call, was followed by the logically second step, man's break with that call and the logical consequence was broken, sinful man. All men are united in a historical oneness in sin and have a solidarity in guilt which is shown in the typology of the Bible. The sin of Adam is the sum of all actual sins and therefore the cause of the disastrous situation in which mankind finds itself. Man is not, however, simply outwardly involved in this solidarity of sin and guilt. His relationship with God is also existentially broken and this situation is revealed in his inability to believe and to love.

Schoonenberg's interpretation of the theology of sin seems to be closely in accordance with Paul's hamartiology. We cannot unfortunately discuss here whether it is also in conformity with the teaching of the Council of Trent (DS 1510–1516).[2] The doctrine of original sin is, after all, essentially an "abbreviated formula for the fundamental theological understanding of history according to which the situation of death, greed, the law, futility and so on, a situation partly determined by guilt, together with the empirical difficulty of good separated from evil in history that is the result of man's concupiscence, cannot be terminated."[3] We may summarize this teaching by saying that man himself is not able to put an end to his historical situation, which is at least partly conditioned by his guilt. This situation forms a permanent part of the constitution of history. Its historical cause is to be found in the context of man's freedom of choice. It is not possible to say what decision was made or how that decision came about. All that we know in faith is that man's broken situation is overlaid by God's saving will, which is active in the infralapsarian sense. The offer of finality made by Christ continues to exist, despite man's brokenness. The situation in which man is saved is partly determined, before any personal decision is made, by the fall and a call that transcends the fall. We are therefore summoned again and again to jump — luckily.

With regard to his experience of evil, the Christian is not necessarily condemned, individually or collectively, to passive resignation. "On the one hand, the power of grace to overcome suffering and death eschatologically is active everywhere and, on the other, the Christian must create a concrete historical phenomenon and testimony of the presence of grace in the world by his shaping of the future in love and justice. The doctrine of original sin is there to remind us of this task and the fact that it cannot be completed in this world."[4]

B. Man's Struggle against Evil

There would seem to be two alternative ways for man to react to the power of evil in the world — by passive resignation or by hoping against hope. There are many different ways in which man's alienation from himself and from society can appear today, but for this reason the phenomenon is often very difficult to understand. (The examples from modern literature given above in § 6 are evidence of this.) It is, however, not possible for any man living in the modern world to avoid coming into contact with the many inner and outward compulsions in society and their threat to enslave him. The way in which these can be attacked depends to a great extent on our interpretation of the causes and relationships of evil. "Many of the theories evolved to explain the presence of evil in the world within the context of the European theological and philosophical tradition are no longer able to convince man today because they underestimate the phenomenon of evil."[5] The recent attempts to reinterpret the doctrine of original sin are based on the same understanding. I shall therefore examine briefly and fundamentally the connection between the interpretation of the origin of evil and the corresponding strategy that can be used in fighting it. I shall also provide a number of more concrete indications in the following section and when I come to deal in detail with the question of norms.

1. The Exclusive Foundation in the Subject

According to the Kantian philosophy of subjectivity, evil is found exclusively in the subject. Kant was opposed to the doctrine of original sin because it taught that evil did not have a historical

101

origin in time, but originated only in man's reason. "Every evil action must — if its origin is sought in man's reason — be regarded as though man had moved from a situation of innocence into it. For, whatever his previous behavior may have been and of whatever kind the natural causes that may influence him may be — whether, in other words, they are within him or outside him — his action is still free and not determined by any of these causes. It can therefore be judged and must indeed always be judged as an original choice."[6] There is no intelligible foundation from which moral evil can be derived. In the absence of a foundation outside, man himself has to determine what he is — good or evil — in the moral sense. Every influence from outside is excluded. Even "supernatural cooperation" — in other words, grace — was, Kant believed, dependent on the fact that man had made himself worthy to receive it.[7] If the moral law calls for an improvement, we must be able to improve; what applies in this case is "you can because you should." What is certain is that man, as a moral subject, will contribute to the victory of good in the world. Kant's hypothetical explanation of evil cannot, however, "elucidate the connection between the intelligible act and man's experiences of evil in time and history on the basis of the distinction between the intelligible and the empirical aspects of man that has been evolved in transcendental philosophy."[8] Ultimately, the subject remains beyond "history, scientific development and society."[9]

2. Evil in the Social Process

Unlike Kant, Marx believed that evil originated in history and more precisely in the social process. The real subject of history was, for Marx, real man, in contrast to Hegel's idea of the abstract subject of history (see above § 4 B 3). He made no distinction between the conscious and the unconscious event and attributed contradictions and differences to empirical man. Reconciliation through the mediation of opposites did not, in Marx's view, take place simply in ideas. It took place through history, in other words, through society in the concrete. Marx understood history as the space in which man himself made concrete and universal changes in human relationships and as the way to liberation. The historical process is based on the state of the forces of production. The inevitable dialectical conflict is therefore of an economic kind. The real subject of history is the proletariat, a class that has been totally alienated from itself by the sale of its labor. It has therefore to be liberated by regaining its self-consciousness. As soon as alienation is overcome, society will cease to be divided into classes. Alienation will not exist in the classless society.

Marxist teaching has made a deeper impression on history than almost any other doctrine of liberation and redemption. It is active in the various Marxist–Leninist political systems and both individual man who is alienated from himself and society and history have been discovered, through the teaching of Marx, as the place of human self-liberation. This understanding has frequently been linked with Freud's insights into man's psychology and there are many theories of society and culture which seek to provide an explanation for the ills of society today. The fundamental thesis of alienation has been transformed into the universally human element. Whereas Marx believed that alienation was an economic phenomenon, it is now suggested that it is determined by the structures of society as a whole.[10] A demand is therefore made in the negative dialectic tension for the destruction of the existing order.[11] In the positive sense, good is seen as the measure of emancipation, insofar as this is objectively possible by manipulating existing conditions in society.[12] Other theories with different emphases have been suggested by Herbert Marcuse, Wilhelm Reich and Arno Plack. According to these thinkers, the roots of evil are to be found in the suppression of primary impulses. Human freedom will only be achieved as a result of man's liberation from sexual repression. A social and economic revolution is also required if man is to become fully developed and the natural structure of his impulses is to be realized. Such a revolution would make it possible for all classes and ages of people to assert themselves sexually without restriction.

3. The Struggle against Evil in History

Not only the structure of the struggle against evil, but also the outcome of that struggle are determined by our interpretation of the causes and relationships of evil. If the roots of evil are to be found, as Heidegger believed, in the "risk of being being," then it would be foolish to think of trying to get rid of it. If, on the other hand, the cause is attributed to economic structures or the repression of sexual impulses, then the demand for individual conversion can only be seen as cynical. We are left with the revolutionary struggle and this calls for faith in unconditional success.

I am of the opinion that the struggle against concrete evil in history must be kept free from one-sided ideological emphases. In discussing the German bishops' document on hope (see § 8 B 2 above), we pointed out that man tries to hide his own guilt in the shadow of such theories. It is not possible to separate subjective from objective errors made in freedom. The struggle against evil therefore calls for personal conversion and the acceptance of responsibility in a historical and social context. Two important factors have to be borne in mind here.

First, every act performed by an individual, however insignificant it may be, has social consequences. The concrete forms of evil — injustice, oppression, exploitation and violence — cannot all be attributed to the responsibility of an individual. They do, however, combine together as a sum total of individual acts of inhumanity which are apparently harmless as merely individual acts and can be dismissed as simply human. It is the linking together of these individual acts into a chain of inhumanity that puts the future of mankind at risk and destroys man's hope of finding an ultimate meaning in life. It is above all because of this phenomenon that we should not be blind to the warnings given by contemporary literature. Idleness, thoughtlessness and a desire for sensation may not perhaps be intrinsically harmful, but there is always a risk that something far worse may arise from them.

Second, every specifically social act calls for very special attention. There is no collective object of action and consequently no collective guilt. It is, however, right to speak of the guilt of society — in other words, of our co-responsibility for the institutions, regulations, customs and collective convictions governing our life together with our fellow-men which also affect the behavior of the individual. If we bear in mind that these social institutions are our own creation and not simply unquestionable expressions of a previously given and existing order, we are bound to recognize our responsibility for them and at the same time the ambivalent aspect of the whole structure and the possibility that it may be associated with a wrong social consciousness which may in turn develop into a very dangerous power of evil. Words that have entered our everyday language — underdeveloped societies, social economy and the reform of the penal code, for example — point to what this means in the concrete.

I would not like to give the impression by what I have just pointed out that I believe that a consciousness of sin and a wrong social consciousness are one and the same. A Christian theology that aimed to overcome guilt in the presence of God by criticizing ideology and regarding penance as the same as help for the developing countries would clearly be a mistaken form of theology. In the theological sense there can never be a fulfillment of man that is produced by man alone. The phenomenon of sin throws man back again and again to his finite state, that is, to his distinction from God. "The consciousness of this distinction could make contemporary man (insofar as he is directed to the production of his history and the disclosure of the conflicts in this production) aware that 'false consciousness' is removable not through corrective measures or by force, and that history cannot be fulfilled by man alone. So long as there is any consideration of the problem of guilt in the sight of God and of its cancellation, conversion to a 'true consciousness' is not in the hands of fallible and finite men."[13]

§ 10 Sin as a Sign

What we have said so far about the phenomenon of sin and guilt indicates that sin is not to be identified with individual acts that are contrary to normal behavior. Sin is not, either, simply the same as failure nor is it merely action that is contrary to the law. Man himself is at risk when he sins. Confession of sin makes it clear that sin goes to the roots of man's existence and touches him in his longing for ultimate fulfillment and his total relationship with God. The same confession also points, however, to the aspect of the sinful act as a decision, the person confessing is confessing his own decision. No decision is, however, made in isolation. Man's sin involves him in a universal history of salvation and its absence, of freedom and slavery, of being oneself and being alienated from oneself. Faith is borne and made secure by the community of those who believe and in the same way sin prospers in the solidarity of sinners. Another aspect of sin also has to be borne in mind. As a human decision, it shares in the human unity of body and soul, has its external and its inner aspects and exists within the context of an individual historical process.

A. The Signs of a Fundamental Option

The expression of human freedom is perceived by any transcendental analysis as an act of original self-determination (see above § 5 B). I have already called this expression of freedom or original opening of the human will to itself, a desire for transcendental freedom. I have also said that the fulfilling content of transcendental freedom could only be freedom itself and this could also, because of the unconditioned nature of its opening of itself, only be a relationship with unconditioned freedom. Transcendental freedom thus anticipates unconditioned freedom by virtue of its own distinctive form. It can in fact only be understood as finite freedom if it is considered within the situation of dynamic tension between limited and unlimited freedom. In expressing itself, it is able to give consent to its own openness to unconditioned freedom, but it can also close itself to that freedom. If it opens itself to it, it gains itself; if it closes itself to unconditioned freedom, it finds itself in a situation of fundamental contradiction with itself. The central event of sin is to be found in this process of self-contradiction, which cannot be directly grasped empirically.

Man is, of course, a being with a body — it is only in and with his body that he is a person. He is therefore only able to express his freedom through and in his bodily existence. In order to be a person too, he has to belong to the world. He has, in other words, to go out in order to go into himself. It is never possible to divide this personal event; it is only possible to distinguish individual aspects of this event and to relate them to each other in order to understand the whole process more clearly. Karl Rahner has, for example, made a distinction in man between the person and his nature. By "person," he means the "I" insofar as it is able to control itself. By "nature," on the other hand, he means "everything in man that has to be present in this control of himself as its object and the condition of its possibility." [1] In the concrete, what Rahner means by this is man's corporeality with his soul together with its links and relationships with the environment.

Two aspects of this relationship between person and nature in man can be distinguished in connection with the human expression of freedom. On the one hand, there is man's original intelligible act of freedom as such. (This is the aspect to which we have given the name of transcendental freedom.) On the other hand, there is the necessary corporealization in and through nature in human acts.[2] These two aspects of the expression of freedom cannot be separated, nor can they be equated. The original act of freedom — the original opening of itself of transcendental freedom — is not directly accessible to human experience. As we have already seen, it only discloses itself to transcendental reflection. This reflection, however, is the ground of empirical freedom, since it is only in reaching out dynamically to good as such that man achieves freedom in his choice of goods. Subject to the conditions imposed by his nature, he has also to give his consent, precisely through this choice, again and again to his openness to good.

Karl Rahner calls the fundamental dynamic tendency of man toward God, as expressed in his orientation toward good, a "supernatural existential" dynamism. Man's "desiring will" is the sign of his original call and the constant point of contact for his relationship with God. This means that the free opening of the will itself to this dynamism — in other words, the expression of transcendental freedom — can be seen to be a fundamental option.[3] It is situated at a deeper level than man's freedom of will. "It is a misunderstanding of the concept of fundamental option to think of it as a fully conscious, limited act alongside the individual acts in man's life. It points, on the contrary, to a radical and dynamic orientation in man's life to which free consent is given in and through the individual acts in which it is realized. This fundamental option is therefore not situated alongside man's individual acts or parallel to them. On the contrary, it inspires them from within."[4] It can only express itself in the individual acts in man's life. It freely realizes itself. It is man's response to a freedom that is given. In this sense, when man gives expression to it, it is always completely inspired by God's power to attract, and it is borne up by his presence. "The more it grows, the more our own powers are integrated into it and the more simple the multiplicity of our activity is made from within."[5] It can "also become paralyzed, die and make way for a very different kind of option, one that is related to man's self and is radically sinful."[6]

This negative option is, of course, the state or rather the fundamental attitude of the sinner. It originates in an act in which we do away with the positive option by enclosing ourselves within our I and rejecting God's love. Sin is therefore an inversion of the fundamental option, but here again it would be wrong to equate this inverted fundamental option with individual acts or sins. It is rather a consequence of individual sins which also has a marked effect on those sins. The individual acts must therefore be understood as constitutive signs of the fundamental option both in the positive and in the negative sense. They are, in other words, signs of a deeper attitude. They are also constitutive — in other words, they determine and influence that attitude in the direction of consent or rejection.

B. Distinguishing the Signs

It should be clear from what has been said above that man is constituted as a sinner by his own sins. For this reason, it is wrong to isolate and objectivize man's individual decisions and to reduce sinning as such to the fundamental decision itself. What is the act, then, that destroys the fundamental option? What sign has in fact to be regarded as constitutive for the inversion of that fundamental option? This question is really the same as the question about the distinction between venial and grave sins. It is possible to answer it in two ways and we shall follow this approach. The first answer is a relatively easy theoretical one. The second is a much more difficult practical one.

1. The Theoretical Distinction

As we have seen, Thomas Aquinas believed that the essential aspect of sin was an *aversio a Deo*. There is no third possibility between being converted to or turning toward God and turning away from him. The antithesis of this proposition is contradictory in itself. As *aversus*, man is a sinner; as *conversus*, he is justified. There is no possibility of being halfway. The formal concept of sin can therefore only be applied to turning away from God, that is, to what we call grave sin (I–II, 88, 1 ad 1). The so-called venial sin can only be called a sin in the analogous sense.

We can therefore define venial sin negatively in the following way. It is *non aversio* and therefore it is non-sin (in the real sense of the term). It is not possible to provide such a homogeneous definition in the positive sense. Thomas and those who followed him tried to do this by speaking of a state of not being against the law (*actio praeter legem*) or an *inordinatio circa media, non circa finem* or a *deordinatio citra aversionem a Deo* (I–II, 72, 5). In his further explanation of these definitions, he was concerned with when and why there was *de facto* no *aversio*. His reply to this question was that this could only happen if a human act did not destroy the principle of love. This state could be conditioned either by the subject (his ignorance or weakness) or by the matter.[7]

Seen in this light, venial sin would appear to be an attitude and an action by which God's love is not rejected, but man only perceives God's claim and carries it out with a divided heart, because of corporeality in the first place and his historicity in the second. Let us examine what is meant by these two aspects of man's existence in this context.

a) As a corporeal being, man exists in space. His desire is a corporealized desire. The original act of freedom itself is also subject to the conditions of man's corporeality. Man as a whole is marked by the tendency of that act toward good. It is therefore man's nature, which is orientated toward good, that at the same time prevents a concrete human act of freedom from being, under certain circumstances, turned away from God (*aversio a Deo*). The imperfection of a purely venial sin, then, is to be found in the spatiotemporal mediation of human knowledge and desire. In other words, insofar as it originates in the center of man's personal being, the act of freedom has a tendency toward totality, but, insofar as it takes place in the materiality of nature, it is subject to imperfection.

This imperfection may be directly conditioned by the subject. As a corporeal being, man is at the point of intersection between the I and the world, what is peculiar to the human person and what is alien to it. The object or matter can, however, also bring about this imperfection. There may, in other words, be decisions that are unable in the normal course of events to involve man totally, because of their material significance or because of their value or lack of value. This means that an objectively abstract evaluation based on moral principles can to some extent be made. This will, however, only provide an index. In other words, I can, in certain cases, say very generally — and only generally — that anyone who does this (in the case of *materia gravis*) is risking his relationship with God. It is not possible to know, because grace cannot in principle be known through our natural intelligence, whether or not in any individual case there will be an inversion of the fundamental option.

b) As a corporeal being, man exists in time. The original freedom of man is not only limited by the mediation of the materiality of his corporeal being — the totality of his decision is also reduced by his temporal existence. Because he exists in time, he can only make partial decisions, which he may regret and revoke as long as he continues to exist in time. He can neither understand himself as a whole nor fail as a whole by means of an individual decision. His individual decisions are not, however, isolated and unrelated to each other in a uniform *chronos*. In the *kairos* of the present, man has to overcome the past and fashion the future. His decisions are therefore a part of a genuine personal history, a continuity that is preserved by the person who is acting. Each decision has a necessary effect on the following decision and thus determines the ultimate decision. This is the basis of an important aspect of knowledge. All temporal decisions are capable of being changed. This is at the same time a very important point of departure for conversion. It is also at this point that the term mortal sin can be seen in its true light. It does not mean, however, that there is no "relative" totality in turning away from God in time because of man's glorification and idolization of himself and his declaration of his own complete autonomy.

2. The Practical Distinction

This problem has not been solved in contemporary theology. It has, on the contrary, been said in several quarters that it cannot be solved by insisting that hard and fast decisions be made about moral transgressions. Man does not usually encounter God directly. The encounter is mediated by his fellow-men and the world. For this reason, moral theologians have tried to base their distinction on the weight of the material objects that bring about this mediation. They have examined, classified and evaluated the material objects of the pluriform world and have come to the conclusion that a turning toward the creature or the realities of creation is in contradiction to the will of God and leads man to make an existential decision against God. It is, however, never possible to state in general terms that turning toward the created reality in fact brings about this total decision. The conclusions reached by moral theologians in the fairly recent past had and still have only the character of an index nowadays.

The significance of this kind of objectivizing distinction is not generally disputed, but what is often stressed is that it can only be correctly understood if the structure of the personal act is borne in mind. Man is able to refuse to obey God in faith by not recognizing that he is dependent on God's salvation. He can also do this, however, by closing himself in his own self-sufficiency to the claim that God makes through his brother. He does not have therefore to turn away from God by formally denying the material truth of faith. To this extent, then, turning away from God does not need to destroy faith radically. What is, however, destroyed in an *aversio a Deo* is love, which is, after all, the form of faith in God's salvation.

A second factor is, however, also involved here. This is the relationship of every individual decision to the total structure of our moral behavior and our religious situation. Man does not set his individual acts on the foundation of a purely objective substantiality, as though he were stringing real or imitation pearls in succession on the thread of external time.[8] He is one and whole, and his life is based on a single fundamental attitude, with the result that he is turned either toward or away from God. It is, of course, not easy to reflect about this fundamental and decisive attitude — it is possible to contemplate individual acts in our lives, but we cannot look directly at the whole of that ultimate and decisive source of those acts that is situated in our hearts.

This means that the question of venial sin takes on new emphasis. An apparently harmless lack of love of one's neighbor may, when it is seen in this light, be a reflection of fundamental selfishness. This selfish attitude may not perhaps be expressed in the form of horrifying acts violating the middle-class moral code, but it may well be what we mean by mortal sin. On the other hand, however, an externally incriminating mistake may be simply an expression of wrongly understood love and this would certainly not imply a turning away from God. This does not mean that encouragement should be given to a wrong kind of relativism. What it does mean is that our individual acts should be judged on the basis of our fundamental human attitude. Those individual moral acts are the constitutive signs of that attitude, in other words, they not only point to our fundamental attitude, but also determine it. The whole of man's life is therefore a form of self-determination carried out in faith or in the absence of faith and consisting of numerous decisions. Our ultimate and fully conscious decision will in the end result from that self-determination and determine our existence in the presence of God for ever.

Section Three: Fulfillment

In the first section of Part One of this book, we considered the fundamental moral claim made on man. In theology, man is regarded as God's creature and understood in the light of his relationship with God. As a created person, he is claimed in the center of his being by God. In our theological understanding of creation, the moral law is, as a fact of reason, nothing but the dependence of a personally free man, who is totally claimed in this freedom, to have control over himself. Man's existence subject to this obligatory claim can be seen, in the light of this theological understanding, as his necessary structure. He does not have himself to thank for this because he knows that he is constituted as a creature. Creation can be seen as an act of God's freedom which both leaves man free and claims him.

In the second section, we discussed the fact that man does not and, in a mysterious way, cannot conform to this claim. This fact has its origin not in his state as a creature — if this were the case, responsibility and guilt would not be possible — but rather in his broken existence, the consequence of the free contradiction directed against the claim made on him. The transition from the possibility of sin to the reality of sin remains a mystery. All that we can say about it is that "freedom as being potentially outside everything in possibility, freedom as the possibility of possibility (Kierkegaard), the human self as the potential center of the world, freedom as potential aseity — these form the prior condition for the creature's dissociation from God, his breaking with and falling away from God."[1] What is always present in human freedom is the tempting possibility of self-idolization, the conviction that man can become absolutely autonomous and the belief that he can make and do everything. This possibility is so powerfully present that, as Paul insisted in his letter to the Romans, all men without exception have failed in this respect and what might have been the history of man's freedom has in fact become a history of slavery in which all men need to be set free to freedom.

§ 11 The Freedom that Sets Free

Freedom and liberation have become central themes in Christian theology in recent years. In view of the many different religious and secular doctrines of liberation that are propagated nowadays, it is important to outline here the essential meaning of Christian faith with regard to man's liberation. "Restating the Christian faith in the idiom of freedom is a more complex task than merely emphasizing this aspect of salvation in order to show that the Church too is in favor of freedom." [2] Christian faith is not a form of wisdom or a philosophy that can be used in a Socratic manner to explain to man how to break through the dungeon of finiteness. Faith is not capable of developing a practical strategy to overcome fears and compulsions or repressions conditioned by conflicts caused by race or class. And yet Christian faith bears witness to the fact that the life and death of Jesus of Nazareth has a universal significance for the history of man's freedom. This is a confession that can and does cause many misunderstandings, because it contains a suggestion that Christians have a monopoly in the promotion of freedom. [3] The ultimate exodus to the land of freedom seems to many men in recent centuries to have been made possible by the coming of secular humanism without religious attachments. We are therefore constrained to ask, within the framework of our ethical problem, what the real and irreducible contribution made by Jesus of Nazareth may be to the liberation of man. What precisely is the freedom of Jesus that sets free?

A. Jesus' Liberating Effect

The dominant concept of freedom in the Christian tradition is based principally on the teaching of Paul and John. Each of these authors was aware in his own way of the theme of freedom as a consequence of the salvation revealed to man in Jesus Christ. In each case, this awareness was the result of the liberating strength that had come from the encounter with Jesus and his tradition. In each case too, it was an awareness based less on the example of Jesus and his conduct in individual matters and more on the event of Christ as a whole. The circumstances in their communities compelled both Paul and John to clarify the ground and the objective of this freedom and to defend its christological character.

Various attempts have been made in recent years to throw a clearer light on the background to the New Testament message of freedom in the tradition of Jesus without minimizing the importance of the apostolic interpretation. According to K. Niederwimmer, for example, "Our interpretation of the positive aspects of the theme of freedom in the New Testament should not begin with Paul's theology. The so-called Greek word *eleutheros* (free) and its derivatives can only be found in the synoptic tradition in Matthew 17.26, but the 'matter' — or rather the new reality — of freedom, that outlined by John, the so-called 'true' freedom, can certainly be recognized in the synoptic tradition. Paul and John did not initiate this theme of freedom. They found it already present as a reality and tried to express it in conceptual language. Christian freedom did not first come about when Christianity penetrated the Hellenistic world. On the contrary, the new Christian way of life was from the very beginning marked by freedom. Christ and his own initiated it."[4] There is therefore every reason for us to look for the origin of Christian freedom in Jesus himself.

This origin is to be found, according to all the theologians who have examined this question, in the distinctive relationship with God that characterized Jesus' person and activity.[5] The authentic theme of Jesus' preaching was indisputably the kingdom of God and it is this theme that we must examine in some detail here in the context of Jesus' moral message, because the underlying tenor of his proclamation of the kingdom of God is directed toward man's liberation.

Perhaps the most important point that can be stressed in this connection is that where God rules, the powers of darkness lose their control over man. The reports in the gospel of the driving out of demons and of healings and miracles show clearly how Jesus' activity was understood at the time to have a liberating effect. "The blind see, the paralyzed walk again, lepers are made clean, the deaf hear and the dead are raised (see, for example, Mt. 11.5 ff.). This is evidence that the time when Satan and his demons ruled on earth was, at least in principle, past. Man was — at first, it is true, by a sign — free from sickness and death. Freedom here is nothing more than being liberated from demonic powers."[6]

Jesus' relationship with God determined his attitude toward the Torah and its exposition by the rabbis. The living will of God was for him superior to the written law of Moses. Jesus was not concerned with the inadequacy of individual decrees. He was above all preoccupied with liberating obedience with regard to the will of God. "The independent authority of Jesus' 'But I say to you' breaches the power of the dominant religion and frees men from the projections of their fears, releasing them into a life in God's kingdom. Jesus binds his hearers to the freedom of love — that is, to God and their neighbor. Jesus teaches men to be good freely — *etsi deus non daretur* (Mt. 25.31-46). He makes God redundant as a human need, and by so doing both preserves God's sovereign freedom and inaugurates freedom for men."[7]

This message that was proclaimed and practised by Jesus cannot be separated from his person. God's liberating power was first visible in Jesus himself. According to his own interpretation, his own power came from the power of the Spirit of God (Mt. 12.28 par, Lk. 11.20; cf. Mk. 3.29 ff.). His freedom was *exousia* or power and it gave him an original and inner authority, in contrast to the rabbis, who relied on a certain tradition.[8] "Jesus' freedom can only be interpreted as the freedom of this man liberated by the Spirit of God (as God's freedom for men). Jesus' claim to possess the Spirit of God is an expression of his faith, his relationship with God, his freedom which derives from and is directed by the Spirit of God."[9] It is because of this that Rudolf Pesch calls Jesus a "free man." Indeed, Jesus was more free than other men because his will was entirely at one with that of his heavenly Father, who wanted all men to be free. In addition to this appeal to the Spirit, it was above all Jesus' unique relationship with the Father that determined his freedom. He had the freedom to call God his Father and to teach others to do the same. He lived and proclaimed the message of the seeking love of God who, as Father, was united with his Son. The relationship between God and man in the kingdom of God is characterized by such concepts as love, sonship, unity and so on. "It is not man who looks for God, but God who looks for man. God himself restores the destroyed human community. . . . The community realizes itself in the disciples' imitation of Christ . . . Jesus' discipleship is the true *koinonia ton eleutheron*. In it, there is freedom from the law and freedom from the world."[10]

The concepts of sonship and discipleship are given a decidedly christological emphasis in the writings of Paul and John. Jesus is not simply the one who proclaims and teaches freedom in these writings. He also mediates it. "If the Son makes you free, you will be free indeed" (Jn. 8.36; cf. Gal. 4.4-7). Jesus' life and activity was affirmed when he was raised again by the Father. He belonged so completely to God that he could be called his only Son. This affirmed his proclamation of freedom and made it possible for that freedom, which would set men free, to exist. "Paul discovers these dimensions of liberation because he sees Jesus' cross and resurrection as the breaking-in of the age to come when freedom will be actual for all creation. On the other hand, since John's eschatology concentrates on the present, for him liberation is not proleptic. Moreover, he can ground it in the work of Jesus even before his death because for John everything depends on acknowledging who Jesus is." [11] For both Paul and John, however, freedom was only thinkable as a freedom that was mediated and given by the exalted Christ. It was sonship, not only through the imitation of Jesus' liberating activity, but also through acceptance into his community with the Father, the community which he had always had as Son.

B. Christian Freedom as an Offer

The possibility of liberation revealed to men in Jesus Christ was given a decisive theological form by Paul and John. A great number of historical influences had an effect on this concrete theological form in addition to the obvious Jewish influence. I do not intend to enlarge on the Pauline or the Johannine doctrine of freedom here, but regard it as more important to point to three aspects of this offer of freedom which are of considerable significance in the present context.

1. The Change of Rule

Paul and John described the offer of freedom against the somber background of man's life in a state of radical unfreedom. Man had failed in his historical quest for freedom. "The Stoics thought of freedom as man's control over the alien existence that threatened him, by means of a conscious and intentional rule over his soul. Generally speaking, according to the New Testament, on the other hand, man is not free, even when he is in control of his own inner nature. It is clear from the New Testament that freedom is absent from man's existence, not because man has insufficient control over himself, but rather because he is in control of himself and has such a great deal of control over himself."[12]

This paradoxical formulation throws some light on the problem of finite freedom that we have already discussed above. It is not wanting to be free or wanting to be oneself that is evil. But man in his finiteness seeks and desires to be autonomous in independence from God; and that is evil. It was precisely in this control over himself that denied his creatural state that the New Testament authors saw man's lack of freedom, which man in his blindness did not see. This "contradiction in man's existence is the *a priori* structure into which the New Testament concept of freedom is fashioned."[13] The offer of freedom made in the New Testament was an attempt to do away with this contradiction into which man is always entering and from which he is obviously not able to liberate himself.

Attempts were being made at the time of Saint Paul to find a way to freedom and he, of course, knew about them. It is not possible to elucidate his message of freedom in its concrete form without reference to these contemporary attempts which have, moreover, never become obsolete.[14] Basically, these attempts can be summarized under two headings. On the one hand, there was the legal attempt to find freedom and justification through the fulfillment of the law. The law, however, was not able to do away with the contradiction of man's existence, because this contradiction went deeper than the law. It is precisely because it was used as a means of self-justification that the law had to fail in this respect.[15] On the other hand, Paul also had to attack the contemporary doctrine of antinomianism which, under the guise of gnosticism, threatened his own teaching in the early Christian communities. Gnostic freedom arose from the meaninglessness of the relationship between the self and the world. The incalculable world was seen to have no right to claim man and guilt was therefore attributed to the world, matter and the cosmos. The body was regarded as non-self. Man in this way came to be reduced to a thing ruled by physis. An ethical claim could have no meaning for him. Paul's teaching was an emphatic rejection of gnosticism. He proclaimed a liberating freedom which was directed not only against antinomianism, but also against nomianism. Freedom in faith did not come about, he taught, as a result of synthesizing authority and freedom. It was brought about by the sonship that became a

118

reality in Jesus Christ. The dualism of autonomy and heteronomy is really overcome for the first time at the point where heteronomy itself provides autonomy and where the Spirit of God claims man and gives him freedom, in other words, in a theonomous autonomy of man.[16]

This fundamental change from slavery to freedom, the freedom of the sons of God, is very clearly expressed in Paul's theology of baptism. For Paul, baptism was a "saving event as a participation in God's eschatological saving activity in Christ. This is at the same time an action in which man is liberated and existentially taken into service. Both of these aspects are indissolubly united."[17] It is therefore possible to speak of a "change of rule." The baptized person is "by means of his baptism appropriated by God for Christ, the crucified and risen Lord."[18] (See, for example, 1 Cor. 1.12 ff.; Gal. 3.27, 29; Rom. 6.3; 7.4; Col. 1.13.)

The other aspect of baptism, the so-called mystical aspect that is frequently misunderstood as such, must also be taken into account in this context. According to this aspect of baptism, "the sacramental initiation into the community of Christ, a community of being and destiny, is not identical with a personal relationship with Christ."[19] The setting up of the kingdom of God is the founding of a new community primarily between God and men and therefore also between men themselves (Rom. 5.1 f., 6-11; 2 Cor. 5.14-21). It is for this reason that it is understood in theology as the sacrament. The Church as a whole is also, because of the presence of the exalted Christ in that Church as his body, the sacrament for this world. We are therefore bound to say that the Christian is also, in leading his Christian life, a sacrament for his fellow-men. He is existentially destined to become a sacrament by his incorporation into the community of Christ in baptism. The Christian's theological and christological existence, inaugurated in baptism, enables him to participate in the eschatological freedom that has been acquired by Christ's death and resurrection. Although this is, of course, above all a mark of the end of time (Rom. 8.2, 18-23; Gal. 4.1-17, 21-31), it is already tangibly present now, since the future eon dawned with Christ. The Christian, then, is inserted into the already present time and the future of redemption that is not yet present. This divine activity of eschatological salvation is made constantly present in the Spirit. It is in the power of the Spirit that the Christian participates in the death and resurrection of Jesus. It is also clear in the Spirit that Christian existence has to be understood as a participation in an all-embracing movement of salvation which God has set in motion through Christ for the salvation of the world. In the Spirit it is also clear that there are no saving gifts that are separate from God and his Christ, no gifts that are, in other words, able to save or change man naturally. The only eschatological saving gift is in fact the Spirit himself. The Spirit is the way in which Christ is present in us. The various interpretations of the eschatological saving event as forgiveness, reconciliation, justification, liberation, the new life, the new creation and so on are not static qualifications of the human soul, but a dynamic way of interpreting the eschatological reality that God himself is, in and through Christ, with us and for us.

"In this understanding of baptism as a change of rule, a liberation to (fruitful) life and a taking of man into service, the understanding of baptism that was shared by Paul and the pre-Pauline and post-Pauline Christian community as acceptance into the community of Christians or the Church, as the forgiveness of sins by washing (or purification) and as sanctification, justification and the giving of the Spirit must be integrated and therefore reinterpreted." [20] Because the baptized person is incorporated into the body of Christ (1 Cor. 12.13), the new existence of that person is at the same time an existence within the ambience of the Church. As the community gathered in the Spirit by God through Christ, the *ecclesia* is the existential form of those who believe in Christ and have been called to his community (*koinonia tou huiou*; 1 Cor. 1.9), the form that has been given in the finiteness of creation, that is historical and that will persist until the fulfillment. This ecclesial existence is therefore "also the response of the community as a whole and in its individual members to God's action in gathering believers together and founding a *koinonia* through Christ in the world (and also for it)." [21] This existence, which is both theological and christological and which is brought about by means of baptism, is therefore always at the same time eschatological, pneumatological and ecclesial.

2. Freedom for the Whole Man

Christian freedom encompasses the whole man. Paul's teaching was in sharp contrast to that of the gnostics, in that he explicitly included the body in the process of liberation. In this, he used the word body for the whole man. The body was, for Paul, the empirical self, intended for freedom from death by transformation in the parousia. This is the fundamental meaning of his statement: "The body is . . . meant . . . for the Lord, and the Lord for the body" (1 Cor. 6.13 f.). Leander Keck thinks that this Pauline axiom was "the basis of a Christian ethic of freedom." [22] It is at least quite clear that it would be wrong to spiritualize Paul's doctrine of freedom. Even if Paul did not speak explicitly about the social and economic liberation of man in his own period of history, his message of the freedom that is offered to all men in Christ nonetheless contains an explosive power that strikes at the foundations of man's selfish interests and divisions.

It is unfortunately not possible for me to discuss this question in detail here. There is, however, another aspect of some importance in connection with the question of social freedom — that of the Christian claim to have a monopoly in promoting freedom. We have already provided an initial and at the same time fundamental answer to this question by pointing to the christological depths of the Pauline and the Johannine doctrines of freedom, according to which Christ was the way to the Father. Josef Neuner has, however, rightly drawn attention to the fact that Jesus Christ cannot be isolated from the profane and religious history of mankind. According to God's plan of creation and redemption, all men are involved in the same history of sin and grace, slavery and liberation. God has, however, shown once and for all time in Jesus Christ the significance of man and the significance of human freedom. It is a fundamental error to give an absolute value to the historical and cultural situation of Jesus while he was on earth. "Jesus Christ means the acknowledgment, liberation, fulfillment of all that is human." [23] The distinctive nature of Christ has therefore to be understood inclusively, not exclusively. It implies that the whole of mankind is called to freedom. The struggle for this freedom includes the whole of mankind. The Christian welcomes all these attempts to find freedom, but "at the same time he ought to develop a fine sense of discernment and ask whether these messages are genuine, whether they diminish or disfigure the true freedom, whether they are not a masked escape from the hard realities of life, a refusal of service, a retirement to oases of illusionary freedom by which man would absent himself from the drama of actual history." [24] The freedom that the Christian has to announce has no safe refuge, no flight back to the past or forward into the future and no security in interiority because it is a participation in the freedom of Christ who accepted the whole of our humanity and liberated us.

3. The Freedom of Creation

The whole of creation is also to share in the freedom of the sons of God (see Rom. 8.19-23). Without going into the details of this eschatological text, we can say with certainty that it is not possible, in the light of this teaching, to isolate man from the world in the history of salvation. The fate of the world is closely connected with the fate of mankind and with man's slavery and liberation. Christianity and the Church have in recent years been very sharply criticized, above all in the context of man's relationship with his environment. Carl Amery, for example, has spoken of the "merciless consequences of Christianity."[25] In his opinion, the destruction of man's environment by the technological civilization of the West is entirely a consequence of the Judaeo-Christian tradition. He believes that people deduced from the story of creation in Genesis (1.26-28) that man was given total control over creation, a commission, given by God, to rule over the world and mediated subsequently by a series of historical measures (monastic ethics, Calvinism, the morality of production and consumption furthered by recent Catholic teaching and so on), leading ultimately to the contemporary practice of large-scale exploitation. In this thesis, Amery has made use of the criticisms already expressed by the American historian Lynn White and the American theologian J. B. Cobb.[26]

It cannot be denied that the biblical faith in creation has played a very important part in the demystification of the cosmos and the de-deification of this world.[27] The secularization of the world was, however, the most important historical factor in the preparation for technological thinking. It simply cannot be maintained that the tendencies to exploit the environment by a merciless control of nature go back to the priestly documents in the Old Testament or to the promise made in the New Testament (Rom. 8.19-23). Let us briefly consider the priestly account in Genesis and Paul's witness in his letter to the Romans.

The statement made about the *dominium terrae*, according to the priestly account in Genesis 1.26b, 28b, has to be understood in the light of its prehistory in the account of the Yahwist. "The Yahwistic history of the Old Testament desacralized the achievements, making them human achievements. These achievements are ambivalent because, on the one hand, they make man's existence possible and, on the other, they involve man in guilt. Despite this ambivalence, they are, however, the result of God's blessing."[28] The priestly text can be explained against this Yahwistic background: "The achievements of man's culture are not only in accordance with the will of the Creator. They also go back to the Creator's commandment."[29] A consideration of the position taken by the priestly text in its description of God's creation of man can therefore prevent us from "suppressing the ambivalence of the achievements and understanding the text as a total authorization, permitting man to do any kind of violence to the earth."[30] Man's · task is connected both with his being made in God's image and with his guilt.

The same applies quite clearly to the witness borne by Paul especially in the epistle to the Romans. Christianity was for a long time accused of retarding scientific and technical progress. More recently, it has been criticized for favoring this same form of progress and encouraging the exploitation of man's natural environment. This recent criticism gives the impression of being a projection of the critics' guilt onto Christianity. This should not, however, prevent us from reconsidering our responsibility with regard to God's creation. Man is not called by the Creator to exploit the world by presuming on the authority given to him by God. His task is to administer the world as God's image and likeness: "Man will be able to enter a new epoch of history as soon as he changes his attitude toward his environment from exploitation to cooperation."[31]

These are only three of the many aspects of the total offer of freedom that has been made to man in the event of Christ. The liberation offered by Christ means "that there is an alternative for man. Man must, however, turn to this alternative freely, making a fundamental option. The way has been opened. Each man must enter it as a result of his own decision."[32] The offer, the promise of the gospel, also becomes a demand. We shall be considering this question in greater detail in Part Three.

Part Two

Fundamental Problems in the Justification of Norms

Section One: The Biblical Foundation

It is not possible, of course, to deal with biblical themes simply for their own sake in a work that is primarily concerned with the principles of moral theology. The systematic theologian has certain questions to ask the biblical theologian, who ought to be able to help him to understand the significance of the biblical foundation for the special character and validity of moral norms.

CHAPTER 1: MORAL NORMS IN THE OLD COVENANT

According to the Talmud, the Pentateuch or Torah of the Old Testament contains 613 commandments and prohibitions[1] of a cultural, religious, social or ethical nature. They are to be found above all in the great bodies of law — in the Book of the Covenant (Ex. 20.22–23.33) and the Decalogue that precedes it (Ex. 20.1-21), the Law of Holiness (Lev. 17–26), the Priestly Code that is distributed throughout the books of Exodus, Leviticus and Numbers and finally in the Deuteronomic Code (Dt. 12–26). The long tradition of these books of law can be dated back — as in the case of parts of the Book of the Covenant — to the twelfth or eleventh century B.C.

Any comparison made between the norms found in the Old Testament and those prevailing in the Ancient Near East generally reveals striking parallels both in language and in content. These similarities with, above all, the Mesopotamian and Hittite legal texts and treaties[2] show that the Pentateuch provided no genuinely Israelite law but was, rather, the Old Testament expression of the ethos prevailing in each particular society, with an orientation toward the surrounding Ancient Near Eastern culture. In addition to the common law, which was regarded as having an almost judicial foundation, these collections of law aimed "to express the views of the community with regard to law and justice. Their underlying intention was not judicial, but literary and above all educational."[3]

Quite apart from this orientation and aim, however, there are also clear differences between the norms of Israel and those of the Mesopotamian cultures, as expressed in the surviving documents. In the following sections in this chapter, I shall examine the specific features of the Old Testament legal texts and try to delineate the factors leading to the formation of a distinctive ethos. The first task here is to set out these norms in their different formal expressions, especially in the casuistic and apodictic laws. I shall also discuss their origin and their situation in life.

§ 12 The Different Kinds of Norms and their Social Context

A. The Casuistic Law

In addition to the numerous priestly and cultic instructions contained in the Old Testament, a great deal of space is occupied in the Pentateuch by the so-called casuistic clauses, the style of these sentences being common to most of the Ancient Near East.[4] Together they form a body of secular law according to which the "elders of the city in the gate" (see Dt. 22.15) made their decisions.[5] These impersonally expressed legal sentences are to be found in considerable numbers in the Book of the Covenant. They include such themes as the laws concerning slaves, blood, marriage, bodily injury and property,[6] in other words, all cases of man's everyday life with his fellow-men. The Book of the Covenant, then, is a collection of cases of precedent. Many of these casuistic clauses were taken over by the Israelites when they took possession of Canaan from the original inhabitants. Some, however, were already deeply rooted in the clan ethos of the seminomadic Israelite tribes. "Those laws in which the casuistic law has been transformed by faith in Yahweh are of special interest here."[7] It is possible that formulas (in participial constructions) were derived from this casuistic law and that these formulas were applied to crimes that called for a curse or the death penalty, but it is also possible that there were no provisions for carrying out the threatened punishment. They may therefore have been not laws that could be applied in practice, but cultic or magic in character, or else formulas directed toward banishment or excommunication. An example of this kind of punishment is that of extirpation or cutting off (*kareth*), which safeguarded certain tabus and punished the offender who broke those tabus by excluding him from the community.[8] (See, for example, Lev. 17.3 ff.; Ezek. 14.6-11; Dt. 27.11 ff.; Jos. 24.25 ff. and other texts.)

128

B. The Apodictic Law, the Word of God and the Covenant

Albrecht Alt[9] called the apodictic law authentically Israelite, as opposed to the casuistic law, which was not. Since E. Gerstenberger,[10] however, this view has been corrected, not only as far as the origin, but also as far as the term "law" is concerned. Seen from the formal point of view, an apodictic clause can be interpreted as prohibitive or as vetitive and, what is more, is usually expressed in the second person singular form. In the case of formulas expressed in the third person singular or in the plural, these were usually official priestly codes of law or lists similar to the Church's code of canon law and used to decide who was to be excluded from the community. These codes were sometimes extended to include a catalogue of virtues, which provided a portrait of the just man.[11] There are examples of total lists (Ex. 20; Dt. 5) and of special lists such as the "judge's code" in Exodus 23.6-9. In many cases, a certain ethos is defined and summarized in the form of a decalogue or a dodecalogue. These sentences express moral maxims in the categorical form of "Thou shalt" or "Thou shalt not" without any ifs or buts. This is the "primordial form of commandment"[12] that "occurs everywhere, wherever instruction is given and rules of life are composed."[13]

G. Fohrer correctly spoke in this context of "rules of life and behavior in an apodictic form."[14] The elders of the clan have, since the earliest times, always had the task of handing down these religious and social commandments. As Gerstenberger insists, then, we have to look for the origin of the prohibitive law in the association of clans before the existence of the state.[15] The same author has also pointed to a close link between the apodictic sentences and the sapiential tradition, a connection which has made it possible for him to trace the origin of the apodictic law in the traditional wisdom of the clans and families of Israel. Nielsen has, however, pointed out that the so-called prohibitive laws were more concerned with cultic and religious matters and that the Wisdom literature is not preoccupied with serious or violent crimes.

What places the apodictic law outside the sphere of jurisdiction is that its clauses all point, without further reference to any punishment and absolutely categorically, to the prohibitive or the vetitive possibilities and because of this they thrust the aim of jurisdiction into the background, since, as the casuistic law shows, the legal consequence has to be clearly formulated juridically. In the apodictic clause, the moral and religious element is more strongly emphasized. The apodictic clause does not, strictly speaking, belong to the category of a law. It affirms, in a commandment, a prohibition or an admonition, and makes permanently valid what has to be regarded, in the view of the authoritative speaker, as wrong for the community (and never for the individual). The essential difference between Israelite legal texts and those of Israel's neighbors is the personal status of that authoritative speaker.

The Decalogue in the Context of the Sinai Event

It was because of the great authority of Saint Augustine that the ethical decalogue (Ex. 20.2-17; Dt. 5.6-22)[16] — as an outstanding example of apodictic language — has come in the course of time to occupy a special place in the Church's moral teaching,[17] even to the present day in Catholic catechisms and instruction. Modern exegesis has shown, however, that the decalogue was not originally a part of the Sinai pericope and indeed that it was not originally one single whole, but consists of several editorial levels. At a later stage in the editorial process, the decalogue was deliberately placed at the head of the commandments proclaimed by Yahweh on the mountain.[18] Because of this manipulation of the text, the preface (Ex. 20.2), which proclaims Yahweh as the speaker, the real "I" of Israel's jurisdiction, is of great importance not only for the decalogue, but also for the Book of the Covenant and the Sinai event as a whole.[19] It provides a theonomous justification for the norms.

All the individual precepts, all the series of commandments and prohibitions, all the legal clauses and all the liturgical instructions and sacrificial laws in the Book of the Covenant, then, can be classified under the heading of the jurisdiction of Yahweh as the authoritative speaker of the law of Israel (Ex. 20.2). He is the "I" of that law. "This I at the beginning of this divine communication means that all responsibility in Israel is a response to this one God, whose act of salvation at the beginning is remembered in his presentation of himself."[20]

Yahweh's presentation of himself in Exodus 20.2, in which he shows his mercy, is followed by a second statement about himself (Ex. 20.5b, 6; cf. Dt. 5.9b, 10), in which his exclusive claim is stressed: "For I, Yahweh, your God am a jealous God, visiting the iniquity of the fathers upon the children to the third and the fourth generation of those who hate me, but showing steadfast love to thousands of those who love me and keep my commandments."[21] "It is in being bound to the one God, Yahweh, who liberated Israel from slavery and was at the same time jealous for his uniqueness, that the fundamental determination of Old Testament faith is to be found."[22] We are able to know from the preamble, which characterizes the decalogue and the Book of the Covenant as the immediate promulgation of God's will for men, that Israel was called to obedience in faith in quite a special way by the God who revealed himself to that people in the beginning in a supreme act of liberation. By displacing the giving of the law from the beginning of the passage through the desert to the end of that journey, when the Israelites occupied the land of Canaan, the Deuteronomist linked God's commandments closely to the idea of election and the fulfillment of the promise. "Israel's occupation of Canaan was rest after a long period of wandering (Dt. 12.9 ff.). It was a blessing and it was life. It was on the threshold of this life that Israel received the law. Two aspects of that law are revealed in this context. With its good and wise precepts, it is part of the blessing that Yahweh bestows on his people (Dt. 4.7 ff.). At the same time, it is also a challenge, requiring a right decision (Dt. 30.19)."[23]

Yahweh's presentation of himself therefore forms a framework and is clearly secondary, as the change from the first to the third person in Exodus 20.7 shows. It has to be borne in mind that most of the apodictic sentences are connected in a secondary sense with the word of God and that they were given their divine authority at a later stage as the result of further theological reflection. The original ethos, in other words, was situated in the tribe, the clan and the family. The ethical formulations were subjected by a later editor to the covenant, as a protective and legitimizing arrangement instituted by Yahweh. In the consciously wide-ranging series of commandments, those commandments referring to the Israelites' association with their fellow-men and with the things of this world are so closely joined to the four commandments that are religious and cultic in the narrower sense of the words that the connection can hardly be detected. Yahweh therefore not only cut his people off from their environment by cultic signs, but also — this emerges clearly in the Book of the Covenant — subjected the Israelites' entire way of life, their relationships with their fellow-men and their association with the things of this world to his will.

In the form in which it appears in the Old Testament, the Sinai pericope, like Exodus 34.10-28, is the representation of a covenant (*berîth*; see Ex. 24.7) between Yahweh and his chosen people. It is possible to see in the decalogue a basic idea of the J source, a charter for a community of people that saw itself as a *berîth*, in order to protect itself for its own ethical substance and to oppose any influence from the Canaanite environment.

In speaking about God's covenant with Israel, it is important to bear in mind the original meaning of the Hebrew word *berîth*. According to M. Weinfeld, this word does not indicate a treaty or an agreement between two parties. Above all, it contains the idea of an imposition or an obligation. A *berîth* is commanded and the word is therefore synonymous with law or commandment. (See, for example, Dt. 4.13; 33.9; Is. 24.5; Ps. 50.16; 103.18.) The covenant of Mount Sinai, then, is an imposition of laws and obligations on the people of Israel (Ex. 24.3-8). [24]

In general, the word *berîth* points to a relationship between two unequal partners, in which the more powerful partner grants a covenant relationship to the weaker partner. Since G. E. Mendenhall's writings about the covenant, [25] it has been common to speak about an affinity between the decalogue or Deuteronomy and the Hittite treaties and about a covenant terminology. [26] This comparison is, however, basically inaccurate. The literary context, the tone, the ethos and the emphasis are all quite different. In Exodus 19–24, the emphasis is placed on Yahweh's proof of his own power and glory. The central point of this whole account of the covenant of Sinai is Exodus 24.1 ff., with its communal meal. [27] It is precisely this rite of the covenant meal that is absent from the Hittite treaties. Another aspect of the Hittite formulas is that they are all related to one particular person. There is no formation of a series, as in the Old Testament. [28]

There are, however, clear parallels with the apodictic clauses in the Pentateuch with their impersonal and objective sentences and the admonitions of the sapiential literature of the Ancient Near East and the Old Testament. [29]

With the acceptance of these series of warnings, admonitions and commandments into the word of God and the events on Mount Sinai, there is a necessary change in the authority of the one who warns, admonishes and commands. At the same time, the different degrees of obligation are also changed at this stage and emphasized by the authority of God, with the result that the absolute nature of the directives is given a new validity and binding force.

C. Theonomy and the Covenant as the Constitutive Elements in the Authetically Israelite Ethos

The observations made in the preceding section about the decalogue in particular and the apodictic law in general and the literary form of the casuistic law within the theonomous framework point to what is authentically Israelite: (a) the law and its subjection to the God of Israel (this is clear from Yahweh's presentation of himself), (b) the prohibition of foreign gods [30] and (c) the connection between the exclusive claim and the prescriptions regarding social ethics. Because of their experience of what they called their salvation from Egypt and the concluding of the covenant on Sinai/Horeb, the people of Israel believed themselves to be claimed in the whole of their existence in such a way that they could "no longer determine and regulate their ethos and their relationships with their fellow-men in any other way than in the presence of Yahweh." [31] Instead of those in authority in the clan, it was now Yahweh himself who functioned as the only lawgiver and judge. [32] This theonomous justification of norms was not original in Israel; it was rather the result of a theological reflection about the central events of revelation. This reflection was based on the idea that Israel was God's possession and his chosen people. A prohibition of foreign gods and images was the first condition of this new relationship.

D. Consequences

With regard to the question of fundamental moral theology, it should by now be clear that the essence of the moral order under the old covenant arose as the result of a historical process and therefore cannot be understood as an original divine law. In their faith in Yahweh, the people of Israel subjected their inherited clan ethos to the authority of God. This subjection of the moral life of the Israelites to the will of God in the form of a word of God as a formula of his love and kindness is very significant. It means that, because Israel's God set his people free in the past, they are committed to a certain kind of behavior in the future. An appeal is thus made to man as a responsible being who is capable of making decisions. He is called to respond to God's offer of a covenant. The answer must be either yes or no;

there is no halfway reply. It is no longer an achievement to keep God's commandments. His gracious offer makes it possible to keep them without difficulty.[33]

Because of the people's situation with regard to cult (not their original social setting), the decalogue has the character of an ethical creed. The statements are paraenetic, that is, they are consoling and admonitory. They proclaim moral values and make fundamental claims and the validity of these values and claims can be presupposed among those who hear the commandments. The apodictic clauses of the decalogue "precede the formation of the casuistic law in time. On the basis of morality, the law decides whether an action is a crime that has to be punished."[34] In other words, "You shall not kill! You shall not commit adultery! You shall not steal!" In these words, an appeal is made to the hearer, about which there is common consent and which, in this form, also applies without exception. "Because the commandment addresses Israel as a whole and each individual member of Israel in his concrete physical life within the community of the people of Yahweh, it cannot be reduced to an interior ethos in which all that is required is the good will of the individual and a good intention, however good or bad the action may be. Yahweh's demand points above all to that action which justifies itself in the concrete communal life of the people of Israel."[35]

The problem as to when killing, for example, is violent and against the law can only be solved by casuistry. Faith in Yahweh played a very important part in the construction of this concrete body of law and morality. We shall consider this question now, in the following section.

§ 13 Faith in Yahweh and its Influence on the Development and Formation of the Ethos of Israel

The decisive criterion for Israel in the people's confrontation with the culture and religion of Canaan was their faith in the covenant. The ethos of Israel was therefore characterized by a decision for Yahweh that had to be made again and again and by a separation from everything that might endanger that relationship.

A. The Decision for Yahweh as a Unifying Principle

Yahweh's commandment was directed toward Israel as a people. "It does not take the individual, but the whole community that is called by Yahweh as its point of departure. . . . We may look in vain in the Old Testament for an ethos of individual self-perfection or for a doctrine of virtues that takes the individual as the primary element in Yahweh's history." [1] This fundamental principle is particularly clear in the context of the political and social relationships of Israel. The people's political situation and the frequent dangers and crises that resulted from this made it very difficult for direct security to be achieved. Only a decision for Yahweh as the basis of unity made possible a kind of indirect security to guarantee the continued existence of the people of the covenant. Without the strength of an obligatory and unifying faith, the otherwise heterogenous tribes of Israel would never have been able to come together in a relatively firm tribal association against a theo-political background. The central point here was the "arrière-ban" or the summons that every tribe had to obey to serve in the "war of Yahweh" and the shared sanctuary. Israel would hardly have been able to begin its history without the unifying force of faith in Yahweh. This was only possible because the people were certain that God's will would be adequately and reliably revealed to them and that it could be carried out (see, for example, Dt. 27 ff.). This certainty of historical salvation and this confidence of salvation in history were based on the fulfillment of the promise that God had made to the patriarchs, that they would be given a country. The demand that Yahweh made of his people to obey him is justified in the final chapters of Deuteronomy. When the tribes of Israel were given the land of Canaan, Yahweh at the same time passed a very severe judgment on the earlier inhabitants of the country and their idols. "Justice" here has a very clearly defined content and meaning. Ṣᵉdhāqāh is to some extent a form of justice that was carried out in God's court of law and by his judgment. [2] This concept was developed further in an interaction between Israel's social and historical situation and the history of the people's faith. "Ṣᵉdhāqāh or ṣedheq as the norm according to which Yahweh always acted and men ought always to act was without question the supreme — and indeed the only — regulator of public as well as of private life. Everything that happened and all activity was evaluated in accordance with this norm."[3] On the basis of their experience of God's justice as faithfulness to the covenant and grace,[4] the people thought of Yahweh's ṣᵉdhāqāh as going far beyond the idea of the lawcourt. It came to include not only concepts such as ḥesedh or ṭûbh/ṭôbhāh, but also the idea of mercy and forgiveness and finally became concentrated in the all-embracing commandment: "You shall love your neighbor[5] as yourself: I am Yahweh" (Lev. 19.18). The man who kept this commandment was a just man. A concept that is closely related to ṣᵉdhāqāh is misᵉpaṭ, which is identical with the principle or principles on which the community existing between God and men was based in Israel. Misᵉpaṭ therefore became the principle of community relationships.[6]

B. Faith in Yahweh as a Selective Principle

Israel's consciousness of having been chosen and of the obligation to be holy ("Be holy as Yahweh your God is holy") not only led to an increased commitment to the covenant and to solidarity among the tribes — it also brought about an attitude of separation from everything that was opposed to that covenant. This separation was primarily felt with regard to the person of the God who was worshiped and the way in which he was worshiped. It was expressed in a very fundamental way in the prohibition against the worship of strange gods. The idea that Yahweh transcended the world absolutely made it impossible for him to be influenced or manipulated in any way. This is made clearly manifest in the cultic separateness of Israel — as, for example, in the prohibition of temple prostitution (see, for example, Dt. 23.17 f.; Hos. 4.13; 2 Kg. 23.7). Faith in Yahweh was opposed to these mythical elements of theology. Israel's God was not subject to the cycle of natural events. An essential aspect of the ethos of the Old Testament is its stripping away of myth and its giving a profane value to the reality of man and the world. This is strikingly evident, for example, in the Old Testament attitude toward sexuality, as opposed to that of the pagan cultures, with their magic and sacral interpretation. "Divine forces immanent in the cosmos were in charge in every instance of the use of the genital powers."[7] The inhabitants of Canaan tried to ensure the fertility of men, animals and the crops by

136

means of imitative practices. This, however, was directly contrary to the essence of Yahwism. "Revelation placed the sacred character of marriage and fertility on a different basis by linking them with the plan of God the Creator."[8] The power to beget life was, in the Old Testament, clearly derived from the fact that man had been made in God's image (see Gen. 1.27).

Israel's separateness also extended to the political sphere. In assimilating the Canaanite and oriental way of life, the Israelites also took over the oriental form of governing the state and the monarchy. In the traditional culture of Israel's environment, the monarchy had a religious aspect in that the king was believed to be divine and functioned as the priest of the deity, being provided for this purpose with special life-giving and saving powers. Indeed, he was not only the minister of the deity, but also the embodiment of that deity on earth, in other words, either the deity himself or his son. Even at a very early stage, the oriental king appeared as the bringer of salvation. In Israel, however, this naturalistic and magic view of the monarchy was replaced by qualitative characteristics that were not unconditionally based on a moral assessment. Only the best and most capable man was to be chosen as king (see, for example, 2 Kg. 10.3). At first, the preference for Saul was to be found only in his physical size — because "he was taller than any of the people" (1 Sam. 9.2) he could be very impressive as their king. The second king of Israel, David, was lively and had many gifts; he was "skilful in playing, a man of valor, a man of war, prudent in speech, a man of good presence and the Lord is with him" (1 Sam. 16.18).

The fitness of the man chosen to be king was, however, not simply a question of his political leadership. According to 1 Samuel 15.28, Saul had the kingdom torn from him so that it could be given to another who was better than he was. Saul had rejected the word of the Lord and had broken the covenant. For this reason, Yahweh had also rejected him (15.26). The consequence of Saul's action was that he was deprived of the kingdom. Someone who would keep Yahweh's covenant, observe his law and be obedient to him, then, would clearly be a more suitable king. This is a clear pointer to the position of the king in the closely linked religious and political history of Israel.

The quality of the king is very clearly expressed in Ecclesiastes 4.13: "Better is a poor and wise youth than an old and foolish king who will no longer take advice." According to the Old Testament writers, the king was a man who was in a very special sense subject to the will of God. In this, Yahweh's kingdom was exclusive with regard to all human leadership (see, for example, Samuel and Isaiah).

Israel's separation from magic did not, however, prevent the people from using tabus and magic survivals as a means of discrimination. (Examples of this are the idea of objective guilt, the notion of magical defilement and the conviction of the need for ritual expiation.) These were given a theonomous justification in the course of Israel's history and in this way successively removed. In Deuteronomy 20.16 ff., for example, the demand to place a ban on booty in certain captured towns is clearly made by Yahweh himself. The conquered enemy was to be killed and everything that could be taken as booty destroyed. The ban was a means of consecration to Yahweh and a thanksgiving for the help that he had given his people in battle. War against foreign nations or against those who had broken the covenant was regarded as holy and just.[9]

Even warlike undertakings conducted by individual tribes or blood-feuds between clans were regarded as wars of Yahweh. During the monarchy, the idea of the holy war gradually disappeared together with that of the arrière-ban. Despite the close links with cultic history, however, there was an unmistakable movement to "renew and transform custom and law under the influence of a lively consciousness of God."[10] In other words, the ethos of Israel was transformed by theonomy.

C. Faith in Yahweh as a Principle Leading to the Systematization of Ethics

The covenant operated not only as a selective principle, but also as one which led to a systematization of ethics. The reduction of faith in the covenant to "moral demands by giving priority to charity"[11] as the only true expression of the will of God can be attributed mainly to the preaching of the prophets (see, for example, Mic. 6.8). In the priesthood of Israel too, attempts were made to select the most important articles of the law and to use them to compose a kind of catechism. These texts, which included the decalogue, were then used as liturgies of solemn entry and as codes for confession (see, for example, Ps. 15 and 24). Finally, reduction to an ultimate principle led to a concentration of this faith in Yahweh's covenant. This concentration already existed, of course, in the Wisdom literature. (See, for example, Pr. 20.22: "Do not say, 'I will repay evil'; wait for Yahweh and he will help you.") The demand to love God and one's neighbor is, of course, most clearly expressed in Deuteronomy 6.4 ff.: "Hear, O Israel: Yahweh our God is the one Yahweh! And you shall love the Lord your God with all your heart, and with all your soul and with all your might." It is also found in Leviticus 19.18: "You shall not take vengeance or bear any grudge against the sons of your own people, but you shall love your neighbor as yourself: I am Yahweh."

The most important factors in the covenant and in Israel's faith in Yahweh, we may therefore conclude, were the specific character of Yahweh himself and "his specific function as the God of the covenant, the correlative of which is the inner unity of Israel as the people of the covenant." [12] For Israel, it was "a fundamental aspect of right action to remain in the covenant." [13]

Excursus: The Influence of Israel's Faith in God on the Law of Property

The concept of property in the Old Testament was in no sense abstract. It was always related to the object. In this excursus, we shall confine ourselves to the ownership of land. The evolution of Israel's law in this respect was characterized by the people's occupation of Canaan, the development within the economy of Israel toward an early form of capitalism and the incorporation of the people into the imperial structure of the Ancient Near East. Property was originally seen predominantly in terms of profane legal structures. Private property in the country was recognized as the basic form of property in the Book of the Covenant. There were two kinds of landed property. The first was land that had come to the clan or family, usually by surveying or lottery. This was handed on as an inheritance. It could only be freely transferred in cases of personal distress and if due consideration was given to the interests of the clan. Unowned property returned to the clan. There was also the practice of "taking possession of land on the basis of obsolete or obsolescent property laws." [1] Until the end of Israel's existence as an independent state, only the "free male member of the clan or the nation who was capable of bearing arms and entitled to take part in the cultic practices of Israel"[2] was entitled to acquire land. These and similar regulations, such as the ban on the displacement of boundary marks (Dt. 19.14; Hos. 5.10), show that ownership of land in Israel was a form of private ownership.

Landed property was, insofar as it had been acquired legally and was necessary to ensure life, protected by God. As Israel's economy developed more and more into a form of early capitalism, however, the possession of large estates and an urban aristocracy as a form of capital power arose and led to the "pauperization of the great peasant masses by increased taxation, legal oppression and a deprival of political rights."[3] Faith in the covenant acted as a corrective against this abuse of the law of property and influenced legal thinking by giving a relative value to private property. This took place in the first instance by the inclusion of certain early fundamentally cultic institutions which "in certain cases" had been adapted to "the changed situation" and "in any case had a social and charitable intention."[4]

One clear example of this practice was the emphasis given every week to the sabbath, and every seventh year to the year of Jubilee. This originally took the form of a universal state of lying fallow. According to Kutsch, this custom went back to the time before the occupation of Canaan and was not primarily concerned with the agricultural economy of land management, but with cult. Later, the practice of remission or release from bonds (*šemiṭṭāh*) within the covenant was added. This eventually may have completely replaced the custom of lying fallow under the influence of urban relationships. During the exile, this lying fallow was once again demanded as part of the year of Jubilee, and later remission from debt demands (the year of Jubilee) was again combined with the year of remission. The institution of the sabbatical year does not seem to have had any direct connection with practices in the cultures of Israel's environment. It was justified in Israel by the conviction that it was Israel's God who really owned the land. (See Lev. 25.23b: "The land is mine, for you are strangers and sojourners with me.") Yahweh was also directly connected in the same way with the chosen land — Canaan was the land of Yahweh and no longer the land of the *ba'alîm*.

Property is recognized in the Old Testament and it is justified in "God's need to have and to guarantee the faithful service of free men."[5] It was, however, restricted in cases "where the exploitation of the law of property harmed social charity and man's uninhibited struggle for power disregarded his love of his fellow-men."[6] Social integrity is clearly the prior condition for man's interiorization of his community with God and his fashioning of his life in holiness. With this aim in view, a critical light is thrown on the functions of material norms. They break down, are corrected or are replaced by new norms. Even though their effectiveness may have been only very slight in fact, they are still a qualified expression of a "typical" attitude of a people whose understanding was determined by an epoch-making event which was without parallel in the whole of the Ancient Near East.

§ 14 The Significance of the Prophets

The Old Testament prophets cannot be ignored in any consideration of the connection between faith and ethics. They played an essential part in the religious development of Israel, because they kept the people on the right path of faith in Yahweh and also continued the movement of his revelation.

A. The Preclassical Prophecy of the Historical Books

The concept "prophet" has many aspects. The collective term "man of God" included, in the early period, the title "seer" (rō'eh or ḥōzeh) and nābhî' (see, for example, 1 Sam. 9.9). These men were not simply passively "called" — they were also actively "calling." Apart from individuals such as Moses (see Dt. 18.15, 18; 34.10-12) or Samuel (see 1 Sam. 9), there were also groups of prophets who were frequently connected with sanctuaries. As a phenomenon, prophets were not confined to Israel. In the Old Testament alone, there were, for example, the seer Balaam and the prophets of Baal whom Elijah encountered on Mount Carmel (1 Kg. 18).

The office of prophet was not like that of the priest or the Levite — in other words, it could not be inherited. It was only possible to be called to be a prophet. Even though this call might take place through a human action (see, for example, 1 Kg. 19.19), the one who called the prophet was always Yahweh himself (see 1 Kg. 19.16; 2 Kg. 2.9 ff.; 1 Sam. 3). As the history of the prophet Jonah and the words of Amos, for example, show, it was also possible for the one who was called by Yahweh to avoid the call.

There are many indications in the Old Testament that the prophets accused the people of Israel in a way which was fully in accordance with the covenant tradition whenever they had broken that covenant. In the case of the preclassical prophets, it was the king and not the people as a whole who was accused. These prophets transmitted the judgment of Yahweh in making an accusation. Elijah, no doubt with the old law formulated in the Book of the Covenant in mind (Ex. 21.12), raised his voice against Ahab, who had murdered Naboth for his vineyard (1 Kg. 21.19). This case, like all the others, was one in which no one took measures against the guilty person. The judge was, here as elsewhere, Yahweh. The prophet was his messenger and had no power himself. He appeared as the protector of moral and legal order. Nathan's position with regard to the dynasty of David is of special importance. The prophets of the preclassical period were also political figures, because of the unrestricted rule and the absolute kingdom of Yahweh.

B. The Major and Minor Prophets

Similar accusations to those made by the preclassical prophets occur in the writings of the major and minor prophets. In the case of the latter, however, it is not an individual who is accused, but the whole of the people of the covenant who are judged.

Experience of the God of salvation was partly an alien one for the contemporaries of these prophets because of political and religious influences. The state of Israel had taken over not only the specifically religious institutions, but also the social and political affairs of the nation. "At a time of increasing disintegration and collapse, it was possible for faith in Yahweh to break out again in an entirely new form in the proclamation of the prophets."[1]

The appearance of the major and minor prophets from the eighth century B.C. onward was governed by four main factors: a) the degeneration of faith in Yahweh caused by religious syncretism; b) "an emancipation from Yahweh and his offer of protection brought about by the fact that the state had come to predominate,"[2] the result, in other words, of Israel's political autonomy; c) the economic and social development of Israel and Judah. Since the time of Solomon and the extensive system of official control and

142

taxation that had been built up during his reign, the earlier social order based on the association of the tribes had begun to fall apart. The economic center of gravity shifted from agriculture to the towns. More and more social abuses occurred among the rural population because of oppression by the great landlords who were, at this time, already resident in the towns (see, for example, Is. 5.8; Mic. 2.1 f.); d) the increased power of the Assyrians and the threat to Palestine from the outside that had existed since the eighth century B.C.

The essential themes of the prophets of this period were: social injustice (Amos, c. 750 B.C.); decline into the natural religion of Canaan and syncretism (Hosea, c. 730 B.C.); a misplaced confidence in military alliances instead of in Yahweh's protection (Isaiah, c. 730 B.C.; see especially Is. 7).

The prophets went back to the early tradition of Yahweh, but, by applying it to their own time, gave it a different form. At the center of the preaching of all the prophets was the conviction that Yahweh was the only God and the Lord of creation, who determined the course of history. As Israel's partner in the covenant, he was first and foremost their God. In the prophetic writings, however, what emerges more and more clearly in the threats and proclamations of salvation is the universal concern of this God for all peoples. One of the consequences of this is a reinforcement of the struggle against syncretism. (This is especially noticeable in Hos. 2.7 ff.; see also Jer. 2.5.) The transcendent God is holy (qādôš). In his glory and power (kabhôdh), he turns toward man. This theme is strongly emphasized in Isaiah (See, for example, Is. 6), but it also occurs in Hosea (see, for example, Hos. 11.9), Jeremiah and Haggai. He is God and not man. That is why his judgment is not irreversible. It can be overruled by his mercy and kindness. The image of the covenant of marriage occurs frequently in Hosea, Jeremiah and Ezekiel for the love of God that is directed toward man.

C. The History of Salvation and the Prophetic Expectation of the Future

The message preached by the prophets can only be understood if it is seen against the background of the traditions of Israel. The prophets were not representatives of an independent law or ethos. They furthered God's will and promoted his covenant by enabling

143

his law to break through. They bore witness to God and his activity in the history of Israel as the people whom he had chosen. In their preaching, they proclaimed the end of the earlier election of Israel.[3]

Their words were directed toward the future, but were as such intimately linked with the history of Israel's salvation in the past and the present. They cannot be disentangled from their roots in Israel's history (see, for example, Ezek. 20). The promises of salvation in the future are always associated with the ideas of Israel's tradition.[4] Signs of a new orientation toward salvation can be recognized as a completely new element especially in the prophetic proclamation of God's judgment.[5] "A new exodus replaced the earlier exodus from Egypt and a new covenant replaced the old covenant."[6]

Amos's words of warning contain the suggestion of God's renewed activity in the salvation of man: "Seek good and not evil, that you may live; and so Yahweh, the God of hosts, will be with you."[7] The good to which Amos was referring here was not to be found in the sphere of worship — in other words, it was not Bethel or Gilgal (see Am. 5.5). The only way to Yahweh was to return to his law, which was valid at all times. Seeking good, which was identical with seeking Yahweh himself, was loving his law, what is right (*mišᵉpaṭ*), and making it valid and hating evil, in other words, false witness, injustice, malice and indifference to worship.[8] Amos regarded the "establishment of justice in the gate" (5.15) as a "fundamental demand of obedience"[9] and the basis of his theological and social teaching.[10] For him, what was good (*ṭôbh*) was identical with what was right (*mišᵉpaṭ*), and this identity was based on the demand that there should be solidarity within the community. "Just as evil in Israel was always wrong because it was an offence against the idea of community, so too was good only right because it was in accordance with the principle of community."[11] According to Ezekiel 20.25, "statutes and ordinances that were not good" were a reversal of the way to life into the way to death. God's effective judgment and rule were reflected in his judgments (*mišᵉpaṭîm*; see, for example, Ps. 119.39). His rule was, moreover, in accordance with the nature of every man.[12] Here, as generally in Deuteronomy, the Torah is seen to be the highest good, more valuable than all possessions (see Ps. 119.72).

It is quite clear from Amos 5 that the threat from outside to Israel's existence and the increase in the number of social abuses led to growing criticism from within. This criticism was directed above all at official life — the monarchy, the ruling classes and the power structures — and at Israel's cultic praxis.[13] "Israel was reduced, with all its religious apparatus, to the level of zero. The prophets created a vacuum by proclaiming God's justice and by sweeping away all false security."[14]

The proclamation of the prophets of Israel was not, however, primarily aimed at moral, social, political or religious criticism. The prophets of the eighth century B.C. should not at least be regarded as calling Israel to repentance and as beginning their statements with the word if and concluding with a threat. They did call upon Israel to be converted, but this call was not directly linked with a proclamation of God's judgment.[15] Conversion was not expressed as a condition for salvation. The prophets' pronouncements of disaster made an appeal to man's power of decision without any reference to an alternative. It is, after all, only in this way that it is possible to make a free decision to be converted.[16] In essence, their message was directed toward an interiorization and a reliving of the people's lost ideas of the covenant and toward a recovery of their perspective of the history of salvation. The ethics of the prophets can be summed up as an "exposition of God's claim and a message of mediation, judgment, peace and mercy as a result of that claim."[17] Their ethics gave rise to a criticism of religion based on religious motives. The culmination of their message was the proclamation of a new salvation and peace, a new covenant, not only for Israel, but also for all people.[18]

§ 15 The Contribution Made by the Wisdom Literature

In basing their proclamation on the evil that had been set in motion by man himself, the Old Testament prophets were not speaking of a "mysterious experience," but were rather practising "an elementary knowledge that already existed for them and also basically for everyone who had some experience of the world and of human life — in other words, a knowledge of the fundamental divine laws to which all human life is subject. It is here that prophecy and wisdom come into close and vital contact with each other."[1]

The Wisdom literature of the Old Testament includes the Psalms, the Proverbs, the book of Job, Ecclesiastes and the Song of Songs. It is in these books and also, of course, in many passages scattered about the Old Testament as a whole that human experience was applied to the task of bringing order into the events of the world. They form a literary deposit of that experience in the form of sayings, proverbs and "sentences."[2] "They are among the most radical expressions of the human spirit and their practical purpose is to keep the threat of harm and the possible reduction of life at a distance."[3] This, of course, applies equally to all the other people of the ancient world. What, however, applies particularly to Israel is that these most radical experiences were expressed in a different way from that of the other cultures in the ancient world and within the framework of Israel's own specific understanding of religion.[4]

To judge by their content alone, the Old Testament Wisdom sentences (in the sense of expositions of proverbial religious truth) can be dated over a very wide period stretching from the pre-exilic period of Israel's kings (Pr. 10–29) to the later post-exilic period. The appearance of the earliest Wisdom writings marked the "emergence of a scholastic wisdom in the early period of the kings,"[5] which has often been called the period of Israel's "Enlightenment." Gemser has pointed in this context to a connection with the establishment in Israel of an official administration that had become necessary. It is clear from the various problems that have arisen in connection with the Wisdom literature, however, that it did not originate among the official administrators of Israel, but rather among those Israelites who lived in the cities and on large farms. The word wisdom is very extensive in meaning and includes a wide range of phenomena.

There was no foundation of special knowledge in the earlier Wisdom sentences, which were concerned with worldly objects and questions of everyday life. It was man's task to acquire wisdom.[6] "The formulas point clearly to the human source of the questions asked. . . . They are obviously concerned with man and with the need to determine man's possibilities."[7] "Just as God's wisdom (see, for example, Pr. 21.30; Jer. 8.9; Is. 31.2; Dan. 2.20-23) was closely related to his creative power (see Pr. 3.19; Is. 40.13 ff.; Jer. 10.12; 51.15; Job 9.4; 12.12-16; Ps. 104.24), so too did wisdom given by God to men bestow on them the power to fashion their life into something happy and successful."[8] In this sense, then, wisdom meant primarily specialized knowledge or skill (see, for example, Ex. 28.3; 31.6, etc.) and was above all of a practical kind. It was even applied to magic arts, the interpretation of dreams (see Gen. 41.8, 38, etc.) and to the turning of a staff into a snake or snake-charming (see Ex. 7.11; Ps. 58.6). The concept "wisdom" was originally without any ethical value. It was, in other words, value neutral (see, for example, 2 Sam. 13.3). "Wisdom was human knowledge, common sense, cleverness and so on, often without any ethical content."[9]

Later, however, "wisdom and morality, knowledge and virtue" became "two sides of the same coin."[10] "Whenever he asked questions about himself, Old Testament man recognized himself as a member of Israel, the people bound to Yahweh by the covenant, and the question was simply asked in a different way: as a member of that people, bound by the covenant, and as a member of that establishment that is superior to myself and that gives me an obligation, how am I to fashion my life?"[11] This question was asked by the member of the people of the covenant as autonomous man who had the task of fashioning himself in freedom. In whatever form it occurred, however, whether as a simple statement or as an admonition, wisdom was always regarded as God's gift.[12] This wisdom enabled the leaders of Israel, in their carrying out of their official duties, to distinguish between good and evil, truth and falsehood, and gain and loss. (See, for example, 2 Sam. 14; 1 Kg. 3; Dt. 1.13; 34.9; Is. 29.14; Jer. 9.22; 18.18; 50.35; 51.57.) It was not until later still that the idea of the wise man as a learned teacher first appeared — during the post-exilic period. Under the influence of faith in Yahweh and the message of the prophets, the idea of wisdom became not only ethical but also very religious and became also closely related to the fear of God and justice (see Hos. 4.6; Is. 11.2; Jer. 8.9; Ps. 19.8; 37.30; 107.43; 119).

When the collection and editing of the teachings of the Wisdom literature had been completed, they were used in the instruction of young people. They have, however, no generally didactic value and should not be regarded as imperatives. They are basically no more than rational assertions. "In their own way and within their own limitations, they aim to express what is undoubtedly valid and certain."[13]

What is particularly striking about the Wisdom is its closeness to the compilations of the law of Israel (cf. Jer. 2.8 and 8.8 ff., for example; see also Is. 10.1). There is a close connection in Israel between the praxis of the law and the proverbial wisdom.[14] It is remarkable how often the Wisdom writings are described as "Torah" (see Pr. 1.8; 3.1; 13.14; 28.4, 7, etc.), as is the law, the authoritative admonition.[15] The legal texts of the Pentateuch (such as Lev. 19) are also full of $m^e\check{s}\bar{a}l\hat{\imath}m$, wisdom expressed in the form of proverbial statements.[16] The dialogue in the Book of Job is also reminiscent of the way in which the lawyers of Israel discussed insoluble problems in the gate of the city.[17] The similarity between the content of the Wisdom writings and that of the law[18] has been stressed by Fichtner and others.[19]

Two different kinds of proverbial expressions of wisdom can be distinguished. In the first place, there are those cases which deal with the norms set by men and directed toward their own inclinations, norms of what is good and evil or useful and not useful, which have no special purpose and therefore no absolute claim. They are the consequence of purposeful ethical thinking (see, for example, 2 Kg. 10.3). There is clearly a scale of values within the Wisdom literature.[20] The rule of wisdom is often characterized as counsel and it is therefore clear that it could be disputed. Although the wise man listened with concentration, his virtue was not so much obedience as knowledge and insight or reflective understanding.[21]

In the second place, the statements made in the Wisdom literature are sometimes based on the contrast between obedience and disobedience and are therefore concerned with an ethical sphere in which there can be no relative or intermediate values and in which man is unconditionally bound (see 1 Sam. 15.22; Ps. 69.32; Pr. 17.1). In the proverbial statements in which something is, "in the style of a congratulatory sentence,"[22] designated as $t\hat{o}bh$ (how good it would be if . . .), we see a reflection of life rooted in $\dot{s}^e dh\bar{a}q\bar{a}h$ and $mi\check{s}^e p\bar{a}t$ (see Ps. 112.5; 133.1; Is. 3.10; Lam. 3.20), a harmonious communal life (Gen. 2.18; 2 Kg. 2.19) in which the individual is not isolated and does not live for himself alone, but is always there as *pars pro toto* for the whole community and able to determine the fate of that community by his actions. The phrase that occurs so often in Proverbs, *lô'-ţôbh* (it is not good), has very much the same meaning as unjust in legal statements, especially when an innocent party has to pay (see Pr. 17.26; also 18.5; 24.23; 28.21). In the Wisdom literature, there are also considerations, expressed in the way that is characteristic of that literature, concerning what is in fact *ţôbh* for man (Pr. 24.13; 25.27; Ec. 2.3, 24; 5.17; 6.12; 11.7; Lam. 3.26 etc.). One of the main themes in the many proverbs containing the words *ţôbh-mîn* ("better than" or "it is good . . . and not . . .") is that of the judgment of poverty and wealth (Ps. 37.16; Pr. 15.16; 16.8, 19; 19.1, 22; 28.6; see also Ec. 6.9). In the treatment of this question, the contrast between just and evil often amounts to the same as a contrast between poor and rich. In this antithesis, wealth as such is not generally condemned. What is condemned is the illegally acquired property of the godless. It is clear, then, that these authors were not criticizing society as, for example, the prophet Amos was. In the book of Ecclesiastes, there is a clear expression of man's striving for the worldly good of happiness and satisfaction (see especially Ec. 2.24; 3.12, 22; 5.17; 8.15) and Ellermeier has spoken in this context of *ţôbh* (good), in the specific sense in which the word is used in Ecclesiastes, as the "place of unreflecting life." [23] The author — or authors — of this transitional work found the meaning of life on this earth in pleasure in the goods that had been bestowed on man and believed this to be so in view of the discrepancy between justice and prosperity, evil and misfortune and especially in the sequence of action and consequence (see Ec. 2.1; 3.13; 4.8; 5.17; 6.3, 6; 8.12, 13, 15). It is quite clear that the author — or authors — of this book regarded worldly goods as gifts from God, however profane the tenor of the work may be.

The admonitions in the Wisdom literature to be humble and kind toward the lowly (Pr. 3.27; 16.19) and to control one's emotions and not exploit one's position of power unscrupulously (Pr. 14.17; 16.32; 24.5 ff.; 25.28; Ec. 7.8) should obviously be seen as ethical statements.

The man who possessed wisdom and understanding, taken in the full spectrum of their practical and ethical implications, had a certainty of life and happiness that transcended all material goods and any position of power. (See, for example, Pr. 3.14; 8.10 ff., 19; 16.16; 19.8; Ec. 4.13; 7.5, 11; 9.16, 18; Pr. 15.2.) Wisdom and understanding are given by God to the man who pleases him (Ec.

2.26) and are as such the supreme good alongside the fear of God and trust in God. The validity of the relationship in the covenant between God and man was expressed in man's fear of and trust in God and there are many references to these in the Wisdom literature. (See, for example, Ps. 63.4; 84.11; 118.8, 9; 119.72; see also Pr. 16.20; Ps. 111.10; Pr. 3.4.) Perhaps the clearest instance of the connection between wisdom and the fear of God and man's reward for acting in accordance with God's will can be found in the exilic or post-exilic Psalm 111.10: "The beginning of wisdom is the fear of Yahweh; the reward for the good of all who act according to it. His praise endures for ever." [24]

Wisdom, then, was seen by the Old Testament authors of this period as closely connected with the fear of God and the latter as being the point of departure for wisdom. This intimate link with God has "an important function with regard to human knowledge" [25] and makes it possible for man to grasp reality in its objectivity (see Pr. 28.5). It is, however, not simply a distinction between what is just and what is unjust that is emphasized by faith. Faith makes knowledge autonomous and activates reason. Nothing fundamentally new is added to the contents of the Book of Proverbs by the statement about the fear of God as the beginning of wisdom. All that this statement does is to express in a concentrated form what is taught in the individual Wisdom sentences. What is, however, particularly striking is that "questions about the presuppositions of man's knowledge and wisdom are asked and answered in a very radical and above all anthropological way in the earlier Wisdom literature, whereas the answer that is given in the later Wisdom writings is theological (wisdom, in other words, comes from God). Wisdom stands or falls by man's attitude towards God." [26] What is particularly true of Israel's wisdom — as compared with that of ancient Egypt, for example — is that it was based on faith in the God of Israel and the understanding of the reality of the world and man which resulted from that faith and according to which there was no separation in wisdom between life and nature. [27] The ancient Egyptians were conscious of an objective certainty in the way the world was ordered. The Israelites, on the other hand, had an understanding of reality that was enriched by their awareness of the mystery of God's activity in human history.

The way in which the norms of human activity were mediated and justified in the Wisdom literature was determined by the "tension . . . between Yahweh's presence and the autonomy of the reality of the world."[28] Human behavior was not, according to these authors, regulated by universal ethical principles, such as those contained in the decalogue, but rather "by man's experience of immanent laws,"[29] in other words, by social institutions that were regarded as given, unchangeable and universally valid. As soon as norms of human behavior are based on the reality of creation, the question as to whether the ethics of wisdom can be described as theonomous is bound to arise. This question can only be answered if the distinctive character of Israel's understanding of wisdom is taken into consideration. To quote Gerhard von Rad once again, "according to the authors of Israel's Wisdom literature, Yahweh delegated so much truth to his creation, indeed, he was himself present in it to such a degree that man was on a very solid ethical foundation when he had learnt to interpret these laws and to adjust his behavior to the experiences that he had acquired."[30] The law and order that prevailed in all things was typically enough never defined as such, but only made visible and effective in a multiplicity of individual cases. The reality was constantly making its presence felt and urging man to act, while at the same time enabling him, in a slow process of understanding, to know by the fruits of his activity what was good and what was evil. (This is the so-called sequence of action and consequence.) It was on the basis of these movements that Old Testament man was able "to recognize laws from which he could derive norms for his behavior; Yahweh himself was active in these movements of reality."[31] It was ultimately this fundamental trust in Yahweh's active and effective presence in the reality of creation that formed the basis of the Old Testament Wisdom sentences as expressions of proverbial truth. We can therefore summarize this brief exposition of the ethics contained in the Wisdom literature by saying with von Rad that it was "a theonomous ethos expressed in a distinctively dialectical way."[32]

CHAPTER 2: THE MORAL MESSAGE OF JESUS

The ethos proclaimed in the New Testament was to a very great extent determined by the authors' confession of faith in Jesus the Christ and by the resulting teaching given in the early Christian communities. Paul's doctrine of Christian freedom was, for example, based on his faith in the death and resurrection of the Lord. It is clear from the history of traditions that this liberating faith had its roots in Jesus' own proclamation.[1] If, then, the primitive Christian tradition can be traced back to the words and deeds of Jesus (both in its message of salvation and in its moral demands), this historical origin has clearly to be questioned. In this chapter, we shall therefore ask a number of questions within the general framework of our aim in this book. The fact that the New Testament message makes certain claims on man is beyond dispute. The questions that have to be asked are rather concerned with the distinctive character of that claim and the obligatory nature of the moral directives contained in the New Testament. Our main aim in this chapter, then, will be to try to find a satisfactory answer to these questions.

§ 16 The Proclamation of the Basileia of God

At the heart of Jesus' message was his proclamation of the Basileia of God. This very full concept signifies God's present rule and the aim of history — his kingdom. God's Basileia then, is the quintessence of his historical activity with and through man while at the same time it points to the state at the end of time, which is exclusively controlled by God, a state in which the world will no longer be dominated by the powers of evil and God will rule. Jesus' moral message forms part of this proclamation of the rule and kingdom of God and its claim is essentially determined by it.

A. The Inseparability of Jesus' Moral Message from his Person and Activity

According to the gospel of Mark, Jesus began his public life with a call to eschatological fulfillment. Mark summarizes Jesus' preaching in two sentences expressed in the style of prophetic calls: "The time is fulfilled and the kingdom of God is at hand! Repent and believe in the gospel!" (Mk. 1.15).[2] The content of his message, then, is, on the one hand, a proclamation of salvation and, on the other, a demand for conversion. The order in which these two aspects are presented is not unimportant, since "the movement of conversion was, for Jesus, in accordance with the anticipatory movement made by God himself (Lk. 15.11-32)."[3]

The foundation of salvation was the fact that the kingdom of God had come (*ēggiken hē basileia tou theou*) and this proclamation has to be taken within the context of the whole of Jesus' preaching of "God's liberating law of love."[4] According to Jesus, then, it was that new beginning, that fulfillment of justice in the world, that only God, as the Lord of history, was able to give. The concept of God's kingdom therefore means that "God is God and Lord and that, for this reason, man is human and the world is saved, because God's state of being God and Lord sets man and the world free from the powers of evil that are hostile to creation and reconciles them in their division and absence of salvation."[5] The call to conversion, then, is based above all on this proclamation of salvation and not, as in the preaching of John the Baptist, on a threat of judgment.

Jesus associated this proclamation of the rule and kingdom of God indissolubly with his own person.[6] In the gospel of Luke, the passage about Jesus at Nazareth replaces the summary of Jesus' teaching provided by Mark (Lk. 4.16-30). In this passage, Jesus reads from the scroll of the prophet Isaiah (the well-known text, Is. 61.1-2a) and says, with emphasis, that this promise is fulfilled in his coming.[7] This corresponds to an authentic part of his inaugural sermon in public (Lk. 6.20 ff.), in which he promises the Basileia to the poor and in so doing makes a direct reference to the same prophetic words. This, however, is not simply a prophetic promise. It is rather the "dawn of the time of fulfillment (see Mk. 1.15a) . . . that is announced. What we hear in this eschatological call to fulfillment which refers back to Isaiah 61.1 is Jesus' proclamation of the Basileia in its most primitive form."[8] It is for this reason that those who witnessed it, by seeing and hearing, were blessed (see Lk. 10.23 ff.; Mt. 13.16 ff.). It is, after all, the power of God himself that was made effective in Jesus' activity. In his action of driving out devils, for example, the Basileia of God was being realized (see Lk. 11.20; Mt. 12.28). Jesus proclaimed the kingdom of God, in other words, and made it present by his praxis. His activity was permeated by a present and a religious eschatology. The *eschaton* or time of salvation was given to the world with his coming into the world and his being present there. The present is, in other words, the place of the future and it is that only because what is at stake is the present of God's saving activity and the universal kingdom of God that is expected in that activity.[9] It would therefore be right to anticipate a post-paschal confession and say that Jesus is God's great saving work in this world.[10] Jesus' words and deeds can be understood in the light of his whole life.

The distinctive aspect of his proclamation of the kingdom of God can therefore be found in the special connection between eschatology and theology. "Because Jesus knew about the God who 'is' transcendentally present and who 'comes' to give grace and direction to man, there are two closely integrated series of statements in his message — the proclamation of the revelation of God and that of the kingdom of God."[11] The point of contact at which these two sets of statements are held together is Jesus' consciousness of being Son.[12] His message, praxis and prophetic self-understanding all point to the special aspects of this consciousness of sonship, which was expressed appropriately in the early Christian communities in the title "Son of God."[13] In this context, there is the christological principle — the so-called hermeneutical principle — which directs our attention to the interrelationship that exists between eschatology and theology. Jesus' ethics were also determined by this fundamental interrelationship. Like the whole of his proclamation, his ethics cannot be separated from his person. Even when the individual demands made by Jesus do not, as far as their material content is concerned, go beyond the Old Testament and Jewish ethos, there is still a newness and a difference in his ethics. "Jesus' ethics can be seen as distinctive only in the light of his eschatological message and messianic task."[14]

B. The Specific Aspect of Jesus' Demands in their Radical Relationship with the Coming of the Basileia

The *eschaton* or the time of fulfillment dawned, as we have seen, with Jesus, but the realization of the kingdom of God is still to come. According to the biblical understanding of time and history, this coming is not simply a future event. Time, in the Bible, is not merely quantitative — it is also qualitative. There is, for example, the "right time" or *kairos*, the opportunity which should not be missed. In this sense, then, the future has already begun and the necessary decisions have to be made. This qualitative aspect of time is given greater emphasis by Jesus' use of the hope that was expressed in the apocalyptic tradition and his interpretation of that hope in the light of his faith in creation which was influenced by the Wisdom literature. "He was therefore able to unite the creative power of the apocalyptic Utopia to the present, without giving way to the apocalyptic temptation to seek flight from the present." [15] This marks a considerable departure from the apocalyptic vision both of John the Baptist and of the entire Jewish world. The apocalyptic teaching of Jesus is without the esoteric and enthusiastic elements of the latter on the one hand and the rigoristically legal aspects on the other. Instead of separating himself from society, perhaps in the company of a few followers, he went up and down the country and took the message of salvation to all men. He did not use the threat of imminent judgment, but proclaimed the good and joyful news of God's universal love of all mankind. This love was revealed to everyone who seized hold of the present moment as God's presence and as the hour of salvation. The promise of the coming of the kingdom of God was a judgment only for those "who do not accept God's present moment and who cling to their own present, their own past and also their own dreams of the future." [16] Jesus' call to conversion was full of this offer and this claim and demanded an acceptance in faith of God's offer.

The basic claim of the Basileia of God is faith. At the very heart of Jesus' mission on earth was his aim to arouse in men an unconditional faith in God. His powerful deeds also serve to arouse faith and the reports of these acts in the gospels point again and again to the faith that they stimulated and that was required by Jesus himself. The content of that faith, however, was simply the Basileia of God — the revelation of God's liberating law in love. This Basileia is the theme of many of the parables in which Jesus depicts God's state of being God as the rule of love in many different images. It is also the way par excellence in which he speaks of God as the Father. [17] When Jesus used the name of Father with regard to God, he was expressing God's "sovereign freedom to love and forgive." [18] It was the love that brought the lost (or dead) prodigal son to life again and made the son who remained at home and was faithful to the law understand that he should not make any claim to reward as the one who had always been given everything (see Lk. 15.31 ff.). God's liberating law transcends all human planning and the coming of the kingdom of God cannot be brought about by human organization. It is also "not a function of human salvation in the sense of God's being possibly useful in the matter of man's salvation. Jesus had the task of doing God's work and man's task is to seek God 'for God's sake.' In other words, the kingdom of God is meaningful in itself and the rest is, as it were, added."[19] This is why it is compared in certain parables to a treasure (Mt. 13.44) or a precious pearl (Mt. 13.45-46) and why, according to one parable, it is entrusted to man like a talent (Mt. 25.14-30 par; Lk. 19.22-27). It is in fact a demand that calls for complete conversion or *metanoia*. Although the kingdom of God can and must seize hold of man totally and despite the important consequences that it can have in praxis, it does not in the first place imply either asceticism or performance. It is expressed above all in faith.[20] What is more, this faith does not imply a religious performance by which one attempts to please God. On the contrary, it means an abandonment of any performance on man's part and an admission that he can do nothing himself, that he cannot help himself and that he is unable to provide a basis for his own existence or bring about his own salvation. If man recognizes his own impotence in this way, his faith can become open to something that is different, new and found in the future. "In expecting nothing from himself, man expects everything from God, 'with whom all things are possible' (Mk. 10.27 par)."[21]

The fundamental claim that is made by the gospel, then, is that man should recognize that his existence is absolutely dependent on God and that God turns toward him and offers him grace and salvation in the event of Jesus. It is this faith that makes the kingdom of God a concrete reality in the world. One consequence of this is that the kingdom of God calls for a committed orientation toward man.

The eschatological claim made in Jesus' proclamation of the Basileia of God was not separate from the reality of the world of man. On the contrary, that claim was directed toward all aspects of it. An orientation toward man is basically the visible form of the coming of the kingdom of God. Jesus did not preach a social revolution, but this does not in any way mean that the goods expressed in the beatitudes were not to be realized until the arrival of a future situated somewhere beyond human history. The overcoming of poverty, hunger and suffering in the present was intimately connected with Jesus' proclamation of God's kindgom and rule. God's liberating law makes man, in the praxis of his life, subject to a critical claim. His universal love does not allow any barriers to be set up or any confessions or sects to be formed. Indeed, Jesus tore down the religious and social barriers that had been erected at that time by Judaism. He did not reject the tax-collectors and sinners, but accepted them as his partners and enabled them to follow his way. It is quite clear that he did not want cultic and ritual laws to stand in the way of man's service of his fellow-men and that he wanted men to abandon their enslavement to mammon and their anxiety about the future. The freedom given by God was not a right that could be claimed by everyone. On the contrary, it questioned the right of the individual, because it was always primarily the freedom of others.[22] "In his behavior, Jesus provided, not a theoretical, but a practical, proleptic — anticipatory — realization of the 'new world' of the humane, good and true life, although this was given in a very concrete historical contingency that could, as such, not be repeated by us."[23] His message was not directed toward an improvement of man's moral existence that could only always be relative, but toward an eschatological claim. It was not aimed at a successive struggle, but at the definitive overcoming of self-alienation.[24] In his attempt to express God's absolute claim in a radical way, he aimed to make men more intensely conscious of the law and at the same time to set them free from the law.

Jesus' proclamation did not provide a positively developed ethos of the kingdom of God. In Jesus himself, God's rule was already present, but, until it was completed by God himself, it was to be realized by men subject to the conditions of finiteness. In the first place, however, the connection between the proclamation of the Basileia and concrete action was exclusively realized in the person and activity of Jesus himself. "Jesus' proclamation and his activity were not mediated — until his death, the death on the cross. Mediation only arose as a problem in the post-paschal tradition."[25]

§ 17 The Torah and the New Law

A. The Fundamental Structure of Jesus' Criticism of the Law

The presence of the Basileia calls for a critical examination of the Jewish and pharisaical understanding of the law. According to Matthew's gospel, Jesus came not to abolish the law of Moses or the teachings of the prophets, but to fulfill them (Mt. 5.17). In making this statement, the evangelist was clearly following the earliest theological doctrines of the first Christian communities, according to which the contrast and the relationship between the old and new covenants were regarded as a sequence in the history of salvation, of promise and fulfillment. The Matthaean statement was able to preserve the continuity of the history of salvation on the one hand and to relativize the validity of the old covenant on the other by interpreting the whole of that history in the light of its fulfillment in Christ.

This understanding seems to be quite without complications in the context of the life, suffering, death and resurrection of Jesus, but its application to the question of the law clearly raises considerable complications.[1] In the latter case, it is not simply a question as to whether what was required by the law of Moses was fulfilled under the new dispensation. It is rather a question of the validity and the orientation of both dispensations. In what way, then, was the old law included in the validity of the new law? Did the morality that was required by the old dispensation — a morality based mainly on individual laws — have to be mediated in a different way in the period of the history of salvation initiated by Jesus? What did Jesus himself say in reply to this question?

A good point of departure for any attempt to resolve this difficulty is provided by the antitheses contained in the Sermon on the Mount, since they "express most clearly Jesus' criticism of the law."[2] Different sources in the history of traditions have, of course, to be considered and it may be assumed, on the basis of a comparison with the Lucan text, that the antithetic form first appeared in Matthew's gospel.[3] It is also clear from various analyses that have been made that "Jesus' words were clarified and applied in accordance with their real meaning by this whole adaptation."[4] We may therefore be sure that the Sermon on the Mount in its final form, as edited by the last editor of the gospel of Matthew, provides us with a good introduction to the authentic intentions of Jesus in his specific moral message. His principal intention is made particularly clear in the formal contrast (or antithesis) of the Sermon on the Mount. In the original antitheses (I, II and IV), Jesus contrasts his position with the traditional Jewish understanding of the law,[5] which had been fundamentally fashioned during the Babylonian exile and the period that followed it.[6] The law was constitutive for the community and any criticism of it was regarded as an attack against the faith of the Jewish people. The written version of the Torah was therefore regarded as identical with the will of God as revealed on Mount Sinai. This resulted in "the obligatory nature of the established written version of the Torah, even when its demands could not be understood by men."[7] In religious, political and social life, then, the chief concern of the Jewish people was to interpret and practice the Torah as the established written form of God's will. It is therefore not difficult to understand how provocative it must have seemed when Jesus, conscious of his messianic power, contrasted what "had been said" (*errethē*), in other words, the will of God as established in the written word, with the clear statement "I say to you" (*legō gar humin*) of his antitheses. For Jesus, the will of God was not a letter of the law, but a living reality. For him too, that living will of God that was active in the history of man's salvation was the factor that bound the old and the new dispensations together. There is a clear difference "between the rabbinical way of thinking and that of the authors of the gospels. . . . In Matthew, what is stressed is never the fulfillment of the law as such, but the fulfillment of the will of God."[8] Jesus called the legal clauses of the Old Testament into question and contrasted them with his theses, but he did this because his claim was more in accordance with the will of God as expressed in the presence of the Basileia. He did not see himself as a scribe of the law who used casuistry to interpret the law. On the contrary, he initiated a new principle. The will of God was no longer established in the Torah. This meant that "the principle of the will of God himself replaced the principle of the Jewish tradition. This was justified by the mission of Jesus and his position in the history of salvation."[9]

B. Corrections in the Traditional Ethics

1. The Depth and Refinement of Jesus' Ethos

Jesus' criticism of the law called for certain radical corrections to be made in the traditional ethics. In the first place, his claim had greater depth. An external functioning of the law was not sufficient in the Basileia that had begun with Jesus. Man was confronted with God and had to examine himself and particularly his innermost self. A demand was made on him, in his heart, his thinking, speaking and acting. In his original antitheses, Jesus made use of the decalogue: "You shall not kill . . . You shall not commit adultery . . . You shall not swear falsely . . . Not a dot, not an iota will pass from the law" (Mt. 5.21, 27, 33, 18). But he stressed that it was not simply the external acts that had to be taken into consideration. Even more important was the inner state of man — the origin of the external acts had to be kept in order.[10]

In addition to this aspect of depth, there is another dimension of Jesus' ethical teaching. Justice could not be done to the refinement of the ethical reality by a carefully prepared casuistic law. The scribes and teachers of the law had sincerely tried to measure the law against the possibilities and limitations of those who would practice it and even to adapt it by means of exegesis to what man was able and had to do in order to preserve order in society. Jesus, however, was not content with this. The will of God could not be discerned simply by observing the letter of the law. "Man is confronted with God, himself and his fellow-man in constantly changing situations . . . The other with his needs, expectations and hopes, all of which he brings to me, consciously or unconsciously, when he encounters me, is, as it were, a 'text-book of God's will.' This text-book is always concrete in the individual, but can only be experienced in each case in the action of that particular individual and can never be anticipated and established in advance."[11] The moral claim is therefore never exposed to arbitrary choice or set free from all obligatory directives. The interiorization of the ethos and man's liberation from the law are based above all on the presence of the Basileia. The parables of the treasure buried in the field and the pearl of great value (Mt. 13.44-46) show how serious and uncompromising Jesus' call to decision was. It was not possible, he emphasized, for a man to serve two masters (Mt. 6.24). "Man can only make a decision that measures up to the offer of the Basileia or the demand made by God himself when he enters fully — in all the aspects of his being — into that decision. Half promises, reservations and compromises are out of the question, as is a correct fulfillment of the law which is only concerned with its letter (see Lk. 18.9-14; Mt. 21.28-32)."[12] The liberating power of the ethics proclaimed by Jesus results from man's decision to accept God's offer of salvation.

2. A Separation from Evil

This decision calls in addition for a fundamental separation from evil. This is quite clear from the so-called secondary antitheses of the Sermon on the Mount (Mt. 5.31 ff., 38-42, 43-48). In this case, it was not the apodictic demands of the decalogue that were selected as points of departure, but rather such cases of the casuistic law as the praxis of sending a letter of divorce (Dt. 24.1), the law of retaliation (Lev. 24.19) or a statement such as that advocating hatred of one's enemies, which is not accredited in the Old Testament. These are basically instructions in the controversy with certain forms of evil in interpersonal relationships.

It has correctly been pointed out that evil was regarded as a datum that could not be eliminated, but only restricted.[13] It was the task of the legal prescriptions to make it possible for men to live together, even though evil could not be overcome, by containing evil by means of the law. Jesus was not satisfied with this situation. His intention was to conduct the struggle against evil at a much more radical level in the presence of the kingdom of God. It was not sufficient simply to fight against aggression between men by limiting the principle of retaliation to the level of an eye for an eye. The struggle could only be won if man was ready to offer the other cheek. The same applied to dissensions in marriage. Real help in such cases was not provided by applying the praxis of divorce or by regulating the possibilities of divorce quantitatively. The only solution was a complete change of attitude, a qualitative alteration in man's thinking and behaving. Jesus was not entirely condemning a legal settlement of marital conflicts here, nor was he concerned with a reform of the legal structure. In his proclamation of the Basileia of God, he was not primarily thinking of law as such. He was above all going to the root of evil itself, which originates in man's thought and will. "He was radically concerned with man as such and that man should have a new understanding of himself in the presence of God and among his fellow-men."[14] He called on man to reexamine his values critically. These calls or radical demands[15] made by Jesus, which go to the root (*radix*) of man's moral responsibility cannot as such be transferred to the categorial form of interpersonal laws. They are a promise which makes a demand or a demand which contains a promise and show that, on the basis of faith, an expectation can be experienced as encouragement and not simply as a burden. What we have here are purposeful demands or antitheses to the law that need a concrete form in moral balance on the basis of this antithetical structure. In these demands, the values that should be given special attention by those who have decided in favor of God's rule and kingdom are particularly stressed. The system of norms employed in a specifically Christian ethos should clearly express this antithetic structure,[16] so that the progressive character of that ethos can in this way be made clear. It is possible for morality to progress only if it is radical in a way which, in this case, cannot, to begin with, be precisely justified. What, however, is evident here is that the believer can, by means of a certain factor and without departing from the reality of the situation, go beyond himself with a courage that defies radical analysis. That factor, which undoubtedly penetrates the whole of Jesus' eschatological message, has been called "God's radical rejection of all forms of evil and all forms of poverty and hunger."[17]

Research into the history of traditions has shown that the legal statements were included in the first place as prior statements preceding Jesus' demands when the gospel of Matthew was being edited. The aim of the antithetic form, then, was to give greater emphasis to the statements made by Jesus. The fact that Jesus or Matthew formulated their own counter-thesis in legal language does not necessarily mean that the author wanted in this way to contrast a new law with the old law. On the contrary, the contrast assimilated in this way into the style of the statements was used to destroy faith in a possible improvement in human relationships brought about by means of divorce or retaliation[18] and to point to the new possibilities, provided by the Basileia of God, of forgiveness, reconciliation, faithfulness and brotherly love.

A great deal of research has been done in recent years into the meaning of Jesus' prohibition of divorce. The result of a reconstruction of what is probably the earliest form of the logion to which both the Q and the Marcan traditions go back is a casuistic legal statement: "Whoever dismisses his wife commits adultery and whoever marries a dismissed woman commits adultery."[19] In this form, the statement is entirely orientated toward the Jewish concept of law and is at the same time fundamentally opposed to it. Jesus apparently wanted to treat any arbitrary divorce whatever as adultery, in this way going contrary to the Jewish praxis of divorce, according to which only the man was entitled to issue a letter of divorce and the woman was thus released so that another man could marry her. According to the valid law, the Jewish man could not commit adultery against his own wife.[20] It is, however, hardly possible that Jesus would have wanted, in making this statement, to intervene in a political legal battle and to change the Jewish law of marriage. We do not, after all, know the concrete situation in Judaism that provoked Jesus to make this statement. Some indication as to what Jesus' intention was is perhaps provided by the controversy with the pharisees, in which the logion occurs both in Mark (10.1-12) and in Matthew (19.3-9). It is clear that those who were asking him questions knew his attitude already and wanted to provoke him to take a stand publicly against a clear regulation in the Mosaic law.[21] Jesus replied at first with a counter-question: "What did Moses *command* you?" With this reply, he avoided being involved in the controversy about the different reasons for divorce and at the same time did not attack the legal prescription calling for a letter of divorce. He did not, later in the dialogue, ask about what was legally possible or permissible, but rather pointed to the will of God, the God who was concealed behind the commandment of Moses[22] and whom Jesus perceived in two passages from Genesis, which he interpreted freely. God has created the sexual difference and the marital dispensation, according to which the two partners were, in accordance with God's will, one. "What God has joined together, let no man put asunder." Jesus' demand was unambiguous and uncompromising. It could not be reduced to casuistry and was therefore not just a new law within the category of the old law.[23] Jesus' reduction of the old law to the fundamental will of God the creator, which went beyond the casuistic discussion, points to the real theo-logical meaning of his teaching. The deepest reality of community and faithfulness in marriage, which was revealed in God's creation, but was abused by man, becomes, in faith, a new possibility with the coming of the Basileia.[24] Jesus' statement therefore has the character of a prophetic call and a challenging promise. It is consequently possible to understand the original meaning of the traditional logion within the framework of this understanding of Jesus' teaching that prevailed in the early Christian community. His statement about divorce was intended to provoke his listeners, because he described a legal attitude frankly as adulterous. "Jesus did not formulate a new law in opposition to the recognized, existing law. He passed a judgment which rejected a religious, ethical and legal way of thinking and which shattered the current norms. Jesus' saying has a diagnostic and revealing meaning — it discloses what the man who is able to appeal to his right really does. It also has a critical meaning — it makes a distinction between God's will and God's law on the one hand and man's own will and his insistence on his own right on the other."[25] What is said here, defining legalistic divorce in the terms of an antithesis, also applies to Jesus' demand that the believer should not practice violence in claiming his legal right to retaliation.

According to all the statements in the New Testament, Jesus did not, in proclaiming the Basileia, aim directly at changing or abolishing the existing order in society. On the other hand, his radical demands did not simply bypass this question. The demands made in the Sermon on the Mount continue to be related antithetically to that order with its legal norms, at least during the period in which God's rule has commenced, but has not yet reached fulfillment in the kingdom of God. This eschatological framework is constitutive and Jesus' directives cannot be separated from it and transformed into isolated ethical principles (in the particular antithetical cases that we have been considering, principles such as nonviolence or the indissolubility of marriage). His demands function as criteria. They purify man's moral consciousness with regard to the Basileia. In this way, they are able to give inner freedom with regard to the correct use of the law. The ultimate aim is always the renewal of man — the greater justice.

C. The Greater Justice

The first section of the Sermon on the Mount in Matthew's gospel opens with the fundamental demand (5.20): "If your justice is not greater than that of the scribes and pharisees . . ." (*ean mē perisseusē humōn hē dikaiosunē pleion*) and ends with the words (5.48): "You must therefore be perfect, as your heavenly Father is perfect" (*teleioi hōs ho patēr humōn*). Rudolf Schnackenburg has pointed out[26] that the more original version is probably to be found in Luke 6.36: "Be merciful, even as your Father is merciful" and that Matthew deliberately changed "merciful" to "perfect." The Judaeo-Christian evangelist must have been influenced in this by Leviticus 19.2: "You shall be holy as I the Lord your God am holy." In this way, he linked the decalogue with the law of holiness. The holiness required by the Old Testament was, under the new dispensation, to appear as perfection. Again, according to Schnackenburg, perfection is "an all-embracing term for the obligation arising from the message of the kingdom of God proclaimed by Jesus to be worthy of the salvation offered by God, to love God with one's whole heart and above all to 'seek his kingdom' (Mt. 6.33)."[27] Taking this "all-embracing term" as our point of departure, then, we shall now try to summarize the most important aspects of Jesus' message.

1. The Form of Reality at the End of Time

Jesus' moral demand for greater justice is the form of reality at the end of time. The end of time began with his proclamation of the Basileia. This proclamation contained "a striking convergence between Jesus' exposition of the law and his message of the Basileia. In both cases, he called the present time the place of God's presence, where God makes demands or comes forward to meet man. God, who was distant and existed in the future, is brought closer and human history becomes the place of his presence."[28] In this historical moment of time, Jesus' call was intended for all men who heard his message. No one was excluded from the kingdom of God, with the result that Jesus' moral demands should not be interpreted as special calls made to individuals. Even the demand made of the rich young man (Mt. 19.21) cannot be broken down, on closer analysis, into a double perfection (based on commandment and on counsel). "In Jesus' twofold reply" (to the question: "If you would enter life" or "If you would be perfect") "there were not two levels of moral concern that had to be reached by the young man, although Jesus left the decision to the young man's discretion, nor were there two degrees of holiness that he could attain by making the right decision."[29] It is, of course, true to say that Jesus called individuals to join the inner circle of his disciples, but the demands made on the basis of his message of the kingdom of God were directed toward all men. Because of this, it is very difficult to make a clear distinction between commandment and counsel in this case. It cannot, for instance, be interpreted in the sense that we are obliged in one case and at the most invited in the other. Jesus' demand is indivisible and mandatory. It can be differentiated in the degree to which we are concerned in a given situation or in a concrete task in life. The same difficulty also applies to the distinction between commandments that can be fulfilled and those which represent ideal aims, which can perhaps be fulfilled at the end of time beyond human history, but which have in the present era to be regarded as Utopian. This distinction is clearly contrary to Jesus' intention. The present time of the Basileia discloses to the believer the Utopia of a real possibility and therefore of an obligatory offer.

2. The Religious Nature of the Demand

The greater justice demanded by Jesus was "not an ethical model, but a religious demand, calling on man to hand himself over to the God who was greater than him and to be subject to him in obedience to his call and in readiness to become pure in heart and radical in action, but also in trust, that he will help and save him."[30] Jesus called on man to place himself unconditionally at the service of the kingdom of God, in other words, to "deny himself and take up his cross and follow me" (Mk. 8.34; Mt. 16.24).

The imitation of Christ means more than simply following a fascinating teacher and his doctrines. In the passages dealing with the imitation of Jesus (Mk. 8.34-38; Lk. 14.16-33; 9.23-26; Mt. 10.38; 16.24-27), it is quite clear that following him was not simply a question of leaving everything and being converted, since that procedure had already become firmly established in Judaism.[31] "The distinctive aspect of the imitation of Jesus was not in leaving everything in order to achieve a master-disciple relationship . . . nor was it simply . . . confessing Jesus (although this was materially correct). It was rather the fact that this confession of Jesus was qualified as a religious conversion, so that the saving dispensation of the Jewish law was in this way seen to be insufficient. The *metanoia* demanded by the coming kingdom of God was a conversion to Jesus — that is the theological relevance of the call to follow Jesus. In this conversion, the kingdom of God that was still to come became a present reality."[32] In this case, too, Jesus' demands should not be seen as isolated, but be regarded as connected with man's need to decide radically in favor of God's rule and kingdom. This fundamental decision is, of course, in the last resort a matter of faith and is therefore not simply a demand, but primarily a gift.

Man responds to God's initiative, which enables him to make that response. "There is no direct expression in the Sermon on the Mount of man's being enabled to become perfect, but it is included in the proclamation, simply in the way Jesus speaks to the disciples about the Father."[33] The beginning of Christian morality, then, is not to be found in man's need to strive toward a humanistic ideal. It is, on the contrary, based on God's offer of greater and greater love.

3. The Promise Contained in the Demand

This is also the main reason why Jesus' demand does not have a legal character. In the context of the eschatological situation, the *nomos* is dead, at least as *nomos*.[34] This does not mean that it no longer exists in the historical or chronological sense — the decalogue is still in force — but it does mean that there is in existence a fulfillment through the one who came in power in order to fulfill the law and the prophets, so that we might be fulfilled in and through him.[35]

The distinction that can be made on the basis of the message of redemption between the claim made by Jesus and the demands of reason — the factor that, for example, qualifies the bonds of marriage in faithfulness as a promise of salvation — cannot easily be contained within the category of a law. The claim made by Jesus could not, moreover, be reflected fully in an institutionally objective definition of marriage which did not include the personal interrelationship between the partners. The statement that this promise which makes a demand cannot have a legal character points in two directions. In the first place, it means that the claim is much more all-embracing than any legal statement could be. Also, it is based on an offer of grace to which the believer has to respond freely. With regard to our example of marriage, this demand means in the case of faithfulness that the partners encounter each other in faith, hope and love because they trust in God's loving orientation toward man and they can hope against hope when all human confidence seems to have reached an end. On the other hand, the claim is also, in a certain sense, less than a law, because it lacks the social compulsion of law. "One thing is common to all the forms of behavior demanded by Jesus — none of them can be forced or prescribed by law. They all appeal to man's goodness of heart which is given freely. In a word, they appeal to love."[36] The fact that Jesus' demands cannot be compelled and cannot as a whole be made law does not mean that the obligations involved are not subject to social and legal constraints. However, this is not in the last resort necessary because the claim of the gospel could not otherwise be passed on in a sufficiently convincing way within the Church. The earliest attempts to do this are clearly discernible in the proclamation of the primitive Christian community.

CHAPTER 3: THE ETHOS OF THE EARLY CHURCH

The essential content of the proclamation of the apostles consisted of the moral message of Jesus in the form in which we have attempted to outline it above. Jesus' life and words became the point of departure and orientation for the apostles' directives and admonitions in the early Christian communities. In this, it was not historical statements that were handed down, but rather the present message of the exalted Christ. The principal theme of the apostolic proclamation was what God had done and was continuing to do through Jesus Christ with man. The fundamental ethical claim resulted from the eschatological saving activity of God in Jesus Christ. Jesus was the bringer of salvation and Lord. At the center of this process was the renewal of man through baptism and conversion. The ethos of the early Church was rooted in man's new existence as founded in Christ (see above, § 11). One of the most striking aspects of that new existence was that it had to come to terms with the concrete demands made by society. The admonitions and directives given by the apostles bear witness to the way in which attempts were made in the early Church to deal with this task.

§ 18 The Special and Obligatory Nature of the Apostolic Directives

The question of the special and obligatory nature of the apostolic directives is one of the essential aspects of the present debate in moral theology about the justification of moral norms within the framework of Christian ethics.[1] The moral message of Jesus is naturally of fundamental importance in any attempt to justify these norms and, to the extent that the directives provided by Paul and others refer back again and again to Jesus's own words and actions, they form a model[2] for the Church and Christian theology. In this section, then, we shall be especially concerned with the origin of concrete directives and demands in the early Church.

The first thing that emerges strikingly from the great number and variety of directives given in the apostolic era is that they were mainly spiritual. "The relatively few operative norms of action and individual directives provided by Paul are embedded in a wide field of categorial spiritual directives and instructions. In addition to this, all these categorial directives and instructions are permeated with admonitions and imperatives with a potentially transcendental orientation."[3] The ultimate norm and fundamental point of departure of all the apostolic admonitions and directives are the words and behavior of Jesus himself and, as we pointed out above, it was the present message of the exalted Christ with its demands that was handed down by the apostles, not historical statements. We are bound to ask whether or not "the environment created both extensively and intensively in the community of the new covenant by this spiritual paraenesis"[4] had an effect on the early Christians' understanding, selection and expression of ethical norms of behavior and to what extent this took place. This is a necessary question if we are to find an answer, on the basis of the ethics of the early Church, to the problem of a specifically Christian ethos that is determined by faith.

A. Jesus' Words and Behavior

The decisive and obligatory norm for the early Church was provided by Jesus' words and behavior.[5] The words of the Lord were in the highest degree obligatory in judging any concrete situation. It is striking, however, that Paul only appeals twice to the word of the Lord — in 1 Corinthians 7.10 and 9.14. In the second case, it is less a question of a moral norm and more a problem of order in the Christian community. "In 1 Corinthians 9.8 and 13, Paul appeals to the Torah in his argument in favor of the right to support of those who proclaim the gospel (Dt. 25.4; Num. 18.8, 31; Dt. 18.1 ff.) and then to Jesus' directive in Luke 10.7b and Matthew 10.10b."[6] "The obligatory and authoritative aspect is emphasized" and its "overriding claim is stressed"[7] by the juxtaposition of the appeal to the Torah and Jesus' directive (9.14). Paul clearly regarded the word of the Lord as obligatory, but it is equally clear that he also regarded it not "as a commandment to be fulfilled, but rather as a permission (*exousia*)."[8] He did not make use of "full powers" mainly "for the sake of higher moral demands."[9] In a different situation, those who proclaimed the gospel in the period after Easter — unlike the disciples who followed Jesus (see, for example, Lk. 10.4-6) — were permitted to support themselves. In other words, the obligatory character of this directive given by Jesus had changed and it should be understood in the analogous or intentional sense.[10]

Unlike 1 Corinthians 9.14, Paul understood the word of the Lord regarding the prohibition of divorce (1 Cor. 7.10; cf. Mk. 10.11 f.; Lk. 16.18; Mt. 5.32; 19.9) as a commandment to be fulfilled. It is explicitly described as a "commandment (*paraggelia*; v. 25: *epitagē*) of the Kyrios and because of this it is removed from the sphere of discussion."[11] His only directive, on the other hand, can "only be an 'opinion' (*gnōmē*) (see 7.25), although it is the opinion of one who 'thinks that he has the Spirit of God' (7.40)."[12]

Paul would appear to be dealing, in 1 Corinthians 7.10 f., with an individual case of a divorced woman, "who, as the 'unbelieving partner,' had separated from her husband and had later entered the community in Corinth."[13] Paul clearly regarded the word of the Lord as binding, but he provided (in verse 11) advice for cases in which the commandment had already been transgressed. If it was not possible for the partners to be reconciled (and that would seem to have been so in this particular case),[14] Paul accepted that they should live separately and was satisfied with an approximate fulfillment of the word of the Lord ("not separate"). In any real situation, in which marriages are broken and remain so, life has to continue in a state of moral order. In the following verses (12-16), Paul defines his attitude toward marriages in general between pagans and Christians and does so in his position of apostolic authority. He was ready to accept the situation in which the Christian party was placed by the other party's decision. He applied the word of the Lord to the changed situation on the basis of a consideration of the goods involved, balancing the good of a marriage to be realized in faith and that of marriage with a pagan. This case can be taken as a classical example of the achievement of an adaptive fulfillment of the word of the Lord in a changed situation and of the way in which the directive must be based on a consideration of the values involved.

The words of the Lord clearly had the same significance in the early Church as the words of God (the commandments or decalogue) had in the community of Israel in the Old Testament. They formed a kind of ethical creed, proclaiming indispensable insights and value judgments, but not providing directly practical instructions. This is a characteristic of the casuistic law, in other words, of adaptive application.

Just as the word of the Lord was seldom interpreted in the nomistic sense as a law, so too were "reminiscences of the words of the Lord," which occur quite frequently in Paul's writings, "not understood legally — in the rabbinical sense — as norms."[15] In this context, Paul characteristically refers to those words of the Lord in which Jesus' demand of love is expressed.[16] The apparent reason for this strong emphasis and for the fact that Paul makes so few direct references to the words of the Lord is that he saw Jesus' words and directives primarily in the context of Jesus' behavior, in other words, "from the point of view of the behavior of the Son or the Son of Man who emptied himself (Paul) or who descended (John)."[17] The event of Christ was, for Paul, of central importance. Jesus' words and examples were primarily understood as the message of the exalted Christ making demands on man in the present. "The admonitions contained in Philippians 2.1-4 — and especially the demand of *tapeinosis* made in v. 3 — are motivated in 2.5: 'Have this mind among yourselves which you have in Christ Jesus.' According to Philippians 2.6 ff., Christ's behavior consisted of the *kenosis* and *tapeinosis* of the one who pre-existentially had the form of God and who 'emptied himself' and 'humbled himself' by accepting human existence and was 'obedient' to death. Again, according to 2 Corinthians 8.9, this behavior of 'our Lord Jesus Christ' was transformed into 'grace,' in other words, into love that gave itself."[18] On the basis of this behavior, the commandment of love is "both characteristic and radical."[19] Paul called this demand or commandment of love the "law of Christ" (Gal. 6.2). It is clear that he contrasted this "law of Christ" with the "law of Moses" (1 Cor. 9.9), in other words, with the Torah, which is here "directed toward and concentrated on" the all-important demand of love.[20] The word "law" is used here in a paradoxical and analogous way, since it is "in principle a law that has been renewed by Christ."[21] One is reminded of the absolutely obligatory nature of this directive and also of the "law" as deeply marked by the behavior of the Son of God whose "behavior, in emptying and humbling himself did away with all laws."[22] The demand to love acquires a definite form and direction when it is considered against the background of Christ's behavior and the figure of the 'ebhedh or servant of Yahweh (Is. 53).

This "law of Christ" or demand of love is something into which the believer is incorporated as one who is "under the law" or *ennomos Christou* (1 Cor. 9.21). He is, as Schürmann has so aptly put it, "incorporated into the norm of Christ."[23] He is in this way given a new existence founded in the event of Christ and based on baptism. This new Christian existence founded in the death and resurrection of Christ is primarily an inner gift. It also contains a demand in that the existence that has been given has to be led in accordance with the situation in which the Christian is living.

God, then, has included man as a whole in baptism in the love of Christ and it is man's task to lead his new existence with full commitment of body and soul in accordance with this reality. The most striking characteristic of this new existence in Christ is that "it must be constantly preserved and regained again and again."[24] Man himself has actively to seize hold of that which has seized hold of him. He has, in the change that has taken place in him, to reach that toward which he is orientated. He has to let what God has achieved in him through Christ take effect in a fully human way in his new existence. All this is contained in the dialectical indicative and imperative of Paul's ethics. "The change in authority which God guarantees to the baptized believer when he comes to belong to Christ and enters the Christian community and to which the believer in turn freely gives his consent (Rom. 6.17 f.) is developed soteriologically as an indicative and an imperative in various statements about baptism."[25] In Romans 6.1-11, 12-23, the indicative and the imperative alternate constantly with each other.[26] In Ephesians 4.1, we read, for example, "Be worthy of the calling to which you have been called" and "Welcome one another, as Christ has welcomed you" (Rom. 15.7) or "Forgive one another; as the Lord has forgiven you, so you also must forgive" (Col. 3.13). The believer is given the love of Christ, who emptied and humbled himself, in baptism. He therefore has the task of realizing that love in his own existence.

172

It is this demand to give oneself entirely in love, the demand of God's love or the love of Christ and one's fellow-men, that is expressed in the totality of the transcendental or theologically and eschatologically orientated directives,[27] which are "universally and permanently valid and obligatory in their concrete christological and staurological form."[28] They point to the origin of the Christian ethos in the event of Christ and to love as the fundamental form of that event. That love is also the fundamental form of the Christian expression of life. The believer knows that he is loved by God in and through Christ and as such he should also love his brothers in the same love. As one who has experienced forgiveness, he should also forgive others. As one who has been justified in baptism, he should also recognize his debt to justice. In other words, as one who has been moved in the Spirit by God through Christ, he should also move himself in the direction of that movement. This movement is expressed in the form of the coming of the kingdom of God and in Paul's writings in the particular form of the revelation of God's justice and the continuation of Christ's rule in this world so that justice and love can have a form in the world. Christian ethics are expressed in the light of faith given by Christ and in the hope of fulfillment. Existence expressed in the light of faith and hope in love is therefore the distinctive aspect of Christian existence. It is not the fact that we believe, hope and love that is distinctive — this takes place in other religions and ethical codes. What is special to the Christian expression of life is that we understand our human condition in faith and hope, both proceeding from and moving toward Christ, and that the love that we experience is not any love, but the love of God through Christ in us, the love in which we are loved by God and with which we should love others. It is only on the basis of this understanding of Christian existence that we can express that existence distinctively. It is not so much the claim that is made of Christians that is new as the situation within which the claim is made on the believer and within which the believer can and should fulfill that claim and the way in which that claim is made. The believer should no longer — as he did once, when he was subject to the law — serve sin and he is therefore no longer bound to end in death, destruction or judgment, with the end result that the struggle against evil always brings, *a priori*, of defeat (see Rom. 6.6, 12 ff., 16 ff.; 7.5-6; Gal. 5.13

ff.; cf. Col. 2.13; 3.5 ff.; Eph. 2.1 ff.; 5.3 ff., etc.). He no longer has any need to cower in fear (either in cult or morally) in the presence of cosmic powers in order to rise up again to God and salvation. He is already raised up to God (see Col. 2.6 ff.; 3.1 ff.; cf. Eph. 2.1 ff.). What the believer encounters as a claim is the fullness of being given in Christ. "The moral claim, which is, for Christians, ultimately God's claim made on men for their salvation, has been made since Christ in the experience of salvation in and through Christ in the Spirit."[29]

The "law of Christ" which is Paul's definition of the demand of love is therefore ultimately Christ himself as the living norm of Christian action. In imitating him, the Christian experiences what love is. It is loving God, realized in a radical turning toward one's fellow-men. This love is the fundamental form of the Christian ethos and therefore has a decisive effect not only on human motivation, but also on the content of the moral claim as a phenomenon that is included materially within the imitation of Christ and is not arbitrary. This takes place not so much by deriving directly operative norms of action from the fundamental demand of love, as by deriving insights into values that are indispensable to the Christian in his moral action from this personalization of moral norms.[30] The Christian who knows that God has called and redeemed every human being in love in Jesus Christ also recognizes the dignity and value of every human being, without regard to his status and performance. "The distinctively Christian element begins and ends with the revelation that the infinite God loves each individual person infinitely. This infinite love is expressed above all in the fact that, in the form of a man, he died the death of a redeemer (and that means the death of a sinner) for those whom he loved."[31] The material content of this insight — the so-called dignity of man — is not exclusively reserved for Christians, but to doubt it would certainly not be Christian.[32]

Jesus' words and behavior, as the "law" of the exalted Christ, do not simply make a claim on man on the basis of his having been given that law, nor do they simply call on him to imitate Christ in the Spirit. They also point to the future. The demand becomes a promise of salvation when the liberating power of the reconciling love of God is recognized and expressed. Jesus' words and behavior are therefore a promise which makes a demand and this promise can only be acquired in the light of faith in God's action in Christ and hope in the future revealed in Christ. The moral message of Jesus Christ and our understanding of its content are therefore based on christology.

B. The Claim and the Directives

As I have already pointed out above, Paul's operative directives are always incorporated into an ultimate and fundamentally theological claim, on the basis of which his directives and the *tupos didaches* (Rom. 6.17b) of the early Christian community were developed.[33]

1. The Call to Decide in Favor of Faith

The fundamental claim is a call to decide in favor of faith and to be ready to accept baptism and be converted. This is quite apparent from what Paul says about *hamartia*. *Hamartia* is, in Paul's terminology, a refusal to believe and to accept justification. Man's *hamartia* consists in his satisfaction with self-justification, in having no need of a redeemer and in therefore boasting of his own works (*kauchēma*). If it is positively applied, the fundamental claim is expressed in faith, hope and love (see Col. 1.4 f.). "For Paul, the basis of the Christian expression of life was contained in the trinity in unity, faith, hope and love, which he probably derived from the early Christian tradition and which was, in his opinion, a fundamental category of Christian existence, because it contained the very substance of human life."[34] These aspects of the one fundamental claim were, for Paul, unconditional and universal, because it was God himself, in claiming man, who made them unconditional.

2. Confrontation with the Demands Made by Life

The proclamation of the early Church placed great emphasis on the need for the moral subject to change inwardly by becoming orientated in the direction indicated by Jesus Christ. This implied an inevitable confrontation with the demands made by life in the concrete. The claim made by Christ on the new existence of the believer therefore acted as a specifically Christian criterion with regard to the formation of concrete directives. It functioned in this way "more or less directly on the one hand by creating norms and, on the other (and, from the quantitative point of view at least, this was the more important aspect) by being critical toward integration."[35]

The criterion of faith in the risen and exalted Christ and the accompanying knowledge of Christ's way through self-emptying and self-giving for the sake of mankind had the effect of creating norms, insofar as it inspires us to behave normally — that is, according to average or ordinary patterns of behavior. This criterion is not, however, exclusively Christian or peculiar to Christianity as such. It has been called "typically Christian,"[36] mainly because it takes its origin and meaning from the event of Christ. These basic attitudes, which are very much in accordance with God's saving activity in Christ, are expressed in such Pauline statements as: "Be kind to one another, tenderhearted, forgiving one another, as God in Christ forgave you" (Eph. 4.32); "Forbear one another and, if one has a complaint against another, forgive one another; as the Lord has forgiven you, so you must also forgive" (Col. 3.13); "Be subject to one another out of reverence for Christ" (Eph. 5.21) and many other texts.[37]

In addition to creating such norms of behavior, this criterion of faith has another and more important function. As we have indicated above, it is critical toward integration. It is not possible to derive a concrete world order directly from God's saving activity in Christ. All that can be done is to mediate and interpret the claim made by reason enlightened by faith and apply it to the situation as it is at any given time. The way in which this took place is clear from the example of the early Church, which was normative and obligatory. The point of departure was then (as it is today) the ethos of the surrounding world as determined by society and history. Paul's letters to his Christian communities therefore do not contain any new concrete norms of behavior. They tend rather to derive these to a considerable extent from the traditions of Jewish proverbial wisdom and popular Greek philosophy. This is abundantly clear from the catalogues of virtues and vices (in, for example, Gal. 5.16 ff.) and the household codes (in, for example, Col. 3.18 ff.).[38] The most important aspect of the inclusion of such catalogues and codes in Paul's letters is not, however, their inclusion as such, but rather the way in which Paul and other members of the early Church dealt with the ethical material that they found in their environment. They did not simply accept everything that they thought was right or morally good. There was, on the contrary, "a conscious and critical selection (see, for example, Phil. 4.8; cf. Rom. 12.2) . . . In taking over what they thought to be in general and in particular 'good and acceptable and perfect,' the early Christians also believed that they should 'not be conformed to this world, but be transformed by the renewal of their minds, so that they might prove what was the will of God; what was good and acceptable and perfect' (Rom. 12.2; cf. 1 Th. 5.21)." [39] It was the task of reason enlightened by faith to distinguish which concrete directives were, at any time, in accordance with the "law of Christ" (Gal. 6.2) in the Spirit. The inclusion of these values, then, was a critical, selective process, in which modifications were made and emphases were changed. [40] Certain norms were excluded if they were not in accordance with the Basileia that had been made present in Jesus Christ. Others, however, were accepted and justified (see, for example, 1 Th. 4.4 ff.; see also the catalogues of virtues and vices and the household codes). These were frequently transformed, given a deeper meaning or expressed in a new way (see, for example, Gal. 5.14 ff.). New priorities were also established within the values and norms taken over. The virtues and vices were not, for example, grouped under the headings of cardinal virtues or capital vices, love was placed above everything and seen as all-pervasive, wrong forms of sexual behavior were put at the beginning of the catalogues and asceticism was regarded as a particularly suitable form of behavior by which justice could be done to the eschatological situation that had been introduced by Christ. [41]

The apostles, then, made Jesus' words and behavior the fundamental norm for Christian behavior, but at the same time went back to the values and norms that they found in their own environment because they were unable to deal with the event of Christ as a criterion for the expression of moral demands. Moral theologians are therefore still faced with the problem of the extent to which a valid material ethos can be based on the New Testament, in other words, the problem of just how the apostolic directives can be regarded today as obligatory. [42] There can be no doubt that many of these directives are either related to concrete situations that existed at the time or were caused by the existence of such situations. There are many applications in the admonitions of the apostles, including Paul, of the commandment to love that were clearly conditioned by the time, the environment or the situation. Examples of these are the admonition to refrain from sacrificial meat out of respect for those whose faith was weak (1 Cor. 8.9 ff.) or the subjection of the wife to her husband (1 Cor. 11.2-16, etc.). It is out of the question that particular directives and values should be disputed.[43] On the other hand, the fact that they were conditioned by the existing situation should not be given an absolute value. Paul's letters were not simply occasional writings. They were also at least partly written for an exchange of ideas with other communities and precisely for this reason also had a universal regulative function, in that Christians were orientated, on the basis of these letters, toward the way in which witness was borne to faith in the other communities and by the practical activities of the members of those communities. What was universally valid in the letters was especially valid in the case of the apostolic paraenesis. In this sense, then, it would be correct to say that "Paul did not provide paradigms to which a universal obligation can be indirectly attributed as though they were models of behavior. On the contrary, he provided directives and instructions which were directly obligatory, although in very different ways."[44] If, however, the apostolic directives are described as paradigms, this is not because of "the distinctive literary quality of Paul's admonitions and demands"[45] or because they were obligatory in the historical situation that prevailed at that time, but rather because of the theological interest in the meaning that they have for us today. What is their significance with regard to the task that has to be carried out at all periods of history, that of applying the claim made by the event of Christ to the situation prevailing at any given time?

If we say, in reply to this question, that Paul's directives "can only be carried out either analogously or by being adapted or else either approximately or by following only their basic intentions,"[46] this ultimately means that the way in which Christians should live and behave — irrespective of historical changes — in the eschatological situation of what has already taken place and what has not yet taken place in the history of our salvation has obviously not been laid down positively in these biblical directives. It is, on the contrary, clear that they reveal, in paradigmatic form, the way in which the members of the early Christian communities lived in the light of faith in the risen Lord and how they understood his commandments as a task and an acceptance of power. The directives are, however, at the same time also obligatory, since they have, for us today as they had for the early Christians, the character of God's word. They bear witness biblically and it is in this biblical sense that they must always be understood. When they were given concrete form in the early Church, this was not an arbitrary response to the situation. It was a positive attempt to give authentic meaning to the moral message of Jesus himself.

The directives of Paul and the other apostles are also paradigmatic in another wider and perhaps even more important sense. They point again and again to the example of Christ or else to man's new being in Christ. In this way, they indicate a specific aspect of Christian ethics. It is not the only characteristic of Christian ethics simply to include previously existing secular values and norms or critically to transform already existing ethics into Christian moral concepts. Christian ethics go further than this — they make the relationship between specifically Christian values and directives and the reality of salvation in the world intelligible. The person who is made aware of the moral claim of Christian ethics is at the same time able to understand himself as a Christian, that is, as one who is loved, accepted, set free and claimed by Christ. The Christian ethos is therefore bound to be a paraenesis, simply because it began with and was founded on Christ himself. We may therefore conclude by saying that "the ethical kerygma of the gospel can be heard in all Christian (or evangelical) imperatives and the same kerygma gives those imperatives the character of paraclesis, which is more than paraenesis or exhortation. The universal and the concrete directives are different from the moral norms of a non-Christian or secular ethos in that they are also a manner of proclamation of the gospel."[47]

Section Two: Nature, Experience and Reason

The moral norms outlined in the Old and New Testaments were the result of a historical process, to which different factors contributed. These include the original tribal ethos, the historical and social development, the political structures and above all the religious attitude of the biblical people. This process took place within the history of God's dealings with his chosen people, in which history it is clear that God had appointed man to be the acting subject. Faith does not remove man's responsibility for shaping human society — on the contrary, it enables him to carry out that task. In faith, man can know himself and the reality around him in a wider context. He has knowledge of his origin and his end. He knows too that the dualism between autonomy and heteronomy can be overcome in faith, in which heteronomy itself bestows autonomy and God's Spirit claims man and gives him freedom, in a theonomous autonomy. On the basis of this understanding, man has to fashion the reality around him. He is helped in this task by increasing human experience and rational reflection. The concrete rules of biblical ethics were a product of this history of salvation. They were thought out and proclaimed by believers in an attempt to make human society bearable and meaningful. Their material content does not go beyond man's understanding and in this sense it is neither mysterious or exclusive.

We may go further and say with confidence that, from the very beginning, Christianity claimed to be a universal message, addressed to all men. In practice, it is irrelevant to ask whether there are commandments or prohibitions in the sphere of the moral virtues, in other words, in the sphere of human relationships, which only the Christian can know on the basis of his faith and which are therefore only obligatory for him. For us, it is less interesting to know whether the moral norms of Christianity are originally or exclusively Christian than whether or not they can be communicated. I am of the opinion that it must be possible to communicate to all men the consequences for human relationships that result from our faith in God and his liberating love. What is of decisive importance, then, is not whether Christianity has included in its teaching many ethical truths taken from the spiritual and moral history of mankind, but whether the Son, the Logos, came into his own when he became man. According to a very old theological tradition, the content of the moral teaching of revelation is open to rational reflection.[1] It is to this rational reflection that we must turn, within the framework of universal human experience, in this section on nature, experience and reason. Questions of this kind are usually dealt with under the heading of "natural law" and for this reason I shall discuss the problem of the *lex naturalis* in the first chapter. I shall then consider the distinction that was made at the beginning of this book (§ 1) between morally relevant insights on the one hand and morally normative judgments on the other and outline the development and foundation of each (chapters 2 and 3 below).

CHAPTER 1: THE NATURAL MORAL LAW

No moral or legal order can exist without reference to reality. In the elaboration of norms of behavior, the nature of man's existence as a natural and spiritual being, the natural structure of his needs and his self-consciousness and longing for self-determination and social recognition have all to be taken into consideration. There is fortunately a high degree of agreement about these questions. All that is disputed is just how reality is expressed in the moral or legal order. What, in other words, do we mean by "nature"? Has nature in this context a normative character? Are there natural human rights? If so, how can they be known?

All these questions arise in connection with the problem of the natural law. I do not intend to deal in this chapter with the various doctrines of the natural law, as I have done this elsewhere.[2] In one section of this chapter, I shall define the relevant concepts and discuss the complexity of the question as such. This justifies my division of the matter involved in the question of the natural moral law into two parts, which are discussed in chapters 2 and 3, respectively.

§ 19 The Complexity of the Question

Even in the introduction to this chapter above, I have used the concepts "nature" and "natural" correctly with different meanings. There is hardly any other concept in the sphere of moral theology that can be employed in so many ways and in so many different combinations. We are therefore bound to begin this chapter with a clarification of this concept.

A. The Many Different Meanings of the Concept "Nature"

1. Nature in the All-Embracing Sense

The word "nature" (*natura/nasci; plusis/phuein*[3]) points to something that has grown or become. The idea of the universe as an all-embracing and animated being is probably mythological, but this would seem to be at the origin of the concept. This being has become what it is and has developed into what it is. The idea of something original, given and not made or fashioned by man is therefore connected with the word nature — something that is present before all making. Any later making can therefore only be a way of changing what has already been given.

In philosophical reflection, the concept of nature is formally and ontologically related to all being. Nature therefore means the essence of reality as what is becoming real, the ascent of a being to its own reality and therefore the whole of all being in a lasting ascent. This ascent is not a secondary activity of a real being, but the fundamental *actus primus* of the ontological constitution of the being. This fundamental primary act forms the inner principle of all the activity and passivity of the being concerned.[4] This becoming of all reality does not, according to the theology of creation, take place "of its own accord." The ascent is based on God's act of creation which bears nature as something that builds itself up autonomously. As the foundation and ground of all being (*causa essendi*), God is not in competition with the reality of being. There is no collaboration of partial causes in the so-called *concursus divinus*. The creator and creation each acts in its own way — creation acts "in categorial exteriority (having an effect on the state of being so), while the creator acts in transcendental interiority (having an effect on being as such)."[5] This distinction and orientation determine the being of the world and the being of God. "God is divine in that he acts in this way and lets both the world and man have autonomous being and act autonomously."[6] Far from giving the natural world a divine or sacral character, this understanding of nature as creation removes all tabus from the reality of nature and does away with the numinous character that often clings to it in the natural religions. Faith in creation makes the world free, so that its laws can be examined without restraint.

In speaking in this way of the natural reality, the concept "nature" is taken in its material significance. By this, we do not mean a definite dispensation or the inner principle of the reality of a thing. What we mean is the totality of all things in the Kantian sense, that totality that is already given to our observation.[7] Nature understood in this sense forms the all-embracing object of natural science. However different the formal and ontological view is from that of natural science, both concepts of nature are very closely connected, "since the inner principles of everything that belongs to the existence of a thing are at the basis of the totality of phenomena and the quintessence of all things."[8]

This thesis is relevant to man's association with the things of nature. In all the fundamental freedom that he has in investigating and fashioning the world, man is not able to overlook the distinctive character of things. Our insight into the inner principles and laws is a very important presupposition in the question of reliability in our association with the things of nature (and a prior condition for our investigation of the world and technology). We are also beginning to recognize more and more clearly the inherent limitations imposed by the economic system on the exploitation of nature. It is, however, only clear when we look at man how insufficient it is to limit our understanding to the phenomena that can be perceived by our senses.

2. The Nature of Man

Applied to man, the concept of nature bears the imprint of the specific mode of being of a personal being. As a person, man is, in his nature (in the *actus primus* of his ontological constitution), removed from all the things and beings of nature that are simply present. In his nature, he is inwardly open and confronted with himself; in other words, human nature is, in the transcendental and existential sense, ontologically determined. In his transcendental freedom (see § 5 B above), man has a point of reference beyond himself. In expressing finite freedom, he transcends himself. The all-embracing aim of his freedom is perfect freedom. In this expression of himself, he is subject to a factual imperative (although he has to make an unhesitating decision) and, what is even more important, he is also originally affected by an unconditional obligation. In this way, human nature is determined by communication with the Absolute.[9]

In his freedom, man is, however, also confronted with himself and his fellow-men. He has an originally existential relationship with himself or his human nature. This does not mean that his nature is broken down into pure existence. On the contrary, man is always fully present both as nature and as existence. His nature is not the reality of a finished being; it is rather the reality of a possible state of being. It is in this context that the full meaning of the definition of nature as a "reality as what is becoming real" becomes clear. Nature is handed over to realization, but not as a reality that is already previously given. Man has certainly to become what he is, but this only means that he has to fulfill his own possibilities. He has to interpret himself and, as it were, decide about what he is to become. This does not mean that "a closed nature is arbitrarily subjected to variations. On the contrary, it is for the first time clear in this process what nature, as man's ascent to his present being, is."[10] This personal expression of himself takes place within the sphere of interpersonal relationships. Man therefore expresses himself interpersonally. The individual does not acquire his identity by looking introvertedly at himself. Human subjectivity does not seem to be capable of determining itself sufficiently in and through itself. Man therefore looks first at those who are different from himself, his fellow-men, in order to find the determination of his own being in and with him. As a speaking being, he is not blindly impelled to self-assertion. On the contrary, he is orientated toward agreement with other men. Aristotle was of this opinion, when he called man "by nature a political being." According to Aristotle, man was able to find his freedom not in pure nature, but in a free society of rights, laws and duties.[11] Man expresses his nature as an objective reality and historically as human society or culture. The constantly recurring question regarding what can be called unconditionally true or unconditionally good enables man to become conscious, at a deeper level, of his transcendental orientation.

From the point of view of the theology of revelation, it is possible to say "that man's transcendental orientation toward God is extremely inward and is part of man's original existential dynamism.[12] This must, however, be contrasted with his ultimate fundamental existence and therefore, as a consequence of a theological tradition lasting for a thousand years, must be called a supernatural existential dynamism."[13] (See § 10 A above) This enables us to understand the distinction between man's concrete nature as manifested in the history of salvation (in accordance with this concrete, historical nature, man longs for the God whose love fulfills his existence) and the abstract concept of pure nature (*natura pura*), that is, man's fundamental existence which must be regarded as presupposing grace. Both Augustine and Thomas Aquinas believed that man might be dependent on something that necessarily had the character of a pure gift.[14] However justified it may be in theory, the concept of pure nature in fact led to a polarization between nature and grace. In this polarity, nature tended to become more powerful and grace less so. Modern theologians, on the other hand, tend to stress man's concrete, historical nature within God's plan of salvation. In the same way, man's fundamental rightness is to be found in the orientation of his whole existence toward God and the fact that his life is led in the recognition and love of God. Sin contradicts this orientation and represents a fundamental distortion of human existence. Fallen man is turned away from God and turned introvertedly toward himself. If, despite everything, man in sin still remains man, then the preservation of his natural existence, which is still capable of salvation, points to the grace of Christ, when sin would have plunged man into his absolute loss of salvation if it had not been replaced by God's mercy, because of the place that even sin has within Christ's dispensation. The consequences of sin, then, are already included in the sphere of nature that is also borne up by Christ, as the sphere of sin. Human nature, which is present in the sinner and is open to salvation, is therefore not the remnant that is left intact after sin. It is rather the new beginning that is set in motion again and again to save man by God's grace in Christ. This is what operates against sin and its tendency to destroy everything. Creation and redemption, nature and grace, are intimately related to each other in the history of mankind. It is precisely this relationship that is expressed in the concept of man's concrete, historical nature within God's plan of salvation. Within a total view of the history of salvation, this concept enables us to evaluate positively what is natural and to define the limits and location of what can be called natural morality.

This comprehensive understanding of human nature, which includes man's free expression of himself in history and society, helps us also to recognize the difficulties that confront our knowledge and definition of universal human nature. In speaking of our knowledge of human nature, we usually mean man's being or essence in contrast to his concrete appearance.[15] In this case, then, we seek a knowledge of what must always be present in any historical and in any individual process of development, so that we are able to speak about man in a specific sense. It cannot be denied that we always begin with the possibility of acquiring this knowledge of man. This is bound to be the case if we are to speak at all intelligibly or meaningfully about the immanent dignity of man as applicable to each individual. The ultimate content of this human dignity, however — what, in other words, makes man man and what has to be said about each individual — cannot be defined exclusively by an elaboration of purely empirical data, some of which are included and others left out. The only understanding of man that could be acquired in this way would be a universally factual one.[16] Without a transcendental analysis of man's consciousness of himself, it is hardly possible to understand his essential being as that of a thinking and speaking subject. It is only by reflecting about what conditions the possibility of man's free expression of himself that we can learn what belongs unconditionally to man as a moral being. It is only in reflection that man can become conscious of his transcendental orientation or the fact that he is given to himself in his corporeality and historicity. On the other hand, however, he is also bound to know, on the basis of this insight into his essential corporeality and historicity and the intersubjectivity of human relationships that is revealed by that insight, that it is not enough simply to look at himself if he is to understand his essential being in an all-embracing way. If historicity is an important aspect of man's essential being, then this must include what has to be regarded as part of his nature and the basis of action, namely "the intentions that have become indispensable and obligatory."[17] This can, of course, be recognized as such only in an act of historical decision. It is important in this context to bear in mind that Plato's concept of being was closely related to the idea of thoughtful conversation.[18] "Essential being here does not mean a pure possibility or a fact of a higher kind which could be discussed if there were no 'soul.' It is not in competition with our sensory experience of the world. It is not a replacement for this, nor is it simply a method, in the neo-Kantian sense, for its scientific elaboration. On the contrary, being is what proves to be the inner correctness of a matter in dialectical conversation, with regard to what is simply good. An ethical and political orientation is included in this concept of essential being together with the activity of the 'soul' in the medium of intersubjective *logoi*. What is not meant in this context is a universal and systematized ontology of essential beings. It is far more a question of a space being created and made visible in reflected conversations and existing between what is present and its immanently transcendent idea."[19]

3. Man and Nature

The question of the relationship between man and nature is the same as that of the relationship between nature and praxis. Since the teleology of nature has been called into question by natural scientists, the concept of nature proposed by modern practical philosophers has become problematical.[20] Nature is now understood either as a structure of need, which emerges all the more clearly as the cultural superstructure is stripped away, with the result that it has an emancipative character as it did in the past in the teachings of the sophists, and it becomes important for nature to be set free and all human activity to be consistently regarded as natural,[21] or else it is regarded as man's pure and hypothetical original condition that preceded human history. In the case of the second understanding of nature, leaving nature becomes a process of liberation and history itself becomes the place where that liberation occurs.[22] Both of these reductions of the concept of nature have one thing in common — in both, nature and history are seen to be incommensurable. "Naturalism and historicism are only two sides of the same coin."[23] The concept of nature, in other words, is determined by our prior understanding of human praxis. It can therefore be varied arbitrarily. There is, however, a fundamental relationship between nature and praxis that cannot be easily changed. According to its most universal tendency, nature is the reality that is not set free from praxis, but rather presupposes it. By nature, man is predisposed to transcend nature. His actions are not simply natural events; they can only be justified as human actions and not as natural events. How, then, should the activity by which he transcends nature be defined and what is the significance of nature in that activity? Is it simply the point of departure or does it influence the direction of the action itself? The following convincing argument has been suggested: "In leaving nature behind by progressively gaining control over it, man returns to his originally purely natural state. He cannot guarantee his life as man by his progressive domination of nature. It is only possible for him fully to transcend nature when he acts while bearing nature constantly in mind as the norm of his activity." [24] A naturally progressive control of nature always runs the risk of reducing the distinction between man and nature and bringing man down to the level of a natural structure. This form of technical structuralism is, then, no more than a perfected naturalism. A genuine culture has the aim of liberating man and for this reason bears nature constantly in mind and is, in freedom, conscious of its obligation to nature. "Freedom is not an essential remnant that remains behind when the whole of nature has been subjugated. The fundamental act of freedom is not to subjugate what cannot be subjugated. It is above all an act of leaving alone. Natural beings can only transcend nature if they and nature recognize each other and leave each other free." [25]

B. Various Expectations

Our discussion in the previous section about the relationship between man and nature points, in a very general way, to the extremely complex problem presented by the concepts of natural law and the natural moral law. These concepts have a very provocative effect on many people today, who regard them as labels for a conservative attempt to justify norms and the law, whereas such norms are in fact no longer valid and can no longer be made valid simply by being repeated. Such general assumptions cannot, however, advance the argument for or against the use of the natural law in any way. There are many different points of departure that can be used by those who favor the continuation of the theory of the natural law. Of fundamental importance in all these arguments are the expectations and interests by means of which the appeal to human nature and the reality that can be experienced by man are understood. The different views of the natural law are not determined by the various questions to which answers are sought. What, then, do we expect when we have recourse to human nature and what are we able to achieve by going back to the nature of man in this way?

1. Safeguarding Society by Means of an Objectively Correct Law

In any consideration of the natural law, human experience of social norms and laws must always be our point of departure. All theoretical considerations must be based on praxis. The law is bound to define the interests of the individual and society as a whole against arbitrary measures and to act as a protection. The limitations and insufficiencies of all human possibilities impel man to ask serious questions again and again about the foundations of law and order in society. He is constantly looking for the correct law. This question about the correct law is one of the basic concerns of the doctrine of the natural law. This correct law contains two elements — a material and a formal element — which are very closely connected. The correctness of the law points to the content and the truth of the law that should determine human activity. The question is therefore concentrated on the material conditions of human activity. The law itself, on the other hand, points to the establishment of, or to the act establishing, the law and the corresponding question is therefore concerned with the conditions of this establishment or the conditions governing the formation of a consensus.

a) The search for the material conditions of the law, in other words, the question of the truth of the law, is universally regarded as the essential question of the doctrine of the natural law.[26] What is almost always meant by natural law and the establishment of natural law is really the safeguarding of the content of a positive dispensation of law and morality in a pre-positive reality. The various positions within the doctrine of the natural law result from the different possible interpretations of this pre-positive reality. The whole history of the doctrine of the natural law has, to some extent, been accompanied by two formulas, each pointing to a position, although the latter can appear in different variations and combinations.

The first of these formulas is *secundum naturam vivere*. This formula originated with Heraclitus — *kata phusin* [27] — formed the basic position of the Stoics [28] and to a very great extent determined the neo-scholastic doctrine of the natural law. [29] The idea of an order permeating the whole of reality — the world and mankind — or of a natural teleology is the prior condition for this "life according to nature." The "recognition of the existence of a universally valid and universally objective order above time as a state of transsubjective being going back to the normative authority of God is clearly the indispensable fundamental aspect of this doctrine of the natural law." [30] Man's essential existential form therefore has to be rationally inserted into this order of nature and has at the same time to take over certain tasks. The problem of this concept begins with the question as to precisely what is meant by the natural order or the universally objective order. If it is an order that can be empirically verified, then this verification has to be made by natural scientists or anthropologists. The latter have, however, been calling the idea of a natural teleology into question for a long time. Man has had such long and varied experience of himself that it is impossible for any anthropology that is based on empirical scientific observation to be given an absolute value. Certain interdependent and interconnected factors that cannot be overlooked by man without risk to himself are being considered again in a new light within the context of ecology and cultural anthropology and held up as examples of the limits of man's power to make everything. All reflection is, moreover, based on human experience and for this reason alone it cannot be denied that the natural sciences must be consulted in the search for a universal natural order within the framework of the traditional doctrine of the natural law. The aim, however, is always to try to justify an ontological order that transcends empirical experience, at least in the sense of a concept of nature of the kind outlined above (A 1 and 2). The question that is inevitably raised in this case is that of the methodical approach or knowability. If the problem is approached by elaborating and interpreting empirical data, then it is not possible to transcend the status of universal facticity. We have already indicated, in our discussion of the concept of nature above, the problems created by man's essential historicity. The history of the doctrine of the natural law has shown how much has been interpreted in the past as meaning provided by nature. It is not necessary to go back to Aristotle or Plato to learn about the natural rule of the more rational men over those with weaker powers of reason, such as women, children and slaves.[31] It is sufficient to note that the Church was teaching, even as late as the nineteen-fifties, that marriage had a hierarchical structure because of the "divinely established order of creation" and the "essentially different natural qualities of man and woman."[32] An appeal to man's being and to natural qualities of this kind makes one suspect that the structures presupposed in the prevailing praxis have been given a stylized form as natural qualities in order to prove that the norms of praxis cannot be changed and are based on man's essential being. This is clearly a form of "positivism based on the natural law and making a theocratic and magisterial legislation of the metaphysics that are presumed to exist, but the positive aspect of this legislation is only made more dangerous by the metaphysical claim. What could, in other words, be seen as a pragmatic rule can easily become intolerable if it is not regarded as an eternal truth of the natural law."[33] We know, however, that "the mutual functional orientation of the differences between human beings that is to be found at all times in history is extremely open in many different ways and to the most widely varying social patterns. The role of woman in society, for example, is capable of extreme changes."[34] Man's historicity and his cultural openness cannot be suppressed. There can be no doubt that this conviction has gained considerable ground in the past twenty or thirty years in the debate about the natural law. It has been summarized in the following way: "History has come to be recognized as an essential aspect of the natural law and history, of course, implies changeability."[35] The formula *secundum naturam* has, throughout this debate, been less emphasized than human reason which confronts the reality and attempts to deal with the conditions of the natural law by means of an analytical process.

The second of the two formulas used in the development of the theory of the natural law is *secundum rationem esse vivendum*. This formula also has its own history. According to Aristotle, what was naturally right only occurred within the *polis*, in other words, within a rational order of free men. "It cannot be separated and exist for itself alone. It can only exist in the multiplicity of what is regarded as right in the *polis*. It exists therefore as a legal right within the *polis*."[36] We may go further and say that it exists as historical reason in the concrete in the praxis of life and law itself

— in other words, in ethics. The idea of participation by human reason in God's reason was taken over by Thomas Aquinas from the traditional Stoic teaching (and especially Cicero) and Augustine and changed and adapted by him in various ways. Above all, he was struck by the emphasis placed on man's incomparable dignity in his active participation in God's providence. (This question has already been discussed in detail in Part One of this book, § 5 B 2 above.) Thomas called this participation, which is expressed in a natural human inclination to define and impose norms, the natural moral law in the strictest sense of the word. He also preferred to use the term *secundum rationem* for the active law-giving function of reason (*rationis ordinatio*).[37] In this way, he did not exclude the possibility of a material orientation of rational activity toward human nature. The very opposite was, however, in his opinion, true — ideal goods were revealed to man in his natural inclinations and these had to be borne in mind in action. His inclination for self-preservation makes it clear to him, for example, that his life is valuable and that it is necessary to preserve it. His attention is also directed toward the significance of human sexuality and the education of children by the same natural inclination to preserve the species. The fact that human beings exist in two sexes and are able to beget and bring up children — this and other similar data[38] — are goods that precede the responsible moral action of man. Thomas did not claim that all men are aware of this. What he did believe was that these insights into reflection about the most universal form (as the *prima principia*) were self-evident.

This recognition of fundamental legal goods tells us nothing, however, about the concrete way in which they should be preserved or realized. In other words, the natural moral law is not to be found in a natural order from which norms can be deduced, nor is it contained in a summary of rational rules of behavior or universal legal statements. On the contrary, it is an inner law which claims man as a moral being capable of fashioning himself and the world, and which makes him aware, by harnessing his powers of reflection, of the most important aims which, as a responsible being, he has to accept unconditionally, these aims, of course, being the fundamental goods to which we referred above. His fashioning of the order of law and morality is a constant task calling for interpretative and determinative thought and action.

It should be pointed out in this context that Thomas and those who followed him in the scholastic tradition tended to go back to the so-called *rectitudo naturalis* when they were concerned with the moral judgment of concrete human actions. According to Thomas, great care had to be taken, in ordering rationally the corporeal and sensory sphere of human activity (*circa corporalia et sensibilia*), "that every part of man and each one of his acts should attain its appropriate aim" (*SCG* III, 122). His reply to the question as to whether every lie was a sin was quite positive: "Since words are naturally signs for thoughts, it is unnatural and unseemly to express something with a word if it is not intended" (II–II 110, 3). According to Thomas, then, lying was naturally bad.

In the course of history, there has been a strong tendency to extend the range of the natural moral law to cover the *rectitudo naturalis* of individual actions. In the late scholastic period in Spain, for example, this tendency was very pronounced as a result of the justified need to establish as concrete and universal a moral law as possible for the colonial peoples. According to Francisco de Suarez (1548–1619), the judgment of reason pointed to the inner goodness or badness of human actions, and further and *consequenter* to the will of God, who accordingly commanded or prohibited.[39] In the sphere of *naturalis ratio*, then, the natural moral law acts as a means of judging what is suitable or unsuitable to nature.[40] In this, the obligation is not derived from rational judgment or from the inner order of the action itself, but from the will of God. The judgment based on pure reason about the goodness or badness of an action would not be obligatory if the will of God were not contained within that judgment. The philosophical doctrines of the natural law of Hugo Grotius (1583–1645), Samuel Puffendorf (1632–1694) and Christian Thomasius (1655–1728) and the so-called scholastic philosophy of Leibniz as systematized by Wolff in the eighteenth century were not based on an objective judgment of human activity. In their tendency to derive laws that were as concrete as possible from an ideally social form of human nature, they were fully in accordance with the teaching of the Spanish theologians.

I shall return to the question of the justification of concrete norms of action when we come to consider the justification of moral judgments. In this context, I will do no more than simply point out that the extension of the natural moral law to include concrete norms of action has made the universal nature of its validity even more questionable. According to Hans Welzel,[41] this extension to the history of law was responsible for the rapid "breakdown of the natural law" and the material problems were handed over to the representatives of German idealism for a solution. In the neo-scholastic doctrine of the natural law, there was a marked tendency to strengthen this extension in the sense of the essentialism referred to above. It was not until the revival of the natural law doctrine in the immediate post-war period that a clear tendency emerged "to avoid the rigidity that comes about as soon as it is laid down in detail with the boldness of rationalism what always has to take place. The prevailing view was that the natural law should be confined in the narrowest and strictest sense of the word . . . to a summary of fundamental and leading statements or axioms and the principles and fundamental relationships of the legal order that can be inferred by means of pure reason."[42] This summarizes the conclusions drawn from a large-scale investigation into the debate about the natural law as it developed in Germany between 1945 and 1965. We may go further and say that there is an internal dualism in the doctrine of the natural law, between absolutely valid legal principles which are so abstract that they are unable to provide a concrete law on the one hand and concrete legal principles which provide concrete laws that call for a decision before they can be made valid on the other. What lies behind this dualism is the necessary distinction that has to be made between insights into values on the one hand and moral judgments on the other. This distinction has already been discussed in some detail in the first part of this book (§ 1 B 2) and has been mentioned elsewhere in other sections.

In the question of the justification of value insights, we are concerned with the same problem that Johann Messner discussed in his cultural ethics — that of the "knowledge of truth in the moral sphere."[43] Messner did not attempt to justify these fundamental moral insights by means of a metaphysical deduction. He took direct human experience as his starting point and used an inductive and ontological method. Kant believed that the categorical imperative could be inferred from the connection between man's experience as a natural being and the concept of a rational will, and he regarded that imperative as a "practical synthetic statement *a priori*." In the same way, Messner also tried to establish the existence of elemental moral truths on the basis of human experience and reflection and to show that these were "necessary *a priori*."

This seems to me to be a legitimate course of action, insofar as no more is expected of it than it is capable of yielding. In fact, these synthetic judgments do produce necessary insights into fundamental goods and values that exist prior to our rational activity. The most important legal goods can be shown to be necessary in this way by means of experience and reflection. In the same way, it is also possible to demonstrate the existence of indispensable fundamental attitudes (the fundamental values of freedom, justice and solidarity). The fact that value judgments can also be expressed in the form of a categorical imperative or an apodictic law does not in any way change the intention of the statement. We know, for example, from the Old Testament decalogue that in Israel these sentences called to mind fundamental goods and values (life, possessions, faithfulness and so on). What we have here, then, is a natural doctrine of legal goods as a natural doctrine of law. The second restriction is equally important, namely that the synthetic judgment is not able to produce unconditional validity. This was for Kant himself a very great problem. Insight into the necessity of the categorical imperative presupposes the absolute validity of the moral law. It is open only to a transcendental and logical form of justification. It therefore gives rise to misunderstanding if we speak of absolutely valid legal principles. The most that can be meant by "absolute validity" in this context is the unconditionally logical validity that is peculiar to the principles of apodictic law if they are reduced to analytical statements (such as, for example, "thou shalt not kill" or "it is unjust to kill unjustly"). Unconditional moral claims cannot be justified without reference to the validity of material legal statements. Otherwise, we could have dispensed with the first section of this fundamental morality. We shall be returning to this question later, but in the meantime we must consider the formal conditions governing the validity of normative statements.

b) There has been a great deal of interest recently in the question of the conditions that are required if we are to come to an obligatory consensus regarding the norms of action. Questions have, of course, always been raised with regard to the formal presuppositions that are necessary if positive laws are to be valid and legitimate. In connection with this, attempts have been made to explain the origins of legislative authority by means of various theories.

The question of autonomous praxis, which we discussed above in § 4 C, confronted us with the central problem of the basic structure of communicative activity. In the theoretical discussion about the ideal community of communication, many questions have been asked about the *a priori* conditions governing the mutual recognition and justification of acting beings. Are there any indispensable presuppositions that are determined by nature in forming a consensus? Many of those who have considered this problem have come to the conclusion that all that is required for the process of free communication is a recognition that all points of view have only a relative value. There need be no unassailable principles. All that has to be done is to try out the convincing powers of the arguments. "This form of argument, which is used extensively nowadays, cannot be employed, because of its inherent openness, as a way of reasoning about the natural law in the traditional sense, even though it is very suitable for the purpose of criticizing, justifying or anticipating the positive law. Whoever uses such political, legal and social arguments is always conscious of the fact that he exists in the relativity of a practical conviction. He understands that his projects are finite and does not make them unconditional. The new attitude of justice consists of recognizing that one's own projects are relative within the structure of social relationships and that they are, as such, necessary." [44] Ellscheid, who maintains this view, regards as necessary this reference back to the pure structure of communication on the part of arguments used in the question of the natural law, "for as long as it remains impossible to determine man's being definitively." [45]

It is certainly necessary for everyone to be conscious of his own project or projects and to be prepared to subject his argument to critical questioning. The question still remains, however, as to whether there are any anthropological presuppositions for human action that can only be sacrificed at the price of self-destruction. This is, of course, the problem of the approach that will only comply with formal conditions of dialogue. This approach dispenses with a definite understanding of man and and makes use of its own image of man, who is seen as "existing autonomously in unrestricted communication." [46] Does this man really exist? Does this idea of man not take away from man in the concrete his natural *de facto* condition as man? "A Utopia that ignores these natural conditions exposes itself to them." [47] Human identity is not simply the

196

result of a sociopsychological process. A natural identity underlies this process. The socially mediated unity of man's consciousness of himself "can only be kept distinct from systematic theoretical claims as an ontologically irreducible element if it is regarded as a return to what man is naturally."[48]

The first question that we are bound to ask in connection with the natural law is that of the objectively correct law. Clearly it means more than a simple question about the material conditions governing the formation of a consensus. It also means more than a guarantee of the formal conditions. I have already pointed out that the element of positivity is connected in the concept of the correct law with the truth of the law. The real ontological structure of the law can be perceived in the connection between the essence and the existence of the law. The essence of the law, as a positive principle, requires this positivity if it is to be active and effective as law. Positive law can only be valid if it participates in the truth of the law. Both principles condition and encourage each other. "The reality of the law has two poles. This means, on the one hand, that essential being and existence are not identical. This datum is directed both against the positivism of law and against the idealistic (or rationalistic) doctrine of the natural law, which determine monistically the structure of law. The positivism of law determines the structure of law by allowing the essence of law to become merged with its existence. The idealistic doctrine determines the structure of law by allowing the existence to become united with the essence of law. On the other hand, however, our concept of the reality of law also means that the positivity and the essence of law cannot be separated from each other. They are as closely related to each other as the body and the soul of man, which are not ontologically identical (and can therefore be distinguished), but are in the concrete one. This means that any attempt to justify an ideally valid positive (or essential) law in addition to a really valid positive law must be rejected. It was a mistake on the part of the modern doctrine of natural law to separate the two poles of the one law and make them independent. As long as this situation prevails, it will not be possible to overcome positivism."[49]

This has resulted in a distinction between a doctrine of legal goods, concerned with the justification of legal goods and values, and a doctrine of norms or laws, with the task of demonstrating the development of concrete legal statements against the background of previously existing goods and values. To what extent this is feasible within the framework of the science of law cannot be discussed here. In the two final chapters of this section, I shall try to justify this claim in the light of the principles of moral theology. I shall deal with the justification of morally relevant insights in the first of these two chapters (chapter 2) and with the justification of normative judgments in the second (chapter 3). Before turning our attention to these closely related, but distinct questions, however, we must briefly consider the problem of unconditional obligation.

2. The Justification of Unconditional Obligation

"What is expressed in the most emphatic and impressive way in the contrast between a natural and a positive law is the conviction that has persisted throughout the history of human thought that there is not only something that is compelling by virtue of its superior power and is therefore put into practice by us as a result of a deeply rooted habit, something that is more than a purely factual reality, but also something that acts independently of any commandment or habit and obliges us in our innermost being to take certain actions. The idea of an unconditional obligation is at the heart of the natural law and is its central and lasting content."[50]

This important statement shows clearly that there has always been a search for the origin of law itself behind the materially correct law and the truth of the law. The problem cannot, however, be solved by pointing to obligatory goods and values or by looking for the empirical presuppositions of an uninhibited dialogue. This has been proved by the classical doctrine of the natural moral law and the profane doctrine of the natural law that was developed in the seventeenth and eighteenth centuries, as well as by the attempts made by Kant, Fichte and Hegel to find a suitable basis for the moral law. It is easy to see that those who favor scientific theoretical positivism cannot at the same time favor a transcendental philosophical approach. The attempts that have been made to go beyond a pragmatic justification of normative statements and to question the transcendental *a priori* assumptions of argumentation and communication are therefore all the more praiseworthy. We are bound, however, to criticize the neoscholastic doctrine of the natural law for treating the question of the ultimate ground of obligation as already solved and for devoting so much attention to the question of absolutely valid legal statements. In so doing, the neo-scholastic theologians gave the impression of trying to solve the problem of obligation in connection with the natural law by means of these legal principles.[51] This way was difficult if not impossible to follow and is ideologically suspect. We are bound to ask not only "what is correct?" but also "what is law?"

Hans Welzel was right when he claimed that "man is confronted in such a direct and inescapable way in the question of law with a choice between immanence and transcendence that he has to admit, if he has to choose between them, with the whole of his corporeal and spiritual existence: if there is no transcendence, in other words, if obligation based on transcendence of human existence was no more than an illusory projection of psychological or sociological factors, man would be totally exposed, with the whole of his body and soul, to a superior power. The limitations imposed by his fallen nature will persist for as long as there is a balance between the different power blocks, but as soon as one of these powers becomes unlimited, man falls a total victim to it, not only physically, but also spiritually."[52] That is why we gave so much attention to the justification of moral obligation in the first section of this work on fundamental moral theology. It is important to keep in mind what was said in that introductory section about the transcendental justification of obligation. We must now turn to the related questions of the development and justification first of morally relevant insights and second of morally normative judgments.

CHAPTER 2: THE DEVELOPMENT AND JUSTIFICATION OF MORALLY RELEVANT INSIGHTS

If moral activity is not to be exposed to an arbitrary process of self-determination, we are bound to examine the goods and values that are important in our judgment of human activity. Our first task, then, will be to gain an insight into these goods and values. The distinction between insights into values and judgments about actions is based on the structure of human intentions.[1] Our conscious activity develops at various levels and it is extended at each of these levels. The stage of knowledge, which includes experience, insight and the ascertainment of values, is followed by the moral stage, which includes reflection, selection and action. This division is necessarily simplified, because not everything that is physically possible is at the same time also moral and also because different moral decisions are possible in view of the conditioned character of finite goods.

At the very beginning of this book, when I was defining the task of fundamental moral theology (§ 1), I made the suggestion that value insights could be more easily explained if a distinction were made between goods on the one hand and values on the other. Until recently, this distinction has not been made universally; generally speaking, goods and values have been grouped together as a collective concept. This has had an adverse effect on the recent discussion about fundamental values in society and the state.[2] This failure to distinguish between goods and values seems also to have caused serious misunderstandings among moral theologians in their attempts to justify moral judgments. In order to prevent such misunderstandings, then, I would suggest the following further distinction and definition.[3] Goods are realities which have an existence independent of personal thinking and desire, but which exist prior to our activity. The term generally used in the philosophy of law is "legal goods." Included among these real goods are, for example, life itself, physical integrity, both spiritual and material possessions, freedoms such as freedom of conscience and freedom to express one's opinion, and institutional goods such as marriage, the family and the state. These are all realities that cannot be ignored when we act individually and interpersonally. They are given to us as a responsible task in human activity.[4] They were given to the people of Israel, for example, in an apodictic form,[5] but in most modern states they are usually incorporated into the constitutional law.[6] Values, on the other hand, can be defined as stereotyped attitudes (or virtues) which really exist only as qualities of the will. Justice, faithfulness and solidarity are values. Thomas Aquinas defined justice as *constans et perpetua voluntas ius suum unicuique tribuendi* and it has always been regarded in the western tradition as a firm attitude of the will to give everyone whatever is lawfully his.[7] Faithfulness is similarly an expression of a firm attitude of the will, in this case, to keep one's promise. These are both values which are closely related to action and therefore moral. They are not only objectively already given to man in his activity — they are also indispensable to him. There are indisputably certain fundamental social values of this kind.[8] The fact that certain fundamental values are necessary, however, does not imply a concrete moral judgment about a definite action. The decision about whether or not the police should use firearms or whether the death penalty is permissible or just, has to be taken as the result of a process of moral judgment. This points once again to the importance of distinguishing between judgments about values and judgments about actions, even when these values and actions are inwardly very closely connected with each other. We shall therefore concentrate in this chapter on the question of the ways in which these goods and values that already exist prior to man's action and some order can be provided among the various goods. In my opinion, there are three important approaches to this problem and one section of this chapter will be devoted to each. There are certain presuppositions that are present in the nature of man himself (§ 20). There is also a great deposit of historical experience and rational reflection (§ 21). Finally, there is knowledge of faith and this has to be taken seriously into consideration in any theological ethos (§ 22).

§ 20 Presuppositions of Nature

It is essential to go back to nature, as the sphere of man's existence, if we are to obtain any morally relevant insights, but it has to be borne in mind that this procedure is subject to presuppositions based on the humane sciences, our knowledge of evolution, ethology and related subjects and other factors. This knowledge makes us aware, for example, of historical connections between man and other organisms (see below, A) and will affect how we view anthropology (see below, B).

A. Natural Historical Presuppositions

Animal behavior and human behavior take place at different levels. An animal is governed by the dynamism of its impulses and is bound to act correctly. Man, on the other hand, is capable of making decisions and is therefore to a great extent responsible for himself. He can and ought to act correctly and is biologically equipped to do so. With his highly developed and differentiated cerebrum, it is possible for him to shape his own behavior to a great extent and to adapt it to his own ideas. It would be foolish, for example, to measure man's responsible activity against the behavior of a wild goose. This is never the aim of the ethologist in his investigation of animal behavior. He is much more concerned with the causes that lead to certain forms of behavior in the animal kingdom and he tends to investigate the effects that this behavior has. He confines himself, in other words, to animals.[9] The sociologist and the psychologist specialize in human behavior. Whether or not a knowledge of animal behavior can contribute to our understanding of human behavior depends on the importance that we attach to evolutionary processes. What is beyond doubt is that man's midbrain, which plays a decisive part in determining his primary impulses (eating, fighting, running away and sexual urges),[10] has only changed very slightly in evolution. One of the specifically human tasks is the cultivation of these primary impulses. This task, however, presupposes that the dispositions and tendencies that have to be formed are already known, at least as far as their biological origins are concerned. The ethologist can certainly contribute to this knowledge.[11] Careful observations and comparisons between different species may justify "working hypotheses about social laws and behavior mechanisms based on impulsive reaction in animals and man."[12] It is very questionable, however, whether we should go so far as to formulate a "biology of the ten commandments."[13] Quite apart from the fact that only the second decalogue can be used in this way, the rules of communication ("thou shalt not lie") and the laws restricting killing ("thou shalt not kill") do not provide any completely unambiguous reference to definite goods. What is more, although characteristics that are externally the same or different in animals and man can be revealed by the empirical method, it is not possible to use this method to ascertain qualitative values and distinctions. Nonetheless, it is interesting to learn that many fundamental principles of human behavior are connected with mechanisms that are intelligible in the light of biological evolution.

In my opinion, what is more interesting than comparisons between different forms of behavior is the discovery of ethologists of a structure of relationships among animals involving rivalry or competition on the one hand and mutual affection on the other. In the animal kingdom, these modes of behavior serve primarily as a natural means for the extension of the genes.[14] Programming to this end, however, also results in a partial conditioning of the formation of groups and the latter are themselves very variable in relationships between individuals. The dynamic tension between aggression and the bond of affection often emerges as the main formative principle of the relationship between groups and that between individuals within each group. It can be observed that "individuals help each other more if they are closely related to each other and that they are increasingly in rivalry with each other, the more remotely they are related."[15]

This is, however, not the only law that has been observed by ethologists. The propensity to preserve inherited good is guaranteed by an "economical" form of behavior in which individuals act as "profit and loss accounts" and the relationships between them are correspondingly adapted. "Following a complicated process of equilibrium between goods, the relationships are modified in accordance with the prevailing conditions. This applies to the strategy of receiving food and to the strategy of love of one's neighbor. Rules of behavior (laws) that are held to be unconditionally valid are therefore unnatural."[16] If it is correctly observed, Wolfgang Wickler insists, animal behavior is essentially directed toward one principal aim — the preservation of inherited good. A whole series of programmed patterns of behavior can be observed, all tending toward this main aim. These patterns of behavior are not rigid laws, but variable forms, all directed toward the same end. Correct behavior, then, is the behavior that serves the aim of best preserving the species.

It should be clear from what I have said in this section that there is a great deal of ambivalence involved in applying ethological insights to ethics. On the one hand, the ethological insight into the relative openness of the relationship between the end and the means is interesting as a datum of the natural law. On the other hand, however, it is evident that all the values of ethology, insofar as it is possible to speak at all of values, are confined to the purely biological level.[17] Serious problems are therefore often raised and misunderstandings abound when the ethologist applies moral concepts such as love of one's neighbor or faithfulness, even if only in an analogous way, to animal behavior. If, however, the methodological limitations and the different understanding of reality both of ethology and of moral theology are borne in mind, then it becomes clear that "there are no contradictions between knowledge acquired from ethology and that gained from moral theology," but it is equally clear that "theological ethics do not make claims that are contrary to nature — their claims go beyond nature."[18] This does not simply mean that personal values take precedence over vital values. It would be dangerous "to apply the biological principle of the subordination of the good of the individual to that of the group directly to the human sphere and say that the needs of society always take precedence over those of the individual."[19] Any significance that ethological knowledge can have with regard to human behavior is not to be found in the provision of positive norms, but in enabling us to understand the anthropological sphere better.

B. Anthropological Data

We have already tried, in § 19 above, to throw some light on the nature of man. We saw that it was possible to transcend nature in moral activity only when that nature was preserved and borne in mind as the norm of action. In this chapter, what we outlined in that section must be applied in a concrete way to morally relevant insights. We must, as it were, try to sound out the natural sphere of man. The results of anthropological research are widely divergent. Even one aspect of this research — the origin and status of aggression as a phenomenon of fundamental importance to our understanding of evil between men — has produced a great range of results. It would seem that the phenomenon cannot be explained satisfactorily or exclusively by the instinct or the impulse theory on the one hand or by the environment theory on the other. Erich Fromm has shown clearly and convincingly, on the basis of the most important neurophysiological evidence, both in the animal and in the human sphere, that the problem cannot be solved by either theory.[20] The question as to whether aggression is innate or acquired seems to me to be less important than the question as to what in aggressive behavior is innate and what is acquired. The distinctive aspect of human existence is that man is subject to nature and at the same time is able to transcend nature by his reason and his freedom.

If we take this widely accepted thesis as our point of departure, we can make two further comments.[21] The first is concerned with man's constitutional weakness. By this, we mean that man is, biologically speaking, born prematurely and needs at least three years before he is born socially. He is also dependent on sociocultural patterns of meaning such as language, morals and so on. He needs the solidarity of the human community to overcome this constitutional weakness. His individual tendencies are expressed in that community, and society is at the same time humanized by means of it. In solidarity with others, individual and personal life is developed in a relationship of pressure and counter-pressure. Social welfare and solidarity are therefore anthropologically indispensable values of fundamental importance.

My second comment is this. Man is always ready to fashion his life and his environment and at the same time to be fashioned. What has developed from this elemental experience is a readiness to take an attitude. In other words, man, both as an individual and in society, is in search of a model by which his natural dispositions and those of the reality of the world can be realized. Only a firm attitude and a corresponding disposition are able to give form and meaning to his natural tendencies. It is only if he is constrained to behave according to valid norms that he can evolve a regular and therefore successful form of behavior that can be recognized by his fellow-men. Social norms as sanctioned patterns of behavior provide the individual with the opportunity to acquire modes of behavior that as a rule have every chance of success and set him free from his search for the best possible solution. They also make it possible for human relationships to be lasting and set man free from uncertainty with regard to the other's behavior. In other words, norms and institutions are fundamental legal goods and man is dependent on them. Another essential value is therefore reliability. We cannot discuss here the extent to which norms can be and in fact are used as means of suppression.[22] The fundamental possibility that such norms will be used positively and meaningfully is, of course, not placed at risk by the possibility of abuse.

It is also important to ask whether anything meaningful can be said about the content of these norms at least from the point of view of the presuppositions of nature. In his examination of the question of the logic of normative reason, W. Korff has considered this problem in detail.[23] In particular, he has stressed that reason is not arbitrary when it is fundamentally anthropological, by which he means the orientation of reason back to its origin in the all-embracing reality of man in his whole complex biophysical, social and spiritual context. Korff included the data of ethology in his study and integrated them into anthropology. Aggression and the desire for affection on the one hand, and competition with and orientation toward others on the other, condition the inner structure of the human personality and the various forms of social relationships between men. In a naturally nonarbitrary way, man appears to his fellow-men as a being with needs, as an aggressor and as one who cares for others. This basic structure, however, does not in itself form a moral norm. It is, on the other hand, what Korff called a "meta-norm," in other words, a kind of structural "guide" or "timetable" for all forms of concrete social behavior. Man, as a being who is given to himself as a task, can only reach the status of being a man by virtue of the norms, institutions and legal and political dispensations that he has himself created. These norms can, however, only set man free so that he is able to attain the status of being a man if they act as a function and a product of reason within the structures of his natural impulses. All social ethics are therefore contained within a fluid equilibrium or a kind of perichoresis of behavior based on objective needs, competition and social care. The necessity of this fluid equilibrium as a foundation for man's life together with his fellow-men points clearly to a naturally nonarbitrary structure of the social order, which has to be borne in mind when any meaningful system of norms is evolved. It is quite possible for one particular element — man's orientation toward objective needs in an objective morality, his drive to compete with his fellow-men in an ethos of justice or his desire to care selflessly for others in a personal ethos of love — to be given priority in this structure of norms. It is therefore possible for a number of ethical systems to exist side by side, although a limit is imposed on this number by the fact that each system has to take all three aspects into consideration at the same time. In any Christian ethos, the ultimate relationship that creates unity between men and the predominance of the caring relationship of love are the consequence of the relationship between God and man that is recognized in faith.

We have, of course, only outlined this problem in general terms, although it should be possible to recognize the fundamental structures. These structures are amplified and modified again and again in the course of human experience. This brings us to our second source of knowledge, one that is very productive of ethical insights — human experience itself.

§ 21 Experience and Reason

Everyone prefers to consult his own experience when he is confronted with the need to make moral decisions. In human experience, we have a source of knowledge that is extremely important to us in our attempt to recognize the goods and values that exist prior to any human activity and are at our disposal. It may be possible to make moral judgments only if, on the one hand, the goods and values involved and, on the other, the factors conditioning human action, are borne in mind against the background of a balanced examination of the goods, which may be in competition with each other. If that is so, then the first question that arises is the hermeneutical one about our correct understanding of the order of these goods and values. In section A below, I attempt to define as precisely as possible the part played in this process of knowledge by human experience. Before doing this, however, I try to throw some light on at least some aspects of this very complex concept, which exists at so many different levels and ultimately seems to resist any effort at systematization.[1] At the same time, I also discuss experience as a point of departure for material ethics. Value insights may, of course, be directly evident, but for the most part they come about within a gradual process of human experience in which these insights differ according to the social and historical situation that prevails at any given time. Human reason enables us to distinguish priorities and obligations (see section B below). On the basis of reason, criteria showing that human experience is an authoritative source of relevant insights have to be formulated. If insights into values come about on this basis, they can only be made intersubjectively obligatory by means of communication. This in turn takes place on the basis of an examination of the situation and its significance. This justification of morally relevant insights is therefore the basis for the establishment of an order of goods and values. The different insights into values must be critically related to each other if this basis is to be established. This integration of the various insights, however, leads to the emergence of clear priorities, so long as it takes place against the background of a clearly defined understanding of man and the world.

A. Experience as the Source of Morally Relevant Insights

1. The Concept of Experience

At first sight, "experience" would seem to be such an obvious category of western thought that no further explanation is necessary. In fact, however, on closer investigation, the concept emerges as one of the "most obscure"[2] and "mysterious"[3] in modern philosophy. It is "such a difficult philosophical concept to grasp on the one hand because it is opposed to all theory and, on the other, because it is so closely allied to theory that it can only escape from its grasp by turning it against itself."[4]

In everyday language, experience is an "indicator of social and technical competence"[5] or the ability and openness to acquire experience. It is based on perception, but not identical with it. It is also always "an experience of connections. . . . Experience is a way of knowing that is mediated. As direct experience, it is based on sensory perception. It is, however, never limited to this. It is capable of drawing conclusions, inferring laws, going back to causes and reading interpretations into data that have already been gained as the result of certain previous interpretations. Any knowledge that we have of experience, then, is inevitably affected by the uncertainty of interpretations. This knowledge is, in other words, historically conditioned — something than cannot be observed by a purely empirical approach."[6] What is more, experience does not take place in a sphere of pure observation. It is always closely related to praxis and structurally marked by it.[7] It includes not only personal, individual experience, but also the concentrated experience of generations that is found in the accepted norms and practices of the community.[8]

"Experience is gained at the expense of time and trouble. What is important in our context is whether or not it is mediated. We have, in other words, not experienced a certain reality until it is introduced to our consciousness without (or after) mediation. According to Henri Bouillard, in any attempt to find a basis by which we can understand the rational structure of this reality, experience appears as unexplained reason or else reason appears as experience that has been made translucent. Experience that has been elaborated in this way provides us with possible insight."[9] In the wider sense of the word, experience is not limited to scientific empirical observation. It also includes concern at the emotional and practical level.[10]

A distinction is sometimes made between experience as an event, as an individual experience and as a datum containing knowledge and ability.[11] "In addition to measured experience (at the cognitive and theoretical level), there are other dimensions of experience, notably lived experience (at the pragmatic level) and fashioned and interpreted experience (at the level of the understanding of meaning). . . . A distinction can be made between the spontaneous and the mediated modes of experience. (Experience of natural basic needs is spontaneous, whereas experience of cultural needs is socially mediated. Both these modes, however, merge into one another.) In the matter of totality, a distinction can also be made between partial and complex experiences, and the total context to which the experience in question refers can be inferred from the fragmentary character of each experience. Finally, experience can also be differentiated according to the degree to which it can be expressed in language and verified cognitively. An important part is also played by the degree of intensity of the experience in question."[12]

Some idea of the complexity and the many different forms of this phenomenon can be gained from these few aspects of the concept of experience. This should be borne in mind if the status of this important source of morally relevant insights is to be determined within the framework of theological ethics.

2. Experience as the Point of Departure for Material Ethics

"Like all sciences, ethics must also have the data of experience as its point of departure."[13] These data of experience can be most easily understood, without being reduced to the individual level, when they are regarded as lived convictions in the moral life of man. Even in the classical tradition, the deposit of experience of lived convictions was known to be relevant in the task of finding norms.[14] "Aristotle thought of *ethos* as the quintessence of the unwritten orders of a community which presupposed the established order of the *nomos* from which the latter proceeded, which was the content of the *nomos* and without which the *nomos* had no power to arouse obedience. Thomas took over this datum in his concept of *consuetudo* as the most commonly practiced and the most constant mode of concrete behavior." [15]

According to Aristotle's view of ethics, [16] "experience played a part not only as a point of departure for ethical reflection, but also as a permanent and necessary precondition for continued thought about ethics at a suitable level." [17] Experience, then, as the point of departure for all practical thinking about ethics, was according to Aristotle, first and foremost a knowledge of the habits and customs of the *polis* that had become the common property of the society in which those customs were practiced. The ultimate aim of all ethical reflection was praxis, the "immanent rationality" of which tried "to raise up and promote" that praxis. [18] Because praxis was so varied in form and so impermanent, however, Aristotle believed that ethics could only become universally valid in the form of "typical" knowledge in outline.

In the same way, Thomas Aquinas regarded experience as "the foundation of all ethical reflection . . . and therefore as the necessary precondition for that reflection. It was for him both the point of departure and the aim of all ethics." [19] For him, the relationship between ethics and experience was not only a pre-moral and morally relevant reality, but also a purely moral element, existing "especially at the level of directly lived morality and *consuetudo*, that is, at the level of factual morality, which Thomas regarded as the most important sphere of ethical relevance." [20] He believed, then, that a part was played not only by knowledge of pre-moral data and its mediation through human experience, but also by the ethical element itself, which was, as the result of reflection, factually experienced and made relevant in the process of determining what was morally correct. It is important in this context to bear in mind that the *lex divina* did not, according to Thomas, do away with experience as the source of relevant insights and that it did not "exclude the concrete process of finding rules of action, but, on the contrary, positively required this process and, what is more, required it precisely in the structures that determined naturally rational morality, in other words, in the form of experience and reflection." [21]

210

Experience did not, therefore, in Thomas's opinion, follow ethics and its fashioning of norms, but rather mediated the normative element and made it concrete. He was not only aware of the value of experience in the process of shaping concrete norms in the sense of the *lex naturalis* — he also tried to determine what experience and whose experience contributed to this task. He concluded that this was not only the experience of the lawgiver,[22] but also the collective experience gained from *consuetudo*. This *consuetudo*, as the complex of communal convictions and collective praxis, was a normative fact and represented "in itself one of the social values that had to be taken into consideration."[23] This is particularly clear from the fact that "the interpretation of the *utilitas communis* may itself be an effect of the *consuetudo*."[24] The constitutive function of the *consuetudo* for the interpretation of the *bonum commune* is clear from this. "The concrete form of the *lex*, in other words, the concrete law-giving as such, is based on the exercise of concrete rationality in any interpretation of what is universally good and useful."[25] This interpretation can, however, only take place via the insight acquired into the goods and values that are at the disposal of our moral judgments and in the light of experience. According to Thomas, this experience was gained within a normative sphere, which it in turn made concrete or modified. "This means, in other words, that this process always takes place within an area of normative and therefore concrete experience."[26]

Even within the framework of the recent discussion about the natural law, the importance of experience for the material fulfillment of the universal principles of the natural law was stressed again and again.[27] It is, after all, not possible for the content of the universal principles of the natural law to be increased. This can only happen if we go back to the content that is already present and available. This existing content is not, however, absolute or universal, nor can it be divorced from history and the world. "Its social context is to be found in the changing public consciousness. It can also be found in the prevailing ethos which has been conditioned by historical, religious, cultural and social factors and has been made appropriate over several generations and which has also become the accepted conviction of a given stratum in society, a whole people or a community of believers within that people. Finally, it can also be found in the experience gained from the ethical and moral mastery of a given situation."[28]

J. Messner was also of the opinion that our understanding of the principles of the natural law by means of synthetic judgments was *a priori* conditioned by our experience. The content and meaning of those principles was, Messner believed, already preconditioned and "induced from historical and contingent experience and moral or ethical structures on the one hand and from either traditionally inherited or newly formed ethical patterns, on the other. It is therefore subject to historical processes of development and change."[29]

In the same way, the secondary statements of the natural law that are derived from first principles can be seen as "commonplaces of a public consciousness which may exist at any time — or be in process of passing away — and which have to be expressed in an increasingly scientific terminology within the sphere of economics and the social sciences.[30] In the scholastic doctrine of the natural law, attempts were made, within the framework of the medieval doctrine of synderesis, to derive these concrete secondary statements of the natural law from the most universal principles by means of a process of making sure of the prevailing situation in the sociocultural environment. We may assume, however, in the light of sociological findings, "that the doctrine of synderesis represents a speculative overemphasis of intuitive insights into the structure of everyday knowledge."[31]

3. Levels of Experience

The process of experience which leads to morally relevant insights takes place at many different levels. In it, at least three fundamental types of experience can be distinguished — experience of contrast, experience of meaning and experience of motivation or intensity.[32]

Perhaps the most important aspect of experience is negative experience, in other words, experience as disappointment or negative event. "By experience in this sense, we mean having an experience with someone or something. It occurs whenever an experience of truth or value that has touched our existence has to be corrected."[33] Everyone has to acquire or go through this kind of experience of life for himself.[34] "Experience in this sense means necessarily disappointed expectations and it will only be gained in this negative way. Although experience is above all painful and

212

unpleasant, this does not point to an especially somber aspect, although this can be perceived directly from the essence of experience as such. It is only by negative factors that new experience can be acquired. (Bacon was aware of this.) Every experience that is worthy of the name always goes counter to another experience. Man's historical being thus contains as an essential aspect a fundamental negativity which is brought to light in the essential relationship between experience and insight. Insight here is more than a knowledge of one or another datum or situation. It always includes a return from an illusion within which one has been held captive. It always contains an element of self-knowledge and at the same time represents a necessary aspect. The latter is what we call experience in the true sense of the word."[35] This negative experience is, in Gadamer's opinion, completed in the fundamental experience of finiteness and historicity.

This philosophical understanding of insight also points to the basically defective aspect of human praxis, which can be experienced in the difference "between individual and universal praxis"[36] or, at the level of insights into values, in the "difference between claim and realization, which may be the difference between value insights themselves."[37] Reduced to the simplest possible formula, this is the "difference between 'it will work' and 'it will not work.' It is also possible to experience at the deepest level in other persons, in the whole of reality and in oneself whether or not value insights are ratified by being expressed in life."[38]

This negative experience is not, however, the end of a process of experience. On the contrary, it is able to operate as a dialectical process of development and produce further insights and reveal new possibilities. In this sense, it is hermeneutical.[39] "It produces not only disappointment and a correction of what was previously known, but also a wider knowledge and therefore an existential enrichment and a deeper understanding of himself on the part of the one who experiences."[40]

This brings to our attention another aspect of experience, since it is obvious that negative experience is in no sense the whole of experience. The experience of contrast presupposes a certain experience of values before it can itself be called into question. Within human praxis, certain models of action have to prove their value or at least have to point to new possibilities within the framework of an experience of contrast. In that case, these data of experience provide an insight which is experienced as a relationship of meaning.[41] In this meaning, the reality that has to be encountered at any given time acquires what Peter Berger has called a "plausibility structure," which is at the same time the basis for moral experience of meaning and is concentrated in the experience of value as a "profile of norms" or a "profile of significance."[42] Possibilities of authentic praxis that may be experienced intensively in the "context of threat"[43] are revealed in the moral experience of meaning. "'It is becoming clear to me . . . ,' 'it dawns on me . . .' and 'that has convinced me' are all exact expressions of an experience of meaning. Justice, mercy and reconciliation are made present in the light of their own testimony and call on us to imitate them as human possibilities."[44] The discovery of new and meaningful possibilities also includes a knowledge of what is simply possible from the empirical point of view.[45] The abundance of empirical data that have been brought to light by the humane sciences to a great degree condition any consideration of traditional insights into meaning and at the same time provide an impetus for new experiences of meaning which are expressed as morally relevant insights into changed value judgments. It is worth recalling how many changes have been made in the penal code on the basis of new experiences of and insights into man and his behavior.

We should, however, recognize that not every experience of meaning is as such a morally relevant insight. Moral experience comes about when an experience of meaning becomes — often through a contrast — so dense for man that it affects him deeply and lets him experience in the center of his being the existential importance of his free realization of himself. The moral factor in this sense is a "universally human, personal and communal experience of the necessities and possibilities of success in man's existence together with his fellow-men that call for an ultimate decision and are therefore obligatory and the meaningful realization of these possibilities."[46] The moral importance of a reality of action experienced in its relationship of meaning is contained within the conscience.[47] The conscience is the experience of intensity or motivation of "what (inevitably) concerns me."[48] "By this we mean that evasions are not admissible here. This forms part of the consequence of my life. If I act differently, I am convicted by myself. It is

214

only when this experience of motivation has a sufficiently high level of intensity that experience of meaning forms an inescapable part of the structural development of the moral person." [49]

In this way, a fund of morally relevant experience is formed in the ethos — either of a person or of a particular sphere in life — and this fund forms the basis of all moral judgment. This is only possible, however, if the experience is accompanied by a process of interpretation in which an attempt is made to understand it within the sphere of experience prevailing at any given time and the experience itself is also reflected in the consciousness as a morally relevant insight or as a value judgment. It is only within a reflection of this kind that the universally obligatory aspect of this experience, in the sense of its socioethical relevance, can be fully revealed. Our critical reason has, however, to be actively applied to this task.

B. Critical Reflection as a Criterion

1. The Foundations of Competent Experience

We have already said that experience is a valid source of morally relevant insights — in other words, that it should lead to a universally recognized order of goods and values. Certain conditions must, however, be present if this experience or practically experienced conviction is to be morally relevant. It would certainly be a "genetical error" to believe that the value of morally relevant insights as truth can be directly inferred from the genesis of those insights themselves. [50] At the most, we would have to rely on conjecture. We have, however, to reflect about and analyze the conditions that are able to show that experience is competent and credible. [51] "Experience is relevant when it points to a reflected and confronted obligation through the experienced consequence of conviction." [52] It is only when it continues to survive in the face of opposition that the real strength of any conviction underlying praxis is revealed. A certain personal strength which the individual subject draws from his roots in authentic experience is required. [53] Moral experience is tested in praxis and clarified in reflection and as such contains a firm obligation which derives its claim not from the simple fact of expression, but from its identity with the personal subject who is claimed. This task, which has to be carried out by reason in reflection, also contains a basic need — we have to reflect critically about the possibility of freedom and conditioning in society.

"Experience is relevant when it has reflected about the conditions which brought it about."[54] The area of possible experience is defined and restricted by the process of socialization and the interaction between groups and institutions. Experience is therefore only credible "when it is not based on authoritarian interaction, but asserts itself in the possibility of critical reflection."[55] It is important in this context to be aware that the possibilities of experience can be manipulated, since one of the necessary presuppositions of authentic experience is that freedom of orientation is safeguarded. On the other hand, however, this freedom of orientation is always in danger of becoming a complete absence of orientation, especially if the sphere of social order is not taken into consideration so that the possibilities of experience are, in other words, restricted to the private area. Experience is limited by society, but is also at the same time made possible by it.

Moral experience is only convincing when it is acquired in personal responsibility. This autonomy or coming of age of man is "the result of a long process of development, the first stages of which can be described in oversimplified terms as a morality of authority and of the group, in other words, as a pre-personal orientation toward internalized patterns of behavior."[56] Part of this personal autonomy is the ability to control one's own emotional impulses.[57] It is important, however, to bear in mind that this autonomy of the subject should not be confined to the individual. Within the framework of communicative praxis, it also includes a respect for the moral experience of others.

This implies that moral experiences can only form the basis of conviction if they can be made communicable by the one who has them. They will be communicable if they can be made translucent. This clarity is particularly important with regard to the content of value of these experiences. The difficulty of mediating experiences is, of course, a matter of everyday knowledge. This does not, however, do away with the fundamental demand that the moral element should be understandable. The problem is really one of the way in which experiences are mediated. This points directly to the importance of "narrative ethics"[58] in the mediation of value statements in the form of a narrative handing on of models as ways of promoting the moral element. All the same, the power of such models of experience to convince cannot replace the argumentative evidence of their validity with regard to certain situations involving a decision.[59]

This very process of mediation also points to the fundamental historical conditioning of all experience, a situation which has to be borne in mind in any consideration of the conditions governing credible praxis, if we are not to make the mistake of giving an absolute value to human experience. I have already discussed the fundamental difficulty inherent in the concept of experience as such, a difficulty that arises as a result of its relationship with theory and which is also present in our experience of values. This experience is made possible by the presence of previously existing, historically developed forms of order, but it can only guarantee its autonomy by being again and again directed against established models of order. An example of this is the development of the doctrine of the "just war" until war was rejected as a means of obtaining peace by the Second Vatican Council. The continuity of traditional insights into values which are often latent in the forms of order that are handed down to us can often only be guaranteed when they can be experienced again and again under different conditions.[60] "The connection between the competence of experience and the dynamism of insights into moral values — a link in which the historical character of man's existence is clearly manifested — should not be condemned as purely relative. These values are not destroyed by an orientation toward the world, but preserved and handed down because of it."[61] We should not, however, overlook the ambivalence of historical praxis in this context, since this is able to "mediate both moral progress and moral decline."[62]

Models of conviction are in this way produced by experience if the latter is competent and these models form a deposit of very varied historical partial experiences. This brings us to the problem of the universally obligatory character of morally relevant insights.

2. The Justification of Morally Relevant Insights

The universally obligatory character of morally relevant insights that are derived from competent experience can only be made translucent in communicative praxis. The principle of transsubjectivity[63] as the basic norm of all communication includes the obligation on the part of all those who participate in rational discourse to resolve by argument "all normative claims to validity according to the standard of the interests that are represented by them and that can be made intersubjectively universal."[64] It is necessary in this context to verify the extent to which fundamental and transcendental pragmatic norms such as truthfulness, for example, are inevitably "compromised by the existing state of human society, because of so many different conventional practices, such as euphemism, discreet silence, devious ways of avoiding explicit truth, understatement and overstatement, exaggeration, dramatization, the use of commercial publicity and political propaganda and Picasso's artistic lie by which the truth is made visible."[65] This is the task of those who specialize in the social sciences, which derive their function to criticize and reconstruct spheres of knowledge in this area from their relationship with the normative principle of transcendental and pragmatic ethics.[66] It is only possible to elaborate the meaning of human experience methodically in the social sciences if the preconditions for this task are present "in the same *a priori* situation in which the fundamental normative principle of ethics was located."[67] In our context, this means that, if morally relevant insights are to be critically reconstructed in accordance with their content and meaning, in such a way that we can aim at communication via their intersubjectively obligatory character, we can only hope to reach a valid consensus on condition that the social sciences, in which this critical reconstruction takes place, take as a basis the same transcendental norms that form the *a priori* situation of any community of communication.

It is only if this presupposition is in force that we can attempt, within the sphere of value insights that are mediated in and by society and are therefore inevitably conventional, "to make a distinction between two kinds of convention. On the one hand, there are those conventions that can be understood and to some degree justified in the light of the historical circumstances that conditioned life at the time they prevailed. On the other hand, there are conventions which deviate radically from the transcendental norm of communication and interaction and thus provide evidence not only of prudence in adapting to the principle of reality (Freud), but of a loss of transparence in the sense of a quasi-pathological objectivization of self-alienation and even perhaps of a return to an already superseded stage of responsible living."[68]

We can, however, only aim at communication via the meaning of statements which have a content of morally relevant insights if we at the same time also aim at agreement about the matter in question.[69] "Signs and intelligibility, statements and truth and experiences and evidence are in this sense . . . aspects of functional language games and cannot be separated from each other. They are, on the contrary, *a priori* interlaced with each other."[70] This interlacing of the two interests "of possible meaning and intelligibility and possible objective truth . . . in the interest of communication"[71] is, according to Apel, a universal and pragmatic constant, the methodological expressions of which can, however, be developed in history and differentiated.[72] This relationship makes the way in which research into meaning and situation can be methodically mediated and used for the purpose of valid intersubjective communication via morally relevant insights.

The social sciences can therefore reach, via a methodical objectivization of the relationship between subject and subject, a certain knowledge, the significance of which is not to be found in the planning side of social technology, but which will undoubtedly make it possible for us to understand at a deeper level the experience of the meaning and content of human life. It may be possible for us in this way to aim at an intersubjective agreement with regard to morally relevant cases of experience, an agreement supported by the need to "bridge the gap between the responsible subject who is always anticipated and the object-subject who is really found in history."[73] If that agreement can be reached, there will at the same time be a continuity in the value insights which we will not be able to abandon if our intention is to give a rational human shape to our lives.[74] This, then, is the basis on which the goods and values that are embodied in the constitutional laws of many states, and are regarded as essential for human society, should be elaborated. These goods and values are defined more and more precisely in a process of increasing knowledge, which is irreversible *de iure*, but not so *de facto*.[75]

3. The Establishment of Priorities in an Order of Goods and Values

If we aim at an intersubjective agreement via morally relevant insights and this leads us to evaluate goods and values, this does not mean that we have established any order of priority among those goods and values. This order should form the basis for our justification of morally normative judgments. The question can be approached in practice by trying to relate differing insights or interpretations of meaning critically to each other.[76] Morally relevant perspectives of the kind that become apparent here have to be seriously considered and can be integrated with other, already existing insights.

Mieth has illustrated this fact by referring to the experience of sexuality. It is possible to interpret the sexual experience of man in contemporary society in three different ways. In the first place, there is the view of sexual freedom, according to which the primary sexual urges will continue to be insatiable for as long as they are not fulfilled. If these urges are subjected to a normative process of restriction by means of social pressures and compulsions, the sexual process will be unable to find its proper form or identity. This process of finding sexual identity takes place within the total framework of the individual's realization of himself as such and this is, according to this interpretation of sexual experience, the most dominant meaning of sexuality. The second interpretation is more common. Its protagonists give primary importance to the fulfillment of eroticism. As a model of human experience, it can correctly be given the name of "enlightened eros." According to the third interpretation, sexuality is institutionally integrated within marriage, as the place in which primary importance is given to the begetting and education of offspring.

What is significant about these three views of sexual experience is that they are not necessarily mutually exclusive. "They can be experienced in successive phases, they can be experienced by mutually excluding each other and they can also be experienced in an integrated way, after one or another has been dominant. There is therefore an abundance of forms determining our experience of historical sexual behavior."[77] The models have therefore to be presented objectively, their aims have to be emphasized and the various ways of experiencing sexuality have to be critically related to each other. It may in this way be possible to show that an integrated institutional model can include the meaningful aspects of both the first and the second way of experiencing sexuality and that this may in the long run be the best way of fulfilling all the dimensions of this experience.

Mieth's example of these three views of sexuality and their possible integration shows that it is only possible to interpret meaning within a particular sphere of human experience and to find the order of goods and values that can be evolved in the light of that interpretation against the background of a definite understanding of man and the world. The priorities within that order can be established on this basis. In this way too, models of meaning which show that man can realize himself primarily by fulfilling his needs without repression inevitably give a higher status to material goods. This is clear from Marcuse's breakdown of the process by which values are translated into needs in two stages: first, material satisfaction, in which freedom is made material, and second, the free development of needs on the basis of this satisfaction, which is a form of nonrepressive sublimation. In this process, Marcuse argues, the relationship between material and spiritual dispositions and needs undergoes a fundamental change. In the process by which man's existence becomes satisfied, the interplay between thought and imagination takes on a rational and leading function. The concepts of justice, freedom and humanity also become the concern of man's good conscience. They can, Marcuse claimed, exist as truth within this framework of conscience and themselves take part in forming a good conscience, in particular as leading to the satisfaction of man's material needs and the rational organization of the realm of necessity. [78]

If, on the other hand, we regard man's realization of himself and his dignity in his free giving of himself to others as the response that he makes to a claim made by moral values such as justice and faithfulness — a claim which he experiences as unconditional — "then he recognizes that he is confronted with demands in his behavior toward his fellow-men that cannot be changed or cancelled out by any consideration of utility or harm to himsef. The demand made by justice and faithfulness is so powerful and unconditional that it cannot be ignored, even if the whole world calls for it to be ignored and, in an extreme case, it can claim man's total commitment, even to the point of death. . . . It is so unconditional in its intensity that man can — and in extreme circumstances must — sacrifice his physical existence rather than abandon the claim of justice and faithfulness." [79]

Another aspect of this problem is indirectly clarified by this contrast — the fact that there are two principles on which a hierarchy of goods can be constructed. These are fundamentality and dignity.[80] The principle of fundamentality gives "priority to the value . . . that is the necessary condition for the realization of all other values. This most fundamental value is life itself and because of this it takes precedence, in any case of conflict, over all values."[81] This points clearly to an order of pre-moral values, that is, physical as opposed to moral goods, with the result that we have to speak of an order of goods. A legal order constituted by an order of goods of this kind aims to "safeguard and preserve peace and therefore to create the material preconditions for a meaningful life."[82] The second of these principles, that of dignity, orders values in accordance with their content of meaning at any given time. Whatever value is higher at the time is made clear because it gives the value that is more fundamental at that time its real meaning. It is, however, only possible to establish this order of values against the background of certain models of meaning. Any interpretation or evaluation of meaning is therefore dependent on man's understanding of the world and himself at that particular period.

It is precisely here that faith has a part to play in justifying and providing a basis for morally relevant insights. We have already seen how this took place in the early Church on the basis of the expression of moral norms. In the following section, we shall reflect more systematically about this function of faith.

§ 22 Knowledge of Faith

Religion is "distinctive in that it can only fulfill its ethical task if it is not defined by it."[1] Religion, in the sense of a living witness to God's saving activity in Jesus Christ, should not be identified with ethics. If we try to define it by its ethical function, it at once loses its function as religion. The expression of Christian existence in faith, hope and love transcends the level of interpersonal order (the sphere of moral virtues) and is entirely directed toward the task of giving form to the world of man. I have been preoccupied in the whole of this work on fundamental moral theology with the need to stress the influence of faith in God. In the light of faith, I have tried (in § 5 above) to provide a deeper insight into moral autonomy and (in §§ 8–10) into the question of human guilt. Our survey of the history of salvation under the old and new covenants also made it possible for us to understand how the biblical ethos was shaped by faith. I do not intend to repeat here what I have already said in previous sections of this book. In discussing our knowledge of faith here, I shall be dealing with the part played by faith in ethics and shall be doing this against the background of the insights that we have already gained.

My aim is to provide a comprehensive answer to the question of the distinctive aspect of Christian ethics: what are specifically *Christian* ethics? This will be my main task in this section, although I am bound to point out at the beginning that my comprehensive answer to this much discussed problem[2] will only be found in the whole of this book.

The fundamental question that has arisen again and again in recent years can be expressed in two ways. Are any original or exclusive moral norms proclaimed in specifically Christian teaching? Or: are the moral demands made of Christians different from those made of nonbelievers, because of the faith of the former? I am of the opinion that, if we are looking for an answer to the question: what are specifically Christian ethics, we should not try to find it by asking either of the two questions formulated at the beginning of this paragraph. If we take the inner unity of the order of creation and redemption as our point of departure, this question will inevitably prove to be illusory. The Christian message is nothing but the fulfillment of man's deepest expectations. It cannot estrange man, nor can it ultimately seem strange to him. At the same time, however, its effect on him is that of a challenge from another world. In his finite freedom, man is confronted, as a self-centered being, with the absolute self. He can only find himself by giving himself. He can only have power over himself when he surrenders himself. As we have already seen, this is not contradictory. On the contrary, it is a source of radical challenge to the deepest contradiction. There is also another aspect to this question — the history of man's salvation takes place as promise and fulfillment. Jesus brought fulfillment with his coming and to this extent his demands were new and different, without being strange to man. In the same way, the promises made with his coming are proclaimed today in a very different way, but still without estranging man. On the contrary, man, as a *laboratorium beatitudinis possibilis*, as Ernst Bloch once called him, is able to fulfill himself through these promises. They were, moreover, made to all men. Openness to them and the possibility of knowing them can be found everywhere.

We cannot therefore say that the fundamental question confronting a specifically Christian ethos is whether the demands made of interpersonal relationships are only applicable to Christians themselves. The question that should be asked is rather: can the consequences resulting from the gospel message and applicable to all men in their relationships with each other be made intelligible because they are in principle open to a consensus with regard to human nature considered in the light of the history of salvation?[3] The problem of specifically Christian ethics, then, is not whether the norms determined by faith are exclusive, but whether they can be communicated.

Before going into the question of the concrete influence of faith on our moral knowledge in section B below, we shall consider how morality should be understood in the context of faith (section A).

A. Faith and Understanding

In § 5 B above, we discussed the God of faith and the difficulty of speaking in the right way about him. How should he who is nameless be addressed and how should he who cannot be expressed be proclaimed? We are unable to apply our words and concepts, directed as they are toward objective human experience, to God, with his complete lack of limitation and objectivity. In theology, we are dependent, in our attempt to bear witness to the God who is concealed and who at the same time reveals himself, on an analogous way (the mode of dissimilar similarity) of speaking about the one who is quite different and about his activity with man. In statements about faith, then, the concepts used have a merely analogous significance with regard to the matter discussed. To what extent does this also apply to moral statements that are determined by faith?

1. Insight as a Presupposition of Moral Action

Acting morally means acting responsibly. This in turn means acting on the basis of insight. This demand for insight does not, however, mean that the one who acts has in every case to understand the objective reasons for his action in order to be able to act morally. It may be quite sufficient for him to be guided by a competent authority with the insight that is required at its disposal. If the person concerned has no positive insight into what he ought to do in a given situation, he cannot be held responsible for his action. His moral decision is in this case reduced to a pure act of formal obedience. An act carried out in obedience can be justified, at least indirectly, in the act of obedience itself, but from the formal point of view it cannot be regarded as a true moral action. It must be possible to have a fundamental insight into and an understanding of what we do if we are to act morally. In the same way, the norms directly regulating our responsible behavior toward our fellow-men and the world must also be open to rational human insight.[4] This does not mean, however, that the individual values that determine these norms are not guaranteed by our faith in God's revelation. It must also always be possible for man to understand without ambiguity the value that determines his action in the concrete or the corresponding good. Our insight into the dignity of man is, for example, made deeper by our faith in God's love of man and in his salvation of man in and through Jesus Christ. If it is to determine our association with our fellow-men in any way, however, this notion of human dignity must be interpreted and made effective by means of unambiguous and universally understood value concepts such as "person," "life" or "corporeal integrity." The validity of a moral norm as such cannot simply be traced back to an authoritative act, nor can it be reduced to evidence for such behavior in Scripture or the Church's tradition. The norm itself must be translucent in the matter itself. Theological positivism is no more valuable in moral theology than legal positivism is in the doctrine of law. One question that inevitably arises in this context, then, is what is meant by "revealed moral demands" in moral theology. Leaving aside the decision itself that is made in faith and religious — and especially sacramental — praxis, what are certainly not meant by these revealed moral demands are demands, the objective content of which is not unambiguously defined and not translucent. According to the traditional theological teaching from Thomas Aquinas onward, the morality of revelation is the true rational morality and is confirmed precisely in this way.[5]

2. Dogmatic and Morally Normative Statements

The need for insight into moral demands leads inevitably to the fundamental question of the relationship between dogmatic statements on the one hand and morally normative statements for which there is evidence in the theology of revelation on the other. Both kinds of statement can only be expressed in human concepts and linguistic forms and both are open to universal interpretation. There are, however, differences between them, at least in accordance with the Church's traditional understanding of revelation. Faith calls for consent to an aspect of reality that could not be known without revelation. We can, for example, only encounter the mysteries of Christ and the Trinity in faith. The dogmatic statements which attempt to express such contents of knowledge have to make use of analogous concepts.[6] For example, when we confess that God loves man, both terms, "God" and "love," have clearly to be understood in an analogous sense. The statement that man is loved by God is also a statement of faith made in analogous concepts. In the same way, we also speak of the "new creation," "grace" or "supernatural" or "infused" virtues. Unlike these dogmatic statements, which cannot be contained within univocal concepts, normative statements, which determine and regulate man's actions in the concrete, are univocal. The correct association with our fellow-man, who is also loved by God, or the correct way of expressing faithfulness in marriage have to be stated precisely. This means that man's right to live must be precisely defined in legal terms and the conditions governing the bond between man and wife have to be laid down unambiguously. In other words, although there are mysteries of faith, there cannot be any mysterious moral norms of action which cannot be positively defined without ambiguity and quite clearly with regard to the demand that they make on man's relationship with his fellow-men. This formal distinction between dogmatic and morally normative statements is of fundamental importance. Dogmatic statements express truths and our insight into those truths cannot be restricted to the fact that there is no evidence proving that they can be contradicted. Moral norms, on the other hand, make objective demands and it is necessary for us to have a positive insight into the content of these demands.[7] A fundamentally constitutive element of responsible interpersonal activity is that each act must be capable of being understood. This is, however, only one element. The fundamental mystery that can only be understood in faith in an analogous sense — the fact that God loves man — has an anthropological significance with serious consequences for moral activity. We must now consider in more detail how faith influences our moral actions.

B. The Influence of Faith

It should be clear from our outline of the ethos of the early Church how the apostles and especially Paul tried to orientate their proclamation toward Jesus' words and behavior (see above § 18 A). Their appeal to the Lord led to a fundamental attitude both toward the individual and toward the community, with the result that it is certainly possible to speak of a distinctive ethos on the part of the Christian community. This ethos, which was based on faith, was and is fundamentally human in its orientation and can be communicated. It is distinctive not because its individual normative statements are exclusive, but because it has a total attitude that is based on and justified by faith and provides an entirely new sphere of understanding which gives a definite status and value to the various behavioral norms.

1. The Justification of Christian Existence

The foundation, meaning and justification of man's expression of freedom can be found in faith in God's saving action in Jesus Christ. Man's continuing memory of the paraenesis of the early Church, reminding him of what God has done and still does for him and his fellow-men in Jesus Christ therefore draws attention again and again to this foundation and motivation of the Christian moral life. He is required to make a fundamental decision — *metanoia* or conversion — which determines the whole of his moral existence as its *fundamentum et radix* (DS 1532). His life, in other words, is a life led on the basis of a decision in favor of God. For the believer, God thus becomes a living reality — by deciding for him and committing himself to him. "Faith seizes hold of the truth of life and accepts the risk of trusting it. According to Scripture, this truth of life is called God. But this is only half correct. In the New Testament — that is, at the climax of the biblical history of revelation — we are told that a man was this truth. It would therefore be more correct to say that this truth was revealed in Jesus of Nazareth, in the way he lived and in the expression of his life."[8]

In this, what we have is not primarily an enlightenment about God, but a human truth. Jesus was and is that truth. "We are bound therefore to say that the Christian will find the specifically Christian element when he discovers Jesus' form of life, not when he finds God or Jesus, but when he finds Jesus' form of existence. That is the meaning of the imitation of Jesus. We can express this idea emphatically by saying that it is not specifically Christian simply to confess him, but to be and to remain in him. These are not mutually exclusive."[9] We have therefore, as Christians, to deduce from Jesus' form of existence what the ultimate reality that determines our own existence is, and what our attitude toward that reality should be. This ultimate reality is what Jesus himself called "Abba, Father." It was from this personally trusting relationship with God that Jesus derived his existence. This fundamental decision for God in the Spirit of Christ, a decision that is experienced in faith, hope and love, forms the heart of the Christian ethos. It is possible to regard this existence as exclusively Christian to the extent that it is based, in a reflected relationship, on the message and the activity of Christ. Man's whole life is given an entirely new orientation in this new existence which he experiences in Christ. "As grace, faith and love, Christian life can only be a life of fullness and therefore of thankfulness — a *eucharistia*."[10] This "subjection of the whole of Christian existence to the direction of the exalted Lord (Jn. 8.12)"[11] as a following of his way is primarily an expression of transcendental freedom. J. Fuchs was right when he spoke of a "Christian intention" and a state of "having and continuing to be decided,"[12] a state that has to be made concrete in individual, reflected and categorially moral decisions. This fundamental decision for God is brought about in man by God himself. It is also man's response to this initiative, but it is inspired and sustained by God's presence and power to attract. It is expressed in many individual acts, although it cannot be identified with any of them. On the one hand, we may therefore say that man's acts do not in themselves have any significance in constituting salvation. We can no more bring about our own salvation than we can, by our own human commitment, achieve the final and complete evolution of the world. For the Christian, this means that praxis can never be the only factor in human life that creates meaning. This factor can only be the contemplation of what always is. On the other hand, however, we are also bound to point out that our activity cannot be in any sense excluded from the structure of salvation. It has the function of sustaining salvation — in other words, it is the commitment of our own freedom, by which we share in the preparation of our own fulfillment, and the realization of our own human history, in which we are moving toward our promised fulfillment.

2. The Deepening of Morally Relevant Insights

Here I would refer the reader to the section on the biblical foundation for the influence of faith on the formation of ethics. It is an undisputed fact that faith had a deep influence on concrete norms of action. Examples of this influence are the Old Testament laws of property and the New Testament demands of faithfulness, the love of one's neighbor and the rejection of adultery. Here we must consider above all the way in which this influence was and is exerted.

From what has been said so far, it should be clear that faith ensures the continuity of the transcendent obligatory claim that the categorial structure of morality — in other words, both the contingency of the goods and values involved and the intelligibility of the objective demand involved — continues to be valid. Christian morality is "in its categorially determined and material aspect a fundamental and substantial human reality, in other words, a morality of authentic humanity." [13] This does not mean, however, that certain goods are not emphasized by our insight into faith or that certain values are not regarded by faith as indispensable. (Examples of these values are the human dignity of slaves and the faithfulness of partners in marriage.) Judged purely on the basis of its content, this influence on the act by which a given value is made real is not exclusively Christian, but when goods and values are considered within the framework of a theological study of man, any such consideration of them undoubtedly forms part of a "distinctively Christian" ethos. [14]

The sphere of meaning that is revealed by faith both limits and modifies the area within which the goods have to be considered before a moral decision can be made. Attempts have been made from the earliest period in the history of the Church to determine in real terms the concrete way in which the human dignity of slaves should be recognized or faithfulness should be achieved in a real marital situation. This has usually been done by a careful and balanced examination of the goods involved (or of the goods and values recognized by faith). In a word, the influence of faith can be discerned within the theological study of man and the anthropological doctrine of goods and values. This is a slow, dynamic process, in which universally human knowledge and faith are inseparably involved. In it, concrete theological statements are made about God, then statements about man and finally unambiguous statements about values. An example of this process is the dogmatic statement that God loves each man and calls on him, despite his sin, to be saved. As a statement about God, this is a descriptive statement and can only be understood analogously. Its anthropological consequence — that is, the descriptive statement about what the fact of divine election and salvation means for man — is also described directly in analogous concepts. The apostolic teaching also described man as renewed "in Christ" or "in the Spirit." This is an analogous way of speaking and so too is the theological concept of "infused virtues." In this idea of a supernatural qualification of natural actions or potential actions that is connected with infused virtue, the relationship with action is only very general. Like a general reference to the love of God and one's neighbor, it touches the transcendental moral act or Christian intention. We are dependent on the formation of an *ordo caritatis* for the concrete moral realization of existence that is justified in this way.[15] Our insights into faith concerning man must also be borne in mind in this process. These can only become a prescription insofar as they are expressed as an unambiguous statement about values. It is, for example, necessary to say that every individual has a personal value that is not dependent on his membership of any social system and that cannot therefore be rejected by any social system.[16]

This insight is understandable in the human sense and it is, nowadays at least, not an exclusively Christian insight.[17] It is, however, as the recent debate about it has demonstrated,[18] in no sense compelling. The struggle to have it acknowledged must inevitably become a political one. This means that Christians cannot be persuaded by any consideration of opportunism or any opinion held by a democratic majority to abandon their attempt to bear witness to human dignity and to fight for the rights of the unborn child or the mentally handicapped adult. What is indispensable for the Christian is also, from the philosophical point of view, translucent with regard to its content of truth, even if it is possibly not compelling. It is therefore not possible for Christians to have a morality if these insights into values are not taken into account. For them as well, life as an absolute value is not in this way necessarily removed from the sphere within which goods can be subjected to a balanced evaluation. The area is narrowed down, it is true, but we continue to operate within the field of humanity, in which ultimate good can only be sought, until the end of time, within a choice between temporary goods.

3. The Demand for Christian Radicalism

Does the condition of rational insight into what is required by the Christian believer also apply to the radical demands made in the Sermon on the Mount? In this example, is the wisdom of the world not overcome by the foolishness of the cross? Does the imitation of the crucified Lord not call for a life led entirely without recourse to reason and calculation? These and similar questions go to the very heart of Christian ethics. In the sense in which they are usually understood, they have to be answered with a simple yes. Whether or not our argument about the intelligibility of moral activity is changed by this fact is, however, a different question.

When we considered the moral message of Jesus himself (§ 16 and 17 above), we showed clearly that his message could only be properly understood within the framework of the proclamation of the kingdom of God as a present and future eschatological reality. The news of the Basileia points to an area in the history of man's salvation in which man's immanent thinking and acting are completely relative. At the same time, however, human thinking is also taken to a very deep and interior level. Any possibility of man's being able to redeem himself is eliminated by the eschatological factor. The expectation of the imminent return of the Lord that flourished in the early Church also compelled Christians to consider the order of goods and to recalculate what was required by the hour of his coming.

There is, however, nothing in the New Testament that suggests that Christians should act without reflection or over-enthusiastically. On the contrary, it contains warnings against this type of action. The objectives revealed by faith call for reflection in action. This, of course, is precisely what I stressed above in the preceding section — that our knowledge of faith modifies our insight into goods and values. We must always, at least in principle, be able to communicate intelligibly our judgment about what is required in this respect for human action. It is only in faith that we can experience the premises that form the basis for a modification of those goods and values. This ought to be perfectly clear with regard to universal ethical statements, but I am of the opinion that it also applies, again in principle, to such decisions made in faith by the Christian as the acceptance of a personal call to marry or to remain celibate or the undertaking to bear witness by nonviolence.

Let me develop what I have just said. In connection with the antitheses contained in the Sermon on the Mount, I have already pointed to the special meaning of Jesus' message with regard to the overcoming of evil. (See above § 17 B 2, "A Separation from Evil.") Jesus' own death, by which man was redeemed, gave a special emphasis to this message. Taking the concrete conflicts of everyday life, the expressions of personal aggression and the human difficul-' ties involved in marital faithfulness and because of deceit and lying as points of departure, he made it clear that none of these problems can be overcome simply by legislation. No really profound help is given to man in a situation of conflict by changing the valid legal norms — either by tightening them or by relieving their tension. No really relevant progress is made by changes of this kind. According to Jesus, only a completely re-orientated way of thinking and acting, made subject to the power of the kingdom of God, can lead men forward. According to his teaching, it was not enough, for example, simply to soften down the practice of revenge by means of a *lex talionis*. He taught that the Christian should be able to do entirely without the need to retaliate for evil and even be ready, on occasion, to offer the other cheek.

The same applies to the laws of divorce and taking oaths. Jesus did not reject either the legal regulation of these two matters or any reform in the law that might be necessary. It is quite clear, however, that he was not primarily or directly preoccupied with the law or with legislation. He was above all concerned with a critical examination of the goods and values in question. His radical demands went to the heart of moral responsibility. They were a challenge to man to criticize and examine himself. They called on man not to be satisfied either with the legal minimum or with a precise estimate of his own insight and strength. He is called upon to extend his vision to the kingdom of God initiated with the coming of Jesus. In this sense, his demand is in striking contrast to the law.

We can only approach the kingdom of God if we trust his promises and in this way overcome our own expectations and fears. A specifically Christian ethos must, in other words, express this antithetical structure of Jesus' proclamation clearly in its system of norms.

CHAPTER 3: THE DEVELOPMENT AND JUSTIFICATION OF MORALLY NORMATIVE JUDGMENTS

Our insight into the goods and values that form the basis of our actions provide the ultimate foundation for our moral judgments about those actions and the norms that are based on them. Without a knowledge of the goods and values involved and of the realities determined by those goods and the attitudes that are made indispensable by those values, we cannot judge whether and in what way our own or other men's actions can be morally justified. Our judgment about the situation, in which we have to consider a definite good such as human life, can, of course, easily be changed into a judgment about action, in other words, a moral judgment. In this case, what has to be taken into consideration simply means what has to be respected in action. Man has a certain dignity which is based on the very fact that he is man and that human dignity has to be respected. Human life and corporeal integrity are, on the basis of our reflection about human experience (see above, § 21), goods with a very high status. They have therefore also to be respected. The obligation to respect these goods is ultimately not based on the goods themselves, but is the result of man's own understanding of the situation and his responsibility. As a moral subject, he is transcendentally called upon to take up a position with regard to the reality involved in the situation. What is revealed in our observation of the situation and our consequent judgment is that a certain good — for example, life itself — is unmistakably the object of moral responsibility. It is morally right to take that object into consideration in action and morally wrong not to take it into consideration.[1] It is possible to do what J. Messner suggests in ascertaining the situation and speak of "synthetic judgments *a priori*," if this situation can be directly ascertained on the basis of human experience and rational reflection (see above, § 19 B 1).

It is also possible, as we have already seen, to express these observations apodictically. The classical example of this is to be found in the decalogue. "Thou shalt not kill" and "thou shalt not commit adultery" are statements which aim to remind the people of the most important goods and values. In this very universal form, apodictic statements can therefore be reduced to analytical judgments, since, according to the meaning at least, what is said is: "thou shalt not kill unjustly" and this can be expressed as "it is unjust to kill unjustly." In the same way, "thou shalt not commit adultery" can be expressed as "it is unfaithful to leave your wife unjustly." Analytical judgments of this kind are, of course, always valid. It is never valueless to make use of this kind of tautology. It had an important part to play as appellative statements within the framework of moral teaching, in which they serve mainly as admonitions.

In considering the justification of morally normative judgments, however, we have to bear in mind man's concrete actions and his practical association with already existing goods and values. How should human dignity be respected in the concrete? How, for example, should we interpret "killing unjustly"? Should the police be allowed to carry and use weapons? Can the death penalty be justified from the moral point of view? What should our attitude be toward tax avoidance, the building of atomic power plants, sexual intercourse between engaged couples and the making of false statements?

If an answer is to be found for these and similar moral questions, we have first to ascertain which goods and values are involved and how they should be assessed. They may, for example, be in competition with each other and this relationship has also to be evaluated. The only possible way of answering these questions is by means of a synthesis of judgments, in other words, in a synthetic judgment *a posteriori*. If we generalize on the basis of this answer, we can make certain normative statements — for example, that tax avoidance is as a rule morally wrong or that armed intervention on the part of the police is, under certain circumstances, morally right. In this chapter, we are particularly concerned with the way in which normative statements of this kind can be justified. In the traditional moral theology, this question was usually discussed in connection with the determination of the *actus humanus* as an *actus moralis (de moralitate actuum humanorum)* and both the object (the objective aim) and the intention of the person acting (the subjective aim) were, under certain circumstances, taken into account. This approach was, in my opinion, correct in principle, but I would prefer to define more precisely the observation that a definite good is already present as an object for the person acting and clarify its importance with regard to the objective justification and validity.

These preliminary remarks should show clearly enough that the justification of norms with which we are concerned in this chapter is only one partial aspect of ethics as a whole. It presupposes an answer to the problem of the justification both of ultimate obligations and of insights into values. It is therefore only with great caution that what I have to say in this chapter should be judged. It is not possible to speak here of an ethical utilitarianism or eudaemonism, if only because a central part is played by the balanced consideration of goods as a way of justifying norms. What I have already said about the justification of obligations and the doctrine of goods and values should also be borne in mind in this chapter. I am of the opinion that it is not possible to construct an ethos on the basis of a single point of view. There are in fact three closely interconnected and fundamental problems that have to be solved and each of them calls for its own method. My attempt to develop a fundamental moral theology could be summarized as an approach to a theologically justified and realistic rational ethical system. In this, the concept of reason[2] should be understood in the relationship with faith that was defined in the preceding section.

§ 23 Two Types of Justification

We are greatly indebted to B. Schüller for having discussed the question of the justification and validity of morally normative judgments in a number of articles.[3] It was he who initiated the debate that has taken place on this subject during the nineteen-seventies.[4] His investigations have shown that two distinct types of argument can be distinguished in the long tradition of Catholic moral theology. Certain actions are judged by an examination of the consequences, whereas in other cases the moral definition seems to exist *a priori* and is independent of the consequences. These forms of justification have, interestingly enough, played an important part in the recent ethical debate.[5] They have been, it is true, very closely interconnected in this discussion, with the result that they have functioned rather as a fundamental principle determining the system. In Catholic moral theology — both in the traditional theology and in that discussed in the recent debate — these two types of justification have the status that I have given them within the framework of ethics as a whole for the justification of norms. Here, in what follows, I shall confine myself to this discussion about moral theology and only marginally refer to analogies and similarities in the debate that has taken place mainly in the English-speaking world about utilitarianism and consequentialism.

A. The Teleological Justification

The theory that all actions must be judged exclusively on the basis of the consequences is the teleological theory, so called because the word is derived from *telos*, end or aim.[6] More and more Catholic moral theologians are becoming convinced that moral norms in the interpersonal sphere[7] can only be justified when all the predictable consequences of the action in question are taken into consideration.

1. The Principal Argument

These theologians' principal argument is based on the assumption that the goods and values that form the foundation of our actions are exclusively conditioned, created and therefore limited goods. Our moral judgment of the action in question can therefore only take place if this conditioned state is taken into account and the goods, which may be in competition with each other, are carefully examined. It is true, of course, that man is unconditionally called on by the absolute ground of all morality. As a contingent being, however, he is only able to realize the absolute good in the goods, which, as contingent goods or values, are "relative" values and as such can never be identified *a priori* as the greatest and highest value which can never be in competition with a higher value. With regard to the goods, the only possible question that remains is that of the good that should be preferred. This means that, if it is not to err by giving an absolute value to what is merely contingent, every concrete categorial decision must ultimately be based on a preferential selection in which a choice must be made according to priorities in goods and values.

2. The Obligatory Nature

This means that there can be no doubt about the relevance of obligatory goods and values or about universally obligatory norms. If norms are called universally obligatory, this does not in any sense mean that they are so for all times in exactly the same way, nor does it mean that a particular form of behavior is independent of every possible condition that is imposed on it and that it is therefore bound to be accepted as obligatory (or as prohibited) without exception or as an absolute. Let us take the death penalty as an example. Until quite recently, there was a general conviction that law and order could only be safeguarded in fact if those who broke the law had to reckon with the death penalty as an ultimate sanction. This meant that the general judgment that the death penalty was, generally speaking, permissible, was a correct judgment. Nowadays it would be very difficult to convince most people of the plausibility of the statement that the only way of guaranteeing the continued existence of law and order was to put those who broke the law, in extreme cases, to death. We therefore have to generalize and express our present conviction in the following way: the death penalty is, generally speaking, not permissible. These judgments are apparently contradictory, but, in view of the conditions presupposed in each case, both are correct. They express a moral norm that is valid *ut in pluribus*. In other words, the universal validity of moral norms really means, when we examine the significance of this concept more closely, a state of being valid in general. The norms are valid insofar as they express what is general or universal and insofar as they include the necessary conditions and take them fully into account. Norms are in this sense not simply well-intentioned pieces of advice which we can treat as we wish. They express obligatory values which we cannot ignore if we wish to act responsibly. They help the individual in his difficult search for morally correct action, but they do not relieve him of the need to examine for himself whether and to what extent the universal prescriptions apply to him in his own concrete situation. He is only able to decide how he should behave in the most moral way if he considers all the values and all the circumstances that are involved.

In connection with this teleological justification of morally normative judgments, it should be clear what may be a good action "in itself" or what may be a bad action "in itself." "In itself" (*in se* or *intrinsece inhonestum*, for example) means that this particular action is determined by an objective value content. Since, however, every created value is conditioned, our judgment about the action in question can only be valid if we presuppose the conditions imposed by the corresponding value. There can therefore not be any actions in the sphere of interpersonal activity that can be called, independently of all conditions, circumstances or motives, *a priori* always and without exception bad in themselves. [8]

On the other hand, there are many statements in the pronouncements of the Church's teaching office which amount to a moral condemnation of individual actions that is unconditional. In the encyclical *Humanae vitae*, for example, we read that sexual intercourse that is deliberately or intentionally made infertile is an immoral act in itself (*intrinsece inhonestum*) and that it is never permissible, however serious the reasons may be, to do evil for a good purpose, in other words, to want something which will harm man's nature according to the moral order (see paragraph 14). This is correct insofar as a morally bad action can never be justified by a good intention. This is not explicitly stated in the text of the encyclical, but the concept *intrinsece inhonestum* is insinuated as meaning without any conditions, in other words, absolutely contrary to morals, because the argument comes down ultimately to a prohibition of artificial means of preventing conception under all circumstances and without taking the possible consequences into account.

Anyone who is convinced of the validity of the teleological form of argument is bound to have reservations regarding this type of justification. Whoever recognizes the contingent nature of all the values that determine human activity must inevitably be open to the need to take conditions into consideration and to examine the goods in question. This applies to all contingent goods, including the good of procreation. We cannot say, in other words, that it can never contradict a greater good and therefore that it is obligatory for everyone in an absolute way (that is, the absolute way implied in the encyclical with regard to the norm of regulation of conception). [9]

3. Objections

a) The commonest objection nowadays to the teleological form of argument is based on the fact that it seems to give a relative value to all norms. These norms have teleologically only hypothetical validity — they are valid only for a certain period and in a certain situation. This objection is correct in principle and the fears of those who suspect the teleological argument are not without foundation. They do not, however, constitute a valid argument against the correctness of teleology. A conditioned universal validity does not mean a complete absence of obligation. Everything depends on how it is proclaimed and presented. For centuries, moral theologians have justified most operative norms of human action by a balanced consideration of the goods involved. This is unquestionably the most obvious way of dealing with life itself as the most fundamental of all goods. For this reason, it occurred to nobody that life was at our disposal or that the norms involved had no obligatory force. The teleological argument is basically concerned with a criticism of wrong attempts to give an absolute value to norms, when such an absolute value is ultimately given only to lying and the use of sexuality that is contrary to nature. We shall return to this question later, but in the meanwhile let me underline the fact that the believer knows that there is only one highest and absolute good — God himself, who calls on us to prove our worth unconditionally in faith, hope and love in this world of relative goods and values and to behave in this way in a permanently provisional situation.

b) There is also a second objection to the teleological justification, based on the argument that fundamental human goods should not be directly harmed. If there is a conflict between two values and both cannot be realized, it is only permissible to harm one of those values indirectly. This objection has been raised by G. Grisez especially[10] but it is not easy to see precisely what he means by fundamental human goods. It would seem that he means "goods and values," without making a distinction between them. Life is also mentioned in the same breath as righteousness and justice.[11]

This, then, is the real problem. No distinction is made between goods and values, nor is each term examined and defined. As they are presented to our consciousness, goods do not have a moral, but a pre-moral character. Even harming them directly is seen to be necessary again and again in life. There has, moreover, never been any objection in the Church's tradition to directly harming life, for example, by the imposition of the death penalty, in which the most fundamental good, if not the most fundamental value, is involved. According to my definition, values, on the other hand, have a moral character. For this reason, they should not be directly harmed. I must not, in other words, be unjust, undisciplined or unfaithful. There is certainly general agreement about this. No one who supports the teleological argument would maintain that this was wrong. We cannot ask, then, whether someone may be unjust or unfaithful, but we can and indeed must ask under what circumstances someone is no longer obliged without harming faithfulness, for example, to a promise. The objection therefore seems to me not to be a valid argument against the teleological justification of morally normative judgments. On the other hand, I would not deny the importance of the way in which a physical evil is caused or a good is harmed, on the basis of legal and therefore also of social and ethical reasons.

The principle of the double effect of an action was evolved in Catholic moral theology for the purpose of judging certain situations of conflict in human activity.[12] According to this principle, a certain evil that may be necessary if an essential good has to be attained is justified or at least tolerated under the following four conditions:[13]

1. The action that results in a bad consequence must be good or indifferent in itself; it should not be morally bad;

2. The intention underlying this action must be good; a bad consequence should not be intended;

3. The bad consequence must result as directly as the good effect; otherwise it would be a means of achieving the good effect and in this way intended;

4. There must also be a correspondingly serious reason for taking the bad consequence into the bargain.

In applying this principle of the double effect, the bad consequence of an action is justified, in the presence of a sufficient reason, but by excluding the direct intention of the will, as an unintentional side-effect. The traditional application of this principle in moral theology is therefore based essentially on a distinction between what is directly and what is indirectly intended. In this way, a collision with deontologically interpreted norms is avoided.

If this distinction between what is directly and what is indirectly intended — a distinction that would seem to be essential to the argument used by traditional moral theologians — is examined more closely, a certain lack of logic becomes apparent in the criteria used and what is presented as a side-effect that is taken into the bargain is seen to be in fact — perhaps indirectly, but nonetheless — an intention or a means.[14] "Either the good effect is brought about via the bad effect or the bad effect must also have been intended as a *conditio sine qua non*, however little it may have been desired."[15] This is the point of departure taken by those who have participated in the recent debate about the principle of the double effect.

In one article, P. Knauer[16] rejected the distinction made in the traditional argument based on the principle of the double effect between direct and indirect in the matter of intention as the decisive criterion for the moral evaluation of actions and replaced it with the concept of the adequate reason. He said: "If the reason for an action is adequate, it only determined the *finis operis*, with the result that the action will be morally good."[17] He also believed that the answer to the question raised by this problem, namely, how should the adequacy of the reason for the action be judged, was to be found in Thomas's formula, *actus . . . proportionatus fini* (*Summa Theologiae* II–II, 64, 7). This, in Knauer's opinion, meant the same as "the action is in accordance with its reason."[18] It is clear that a reason is adequate "insofar as the action is adequate to the value that it follows."[19] The moral content of an action has therefore not to be measured against the bad consequences that result from it, but against the adequate reason for permitting the consequence.[20]

L. Janssens[21] took a somewhat different point of departure, but reached a very similar conclusion. His point of departure was in fact Thomas's theory of action, which is based on the inner act of the will,[22] composed of man's striving toward his aim (*intentio*) and his choice of means (*electio*),[23] *electio* and *intentio* being two aspects of the one act,[24] the formal object of which is the aim or end (*finis*). This aim also determines the *actus exterior* as the means of reaching the aim. This external act, then, forms the material object of the action as a whole.[25] The aim or end is ultimately what determines whether an action is moral.[26] This aim of the inner act of the will can, however, never be ontically bad or evil, in Janssen's opinion, if what is meant by the end or aim definitively gives an aim, in the full sense of the word, to the activity of the subject. What is ontically bad or evil can, however, be the aim, Janssens insisted, if that aim is not intended as the ultimate aim, but is only a *finis medius et proximus* toward a higher aim.[27] It is precisely in this way that the material object has to be adequate to the formal object. Janssens' criterion is therefore the *debita proportio* of the means compared with the aim.[28] It is this which determines whether an evil in the moral sense is intended or not.[29]

In his argument, B. Schüller[30] made use of the distinction between what is morally bad and what is nonmorally evil that is implicit in Knauer's article.[31] With regard to collaboration with another in what is morally bad, the distinction between what is directly intended and what is permitted and indirectly intended is a correct one. Sin should never be positively intended. For a sufficiently important reason, however, giving occasion for sin may be taken into the bargain. The distinction between direct and indirect, however, ceases to have any meaning when it is a question of causing nonmoral evil. Physical evil of this kind can also be directly intended and caused when an appropriate reason exists. This in brief is Schüller's argument.

All three examinations of the problem — Knauer's, Janssens' and Schüller's — show clearly that what is indirectly intended according to the classical argument based on the principle of the double effect is in fact a direct intention in all those cases in which there is an essential connection. "What is seen as a secondary consequence that is taken into the bargain proves to be a means that has been chosen silently and without open confession, in other words, an evil means or an indispensable presupposition by which the aim in view can be attained."[32] In the fourth condition governing the principle of the double effect, any dependence of the good effect on the bad effect is explicitly rejected, but this dependence in fact exists, showing that the indirect intention is directly intended for the sake of the aim, which takes precedence. The earlier statement "never directly" therefore has to be replaced by the new version: "directly on the basis of an adequate reason."

I believe that these three authors' analysis of the concept of the double effect is fundamentally correct. I would also agree with Schüller that a balanced consideration of the goods, in other words, a teleological justification of the moral quality of the action, is of first importance in cases where a physical evil is caused. I think too, however, that it is also important to take into account the way in which nonmoral, physical evil may be caused. The distinction that has to be observed in this case is between a voluntary action (*volo agere*) as the cause and a voluntary omission (*volo non agere*). It is not a matter of indifference whether a patient's intravenous infusion is turned off and his death is therefore hastened or whether he is given an injection that will be immediately fatal. As far as the law is concerned, it is clear that a person can be held responsible for omitting or ceasing therapy only to the extent that this can be proved contrary to his or her duty. The same person can, however, in every case be held responsible for an action that has a direct effect. As far as the moral aspect is concerned, I am unable to recognize any essential difference. The difference can only be conditioned by the principle of *periculum commune* or legal safety. Since, however, there can be no action that is entirely free from the social structure, this distinction, which is not essential, is, in my opinion, also of importance in respect of moral responsibility.

B. The Deontological Justification

The theory that not all actions are morally determined exclusively by their consequences is known as the deontological theory. The name is derived from *to deon*, duty. The theory recognizes that many actions have to be judged teleologically. It does not, however, recognize that this is generally the case. Those who support it are convinced that there are actions that are, independently of all possible circumstances, in themselves contrary to morals, whatever consequences may result from them. Among such actions they include, for example, the false statement (or lying) and the exclusion of procreation from the sexual act (masturbation or sterilization). In their view too, there are also actions that are, at least under certain circumstances, always and without exception forbidden, irrespective of the consequences. The killing of an innocent person (*occisio innocentis*) is such an action. In public discussion on this question, actions are often said to be obviously always forbidden under all possible circumstances, but such actions can frequently and without difficulty be traced back to analytical judgments. Examples of such actions that are regarded as always bad are murder, perjury and adultery. There can be no doubt about the moral evil of murder, for example, which is called "unlawfully killing" or adultery, which is known as "unlawful sexual intercourse." An immoral action is, of course, always immoral. It is possible to formulate any number of statements in which the value judgment expressed in the predicate is also included in the subject (see above, note 8). What is not possible is to conduct a meaningful scientific discussion about this question within the framework of the question of the justification of moral judgments. We have to confine ourselves here to a discussion about the justification of these two categories of action.

1. The Argument Based on the Threat of Universal Danger

This argument takes a consideration of the goods involved as its fundamental point of departure. It is therefore really a teleological argument. The assumption that the legal and moral order of society is threatened, however, excludes all possible exceptions. Many writers have attempted to justify the prohibition, without exception, of all extramarital sexual relationships in this way.[33] There are undeniably cases where neither the well-being of the children (*bonum prolis*) nor the personal well-being of the lovers would appear to be threatened, but, so these writers argue, to leave the decision to those concerned in such cases would constitute a serious danger to the social order. However important it may be for the universal well-being of society and for the institutional values to be included in any examination of the goods in such cases, a reference to these goods cannot justify the fact that there can be no exceptions to the norm. There is always the possibility that any harm that may perhaps be caused might even be averted by those concerned (for example, by preserving silence) or so diminished that it could be outweighed by a positive good. This argument based on the threat of universal danger is ultimately teleological.

A very similar argument is based on defective justification. Here too, suicide and the killing of an innocent person is forbidden without exception. As Schüller has correctly pointed out, a false understanding of human responsibility is often to be found at the base of this argument.[34] What I have said above about theonomous autonomy (§ 5 B 2) applies here. A further factor, however, is also to be found underlying this form of argument. Moral theologians, who are responsible for the justification of norms, are bound to ask whether, in the case of a definite action such as the killing of an innocent person and when all the various possibilities have been taken into account, there may be any situation in which an exception could possibly be found after all the goods involved have been responsibly considered. If such an exception cannot be found, then the prohibition can be regarded factually as being valid under all circumstances and without exception. Yet even this practical form of the argument, which is to some degree correct because it is pragmatic, does not in principle go beyond the teleological argument. Among all finite goods, there is not one of which it may be said that there cannot be another that is more important. Deontology, then, can only be served by a particular understanding of the natural order.

2. The Appeal to the Natural Order

The traditional Catholic teaching about the natural law has for centuries formed the basis of the practice of considering goods in order to evolve operative rules of behavior. As we have already seen (for example, in § 19 B above), this does not mean that we have to go back to the *rectitudo naturalis* for this. With regard to lying, for instance, Thomas Aquinas was able to say that it was the natural intention (*intentio naturae*) of speech for man to say what he was thinking and feeling. For this reason, Thomas maintained, a lack of truthfulness was contrary to the nature of speaking and therefore also contrary to human nature as such (see *Summa Theologiae* II–II, 110, 3). He consequently rejected the false statement made in order to avoid a great evil (II–II, 110, 3 ad 4).

In this example, Thomas made use of an argument that would be called "essentialist" if it had been used by a neo-Thomist. From the whole body of Thomas's teaching, however, it is clear that the appeal to nature has to be seen in the context of the rational order.[35] Even Francisco de Suarez, who concentrated on the morality of the objectively existing act itself in a way that had a decisive influence on moral theology in recent centuries,[36] explicitly emphasized the need "to examine the conditions and circumstances under which the act concerned may be in itself bad or good"[37] if that act was to be fully understood. It should therefore be clear that the inner determination of the action (*malitia intrinseca*) cannot be equated with an unconditional (or absolute) moral determination.

A new understanding of the natural law evolved for the first time at the end of the nineteenth and at the beginning of the twentieth centuries. The divine order of nature, in which the will of God himself was included, gradually replaced the earlier objectively justified rational order. Vermeersch, for example, criticized the moral theologians of the eighteenth and nineteenth centuries for regarding the moral order as an objectively justified legal order. In his opinion, the moral order was presented as a secondary order that was justified by moral reason on the basis of a previously existing reality. Individual actions were judged according to the significance of their objects and the possible consequences. On the other hand, the true nature of God's moral law had to be recognized. This, Vermeersch insisted, was already given in the order of man's being. It arose directly from the being of man and the world surrounding him. It could be known by abstracting and generalizing from human experience. In principle it was unchangeable. It was also above all God's order and to harm it was therefore always and in every case bad. The only difference that existed was concerned with the *gravitas materiae*. Finally, Vermeersch believed that the moral order could only be harmed in its substance or in its integrity, a substantial harm, concerning man and his natural disposition, being always a grave sin and a harm done to the integrity of the moral order being only a venial sin.[38]

All that I would wish to add here is a reminder of what I said above (§ 19) about the natural law. In particular, I would draw attention to the difficulty — even impossibility — of knowing an essential order of being of such a concrete kind. Moral theologians do not dispute the fact that the moral order is rooted in fundamental values that are previously given to man, are not at his disposal and are obligatory. This link with values is, however, weakened by placing too much reliance on metaphysical knowledge. As long ago as the nineteen-fifties, Karl Rahner pointed to the danger of depending too much on the argument based on natural law in moral theology.[39] Only recently, J. Ratzinger pointed to the possible consequences of this procedure: "If we try to justify values metaphysically and derive them from metaphysical knowledge without giving sufficient attention to the fundamental possibilities of metaphysics, the whole structure will be in danger of being reduced to an unfounded, unreal and even fictitious level."[40] At the point where it is very difficult to apply fundamental values to concrete human action, it would be wrong to try to replace a plausible justification by a form of positivism based on the natural moral law "that might attempt to base a theocratic magisterial legislation on a presumably metaphysical knowledge. . . . What might be accepted as a pragmatic rule could not be accepted if it were suggested as an eternal truth of the natural law."[41]

Section Three: The Church's Contribution

Theology is not a private affair, but a science that takes place within the framework of the Church. It is one of the essential functions of the Church. Because the Church is built on faith in God's saving activity in Jesus Christ, its constantly renewed understanding of God's revelation in history inevitably enables it to express itself as a community of believing people who are bound together in the same faith. Theology has the task of furthering this understanding of the Christian message in the widest sense. As theological ethics, moral theology is therefore fundamentally concerned with the Church's moral and religious consciousness of faith. According to the manuals, the "direct source" of this consciousness of faith is to nourish the whole of theological study. This can be done in various ways. The situation in contemporary secularized society, in which this moral consciousness of faith is often either challenged or critically questioned, has always to be taken seriously into account. It is important to listen to people's questions and doubts and to give a convincing answer in faith. In this, theologians have to take care neither to adapt their thinking too easily to the norms of society nor to give it an absolute value which might be false. This, at least, has been my endeavor throughout the whole of this work, which I regard as no more than a contribution written in the light of the Church's understanding of faith. This final section is added only in order to clarify a few of the points that have arisen in recent years in the debate within the Church about a number of questions connected with moral theology.

§ 24 The Church and Moral Norms

Our examination of the Bible and the doctrine of the natural law has shown clearly that the moral content of God's claim cannot simply be preserved and handed down either in a collection of biblical statements or in a selection of pronouncements about the natural law. The message of God's rule and kingdom, the Basileia proclaimed by Jesus and the most important commandment to love God and one's fellow-men has to be made concrete again and again in new historically conditioned forms. The discovery and formulation of concrete moral directives is therefore a historical process in which the various offices and branches of the Church have an important part to play. The only valid point of reference here is "the event of Jesus himself . . . not an abstract *lex aeterna* existing outside or above history and communicating absolute values directly deduced from historical norms. In other words, the direction of our thought should not be from an order of being that is above history to a situation within history, but from the ontological aspect of the event of Jesus in the past to the present, in which we are responsible for our own insights and decisions. For believers, the order that transcends history is contained within the historical event of Jesus."[1]

The experience of faith of the whole Church is therefore of great importance. It enables us to know the moral truth and to make this truth concrete in practical norms of action. This experience of faith is discussed below in section A. This truth has also to be communicated and has therefore to be incorporated into social thinking and acting (see section B). The Church's teaching office also has a specific function in applying the truths of faith to morality (section C).

A. The Experience of Faith of the Whole Church

The task of finding concrete norms of behavior in order to solve the very difficult problems confronting contemporary society cannot be left exclusively to the Church's teaching office or to moral theologians. The whole of the Church has to share in this responsibility, despite the great degree of uncertainty that exists between the traditional view of the teaching office and the co-responsibility of the Church as a whole. A clear distinction can, of course, be made between the process of discovery of the truth on the one hand and a necessary decision, when the circumstances point to the need for this, on the part of the authentic[2] teaching office of the Church on the other. In accordance with a generally accepted theological procedure, the Church's teaching office has an irreplaceable function only in the formal act of presenting a truth of faith. There can be no doubt that all members of the Church are called upon to discover the truth and that they are given the power to carry out this increasingly comprehensive task. "In principle, there are no different grades of perfection that are mutually exclusive and there is also no knowledge that is reserved for a minority in the body of Christ."[3]

The truth that is contained in the moral message of Christianity is one that has to be experienced in Christian life and ultimately also verified in a life experienced in faith. The witness borne by committed Christians cannot therefore be ignored. They are able to discover norms "from below" in the way we discussed at some length above in the section on experience. In principle, the same rules also apply to this procedure. Here too factual behavior as such has, of course, no normative or at least no direct normative power. What is important in the contribution of the whole Church is the conviction that is inherent in a factual attitude and its struggle for recognition in society, where it can develop a normative power. Within the Church, however, it would be difficult to say that a conviction of this kind is without insight into faith or irrational, because the life of the Church is determined by it long before it is given legal or official recognition in the Church. This movement from below has always made a most important contribution to the evolution of concrete forms of behavior in the sphere of moral order throughout the history of the Church. A very important part has, of course, been played by saints and heretics. There have also been many movements stressing poverty and one of their main aims has been to remind the Church of the relative nature of wealth and possessions. In the nineteenth century, "social Catholicism" was a striking movement from below and, more recently, there was the struggle for the recognition of religious freedom and the active preparations for the Second Vatican Council. It is to be hoped that in other spheres of the Church's life the striking discrepancy that exists today between the values of so many believers and the pronouncements made by the Church's teaching office[4] will eventually lead to the development of further normative statements. These and similar developments within the Church are naturally closely connected with certain social presuppositions. Man is both a Christian and a citizen and for this reason the process within the Church is necessarily an important factor in the development of society as a whole. The way this debate within the Church takes place is therefore also relevant to the social task.

B. The Social Task

Our aim as Christians should not be to cause social divisions by means of Christian ethics, but rather to build up an order based on a universal consensus. The Church must therefore be given the right to take part in the debate on moral reason. The fact that we have become emancipated from the power of the Church and its function in guiding and teaching all members of society and that our moral consciousness has become secularized should not lead to the Church's exclusion from the task of providing an ethos for society. No one really wants this to happen. No theologian has ever suggested that the Church should not play any part in formulating social ethics and the Church's critics are the first to raise their voices against the bishops and Christians generally whenever the latter are silent about concrete moral questions.

It is not this, however, that is the real object of controversy. The subjects in dispute are the authority, the reasons and the degree of certainty with which the Church is able to make pronouncements and even firm decisions about concrete moral questions. This controversy became particularly urgent and heated in connection with the encyclical *Humanae vitae* over ten years ago. Following the First Vatican Council, theology became restricted to asserting formally the authoritative (and infallible) pronouncements of the Church's teaching authority about questions to do with the natural law. The manuals of moral theology of the period that followed the council quite firmly subordinated their moral doctrine as such — and this included everything that came within that category — to the teaching authority of the Church. Such statements as this were frequently made: "If the Church has the task of leading men on their way to eternal salvation, then she leads, teaches and decides with divine authority."[5]

Three stereotyped arguments can be found in the manuals, illustrating the Church's authority in questions connected with the natural law. The first is that the Church is competent to judge about the natural law because it is confirmed by supernatural revelation,[6] is organically connected with revelation,[7] is contained in it[8] and is perfected by it.[9] The second argument is that, because the supernatural aim also calls for the fulfillment of the natural moral law,[10] the Church, as the "infallible guardian of morality"[11] and the institution responsible for proclaiming "the whole truth of God,"[12] has also to pronounce about the natural law. The third of these stereotyped arguments is that, because it would be contrary to the holiness of the Church if it taught "what is not honest,"[13] the whole *honestum* is within its competence. The Church therefore claims to be able to make infallible decisions.[14] In all the editions, from the first to the last, of the manual of moral theology compiled by J. Mausbach and G. Ermecke, we read, for example, that "the infallible decisions of the Church's teaching authority can be applied not only to the revealed truths of Christianity, but also to the truths of natural ethics."[15]

Such statements can be found in all the Catholic moral teaching of the period and what is common to them all is this broadly based claim that the Church's teaching office has the highest authority to judge in moral matters. This claim was made on the basis of very generalized theoretical considerations, but nothing precise was ever said about when this authority should be used or what the consequences might be. Concrete examples were very rarely given[16] and indeed it was often stated explicitly that it would be difficult to indicate precisely the degree of certainty that should be attributed to moral statements.[17] The division between what is fallible and what is infallible is never very clear.

This lack of clarity is of no real practical significance for members of the Church. In cases where there is no certainty of infallibility, absolute consent is not required. Catholics should not, however, "appeal to the statement (customarily applied as an argument against private opinions) that 'the authority is as valid as its reasons.' Even if one of the Church's directives seems not to be justified on the basis of the reasons supporting it, the obligation to obey it still remains."[18] It is hardly necessary to discuss this obligation to obedience in the case of the need to observe a positive law in the Church. What is open to question, however, is what this declaration means when an interpretative statement or an opinion about the natural law is contained within a directive of the Church. The mature person must, in such a case, act responsibly and morally above all in accordance with his insight and in this objective reasons are of first importance. In such questions, a competent leader will be trusted if he is convinced that only objective reasons have played an essential part in establishing the authoritative norm. Even if an appeal is made to the rational aspect of faith, morally normative statements must be used rationally. At every stage of the argument, their categorial structure must be taken fully into account. The natural moral law must be demonstrated by argument. It is no longer possible to appeal to a rational insight in the case of believing or unbelieving man in contemporary society and at the same time to call for a moral allegiance that is not capable of following the rational reasons provided. This, then, is the fundamental cause of the crisis of authority brought about by the publication of *Humanae vitae*.

There are clear signs that a change has taken place in recent years in the attitude toward the teaching authority of the Church, both with regard to the association between the laity and the bishops and with regard to the interpretation of the documents of the Church. This change has been observed at several of the recent diocesan synods that have taken place in West Germany.

One clear example has been the changed attitude of the German bishops toward the question of contraception. It is well known that, according to the Church's teaching authority, only one method — complete or partial continence within marriage — is permitted. What is remarkable, however, is that no lay person is completely committed to an exclusive application of this one way permitted by the Church. The only conclusion that can be drawn from both the findings of the survey that preceded the most recent joint synod and the discussions of the preparatory commission and both of the plenary sessions is that an overwhelming majority of Catholics regard it as right that there should be greater freedom of personal decision in the choice of contraceptive methods. This raised the important question of how to do justice to this conviction without going directly against the papal decision.

According to the draft of the first reading, the husband and wife were responsible for the choice of method, but the choice should not be made for selfish reasons. This was regarded by the bishops as a "privatization" of the decision and they pointed to their right of veto and at the same time insisted on the statement: "the decision . . . must be sought and found in a conscientious examination of objective criteria and in accordance with the norms proposed by the Church's teaching office." This statement, of course, makes the norm of the Church's authority exclusively the basis of any judgment about the method used. The commission was not able to give its consent to this statement. Although it admitted without hesitation that no Catholic should simply ignore a norm proclaimed by the Church and treat it as though it was irrelevant to his or her life, the commission was unyielding in its insistence on the possibility of a different judgment being reached by a Catholic after a conscientious examination of the Church's norm. The members of the commission believed that justice could be done to this possibility by the statement: "judgment about the contraceptive method must include in the conscientious examination the objective norms proposed by the Church's teaching office." Here, the word "include" is of central importance. It gives quite a different emphasis to the idea of a divergent judgment from that given by the statement that the decision must be "sought and found" in accordance with the Church's objective norms. It proved difficult in the debate in the plenary assembly to convince a powerful opposition that the statement suggested by the commission did greater justice to the contemporary situation in the Church. One counter-argument was that it was in principle too theoretical and not sufficiently helpful for the "ordinary Christian" and another was that it was not consistent with the papal decision. The great majority of bishops, however, recognized that the synod could not pass a resolution that directly contradicted the papal decision and that it would have to be satisfied with a general principle that would express the way in which Christians should approach a statement made by the Church's teaching authority. This, then, is the inestimable importance of this decision — it makes it clear that a Catholic who is faithful to his Church can make a decision different from that of the teaching office of the Church and that he can also hold this view and even put it into practice either personally or, for example, as a doctor, in which case he can recommend it to his patients.

If theologians — or the teaching authority of the Church — believe that they have a greater knowledge of a moral question from other sources than those providing objective reasons, they are bound to make it clear to Catholics and to all men of good will where this greater knowledge is obtained, what they have to say that is more than the knowledge based on objective reasons and why they assert it with such confidence. Otherwise, the arguments will only convince insofar as they are able to demonstrate their validity. No one with really good arguments needs to be frightened by this. The way in which the Church has, for instance, adopted an

254

attitude toward questions of social justice or peace and the echo that its pronouncements on these questions has aroused in men's hearts show clearly enough that the Church is able to increase its moral authority to the extent that it is prepared to take part in open debate and argument.

C. The Specific Teaching Authority of the Church

According to the same teaching of both Vatican Councils,[19] the Church's specific teaching authority is concerned with the application of faith to morality. The Constitution *Lumen gentium* says explicitly that the teaching office has *fidem credendam et moribus applicandam praedicare* (para. 25). Two questions arise from this statement. The first is: what is the consequence of this specific insight into faith for moral knowledge? The second, more oblique question is: what are the possible reactions that an increase in knowledge in secular ethics might have on the message of faith (*sancte custodiendum et fideliter exponendum*)?[20] An objective answer can only be given to these questions if the distinctive character of the moral reality is carefully considered. (See above, § 22.) Bearing these insights into the distinctive nature of morals in mind, we may say that there are several ways in which faith can be applied to morality. We can also indicate the Church's task here.

In the first place, faith throws light on the fundamental and all-embracing aim of transcendentally moral activity. The structure of salvation revealed by this belongs, together with the doctrine of grace and justification, to the teaching office of the Church. In the second place, man's theonomous claim in expressing his freedom is also guaranteed by this aim. The Church has the task of defending this theonomous claim against any attempt to interpret the claim of obligation ideologically and thus to make values that are merely contingent absolute. The Church must, however, also recognize that a theonomous justification of the claim of obligation does not in any way change or restrict reason as an attribute of the creature, but on the contrary sets it free precisely as a creaturely attribute.

Thirdly, the content of concrete moral norms of action can be justified and confirmed at a deeper level and given a firmer basis by the Church's teaching office. (Examples of this are man's right to dispose of his own possessions, marital fidelity and so on.) It is the task of the Church's teaching authority to safeguard these norms. Insights into man and his behavior are therefore of great importance. These insights, however, can only help to determine the content of a directive when they are expressed in an unambiguous statement about values. It should also be borne in mind that moral norms are never made absolute simply because they are proclaimed by the Church's teaching office. The official procedure does not as such mean that they become valid under all circumstances and without exception.[21] They are, in general, valid subject to the conditions that apply to them and the contingency of these conditions makes them open to further development. Insofar as this validity is safeguarded by a value that is, in turn, guaranteed by an insight into faith, norms can be proposed as universally valid with an ultimately obligatory force.[22]

Each generation of Christians has to experience the moral message of the gospel in accordance with the practical and critical spirit of the age. This horizontal dimension of the message of Christ that is experienced again and again in the present is at the same time connected in a vertical dimension with all the periods of the past. There is an irreversible process in our rational knowledge of man and his world and this process also influences our understanding of Jesus' message. The history of the Christian gospel forms part of the whole cultural, intellectual and spiritual history of the West. They are interdependent and each has always conditioned the other. In this relationship, insights of lasting importance in interpersonal behavior have been gained. There is also a reciprocal process of knowledge in the application of faith to morals and it is difficult to say — and hardly worth while to dispute — whether the impetus is provided in any particular case by a theological insight or by an advance in moral reason. The most important and indeed the only important factor in this process is that the Church should recognize and undertake its task again and again. In this way, the Church can continue to be a sign of hope for the world.

List of Abbreviations used in the Notes

BK	Biblischer Kommentar	THAT	Theologisches Handwör-
BZAW	Beihefte zur Zeitschrift für		terbuch zum Alten
	die alttestamentliche Wis-		Testament
	senschaft	ThLZ	Theologische Literatur-
Cath	Catholica		zeitung
Coll Gand	Collationes Gandavenses	ThPh	Theologie und Philosophie
DThA	Deutsche Thomas Ausgabe	ThSt	Theologische Studien
EKK	Evangelisch-katholischer	ThWAT	Theologisches Wörterbuch
	Kommentar zum Neuen		zum Alten Testament
	Testament	ThWNT	Theologisches Wörterbuch
FZPhTh	Freiburger Zeitschrift für		zum Neuen Testament
	Philosophie und Theologie	VTS	Vetus Testamentum Sup-
Gr	Gregorianum		plementum
HAT	Handbuch zum Alten	WiWei	Wissenschaft und Weisheit
	Testament	WMANT	Wissenschaftliche Mono-
Her Korr	Herder Korrespondenz		graphien zum Alten und
HPhG	Handbuch philosophischer		Neuen Testament
	Grundbegriffe	ZAW	Zeitschrift für alttesta-
HThG	Handbuch theologischer		mentlichen Wissenschaft
	Grundbegriffe	ZEE	Zeitschrift für evangelische
HThK	Herders theologischer Kom-		Ethik
	mentar zum Neuen		
	Testament		
HWP	Historisches Wörterbuch		
	der Philosophie		
LThK	Lexikon für Theologie und		
	Kirche		
LUÅ	Lunds Universitets Års-		
	skrift		
MS	Mysterium Salutis		
MThZ	Münchener Theologische		
	Zeitschrift		
NovT	Novum Testamentum		
NZSTh	Neue Zeitschrift für sys-		
	tematische Theologie (und		
	Religionsphilosophie)		
NZZ	Neue Zürcher Zeitung		
PhJ	Philosophisches Jahrbuch		
QD	Quaestiones disputatae		
SBS	Stuttgarter Bibelstudien		
Schol	Scholastik		
SM	Sacramentum Mundi		
StZ	Stimmen der Zeit		

Notes

§ 1 The Concept and Task of Fundamental Moral Theology, pp. 1–11.

1. B. Casper, K. Hemmerle and P. Hünermann, *Theologie als Wissenschaft. Methodische Zugänge, QD* 45, Freiburg 1970; G. Sauter, ed., *Wissenschaftstheoretische Kritik der Theologie. Die Theologie und die neuere wissenschaftstheoretische Diskussion. Materialien – Analysen – Entwürfe*, Munich 1973; W. Pannenberg, *Wissenschaftstheorie und Theologie*, Frankfurt 1973; H. Peukert, *Wissenschaftstheorie — Handlungstheorie — Fundamentaltheologie*, Düsseldorf 1976.

2. See D. Mieth, "Der Wissenschaftscharakter der Theologie," *FZPhTh* 23 (1976), 13–41, 31; H. Rombach, "Der Glaube an Gott und das wissenschaftliche Denken," H.-J. Schultz, ed., *Wer ist das eigentlich-Gott?* Munich 1969, 192–208.

3. See D. Mieth, *op. cit.*, 30.

4. F. Böckle, "Bestrebungen in der Moraltheologie," J. Feiner, J. Trütsch and F. Böckle, eds., *Fragen der Theologie heute*, Einsiedeln, Zürich and Cologne, 1960, 425–446, 426.

5. The basic principle applied by F. Tillmann was taken to a deeper level and correspondingly changed. This principle of the imitation of Christ is understood as a realization of the life of Christ based on a sacramental way of life. Man was understood in the concrete and within the history of salvation as a member of the mystical body (see E. Mersch, *Morale et corps mystique*, Louvain 1937) or within the context of his vocation to the kingdom of God (see J. Stelzenberger, *Lehrbuch der Moraltheologie. Die Sittlichkeitslehre der Königsherrschaft Gottes*, Paderborn 1953) or as man created and renewed in and through Christ (see N. Krautwig, "Entfaltung der Herrlichkeit Christi. Eine Wesensbestimmung der katholischen Moraltheologie," *WiWei* 7, 1940, 73–99; B. Häring, *Das Gesetz Christi*, Freiburg 1954). The corresponding principle on which moral theology could be built up was "the fashioning of man's life into Christ as a fashioning with him to the glorification of God in the Church and the world" (see G. Ermecke, "Die Stufen der sakramentalen Christusbildlichkeit als Einleitungsprinzip der speziellen Moral," T. Steinbüchel, T. Müncker, eds., *Aus Theologie und Philosophie. Festschrift für F. Tillmann*, Düsseldorf 1950, 35–48) or a fashioning brought about by grace of the "old Christ" as a member in the mystical body of the Lord (see R. Egenter, "Moraltheologie," *LThK* VII, 613–618).

6. In strictly christological concentration, Karl Barth formally defined creation as the presupposition of redemption, nature as the presupposition of grace. Creation is presupposed in God's eternal decision that the Son should become man. The eternal presupposition of Jesus Christ before and in the foundation of the world is the eternal guarantee of a good world that cannot, in its nature, be destroyed. The problem of this presupposition is

that what is presupposed must be considered in the light of its setting if it is to be understood. On the other hand, we have to take care not to identify it with that setting. The whole doctrine of the creation is enclosed within a double impossibility — on the one hand, it is impossible to deduce the natural order from the order of redemption and, on the other, it is also impossible to separate these orders and determine the essence and meaning of nature from below. This concept of presupposition therefore includes a duality of orders. All that it means is that there is an authentic, but only relative independence of the natural order within the order of grace (see K. Barth, *KD* I/1, 431; II, 172). The whole of creation is simply a sign of the promise and expectation of grace. All true humanity is simply an epiphenomenon of Christ. Barth is inclined to oppose an order of creation that is evident to the natural reason of all men on the basis of his dogmatic approach, but he is none the less ready to use the concept of an order of creation, in particular as "the special sphere of divine command and human action, in which God, who is gracious to man in Jesus Christ, commands as creator and man, to whom God is gracious in Jesus Christ, stands in God's presence as his creature and is sanctified and liberated through his commandment. . . . We do not have to leave the closed circle of theological knowledge in order to become aware of this order" (*KD* III/4, 49). It is clear from this that there could be no other form of theological ethics than ethics of faith.

7. See J. B. Metz, "Christliche Religion und gesellschaftliche Praxis," *Dokumente der Paulus-Gesellschaft* XIX, 30; D. A. Seeber, "Was will die politische Theologie?" *Her Korr* 22 (1968), 345–349.

8. "The impossibility of a 'scientific' representation of practical positions — apart from cases in which means for a firmly given and presupposed aim are discussed — has far deeper reasons. It is therefore meaningless because the different orders of value in the world are indissolubly in conflict with each other" (M. Weber, "Wissenschaft als Beruf," *Gesammelte Aufsätze zur Wissenschaftslehre*, Tübingen 1968, 603).

9. See R. Carnap, *Philosophy and Logical Syntax*, London 1935, 24.

10. R. M. Hare, for example, has demonstrated that the meaning of prescriptive statements is constituted by an act of self-obligation that in itself gives meaning. (See the detailed discussion of this problem in § 2.)

11. F. Kambartel, "Moralisches Argumentieren. Methodische Analysen zur Ethik," F. Kambartel, ed., *Praktische Philosophie und konstruktive Wissenschaftstheorie*, Frankfurt 1974, 54–72, 60.

12. We have to make a distinction here between the operational conditions of rational discourse, as discussed in the school of P. Lorenzen, and K.-O. Apel's "conception of linguistic transcendentalism," in which the *a priori* criteria of our knowledge of reality is conceived as communicative knowledge, in other words, the question of the *a priori* of the community of communication points to the constitution of a "transcendental intersubjectivity," in which the conditions governing the possibility of intersubjectively valid knowledge are established within the framework of a commu-

nity of communication. (For this, see C. F. Gethmann, "Realität," *HPhG* (Studienausgabe) IV, Munich 1973, 1168–1187, 1186 ff.)

13. F. Kambartel, *op. cit.*, 68.

14. We are deliberately avoiding the use of the concept "value knowledge," because its meaning has been determined by a particular movement in philosophy.

15. This distinction must prove its value with regard to the present discussion of fundamental values, in which moral and pre-moral values are frequently juxtaposed and not distinguished. If, in this context, we are required to protect a fundamental moral value such as justice, this demand may remain in a vacuum for as long as it remains unclear what everyone's rights are. The most important constitutional laws that are everybody's rights are contained, for instance, in the catalogue of the constitution of the Federal Republic of Germany. One of these laws, which is normative for all the other laws, is the right to human and personal dignity of every individual. Related rights are those to the free development of the human personality, to life and intactness of the body and to the protection of family and spiritual and material goods. Men are the bearers of all these rights. Only people can have rights. These rights are, however, related to particular goods, from which they also derive their names. These are personal, spiritual and material values. The constitutive supreme value is the life of the individual. This cannot be destroyed. This is followed in order of priority by the human personality, which must be allowed to develop, and then by all the other goods, as listed in the West German constitution. These determine the constitutional laws and are therefore sometimes known as constitutional or fundamental values. It would be perhaps more correct to speak here of right goods. This does not mean that they are unimportant for moral action. On the contrary, they are of great importance morally because they demand respect. They do not, however, exist as qualities of will, but as realities that are previously given as obligations to human action. Rights and social ethics (morality) are indissolubly bound together in these fundamental values.

§ 2 The Distinctive Character of Normative Reality, pp. 15–23.

1. F. Kambartel, quoted in W. Kern, "Über den humanistischen Atheismus," K. Rahner, ed., *Ist Gott noch gefragt? Zur Funktionslosigkeit des Gottesglaubens*, Düsseldorf 1973, 9–55, 17.

2. See R. Spaemann, "Überzeugungen in einer hypothetischen Zivilisation," *NZZ*, 26 November 1976, foreign edition No. 277, 27 f.

3. *Id.*, "Sinnstiftung in einer hypothetischen Zivilisation," *NZZ*, 10 December 1976, foreign edition No. 289, 38.

4. See A. Gehlen, *Der Mensch seine Natur und seine Stellung in der Welt*, Frankfurt 1966.

5. See E. Durkheim, *Soziologie und Philosophie*, Frankfurt 1970; T. Parsons and R. F. Bales, *Family, Socialization and Interaction Process*, Glencoe 1955.

6. I. Craemer-Ruegenberg, *Moralsprache und Moralität*, Freiburg and Munich 1975, 16.

7. This is the position of A. J. Ayer, *Truth and Logic*, London 1946; *id.*, *Logical Positivism*, Glencoe 1959.

8. See C. L. Stevenson, *Ethics and Language*, New Haven 1960; *id.*, *Facts and Values. Essays*, New Haven 1963.

9. J. L. Austin, "Performative Utterances," J. O. Urmson and G. J. Warnock, eds., *Philosophical Papers*, London 1961, 233–252, 233.

10. "For Austin, there are no semantics of moral linguistic or moral linguistically relevant utterances. These belong to the sphere of the illocutionarity or performativity of utterances as such and are exposed to the conditions imposed by success and failure" (I. Craemer-Ruegenberg, *op. cit.*, 46).

11. *Ibid.*, 47.

12. Descriptive sentences can be analyzed and complemented by the addition of "it is the case." Prescriptive sentences can be complemented by the addition of "do it." I. Craemer-Ruegenberg has similarly defined prescriptive sentences as those "whose predicate has a meaningful part that can be explicated in an imperative formula" (*ibid.*, 54).

13. *Ibid.*, 71.

14. *Ibid.*, 90.

15. A neglect of the question of the ultimate justification of obligation, which is characteristic of the transcendental philosophy, is a feature of the method followed by the representatives of operationalism. See F. Kambartel, "Moralisches Argumentieren. Methodische Analysen zur Ethik," F. Kambartel, ed., *Praktische Philosophie und konstruktive Wissenschaftstheorie*, 59 f.

16. See E. Durkheim, *Die Regeln der soziologischen Methode*, Neuwied 1965, who clearly regarded the concept of "social norm" as a moral standard within the "collective consciousness" and stressed the aspect of obligation (see *ibid.*, 112, note). For the concept of "chance," see M. Weber, "Soziologische Grundbegriffe (1921)," M. Weber, *Ausätze zur Wissenschaftslehre*, Tübingen 1968, 567 and 570 f. T. Parsons stressed the aspect of safeguarding social norms by means of the process of internalization (see T. Parsons and R. F. Bales, *Family, op. cit.*).

17. See H. Popitz, "Soziale Normen," *Europäisches Archiv für Soziologie* 2 (1961), Heft 2, 185–198; W. Korff, *Norm und Sittlichkeit. Untersuchungen zur Logik der normativen Vernunft*, Mainz 1973, 113–128.

18. See F. Tönnies, *Die Sitte*, Frankfurt 1909; M. Weber, "Soziologische Grundbegriffe (1921)," *op. cit.*; G. Heilfurth, "Sitte," *Wörterbuch der Soziologie*, W. Bernsdorf, ed., Stuttgart 1969, 931–933.

19. See W. Korff, *op. cit.*, 123.

20. See T. Parsons' and N. Luhmann's attempts to evolve a systematic theory and R. Dahrendorf's conflict model.

21. See H. Albert and E. Topitsch, eds., *Werturteilsstreit*, Darmstadt 1971.

§ 3: Freedom of Choice as a Precondition, pp. 23–31.

1. W. Schulz, *Philosophie in der veränderten Welt*, Pfullingen 1972, 756.

2. See H. Kuhn, "Freiheit — Gegebenheit und Errungenschaft," K. Forster, ed., *Freiheit und Determination*, Würzburg 1966, 57–88.

3. All goods that are encountered in this life display an objective indifference to the good and for this reason our will is subjectively indifferent to them. On the basis of comparative insights, it has to make a choice.

4. H. Kuhn, *op. cit.*, 63.

5. *Ibid.*, 65.

6. See F. P. Fiorenza's and J. B. Metz's detailed treatment of this theme in *MS* II, chapter 8, section 2, especially 618–625.

7. *Ibid.*, 621.

8. *Ibid.*, 623.

9. J. B. Metz, "Leiblichkeit," *HThG* II (1963), 30–37, 36.

10. *Ibid.*, 36. The ontological status of corporeality is denied by all tendencies that are in themselves justified and are directed against latent Manicheanism, toward a complete moral neutralization of corporeality.

11. See W. Brugger, "Dei Verleiblichung des Wollens," *Schol* 25 (1950), 248–253.

12. K. Rahner, "Die Gliedschaft in der Kirche nach der Lehre der Enzyklika Pius XII 'Mystici Corporis Christi,'" *Schriften* II, 1955, 7–94, 87.

13. *Ibid.*, 87.

14. See F. Böckle, "Bestrebungen in der Moraltheologie," J. Feiner, J. Trütsch and F. Böckle, eds., *Fragen der Theologie heute*, Einsiedeln, 1960, 434 ff. See also the detailed discussion of this question below, § 10.

15. See M. Müller, *Erfahrung und Geschichte*, Freiburg 1971, 300: "Freedom as absolute distance, transcendence, absolute reflection and being placed in the absolute is identical with what is called spirit or spirituality."

16. *Ibid.*, 301.

17. In an original sense, freedom is of course opposed to itself in indifference (and is identical here with all its possibilities), with the result that it can choose its own negation by choosing that possibility that is not the authentic possibility of freedom.

18. Two different forms of necessity can be distinguished: "what must be done" (*necesse est, necessitas*), which corresponds to "not being able to act differently," and "obligation" or "what ought to be done" (*debere, obligatio*), which corresponds to "not being permitted to act or decide differently" with, at the same time, the possibility of being able to act differently.

19. B. Schüller, in his *Gesetz und Freiheit. Eine moraltheologische Untersuchung*, Düsseldorf 1966, 17, has made the following pertinent comment: "As something planned from freedom, not one of these possibilities has anything in itself because of which it would in advance merit being preferred to other possibilities. Freedom can be seen precisely as freedom by the fact that it is equally open to all its possibilities. . . . It is only as

decision that freedom is able to make a distinction between all its possibilities between what merits being preferred and what merits being set aside."

20. M. Müller, *op. cit.*, 303.

21. According to M. Müller, *op. cit.*, 304, "Freedom of action is so completely determined by its motives, although these motives are in the first place motives in the pre-determination by fundamental choice or fundamental consent of the freedom to decide."

§ 4 The Claim to Autonomy, pp. 31–46.

1. See R. Pohlmann, "Autonomie," *HWP* I, 701–719, 701.

2. Autonomy (or the "emancipation of different religions and faiths") was rejected in the debate about the interpretation of the Peace of Augsberg (1555). Since the Peace of Westphalia (1648), autonomy, as freedom of conscience, has been regarded as a positive achievement. See R. Pohlmann, *op. cit.*, 702 ff.

3. See G. Rohrmoser, "Autonomie," *HPhG* (Studienausgabe) I, 155–170, 156.

4. See M. Forschner, *Gesetz und Freiheit. Zum Problem der Autonomie bei I. Kant. Epimeleia, Beiträge zur Philosophie*, Munich 1974, 24. During the seventeen-fifties, the objectivism of the Enlightenment dominated Kant's thought, but his writings in the early seventeen-sixties (including *Der einzig mögliche Beweisgrund* of 1762 and the *Untersuchung über die Deutlichkeit der Grundsätze* of 1762–1763) show a deeper penetration into the problems of moral philosophy. It has been said that the decisive aspects of Kant's thought at this period were "the change in the concept of perfection and, as a result of this, a reformulation of the idea of obligation and that of the necessary purpose, according to which an action can be qualified as morally good. This change in Kant's thinking can be described as an anthropological change or better as a change to subjectivity, since, from that time onward, perfection, order, obligation,the good and so on were conceived essentially in the light of the knowledge and will of the subject," *ibid.*, 64.

5. Even in the precritical phase, "the fundamental concepts . . . of morality . . . are the essential laws of the spirit itself. Their structural aspects . . . resemble those of critical morality" (M. Forschner, *op. cit.*, 129). The concept of reason itself is still totally committed to scholastic philosophy. "Divine Spirit and divine will . . . are not used in a critical sense (that is, as limiting the human spirit as a possibility of thought) or in a regulative sense, but with a constitutive meaning. Human morality constitutes and realizes itself as participation in the divine Spirit and as a realization of its creative teleology. The categorical imperative had not yet been formulated as an expression of human autonomy" (*ibid.*, 129).

6. This distinction was first reduced to a theme in the dissertation *De mundi sensibilis*. In this, according to M. Forschner, *op. cit.*, 239, "the *mundus intelligibilis* represents the object of conceptual thought and reveals its

being in itself to a purely conceptual determination independent of any sensually conditioned possibility of experience. . . . . After the critical change in his thinking, Kant restricted the validity of the categories to the world of phenomena and maintained that the noumenal was unknowable. The thing in itself became a purely marginal concept, something that we have to assume as the ground of all phenomena and their determination, without being able to determine it positively, in accordance with its being."

7. I. Kant, "KrV," *Werke in zehn Bänden*, W. Weischedel, ed., IV, Darmstadt 1968, 675 (A803 B831).

8. "We know practical freedom from experience, as one of the natural causes, that is, a causality of reason in determining the will, whereas transcendental freedom calls for independence on the part of this reason . . . from all determining causes of the world of the senses; it is also contrary to the natural law and all possible experience and is therefore always a problem" (*ibid.*, 675 ff.; A803 B831).

9. M. Forschner, *op. cit.*, 195. Kant generally used the term "practical reason" only to describe the fact that reason functions for itself exclusively as the basis of determination. For Kant therefore, "practical reason" did not mean the same as it does in modern terminology. Kant's "theoretical autonomy," as the autonomous connection between empirical ideas and the autonomy of ideas through reason alone, can also "only be combined in an analogous sense with practical autonomy" (*ibid.*, 196).

10. I. Kant, "GMS," *Werke, op. cit.*, VI, 51 (BA 52).

11. M. Forschner, *op. cit.*, 209.

12. I. Kant, "GMS," *Werke, op. cit.*, VI, 59 (BA 64).

13. M. Forschner has pointed out (*op. cit.*, 250) that the "metaphysical structure of morality underlying the foundation text is based on a moral structure of metaphysics. Freedom and its structure of being (autonomy) is a postulate that raises the level of meaning of the moral law. . . . The 'suprasensual objects,' which are introduced in Kant's criticism of pure reason simply as possibilities and as marginal concepts, are 'confirmed by a fact.'"

14. *Ibid.*, 259.

15. J. G. Fichte, "Das System der Sittenlehre nach den Principien der Wissenschaftslehre," 1798, in *J. G. Fichte's Sämtliche Werke*, J. H. Fichte, ed., IV, Berlin 1845, reprinted 1965, 12.

16. J. G. Fichte, "Zweite Einleitung in die Wissenschaftslehre," 1797, *op. cit.*, I, 468.

17. *Id.*, "Die Staatslehre, oder über das Verhältnis des Urstaates zum Vernunftreiche," 1813, *op. cit.*, IV, 389.

18. *Ibid.*, 387.

19. *Ibid.*, 385.

20. See J. Ritter, "Ethik," *HWP* II, 759–795, 786.

21. J. G. Fichte, "Das System der Sittenlehre," 1812, *op. cit.*, XI, 42.

22. J. Ritter, *op. cit.*, 787.

23. See E. Simons, "Gott (2)," *HPhG* III, 616–629, especially 623–627.

24. *Ibid.*, 623. E. Simons also says (*op. cit.*, 624): "Although Fichte's idea of God is similar, as far as its content is concerned, to the Platonic and Augustinian tradition, he goes far beyond this tradition and the whole of the so-called *philosophia negativa* in his methodical reflection, that is, his mediation of immanence and transcendence (which at the same time also has a radically interpersonal and historical aspect). For this reason, the content of his concept of God is essentially different. Fichte does not show God to be light and life as the (transcendental) *a priori* condition of all human action and knowledge, as though the latter had always been exclusively based on God. On the contrary, this light and life could, according to Fichte, only take place subject to shared conditions of freedom. It could therefore only be creatively produced by finite freedom."

25. See G. W. F. Hegel, "Phänomenologie des Geistes, A. II. Die Wahrnehmung, oder das Ding und die Täuschung," *Sämtliche Werke*, H. Glockner, ed., II, Stuttgart 1951, 92–107.

26. See "Glauben und Wissen oder die Reflexionsphilosophie der Subjektivität," *Sämtliche Werke* I, Stuttgart 1958, 277–433. In this essay, published in 1802–1803, Hegel continued and took to a deeper level the controversy with contemporary philosophers that he had begun when he first considered the difference between Fichte's and Schelling's philosophical systems.

27. *Ibid.*, 280.

28. *Ibid.*, 293.

29. *Ibid.*, 420.

30. *Ibid.*, 425.

31. J. Ritter, "Ethik," *HWP* II, 792.

32. G. Rohrmoser, "Autonomie," *HPhG* I, 155–170, 161.

33. W. Schultz, *Philosophie in der veränderten Welt*, Pfullingen 1972, 506.

34. K. Marx, "Die heilige Familie," chapter 6, *Werke*, H. J. Lieber and P. Furth, eds., Darmstadt, 1962, 766 ff.

35. "The philosopher functions simply as an organ in which the absolute spirit that makes history subsequently comes to consciousness after the movement has run its course. The philosopher's share in history is reduced to this subsequent consciousness, since the real movement is unconsciously perfected by the absolute spirit. The philosopher therefore clearly arrives too late" (*ibid.*, 767).

36. K. Marx, "Thesen über Feuerbach," *Werke* II, Darmstadt 1971, 4.

37. *Id.*, "Die deutsche Ideologie," *Werke* II, *op. cit.*, 29.

38. *Id.*, "Kritik des Gothaer Programms," *Werke* III/2, *op. cit.*, 1024.

39. W. P. Eichhorn, "Bedürfnis," *Philosophisches Wörterbuch*, G. Klaus and M. Buhr, eds., Leipzig 1975, I, 206.

40. "The system of needs in all spheres of man's social life develops in accordance with certain laws; it is dependent on and interacts with the economic structures of the society of the period" (*ibid.*, 206).

41. M. Scheler said, in "Der Formalismus in der Ethik und die materiale Wertethik," *Werke* II, Berne 1966, 72 f., that "the sphere of *a priori*

evidence has nothing whatever to do with the 'formal' and the antithesis between *a priori* and *a posteriori* also has nothing to do with the contrast between 'formal' and 'material' . . . One of the fundamental errors in Kant's teaching is the identification of *a priori* evidence and the 'formal.'"

42. M. Scheler, "Absolutsphäre und Realsetzung der Gottesidee," *Werke* X, Berne 1957, 179–253, 197.

43. See I. Craemer-Ruegenberg, "Über methodische Schwierigkeiten bei der Auslegung von moralischen Urteilen," M. Riedel, ed., *Rehabilitierung der praktischen Philosophie* I, Freiburg 1972, 133–158. Scheler made a distinction between the concept and what was conceived, and believed that the second was accessible *a priori*. "Its evidence can only be used to demonstrate the *a priori* nature of value concepts . . . We cannot conclude from the *a priori* nature of certain concepts . . . that what is conceived by these conepts can also be known *a priori*" (*ibid.*, 136).

44. *Ibid.*, 139.

45. G. Rohrmoser, "Autonomie," *op. cit.*, 155.

46. H. Peukert, *Wissenschaftstheorie — Handlungstheorie — Fundamentale Theologie*, Düsseldorf 1976, 106.

47. According to the thesis of physicalism, all statements can, insofar as they have any claim to scientific truth, be formulated in the language of physics; see H. Peukert, *op. cit.*, 107.

48. *Ibid.*, 126.

49. *Ibid.*, 146.

50. See L. Wittgenstein, "Philosophische Untersuchungen," 1935, *ibid.*, *Schriften* I, Frankfurt 1969, 292: "We can also imagine that the entire process of the use of words is one of those games by means of which children learn their mother tongue. I intend to call these games 'language games' and to speak of a primitive language as a language game."

51. For the terminology, see *Sprachpragmatik und Philosophie*, K.-O. Apel, ed., Frankfurt 1976, editor's foreword, 7–9.

52. H. Peukert, *op. cit.*, 201.

53. The attempts made by the members of the Erlangen school to evolve a constructive theory of science, K.-O. Apel's program to transform philosophy in the direction of transcendental and pragmatic thought and J. Habermas's idea of an ideal community of communication can all be seen in this light.

54. H. Peukert, *op. cit.*, 253.

55. *Ibid.*, 255.

56. K.-O. Apel, ed., *Sprachpragmatik und Philosophie, op. cit.*, editor's foreword, 8.

57. See the beginning made by H. Schnelle, *Sprachphilosophie und Linguistik*, Reinbek 1973.

58. This is the main emphasis of the research done by the members of the Erlangen school; see K.-O. Apel, "Das Apriori der Kommunikationsgemeinschaft," *Transformation der Philosophie* II, Frankfurt 1973, 358–435, 426.

59. K.-O. Apel, "Sprechakttheorie und transzendentale Sprachprag-matik zur Frage ethischer Normen," *Sprachpragmatik und Philosophie*, K.-O. Apel, ed., 10–173, 122.

60. *Ibid.*, 126: "This principle can, with P. Lorenzen, be called the prin-ciple of 'transsubjectivity' and understand by it a reconstruction of Kant's categorical imperative."

61. *Ibid.*, 124.

62. K.-O. Apel, "Das Apriori der Kommunikationsgemeinschaft," *op. cit.*, 416 ff.

63. *Ibid.*, 416.

64. *Ibid.*, 420.

§ 5 The Theological Justification of Moral Autonomy, pp. 46–63.

1. As we have pointed out above in § 4, K.-O. Apel for this reason regarded it as essential to analyze the subject transcendentally.

2. It is remarkable that the neo-Marxists have been the sharpest critics of the immanent "Godlessness" of positivism. "Even in the nineteen-twenties, Lukács called the reduction of thought to the application of the categories of natural science a middle-class ideology that was blind to the total context of human praxis, the science of which science itself is a de-rivative" (see R. Spaemann, "Gesichtspunkte der Philosophie," H.-J. Schultz, ed., *Wer ist das eigentlich-Gott?* Munich 1969, 56–65, 60).

3. R. Spaemann, "Sinnstiftung in einer hypothetischen Zivilisation," *NZZ*, 10 December 1976, Fernausgabe, No. 289, 38.

4. K. Marx, "Kritik der Hegelschen Rechtsphilosophie," *Werke, op. cit.*, I, 489.

5. *Ibid.*, 489.

6. *Ibid.*, 497.

7. *Id.*, "Zur Kritik der Nationalökonomie. Ökonomisch-philosophische Manuskripte: III, Privateigentum und Arbeit," *Werke*, I, 607.

8. See W. Kern, "Über den humanistischen Atheismus," K. Rahner, ed., *Ist Gott noch gefragt?* Düsseldorf, 1973, 9–55. If Marx regarded atheism, at least to some extent, as meaningless, then we may conclude that it is not necessarily linked to the Marxist theory of society. His denial of faith in God may therefore possibly be explained on the basis of "experience of the sanction of unenlightened (pseudo) Christian religion to social conditions that were urgently in need of change." It may not have been a rejection of Christian faith as such. Marxism may therefore be able to reconsider its attitude toward religion in the light of recent changes in historical condi-tions. According to the investigations made by J. Kadenbach, *Das Reli-gionsverständnis von Karl Marx*, Paderborn 1970, and W. Post, *Kritik der Reli-gion bei Karl Marx*, Munich 1969, religion was for Marx above all part of the ideological superstructure of society (*op. cit.*, 28).

9. See H. Krings, "Freiheit. Ein Versuch, Gott zu denken," *PhJ* 77 (1970), 225–237, 227: "The characteristic aspect of this concept is to think of the logical maximum of an ontological idea."

10. W. Schulz, *Der Gott der neuzeitlichen Metaphysik*, Pfullingen, 1974, 27.

11. H. M. Baumgartner, "Über das Gottesverständnis der Transzendentalphilosophie," *PhJ* 73 (1975–1966), 303–321, 306.

12. In this Kantian concept, the God of the philosophers seems to have disappeared and to have become simply a rational idea. Philosophical knowledge of God seems to have been totally destroyed. On the other hand, it cannot be denied that reason points here in the direction of unity and that consent is given to this unity or striving for unity. "There is, according to Kant, a connection between rational unity and the idea of God. And because consent is given to the idea of God, faith in God is possible" ("J. Möller, Antworten des 19. Jahrhunderts," H. J. Schultz, ed., *Wer ist das eigentlich-Gott?, op. cit.*, 165–177, 166).

13. *KrV, op. cit.*, 681 (A810 B838). "Absolute being in and from itself, simple being through something else, autonomous spontaneity and radical receptivity represent the two ideas in which finite reason is impelled to its limits. If they transcend their character as related concepts, they are hypostasized into substances that are in themselves, they lose their sense and meaning for human knowledge and they change into concepts that are in themselves full of contradictions" (M. Forschner, *op. cit.*, 220).

14. See H. Krings, "Freiheit," *op. cit.*, 230: Kant based "his real concept of God not on a knowledge of natural objects . . . but on a knowledge of man as a moral being. The framework of thought in which Kant tried to think of a concept of God did not give rise to a series of ontological concepts in an attempt to think of a first principle along a *via eminentiae*. On the contrary, it allowed the series to remain, then left the series and thought of what that series in the first place made it possible to think of meaningfully."

15. See H. M. Baumgartner, *op. cit.*, 309.

16. E. Simons, "Gott (2)," *HPhG* III, 616–629, 625.

17. W. Schulz, *Gott, op. cit.*, 25, saw in the development of the idea of God from Kant to Hegel a typical movement on the part of modern metaphysics toward self-consciousness. It was not a straight line, but rather a line oscillating between two poles. One pole was represented by thinkers who placed human subjectivity in the central position, but allowed it to be limited by a higher form of subjectivity. (These thinkers included Nicholas of Cusa, Descartes, Kant, Schelling and Heidegger.) At the other pole were systematic thinkers (Giordano Bruno, Spinoza, Hegel and Nietzsche) who tried to mediate human subjectivity and the higher subjectivity that limited it within a systematic whole.

18. E. Simons, *op. cit.*, 628.

19. W. Schulz, *Gott, op. cit.*, 55.

20. K. Rahner, *Grundkurs des Glaubens*, Freiburg 1976, 81.

21. *Ibid.*, 80.

22. *Ibid.*, 86. This, however, blocks the way to any dualistic interpretation of the event of creation. God and the creature are not in competition.

God's creative act transcendentally encloses the categorial evolution of the world.

23. I follow here H. Krings's outline of a transcendental doctrine of freedom as set out in his "Freiheit," *op. cit.*, 225–237. See also *id.*, "Wissen und Freiheit," *Die Frage nach dem Menschen, Festschrift für M. Müller*, Freiburg and Munich 1966, 23–44; *id.*, "Freiheit," *HPhG* II, 493–510; *id.*, "Gott (3)," *HPhG* III, 629–641.

24. W. Schulz, *Philosophie in der veränderten Welt, op. cit.*, 330, in which the author follows Fichte.

25. H. Krings, "Freiheit," *op. cit.*, 231.

26. *Ibid.*, 231.

27. *Ibid.*, 232.

28. *Ibid.*

29. "The term 'unconditioned freedom,' like the concept 'transcendental freedom,'" does not describe an object or a being. Nor does it describe a transcendental event. It rather describes the idea of the unity of unconditioned form in the act of opening itself, carried out by freedom and in the unmediated fullness of content. The concept of perfect freedom enables us to grasp the meaning of identity. Insofar as empirical human freedom is justified by transcendental freedom, it can, because of its form, receive an anticipation of perfect freedom" (*ibid.*, 233). In this, we do not come to understand the concept of finite freedom along a *via eminentiae*, by raising the concept of finite freedom to that of absolute freedom, but rather by returning to the idea of the formally unconditioned character of finite freedom. If the original relationship within which we are confronted with the aim of our transcendence is indicated by analogy, then transcendental freedom is an analogon or an anticipation of absolute freedom.

30. *Ibid.*, 233.

31. "The concept of perfect freedom is a necessary one insofar as freedom should be (and that is the same as wants to be). The idea of God, thought of in the concept of perfect freedom fulfilling transcendental freedom, is not objective. It only becomes necessary in the expression of freedom. It is not a necessary concept of theoretical thinking. It is only a necessary concept of practical thought. Insofar as a concept of God is thought of within a process of thinking about freedom, that concept is thought of as a necessary aspect of the transcendental structure of freedom and as the idea of the fulfilling content of transcendental freedom" (*ibid.*, 234).

32. *Ibid.*, 236.

33. A certain aseity is present in freedom as the expression of universal distance and as the possibility of absolute reflection about everything and about itself. According to Fichte and Hegel, the I had creative power on the basis of freedom. According to Schelling, on the other hand, freedom existed at the point of indifference between God and nature, being and nonbeing. (See R. Spaemann, "Freiheit," IV, *HWP* II, 1088–1098, 1092 ff.)

34. W. Kern, "Über den humanistischen Atheismus," K. Rahner, ed., *Ist Gott noch gefragt?, op. cit.*, 47 ff.

35. The unconditioned claim that man experiences in his freedom has to be carried out in individual contingent acts. The absolute character of the claim is not, however, derived from the individual act, but from the claim made on contingent man by the absolute God.

36. In this, I base my outline on K.-W. Merks's as yet unpublished dissertation, "Theologische Grundlegung der sittlichen Autonomie, Strukturmomente eines 'autonomen' Normbegründungsverständnisses im Lex-Traktat der Summa Theologiae des Thomas von Aquin," Bonn 1976.

37. The different laws are interpreted according to the idea of a graded participation and derivation. It should, however, be noted that "this interpretation is an attempt to find a basis for the factual laws that are encountered in concrete which was represented as quasi-deductive, but was achieved by reduction and reflection" (*ibid.*, 120).

38. In this approach, the *lex divina*, the so-called divine law of revelation, retained its teaching function, but lost its alienating aspect in the justification. (See *ibid.*, 336–360, in connection with 38–90.)

39. W. Korff, *Norm und Sittlichkeit*, Mainz 1973, 61.

40. I–II, lc: "*ratio, quae est primum principium actuum humanorum . . . rationis enim est ordinare ad finem, qui est primum principium in agendis.*" The regulating factor that is expressed by *ratio* and the *lex* does not function in the same way. It should rather be thought of as a stage in the sense of fundamental and derived (see K.-W. Merks, *op. cit.*, 126).

41. In an attempt to clarify the meaning of ratio in the definition of law, Merks provides a detailed analysis, in which he also includes the *Quaestiones de ultimo fine et de actibus humanis* of Ia–IIae.

42. In this statement, Thomas followed Aristotle's analysis of the *proairesis*, which, according to Aristotle, was "striving reason" or "rational striving." It was therefore in this way that man was — because of his *proairesis* — the origin of his actions.

43. K.-W. Merks, *op. cit.*, 139.

44. See EN VI, 1.2, n.1131: "*finis . . . determinatus est homini a natura. . . . Ea autem quae sunt ad finem, non sunt nobis determinata a natura, sed per rationem investiganda.*"

45. K.-W. Merks, *op. cit.*, 157.

46. *Ibid.*, 161.

47. *Ibid.*, 165.

48. See the interpretation of the *lex aeterna* (*ibid.*, 184–217) in its connection with the *lex naturalis* (229–240).

49. U. Kühn, *Via caritatis. Theologie des Gesetzes bei Thomas von Aquin. Kirche und Konfession IX*, Göttingen 1965, 146, with reference to I–II, 93, 2 ad 1 and therefore critical of M. Wittmann.

50. See I–II, 90, 1. A law is always *aliquid constitutum per rationem* (ad 2), that is, neither *ratio* itself, nor the human act of understanding, but what is constituted by the legislator and insofar as it is constituted by him — the *ordinatio*.

51. See K.-W. Merks, *op. cit.*, 229–240, including his analysis of *ratio* in the *lex naturalis*.

52. To this extent, it is *aliquid per rationem constitutum* (I–II, 94, 1).

53. In our understanding of faith in creation, the unconditioned obligatory claim is simply the dependence of a personally free self who in his freedom totally claims to have control of himself in freedom.

54. In the conflict about grace, the anthropological aspect (freedom as control of oneself) and the theological aspect (freedom as being controlled by God) were seen as competing factors. Even ingenious attempts to harmonize the two aspects have proved to be unconvincing. (See H. Holz, "Omnipotenz und Autonomie," *NZSTh* 16, 1974, 257–284.)

§ 6 Reflected Experience of Guilt, pp. 64–76.

1. See K. Lorenz, *On Aggression*, New York 1966; A. Mitscherlich, *Auf dem Wege zur vaterlosen Gesellschaft*, Munich 1965; H. Marcuse, *Kultur und Gesellschaft* I and II, Frankfurt 1965; id., *Triebstruktur und Gesellschaft. Ein philosophischer Beitrag zu S. Freud*, Frankfurt 1967; A. Plack, *Die Gesellschaft und das Böse. Eine Kritik der herrschenden Moral*, Munich 1967; E. Fromm, *Anatomie der menschlichen Destruktivität*, Stuttgart 1974. There is a strong movement in contemporary thinking to transfer Freud's insights into the psychology of the individual to the structures of society. See especially W. Czapiewski and G. Scherer, *Der Aggressionstrieb und das Böse*, Essen 1967; M. Oraison, *Was ist Sünde?* Frankfurt 1968.

2. W. Korff, "Erfahrung von Schuld und Sünde in der Schulderfahrung des einzelnen und im Schuldigwerden der Gesellschaft," S. Rehrl, ed., *Sünde — Schuld — Erlösung*, Salzburg 1973, 18.

3. P. Kurz, "Das Böse und die Schuld in der zeitgenössischen Literatur," *StZ* 190 (1972), 20–34, 21.

4. *Ibid.*, 22.

5. M. Frisch, *Tagebuch 1946–1949*, Frankfurt 1971, 37.

6. *Id.*, *Andorra. Stück in zwölf Bildern*, Frankfurt 1961.

7. *Id.*, *Stiller. Roman*, Frankfurt and Hamburg 1971, 47, 75, 96, 113 ff., 195, 317, 318, 319, 328, 325.

8. P. Kurz, *op. cit.*, 32. Several examples of this can be quoted in contemporary German language literature: Friedrich Dürrenmatt, *Die Panne; id., Der Besuch der alten Dame*; Heinar Kipphardt, *Joel Brand. Die Geschichte eines Geschäfts*; Peter Schneider, *Brief an die herrschende Klasse in Deutschland*; Heinrich Böll, *Gruppenbild mit Dame*.

9. Relationships, as a well-known term in the Marxist criticism of society, "mean in the first place relationships of production and only secondarily social relationships as such. They are therefore, for the Marxists, the embodiment of evil in the capitalist society" (P. K. Kurz, *op. cit.*, 28).

10. J. Kopperschmidt, "Schuldhafte Schuldlosigkeit. Das Thema 'Schuld' in der modernen Literatur," J. Blank, ed., *Der Mensch am Ende der Moral*, Düsseldorf 1971, 35–61.

11. F. Dürrenmatt, *Theaterprobleme*, Zürich 1955, 47 ff.

12. J. Kopperschmidt, *op. cit.*, 35. H. Broch has also written in a similar way about the problem of guilt in *Die Schuldlosen*, Zürich 1950.

13. Martin Walser, *Gesammelte Stücke* 6, Frankfurt 1971, 215–246.

14. *Ibid.*, 220.

15. Literary critics have also made very different pronouncements. Stiller "disregards his guilt" and this is a "blind spot in the eye of the I-man Stiller" (K. L. Tauh, "Schuld: ein Weg zur Wirklichkeit Stiller — ein Roman," *Sonntagsblatt*, 16 January 1955). Or Stiller cannot elaborate his examination of himself to the point where he has an authentic feeling of guilt (W. Kohlschmidt, "Selbstrechenschaft und Schuldbewußtsein im Menschenbild der Gegenwartsdichtung," A. Schaefer, ed., *Das Menschenbild in der Dichtung*, Munich 1965, 184). Or "guilt as a result of neglect is part of his history — an essential and indispensable part" (M. Wintsch-Spieß, *Zum Problem der Identität im Werk Max Frischs*, Zürich 1965, 91).

16. J. Blank, "'Am Rande des Kontinents' oder 'Die spätbürgerliche Hölle.' Zur Interpretation von A. Camus' 'Der Fall,'" *id.*, ed., *Der Mensch am Ende der Moral, op. cit.*, 9–33, 24 ff.

17. *Ibid.*, 25.

18. The superego accuses and judges the ego or I. In this strange situation of accusation, the accused I reacts as a bad conscience. This bad conscience is therefore the repressed, inward-turning and as yet unburdened instinct of freedom. This repressed and inward-turning instinct makes a place for itself in acts of aggression. This aggression, as a means of defence against fear, produces new feelings of guilt and these produce new fear and anxiety. This vicious circle of guilt, anxiety and aggression is what we call "proto-ethical mechanical morality."

19. K. Demmer has dealt with this question in a striking analysis, *Entscheidung und Verhängnis. Die moraltheologische Lehre von der Sünde im Licht christologischer Anthropologie. Konfessionskundliche Studien XXXVIII*, Paderborn 1976.

20. P. K. Kurz, *op. cit.*, 29 f.

21. *Ibid.*, 30.

22. J. Blank, *op. cit.*, 26 f.

§ 7 Symbolism and Concepts, pp. 76–86.

1. See P. Ricoeur, *Symbolik des Bösen. Phänomenologie der Schuld* II, Freiburg 1971; *id.*, "Guilt, Ethics and Religion," *Concilium* 6 (1970), 11–27; *id.*, "Hermeneutik der Symbole und philosophisches Denken," *Kerygma und Mythos* VI–1, 1963, 44–68.

2. Ricoeur's research is connected with his philosophy of the will, the first work that he wrote on this theme being *Philosophie de la volonté. Le volontaire et l'involontaire*, Paris 1950. It is clear from Ricoeur's philosophy of the will that only the eidos or the essential being of the will can be perceived when a phenomenological and eidetical method is used and that everything that does not form part of this being of the will is disregarded. Failure or fault also belongs to the part that has to be set aside. It is a phenomenon that can only be attained with the help of the empirical method. This empirical method, however, is not capable of solving the

problem that Ricoeur regarded as the central problem of the whole philosophy of the will — the problem of the transition from innocence to failure or fault. This problem, Ricoeur hopes, can be grasped with the help of a concrete mythicism so that the empiricism of the will can then be attacked from this standpoint. See J. Rütsche's review of P. Ricoeur, *Phänomenologie der Schuld* I and II in *PhJ* 80 (1973), 415–422, 415 ff.

3. P. Ricoeur, "Guilt," *op. cit.*, 12; see also *id.*, *Symbolik*, 13 ff.: "The experience of the penitent is a blind experience. It is covered with emotions such as fear and anxiety. These emotions demand to be objectivized in discursive reason. The confession of guilt expresses emotion, forces it out, when it would otherwise be enclosed upon itself as an impression of the soul. Language is the light of this emotion and through confession our consciousness of guilt is raised up into the light of the word. Through confession man remains word until he.experiences his absurdity, his suffering and his anxiety."

4. *Id.*, "Hermeneutik," 46.

5. *Id.*, *Symbolik*, 14

6. *Id.*, "Guilt," 12.

7. *Ibid.*, 12.

8. *Id.*, "Hermeneutik," 48; see also *id.*, *Symbolik*, 60 ff.

9. *Id.*, "Hermeneutik," 48.

10. *Ibid.*, 48.

11. *Ibid.*, 49.

12. In this section on the Old Testament, I rely especially on Rolf Knierim, *Die Hauptbegriffe für Sünde im Alten Testament*, Gütersloh 1965; *id.*, "*ḥṭ'*, sich verfehlen," *THAT* I (1973), 541–549; *id.*, "*poeša'*, Verbrechen," *THAT* II (1976), 488–495; *id.*, "'*āwōn*, Verkehrtheit," *THAT* II (1976), 243–249.

13. See Knierim, *Hauptbegriffe*, 13 note 1.

14. It is used 237 times in the Old Testament as a verb and 358 times as a noun; see *THAT* I, 542.

15. See Gen. 40.1; 42.22; Ex. 5.16; Jg. 11.27; 1 Sam. 24.12; 26.21.

16. Knierim, *Hauptbegriffe*, 58.

17. *Ibid.*, 59.

18. *Ibid.*, 23; see 2 Sam. 12.1 ff. The singular form is also frequently used in the secular sphere, whereas the plural form occurs twenty-four times and only in connection with cultic or sacral legal events.

19. Knierim, *Hauptbegriffe*, 33.

20. *Ibid.*, 60.

21. The passages in which an unconscious objective failure is expressed belong to an earlier tradition with a dynamistic understanding of the situation; *ibid.*, 68.

22. W. Eichrodt, *Theologie des Alten Testaments* III, Göttingen 1974, 266.

23. Knierim, *Hauptbegriffe*, 70.

24. Köhler was referring here to Ex. 22.8. "Ein Beitrag zur Kenntnis des hebräischen Rechts," *ZAW* 46 (1928), 213–218.

25. Knierim, *Hauptbegriffe*, 143 ff.; "*poeša'*," *THAT* II, *op. cit.*, 489. The use of the plural form in the prophetic pronouncements on the nations in Amos (1.3–2.16) contradicts these translations.

26. Knierim, *Hauptbegriffe*, 177.

27. K. H. Fahlgren, *Ṣᵉdāḳā nahestehende und entgegengesetzte Begriffe im Alten Testament*, Uppsala 1932, 19.

28. Knierim, *Hauptbegriffe*, 178.

29. *Ibid.*, 182.

30. *Id.*, "*ʿāwōn*," *THAT* II, *op. cit.*, 243.

31. *Id.*, *Hauptbegriffe*, 251.

32. *Ibid.*, 252.

33. *Ibid.*, 255.

34. *Ibid.*, 256.

35. *Ibid.*, 248.

36. *Ibid.*, 250.

37. See, for example, W. Grundmann, "*hamartanō* (Die Sünde im NT)," *ThWNT* I, 305–320; K. H. Rengstorf, "*hamartōlos*," *ThWNT* I, 320–337.

38. See W. Grundmann, *op. cit.*, 305; K. H. Rengstorf, *op. cit.*, 333.

39. See R. Schnackenburg, "Die sittliche Botschaft des Neuen Testaments," M. Reding, ed., *Handbuch der Moraltheologie* VI, Munich 1962, 233 ff.

40. See O. Kuss, *Der Römerbrief*, Regensburg 1957, 246.

41. *Ibid.*, 246.

42. See A. Vögtle, "Sünde (IV. Im NT)," *LTHK* IX, 1174–1177, 1176 f.

43. G. von Rad, *Theologie des Alten Testaments* I, Munich 1969, 167.

§ 8 Sin as an Act, pp. 87–97.

1. See B. Welte, *Über das Böse*, QD 6, Freiburg 1958; K. Hemmerle, "Das Böse," *SM* I, 617–624.

2. According to the traditional doctrine of the Church, there is a *libertas contrarietatis* or freedom of contradiction, as opposed to a freedom of choice, in other words, the freedom to act or not to act or to act in a certain way or to act differently.

3. See P. Ricoeur, "Guilt, Ethics and Religion," *op. cit.*, 12.

4. K. Demmer, *op. cit.* (§ 6), 25.

5. See H. Goeke, *Das Menschenbild der individuellen Klage lieder. Ein Beitrag zur alttestamentlichen Anthropologie*, Bonn 1971, 91 ff.

6. See T. Boman, *Das hebräische Denken im Vergleich mit dem griechischen*, Göttingen 1968.

7. P. Ricoeur, "Guilt, Ethics and Religion," *op. cit.*, 12.

8. F. Dürrenmatt, *Theaterprobleme*, *op. cit.*, 47.

9. See F. J. Stendebach, *Theologische Anthropologie des Jahwisten*, Bonn 1970, 218 ff.

10. *Ibid.*, 221 ff.

11. K. Demmer, *op. cit.*, 28.

12. *Ibid.*

13. P. Ricoeur, "Guilt, Ethics and Religion," *op. cit.*, 25.

14. *Beschlüsse der Vollversammlung. Offizielle Gesamtausgabe* I, Freiburg 1976, 93.

15. J. B. Metz, "Vergebung der Sünden. Theologische Überlegungen zu einem Abschnitt aus dem Synodendokument 'Unsere Hoffnung,'" *StZ* 195, (1977), 119–128.

16. *Ibid.*, 120.

17. *Ibid.*, 121.

18. *Beschlüsse, op. cit.*, 94.

19. See O. H. Pesch, *Theologie der Rechtfertigung bei Martin Luther und Thomas von Aquin. Welberberger Studien. Theologische Reihe* IV, Mainz 1967, 468–516.

20. *Ibid.*, 468.

21. *"A theologis consideratur peccatum praecique secundum quod est offensa contra Deum: a philosopho autem morali, secundum quod contrariatur rationi"* (71, 6 ad 5).

22. *"Habet autem actus humanus quod sit malus, ex eo quod caret debita commensuratione. Omnis autem commensuratio cuiuscumque rei attenditur per comparationem ad aliquam regulam, a qua si divertat, incommensurata erit. Regula autem voluntatis est duplex: una propinqua et homogenea, scilicet ipsa ratio humana, alia vero est prima regula, scilicet les aeterna, quae est quasi ratio Dei"* (71, 6).

23. O. H. Pesch, *op. cit.*, 470.

24. *Ibid.*, 473.

25. *"Et ideo Augustinus indefinitione peccati posuit duo: unum quod pertinet ad substantiam actus humani, quod est quasi materiale in peccato, cum dixit, dictum vel factum vel concupitum; aliud autem quod pertinet ad rationem mali, quod est quasi formale in peccato, cum dixit, contra legem aeternam"* (71, 6c).

26. O. H. Pesch, *op. cit.*, 479.

§ 9 Sin as a Power, pp. 97–105.

1. See P. Schoonenberg, *Theologie der Sünde*, Einsiedeln 1966; P. Lengsfeld, *Adam und Christus*, Essen 1965; H. Haag, *Biblische Schöpfungslehre und kirchliche Erbsündenlehre*, Stuttgart 1966; see also a valuable critical essay dealing with various approaches to the problem: L. Scheffczyk, "Versuche zur Neuaussprache der Erbsünde-Wahrheit," *MThZ* 17 (1966), 253–260.

2. See M. Seybold, "Erbsünde und Sünde der Welt," *MThZ* 18 (1967), 56–60.

3. K. Rahner, "Erbsünde," *SM* I, 1104–1117, 1115.

4. *Ibid.*, 1115.

5. W. Oelmüller, "Probleme des neuzeitlichen Freiheits- und Aufklärungsprozesses," J. B. Metz, J. Moltmann and W. Oelmüller, eds., *Kirche im Prozeß der Aufklärung*, Munich and Mainz 1970, 91–143, 131.

6. I. Kant, "Die Religion innerhalb der Grenzen der bloßen Vernunft," *Werke*, W. Weischedel, ed., Darmstadt 1968, VII, 690 (B43/ A39); English trans.: *Religion within the Limits of Reason Alone*, Glasgow 1934.

7. *Ibid.*, 694 ff. (B49/A45).

8. W. Oelmüller, *Die unbefriedigte Aufklärung*, Frankfurt 1969, 236.

9. W. Post, "The Problem of Evil," *Concilium* 6 (1970), 105–114, 107.

10. See H. Marcuse, *Triebstruktur und Gesellschaft*, Frankfurt 1969.

11. See T. W. Adorno, *Negative Dialektik*, Frankfurt 1965.

12. See J. Habermas, *Erkenntnis und Interesse*, Frankfurt 1968.

13. W.-D. Marsch, "Is Consciousness of Sin a 'False Consciousness'?" *Concilium* 6 (1970), 28–44, 43–44.

§ 10 Sin as a Sign, pp. 105–112.

1. K. Rahner, "Zum theologischen Begriff der Konkupiszenz," *Schriften* I, 377–414, 393, note 1; *id.*, "Würde und Freiheit des Menschen," *Schriften* II, 247–277; *id.*, "Schuld und Schuldvergebung als grenzgebiete zwischen Theologie und Psychotherapie," *Schriften* II, 279–297; F. Böckle, "Bestrebungen in der Moraltheologie," J. Feiner, J. Trütsch and F. Böckle, eds., *Fragen der Theologie heute*, Einsiedeln 1957, 425–446; H. Reiners, *Grundintention und sittliches Tun*, QD 30, Freiburg 1966; H. Kramer, *Die sittliche Vorentscheidung*, Würzburg 1970; K. Demmer, *Entscheidung und Verhängnis*, Paderborn 1976.

2. It should be borne in mind that this distinction between the original act of freedom and its corporealization does not coincide with the scholastic distinction between an *actus internus* and an *actus externus*. They are not the same — the scholastic distinction precedes the other distinction and the *actus internus* should be regarded as a corporealization of man's desire. See W. Brugger, "Die Verleiblichung des Wollens," *Schol* 25 (1950), 248–253.

3. See P. Fransen, "Zur Psychologie der göttlichen Gnade," *Die Kirche in der Welt* 11 (1960), 143–150 and 265–274; *id.*, "Das neue Sein des Menschen in Christus," *MS* IV/2, 921–984, 954 ff. For Fransen, the fundamental option is a fresh possibility to discuss sanctifying grace; see, for example, *MS* IV/2, 956.

4. *Id.*, *MS* IV/2, 955.

5. *Ibid.*

6. *Ibid.*, 957.

7. See A. Landgraf, *Das Wesen der läßlichen Sünde in der Scholastik bei Thomas von Aquin*, Bamberg 1923, 135.

8. See K. Rahner, *Schriften* VI, 271.

§ 11 The Freedom that Sets Free, pp. 113–123.

1. K. Niederwimmer, *Der Begriff der Freiheit im Neuen Testament*, Berlin 1966, 106.

2. L. Keck, "The Son who Creates Freedom," *Concilium* 10 (1974), 71–82, 71.

3. J. Neuner, "No Monopoly in Promoting Freedom," *Concilium* 10 (1974), 170–175.

4. K. Niederwimmer, *op. cit.*, 150. See also D. Lührmann, "Jesus: History and Remembrance," *Concilium* 10 (1974), 42–55, 51: "A layer of primitive Christian tradition which expressly handed down Jesus' words and deeds for the sake of salvation *has to be* examined to decide how its tradition relates to its starting-point, the words and deeds of *Jesus*. Only in this way is it possible to decide what 'Easter' meant for these groups, and whence they derived the legitimation for their assertion of continuity with Jesus. On the other hand, another question is also pressing: that of the support such a theology finds in Jesus himself. Is there a road from the circle which Jesus summoned as his disciples to the community of Jesus which confesses him?"

5. See R. Pesch, "Jesus, A Free Man," *Concilium* 10 (1974), 56–70, 63 and 66; K. Niederwimmer, D. Lührmann and L. Keck, *op. cit.*, all have some valuable statements to make about this.

6. K. Niederwimmer, *op. cit.*, 152.

7. R. Pesch, *op. cit.*, 63.

8. K. Niederwimmer, *op. cit.*, 166 ff., with reference to Foerster, *ThWNT* II, 566, 20 ff.

9. R. Pesch, *op. cit.*, 65.

10. K. Niederwimmer, *op. cit.*, 165.

11. L. Keck, *op. cit.*, 76.

12. H. Schlier, "eleutheros," *ThWNT* II, 484–500, 492.

13. K. Niederwimmer, *op. cit.*, 79.

14. "In the New Testament, freedom is a polemical concept. Its place is within the polemics directed against a misunderstanding of the gospel and in the controversy with legalism and libertinism" (*ibid.*, 84).

15. In this sense, the Pauline statement is fundamental. In classical Greece, freedom was primarily a political concept. The laws of Greece acted as a guarantee of freedom. But "the Greek knew that the law could lead him to the insoluble difficulty of his existence. He interpreted this, however, as an inner contradiction in the law itself, as the fact that the law was opposed to the law. The result, that the law could not be fulfilled, was projected into the deity and regarded, not as a guilty situation, but as a tragic one" (*ibid.*, 118 ff.). A good example of this can be found in Sophocles' Antigone.

16. "Being in Christ or in the Spirit is being in freedom. . . . The conflict is to be found in the fact that man is at the same time concentrated on himself and also a creature, that he is his own independent subject and also God's object. This conflict is resolved in the Spirit. Man is completely controlled by God in the Spirit and yet at the same time — not as a restriction of this state of being controlled by God, but rather as the paradoxical other side of this relationship — he is also controlled by himself. In the

Spirit, God is in control of man and, precisely within this control, man is in control of himself" (ibid., 183).

17. H. Halter, *Taufe und Ethos. Eine Untersuchung zu den paulinischen Gemeindebriefen im Rahmen der moraltheologischen Propriumsdiskussion*, Bonn 1975, 279.

18. *Ibid.*, 279.

19. *Ibid.*, 279. "Both aspects are contained in the formula *baptizesthai eis Christon (Iesoun)* (Gal. 3.27; Rom. 6.3; see also 1 Cor. 10.2; 12.13). They are so essential for our understanding of baptism that they appear in some form or other in almost every statement about baptism" (ibid., 279).

20. *Ibid.*, 283.

21. *Ibid.*, 453.

22. L. Keck, *op. cit.*, 75–76.

23. J. Neuner, "No Monopoly in Promoting Freedom," *op. cit.*, 40.

24. *Ibid.*, 41.

25. C. Amery, *Das Ende der Vorsehung. Die gnadenlose Folgen des Christentums*, Hamburg, 1972.

26. J. B. Cobb, *The Structure of Christian Existence*, London 1968. See also G. Altner, *Schöpfung am Abgrund*, Grenzspräche V, Neukirchen and Vluyn 1974, 11 f.

27. "In the light of the biblical message, the world is not the majestic all-embracing reality in the pre-established orders of which man is enclosed, but the reality that is available to man, the material as it were of his becoming historically man in the presence of God and his turning toward man in Jesus Christ" (J. B. Metz, "Die Zukunft des Glaubens in einer hominisierten Welt," J. B. Metz, ed., *Weltverständnis im Glauben*, Mainz 1965, 45–62, 53). For the process of secularization, see F. Gogarten, *Verhängnis und Hoffnung der Neuzeit. Die Säkularisation als theologisches Problem*, Stuttgart 1953; A. Auer, "Gestaltwandel des christlichen Weltverständnisses," *Gott in Welt* I, Freiburg 1964, 333–365; J. B. Metz, *Theology of the World*, London 1969.

28. G. Leidke, "Von der Ausbeutung zur Kooperation. Theologischphilosophische Überlegungen zum Problem des Umweltschutzes," E. von Weizsäcker, ed., *Humanökologie und Umweltschutz*, Munich 1972, 36–65, 42.

29. C. Westermann, *Genesis* BK I/1, Neukirchen and Vluyn 1974, 84.

30. G. Leidke, *op. cit.*, 44.

31. *Ibid.*, 56.

32. W. Beinert, "Freiheit durch Jesus Christus," *StZ* 193 (1975), 467–481, 481.

§ 12 The Different Kinds of Norms and their Social Context, pp. 127–134.

1. Makkoth 23 b.

2. See, for example, the laws of the Bilalama of Ešnunna in Babylonia, twentieth century B.C.; the Code of Lipit-Ištar, middle of the nineteenth century B.C.; the Code of Hammurabi, seventeenth century B.C. See V.

Korošek, *Zakonik mesta Ešnunne in Lipit-Ištarjev zakonik* (*Slovenska akademija znanosti in umetnosti*, Razprave II), Ljubljana 1953; A. Falkenstein and M. San Nicolò, "Das Gesetzbuch Lipit-Ištars von Isin," *Orientalia* 19 (1950), 103 ff.; J. B. Pritchard, *Ancient Near Eastern Texts* II, Princeton 1955.

3. G. Cornfeld and G. J. Botterweck, *Die Bibel und ihre Welt* I, Bergisch Gladbach 1969, 574.

4. Conditional sentences in the third person singular, with a statement of the legal case in the protasis and a definition of the legal consequences in the apodosis: "Given the case that . . . then he/she . . ." (see, for example, Ex. 22.15 f.).

5. See E. Nielsen, *Die Zehn Gebote. Eine traditionsgeschichtliche Skizze.* Acta Theologica Danica 8, Copenhagen 1965, 50: "Jurisprudence in the real sense of the word."

6. G. J. Botterweck, "Form-und überlieferungsgeschichtliche Studie zum Dekalog," *Concilium* 1 (1965), 392–401, 392.

7. H. Schlüngel-Straumann, "Der Dekalog — Gottes Gebot?" *SBS* 67, Stuttgart 1973, 19.

8. See E. Nielsen, *op. cit.*, 51. In the curses and blessings that are connected with commandments and prohibitions, there is no human jurisdiction. If the punishment of *kareth* is directly related to the criminal, then the *bi'ar^eta* formula is applied to the "taking away" of such evils as murder, abduction, improper behavior toward parents and so on. (See Dt. 13.2-6; 17.2-7; 19.11-13 etc.) The *tô'ebhah* or "abomination" formula ("This is an abomination to Yahweh, your God") should be seen in connection with the commandment to extirpate the people of Canaan and can be regarded as anti-Canaanite. (See, for example, Dt. 16.21–17.1; 22.5.)

9. A. Alt, "Die Ursprünge des israelitischen Rechtes," *Kleine Schriften zur Geschichte des Volkes Israel* I, Munich 1953, 278–332.

10. "Wesen und Herkunft des 'Apodiktischen Rechts,'" *WMANT* 20, Neukirchen 1965.

11. See E. Nielsen, *op. cit.*, 61.

12. H. Schlüngel-Straumann, *op. cit.*, 20. One is reminded in this context of the Egyptian moral maxims in the reign of Rameses II, which consist of two series of ten in the formula: "Do not . . ." or "Thou mayest not do . . ." They are concerned with such matters as the moving of a boundary stone, a false measuring cord, false weight, greed for possessions on the part of the poor and so on. These negative catalogues of confessed sins present us with the idea of the dead being judged in the hereafter. They express an ethical order which embraces the whole of human life. The negative catalogue functions as a series of directives and warnings. Such a negative confession of sins presupposes the existence of a series of apodictic commandments and prohibitions; it is, after all, only meaningful to say "I have not . . ." in such a situation. There was in Egypt an ideal biography, expressing the proper order in a particular sphere of life (that of a high-ranking official), and on the other hand the ideal of justice and ethical order which was universally valid and was not

applied to a particular human status. The spread of an ethos expressed in Wisdom formulas throughout the whole of the Ancient Near East shows that there had been since the very earliest period a definite ethos that was expressed in short sentences in the form of moral maxims. Scholars have tried to trace this form back to cultic formulas, clan ethics or covenant formulas.

13. H. Schlüngel-Straumann, *op. cit.*, 20. Nielsen, *op. cit.*, 22, believes that the social context of the decalogue was that of a household code or a collection of rules used within the family circle.

14. See his comments on the apodictic law and the decalogue in *Kerygma und Dogma* 11 (1965), 49–74.

15. See the Rechabite rules (Jer. 35.6 ff.).

16. See the cultic decalogue (Ex. 34.10-28), which is a cultic and liturgical fragment with a paraenesis and at the same time a promulgation of the law.

17. See H. Schlüngel-Straumann, *op. cit.*, 7.

18. See W. Zimmerli, *Grundriß der alttestamentlichen Theologie*, Stuttgart 1972, 95.

19. The function of the decalogue as a summary of God's will in cultic celebrations is especially clear from Psalms 50 and 81. In connection with the prohibition of foreign gods, Yahweh's presentation of himself in the preamble to the decalogue (Ex. 20.2) should be seen as a formula of God's love. The principal examples of this formula will be found in the law of holiness. Again and again the most important places are emphasized by the claim that Yahweh is the God of Israel. For this, see W. Zimmerli, "Ich bin Jahwe," *Geschichte und Altes Testament. Festschrift für A. Alt, Beiträge zur Hist. Theol.* 16, Tübingen 1953, 179–209. In Ezekiel, the formula is anticipated: Yahweh will be known when the people believe in him. Yahweh's presentation of himself is thus a criterion of knowledge that becomes the object of our human behavior. The social context is made clear in Exodus 6 and Ezekiel 20: the really effective power in history is the name of Yahweh. Connected with this is the demand made of the people that they should have no relationship with any other God.

20. W. Zimmerli, *op. cit.*, 95.

21. F. M. Cross, "El," *ThWAT* I, Stuttgart 1973, 259–279, 275; see also G. von Rad, *Theologie des Alten Testaments* I, Munich 1969, 221: "There are clearly no parallels in the polytheism of Canaan for YHWH's exclusive claim to loyalty in the covenant. This epithet may well have arisen at a very early stage in the cult of Israel and have been fashioned on contemporary types of living liturgical language."

22. W. Zimmerli, *Theologie*, 100.

23. *Ibid.*, 97.

24. See M. Weinfeld, "berîth," *ThWAT* I, Stuttgart 1973, 781–808, 784.

25. "Recht und Bund in Israel und dem Alten Vorderen Orient," *ThST* 64, Zürich 1960; also D. J. McCarthy, "Der Gottesbund im Alten Testament," *SBS* 13, Stuttgart 1966, 31 ff., 51 ff.

26. This idea has been developed by K. Baltzer, "Das Bundesformular," *WMANT* 4, Neukirchen 1964; W. Beyerlin, *Herkunft und Geschichte der ältesten Sinaitradition*, Tübingen 1961; D. J. McCarthy, *op. cit.*; E. Nielsen, *op. cit.*

27. See D. J. McCarthy, *op. cit.*, 52 ff.

28. Whereas Wellhausen believed that the covenant between Israel and Yahweh was a form of totemism, D. J. McCarthy believed that the covenant led to the movement of "ethical monotheism," according to which "union with God was neither a matter of natural affinity, nor a magic rite, but rather a moral event, Israel being the privileged friend and partner of God for as long as the people observed God's law," *op. cit.*, 18. According to W. Eichrodt, on the other hand, the covenant necessarily contained a declaration of Yahweh's will and intention, as that of the senior partner. By coming to a knowledge of God's will in this way, Israel acquired a law that guided the people and gave them confidence in an environment in which the deity was usually experienced as arbitrary and terrifying. See McCarthy, *op. cit.*, 22.

29. Compare, for example, Pr. 22.22 with Lev. 19.13; Pr. 22.28 with Dt. 19.4; Pr. 23.10; with Ex. 22.21.

30. A similar situation can also be observed in the Hittite treaties.

31. G. J. Botterweck, "Form- und überlieferungsgeschichtliche Studie zum Dekalog," *op. cit.*, 398.

32. See Ps. 147.19 f.: "He declares his word to Jacob, his statutes and ordinances to Israel. He has not dealt thus with any other nation; they do not know his ordinances."

33. See H. Schlüngel-Straumann, *op. cit.*, 101.

34. See E. Nielsen, *op. cit.*, 61; see also B. Schüller, *Die Begründung sittlicher Urteile*, Düsseldorf 1973, 11 ff., especially 16 f.

35. W. Zimmerli, *Theologie*, 121.

§ 13 Faith in Yahweh and its Influence on the Development and Formation of the Ethos of Israel, pp. 134–139.

1. W. Zimmerli, *Theologie, op. cit.*, 120. According to Zimmerli, the individual and the community in Israel cannot be separated, even in the psalms (*op. cit.*, 121). There is no individual ethos that can be regarded as distinct from the responsibility of Israel in and for the community as such.

2. For ṣ*e*dhāqāh, see K. H. Fahlgren, Ṣ*e*dāḳā, *nahestehende und entgegengesetzte Begriffe im Alten Testament*, Uppsala 1932, 79: "The root ṣdḳ points to a relationship of equilibrium in the community in the world. The nouns Ṣ*e*dāḳā and Ṣaedaeḳ express the norm of this relationship and what is in accordance with that norm; the adjective ṣaddîḳ points to the person who takes up the right attitude in the relationship to men or to God; the verb ṣādaḳ means 'keeping the right norm in accordance with the point of view of togetherness.'" See also E. Nielsen, *op. cit.*, 26.

3. K. H. Fahlgren, *op. cit.*, 83.

4. See, for example, Ps. 116.5.

5. The concept "neighbor" in the Old Testament is always a member of the people of Israel and never a stranger. It is only in the New Testament that the concept is extended to include all people.

6. See Fahlgren, *op. cit.*, 128.

7. P. Grelot, "The Institution of Marriage: Its Evolution in the Old Testament," *Concilium* 5 (1970), 39–50, 43.

8. *Ibid.*, 43.

9. See G. von Rad, *Der Heilige Krieg in alten Israel*, Göttingen, 1965.

10. W. Eichrodt, *Theologie des Alten Testamentes* II, Göttingen 1974, 224.

11. J. Hempel, *Das Ethos des Alten Testamentes*, Berlin 1964, 193.

12. *Ibid.*, 193.

13. H. von Oyen, "Ethik des Alten Testamentes," *Geschichte der Ethik* II, H. von Oyen and H. Reiner, eds., Gütersloh 1967, 97.

Excursus: The Influence of Israel's Faith in God on the Law of Property, pp. 139–141.

1. F. Horst, "Das Eigentum nach dem Alten Testament," *Gottes Recht. Gesammelte Studien zum Recht im Alten Testament. Theologische Bücherei* 12, Munich 1961, 203–221, 209.

2. *Ibid.*, 210.

3. *Ibid.*, 213.

4. *Ibid.*

5. *Ibid.*, 221.

6. *Ibid.*, 213.

§ 14 The Significance of the Prophets, pp. 141–145.

1. G. von Rad, *Die Botschaft der Propheten*, Munich 1970, 7.

2. *Ibid.*, 7.

3. See E. Jenni, "Die alttestamentliche Prophetie," *TS* 67, Zürich 1962.

4. *Ibid.*, 18.

5. See G. von Rad, *Die Botschaft der Propheten, op. cit.*, 10.

6. E. Jenni, *op. cit.*, 18.

7. See Am. 5.14; 5.4, 6; Ex. 15.26; Dt. 6.18–12.28; 12.25; 13.19; 21.9; 1 Kg. 11.33, 38; 2 Chr. 14.1; 19.3, 11; Ezra 8.22; Ps. 4.7; 34.15; 37.3, 27; Is. 1.17; Mic. 6.8.

8. Am. 5.15; see also Ps. 34.11, 14 f.; 36.4; 37.3; 52.5; Pr. 11.27; Mic. 3.2; Est. 10.3; 2 Chr. 30.18.

9. Reinhard Fey, "Amos und Jesaja," *WMANT* 12, Neukirchen and Vluyn 1963, 36.

10. See also Neh. 9.13; Ps. 119.39; Pr. 20.23; 24.23, 25; Mic. 2.1 ff.; Am. 2.6 ff.

11. K. H. Fahlgren, *op. cit.*, 156.

12. See Dt. 30.11-14.

13. See Wolfgang Richter, *Recht und Ethos*, Munich 1966, 157 ff.

14. G. von Rad, *Theologie des Alten Testaments* II, Munich 1968, 129.

15. E. Jenni, *op. cit.*, 12.
16. Martin Buber, *Der Glaube der Propheten*, Zürich 1950, 149.
17. A. Auer, *Autonome Moral und christlicher Glaube*, Düsseldorf 1971, 69.
18. See Is. 2.2-5; 4.2-6; 9.1-6; 11; 35; 43; 65.17-25; Jer. 30.1-31, 40; 33; Ezek. 20; 36; 37, etc.

§ 15 The Contribution Made by the Wisdom Literature, pp. 145–151.

1. G. von Rad, *Theologie des Alten Testaments* II, *op. cit.*, 87.
2. G. von Rad, *Weisheit in Israel*, Neukirchen 1970, 14; H. H. Schmid, "Wesen und Geschichte der Weisheit," *BZAW* 101 (1966), 159; U. Skladny, *Die ältesten Spruchsammlungen in Israel*, Göttingen 1962, 8; W. Zimmerli, *Theologie, op. cit.*, 136 ff.
3. G. von Rad, *Weisheit, op. cit.*, 14 ff.
4. *Ibid.*, 16. See also the Egyptian Wisdom books from the third century B.C. until the latest period of Egyptian culture. Unlike von Rad (*ibid.*, 21), W. Richter, in his *Recht und Ethos*, rightly refuted the suggestion that Pr. 22.17–23.11 had been taken almost word for word from the Wisdom book of Amen-em-ope.
5. G. von Rad, *Weisheit, op. cit.*, 24; see also *id.*, *Theologie des Alten Testaments* I, 427: "as soon as the state of Israel had been organized during the reign of Solomon on the model of an Ancient Near Eastern kingdom, wisdom was introduced and practised." See also B. Gemser, "Sprüche Salomos," *HAT* 16, Tübingen 1963, 2; A. Alt, "Die Weisheit Salomos," *ThLZ* 76 (1951), 139–144 = *Kleine Schriften* II, Munich 1953, 90–99.
6. G. von Rad, *Weisheit, op. cit.*, 81.
7. W. Zimmerli, "Zur Struktur der alttestamentlichen Weisheit," *ZAW* 51 (1933), 177–204, 178.
8. B. Gemser, *op. cit.*, 1. See also W. Zimmerli, *Theologie, op. cit.*, 137 ff.: "In their different forms of parallelism and their playful, artistic and original structure, which is clearly present in their metaphors and similes, the proverbs of Israel have an underlying intention, that of imparting a knowledge of certain laws that operate in nature and in human life. In this intention, the one aspect is related again and again to the other. This process can, for example, be seen at work in the series of phenomena listed in Pr. 30.24-28 as remarkable for their law and order. Knowledge of these laws is not, however, acquired simply unintentionally, but rather with the intention of acquiring a norm for human behavior from a knowledge of such hidden laws and in this way of gaining life by behaving correctly."
9. *Ibid.*, 1.
10. *Ibid.*
11. W. Zimmerli, "Struktur," *op. cit.*, 178 ff.
12. *Id.*, *Theologie, op. cit.*, 138: "The believing people of the Old Testament could only see, in the laws that they recognized in their everyday life, the one whom they addressed in their oral and written praise — Yahweh."
13. G. von Rad, *Weisheit, op. cit.*, 48.

14. See O. Eißfeldt, *Einleitung in das Alte Testament*, Tübingen 1964, 92–94 (*The Old Testament: an Introduction*, Oxford 1966); B. Gemser, "The Importance of the Motive Clause in the Old Testament Law," *VTS* 1 (1953), 50–66, especially 64–66.

15. See W. Zimmerli, "Struktur," *op. cit.*, 181.

16. See G. Boström, "Paranomasie i den äldere Hebreiska Maschallitteraturen med särskild Hänsyn till Proverbia," *LUÅ*, new series Adv. 1, XXIII, 8, Lund (1928), 38, note 2.

17. See J. Hempel, *Die althebräische Literatur*, Potsdam 1934, 177; L. Köhler, *Der hebräische Mensch*, Tübingen 1953, 82 ff., 143 ff.

18. See, for example, Pr. 11.1; 20.10, 23; Dt. 25.13-16.

19. J. Fichtner, "Die altorientalische Weisheit in ihrer israelitisch-jüdischen Ausprägung," *BZAW* 62 (1933), 27 ff., 34.

20. This also applies to proverbs expressed in the form of a comparative ("better than . . .").

21. See W. Zimmerli, "Struktur," *op. cit.*, 183.

22. H.-J. Kraus, "Psalmen," *BK* XV/2, Neukirchen 1972, 773: Ps. 112.5.

23. F. Ellermeier, *Qohelet I*. 1, Herzberg 1967, 87.

24. See M. Dahood, *Psalms III*, The Anchor Bible, Garden City and New York 1970, 125. This is one of the very characteristic statements of the Book of Proverbs, occurring five times in all in the didactic literature of the Old Testament (apart from Ps. 111.10 — Pr. 1.7; 9.10; 15.33; Job 28.28). See G. von Rad, *Weisheit, op. cit.*, 91 ff.

25. G. von Rad, *Weisheit, op. cit.*, 94.

26. *Ibid.*, 96.

27. *Ibid.*, 99.

28. *Ibid.*, 125.

29. *Ibid.*, 122.

30. *Ibid.*, 125.

31. *Ibid.*, 129.

32. *Ibid.*, 126.

§ 16 The Proclamation of the Basileia of God, pp. 151–157.

1. See K. Niederwimmer, *Der Begriff der Freiheit im Neuen Testament*, Berlin 1966, 150.

2. R. Pesch, "Das Markusevangelium," *HThK* II/1, Freiburg 1976, 100 ff. "The first of these statements is a prophetic and apocalyptic call and can be regarded as an authentic statement of Jesus', supported by formal parallels in the Old Testament (Is. 56.1; Ezek. 7.3, 12; 9.1; Lam. 4.18b)."

3. *Ibid.*, 102 ff. "The demand for conversion resulting from the proclamation of the imminence of the kingdom of God forms part of the authentic proclamation of Jesus himself" (*ibid.*, 102).

4. See P. Stuhlmacher, *Gerechtigkeit Gottes bei Paulus*, Göttingen 1966, 255. Stuhlmacher demonstrated that "the same phenomenon was announced in Jesus' concept of the Basileia of God and the Pauline state-

ments about the *dikaiosune theou*. This phenomenon was God's liberating law of love."

5. W. Kasper, *Jesus der Christus*, Mainz 1975, 85.

6. See P. Stuhlmacher, *op. cit.*, 254.

7. See H. Schürmann, "Das Lukasevangelium," *HThK* III/1, Freiburg 1969, 231. This proclamation made in Nazareth, in which Jesus revealed himself, was, for Luke, "unmistakably . . . the solemn inaugural experience" (*ibid.*, 227).

8. *Ibid.*, 332.

9. See H. Schürmann, "Das hermeneutische Hauptproblem der Verkündigung Jesu. Eschato-logie und Theo-logie im gegenseitigen Verhältnis," *Traditionsgeschichtliche Untersuchungen zu den synoptischen Evangelein*, Düsseldorf 1968, 13–25 = *Gott in Welt* I, 33, Freiburg, 579–607.

10. See E. Schillebeeckx, *Jezus, het verhaal van een levende*, Bloemendaal 1974, 212, who says that "this is a way of speaking about Jesus based on an identifying understanding of the whole of his life."

11. H. Schürmann, "Das hermeneutische Hauptproblem," *op. cit.*, 33.

12. See *ibid.*, 34: "Although it never becomes a constitutive exegetical principle, the idea of Jesus' sonship throws considerable light on his problem and points the way to its solution. The relationship between the proclamation of God's revelation and that of the eschatological kingdom of God can hardly be determined simply by listening to the Scriptural message. Scripture can only be correctly interpreted by the one who has the Spirit. It is, however, not a phenomenon that is entirely alien to the Bible, nor is it an assumption that is completely devoid of rationality for someone to promise the Spirit not exclusively to himself, but for him to try to listen to and interpret Scripture within the Church of Jesus Christ. In this matter, however, there has always been only one understanding of Scripture and that is in the light of the sonship of Jesus."

13. See W. Kasper, *op. cit.*, 122 ff., especially 128–131: "The full depth of Jesus' claim and the full mystery of his person are revealed to us as soon as we consider the sovereign title that played such an important part in the confession of Christians in the later New Testament period and in the early Church and that proved to be the most appropriate title for Jesus — Son or Son of God" (*ibid.*, 128). In the Old Testament, the idea of the sonship of God was never based on a purely physical derivation. It was only used of an election and a mission given by God. Jesus' sonship from God should also be understood against the background of this faith in God's choice. In the synoptic gospels, Jesus never explicitly calls himself "Son of God." The statement that Jesus is the Son of God is "unambiguously a confession of faith made by the early Church" (*ibid.*, 129). Even the claim to the title "son" in its absolute form may not go back to Jesus himself. Nonetheless, we may assume, on the basis of the terms "my Father" (Mk. 14.26 par; Mt. 11.26 par), "your Father" (Lk. 6.36; 12.30, 32) and the Johannine "my Father and your Father" (Jn. 20.17), which occur consist-

ently at all levels in the New Testament tradition (see also Mt. 11.27 and Lk. 10.22), that "Jesus spoke about himself in a very unique way as 'son'" (*ibid.*, 130). As the one who believed (Mk. 9.23), Jesus was clearly "in his radical obedience radically derived from God and radically orientated toward God. . . . This orientation of Jesus toward the Father naturally presupposed an orientation of the Father toward Jesus and a communication of the Father with Jesus. The later christology of the Son is simply an exposition of what was always present, although concealed, in Jesus' obedience and self-surrender as the Son. What was expressed ontically in Jesus' life before the Easter event was expressed ontologically after Easter" (*ibid.*, 130). At the same time, however, the one who enjoyed such a special relationship with God was also the one who was sent by God, the one who was given full power by God and the one to whom all things had been given by the Father (Mt. 11.27), the one, in other words, who was "God's being for others" (*ibid.*, 131). "As *the* Son, Jesus was the kingdom of God that had become a person, the kingdom in love that communicated itself to man. As *the* Son, too, he was *the* free man. Our freedom is also to be found in him" (*ibid.*, 131). "What this freedom really meant in the concrete . . . and the deepest significance of Jesus' sonship" first became clear in his death on the cross (*ibid.*, 131).

14. R. Schnackenburg, "Biblische Ethik II," *Sacramentum Mundi* I, 546–552, 546.

15. P. Hoffmann, "Die Basileia-Verkündigung Jesu: unaufgebbare Voraussetzung einer christlichen Moral," P. Hoffmann and V. Eid, *Jesus von Nazareth und eine christliche Moral*, Freiburg 1975, 27–58, 51 (see especially 50 ff.).

16. G. Bornkamm, *Jesus von Nazareth*, Stuttgart 1971, 85.

17. W. Kasper, *op. cit.*, 94.

18. *Ibid.*, 95.

19. E. Schillebeeckx, *op. cit.*, 116.

20. *Ibid.*, 172 ff.; the author points out that faith *in* Jesus, in the sense of *pisteuein eis*, was a post-paschal phenomenon.

21. W. Kasper, *op. cit.*, 96.

22. "It has to be admitted that Jesus, together with his words and actions, will always resist any attempt to misuse them in order to justify theologies that are ultimately based on themselves and derive their content from other sources than scripture. . . . The attempts to interpret Jesus with the help of the category 'freedom' will continue to be futile as long as this concept is not more precisely defined on the basis of Jesus' proclamation of the kingdom of God and his justice" (D. Lührmann, "Jesus: Geschichte und Erinnerung," *Concilium* 10, 1974, 173–181, 180).

23. E. Schillebeeckx, *op. cit.*, 125.

24. K. Niederwimmer, *Askese und Mysterium. Über Ehe, Ehescheidung und Eheverzicht in den Anfängen des christlichen Glaubens*, Göttingen 1975, 32 ff.

25. *Ibid.*, 41.

§ 17 The Torah and the New Law, pp. 157–167.

1. See W. Trilling, *Das wahre Israel. Studien zur Theologie des Matthäus-Evangeliums*, Leipzig 1959, 177: "There is only one major question with regard to the history of salvation and that is: do the events that occurred . . . correspond to the predictions? This is a linear problem on one level. . . . In the question of the law, the problem exists at more than one level."

2. P. Hoffmann, "Die Überwindung gesetzhafter Sittlichkeit in der Auseinandersetzung Jesu mit jüdisch-pharisäischem Gesetzesverständnis," P. Hoffmann and V. Eid, *Jesus von Nazareth und eine christliche Moral*, Freiburg 1975, 73–94, 73.

3. Two levels can be distinguished in the history of traditions in the Matthaean version. The antitheses of killing (Mt. 5.21), adultery (5.27 ff.) and swearing oaths (5.33–36) all go back to an earlier tradition. They were adapted and to some degree extended by Matthew, but in all probability they had already been expressed in an antithetic form before the Matthaean editing. In all three cases, Torah or, more exactly, decalogue sentences were used and made more intensive and radical. Jesus, for example, enlarged the datum in question to some extent by indicating that murder begins with uncontrolled anger, adultery with evil desire and perjury with dishonesty. The other three antitheses of divorce (Mt. 5.31 ff.), retaliation (5.38–42) and the hatred and love of one's enemies (5.43–48) can also be found in Luke without any antithetic introduction. They must therefore have been included in the antithetic conception of the final editing of the gospel of Matthew. This total conception based on the principle of antithesis therefore constitutes an exposition of the tradition of Jesus and that of the proverbs for the Judaeo-Christian community.

4. L. Goppelt, "Das Problem der Bergpredigt," *Christologie und Ethik*, Göttingen 1968, 27–43, 29.

5. Jesus' hearers were addressed as though they had heard (*ekousate errethē*). This is a clear indication of the Jewish traditional faith — the Torah was, of course, part of that tradition.

6. "In the specifically Jewish sense, the Torah was a work compiled during the exile in the Babylonian diaspora. During the period of the reconstitution of the Jewish state under Persian sovereignty in 398 B.C., it was declared by Ezra to be the constitutional law of Israel. In so doing, he "created early Judaism and gave it its religious basis in the Pentateuch" (Fohrer). The Jewish people's commitment to the law and its deep effect on their whole existence were intensified by the crisis that occurred in 175 B.C. in connection with the Hellenistic attempt to reform the Jewish state and the consequent persecution of those who adhered to the law, resulting in the Maccabean wars of liberation. The law therefore became the most important factor in the development of the nation" (P. Hoffmann, *op. cit.*, 81).

7. P. Hoffmann, *op. cit.*, 82 ff.

8. W. Trilling, *op. cit.*, 177 ff.

9. *Ibid.*, 178.

10. This claim for totality was also made clear by Jesus in other statements, for example, like that in which he compared the eye to the "lamp of the body" (Mt. 6.22 f.) or in his criticism of the laws of cleanliness (Mk. 7.15). "This was correctly understood by the community of the people, who believed that 'what comes out of man' meant 'what came out of his heart'" (Mk. 7.20 ff.), where thoughts, words and works originated" (P. Hoffmann, op. cit., 86).

11. P. Hoffmann, op. cit., 89, following U. Luz, "Einige Erwägungen zur Auslegung Gottes in der ethischen Verkündigung Jesu," EKK, Vorabschriften H. 2, Einsiedeln and Neukirchen 1970, 119–130, 125.

12. Ibid., 87.

13. L. Goppelt, op. cit., 31, following R. Guelich, "Not to Annul the Law, Rather to Fulfill the Law and the Prophets," An Exegetical Study of Jesus and the Law in Matthew with Emphasis on 5, 17–48, Hamburg 1967.

14. R. Schnackenburg, "Die Bergpredigt Jesu und der heutige Mensch," ibid., Christliche Existenz nach dem Neuen Testament I, Munich 1967, 109–130, 117.

15. B. Schüller, "Zur Rede von der radikalen sittlichen Forderung," ThPh 46 (1971), 321–341. Schüller was right to call in question all the interpretations of the radical nature of Jesus' demands. What most exegetes mean by "radical" here is a reduction of the purely legal claim to the moral claim, with the suggestion that "categorial Christian behavior has to result in a selfless decision made in the power of the Holy Spirit in favor of God and one's fellow-men" (see J. Fuchs, "Moraltheologie und Dogmatik," Gregorianum 50, 1969, 689–716, 703). This is not, as Schüller appears to think, with reference to Ratzinger (op. cit., 324), a "deontologization."

16. In elaborating and developing normative statements, it is not possible for the theme "law–gospel–law" to be ignored in Christian ethics. There can be no Christian ethics without a discussion of the usus legis. This structural problem also forms part of the specifically group morality.

17. E. Schillebeeckx, op. cit., 146.

18. This is the essence of Guelich's interesting argument; see note 13.

19. "hos an apoluse tēn gunaika autou moichatai kai hos an apolelumenēn gamēsē moichatai." See G. Delling, "Das Logion Mark X 11 (und seine Abwandlungen) in Neuen Testament," NovT 1 (1956), 263–274.

20. See H. Baltensweiler, Die Ehe im Neuen Testament. Exegetische Untersuchungen über Ehe, Ehelosigkeit und Ehescheidung, Zürich and Stuttgart 1967, 63.

21. See R. Schnackenburg, "Die Ehe nach dem Neuen Testament," G. Krems and R. Mumm, eds., Theologie der Ehe, Regensburg and Göttingen 1969, 9–36, 13; the controversy can only in this way be preserved as a dialogue in which Jesus himself authentically participated (and not as composition made by the Christian community).

22. This arrangement was made in order to protect marital relationships. Husbands were compelled by the practice of the letter of divorce to adhere to the divorce. It was therefore not a concession, but a testimony against (pros) their hardness of heart. See H. Greeven, "Zu den Aussagen

des Neuen Testamentes über die Ehe," *ZEE* 1 (1957), 109–175, 114. H. Baltenweiler and R. Schnackenburg are both in favor of this interpretation.

23. See H. Greeven, "Ehe nach dem Neuen Testament," G. Krems and R. Mumm, eds., *op. cit.*, 37–79, especially 61–64.

24. See. J. Ratzinger, "Zur Theologie der Ehe," G. Krems and R. Mumm, eds., *op. cit.*, 81–115, 84.

25. R. Pesch, *Freie Treue. Die Christen und die Ehescheidung*, Freiburg, Basle and Vienna, 1971, 13.

26. R. Schnackenburg, "Die Vollkommenheit des Christen nach Matthäus," *Christliche Existenz nach dem Neuen Testament* I, 131–155, 139.

27. *Ibid.*, 141.

28. P. Hoffmann, *op. cit.*, 91.

29. R. Schnackenburg, "Die Vollkommenheit des Christen nach Matthäus," *op. cit.*, 149.

30. *Ibid.*, 146.

31. See E. Schillebeeckx, *op. cit.*, 183. For the concept of the imitation of Jesus, see *ibid.*, 179–188. Schillebeeckx makes a distinction between the disciples' imitation of Jesus before the Easter event, describing this as a "community of fate" (187) with Jesus, a phenomenon of deep soteriological significance, and their imitation after the Easter event, which he interprets as a conversion to Jesus as the risen and exalted Lord.

32. *Ibid.*, 185.

33. R. Schnackenburg, "Die Vollkommenheit des Christen nach Matthäus," *op. cit.*, 145.

34. See Lk. 16.16. The revelation of God's will by the law and the prophets was superseded by Jesus' proclamation of the Basileia. The new dispensation also surpassed the old order, since the salvation of the kingdom of God became present in Jesus himself.

35. For *plēroun*, see W. Trilling, *Das wahre Israel, op. cit.*, 149.

36. F. J. Schierse, "Das Scheidungsverbot Jesu," N. Uetzel, ed., *Die öffentlichen Sünder*, Mainz 1970, 26. The fact that Jesus' directives do not exert compulsion does not mean that they do not make demands. It is clear that the moral claim can be mediated by various kinds of norms and that this mediation does not in any way diminish the claim as such. The need to express a demand in the form of a compulsion may even point to the fact that too little trust is placed in the matter expressed in the demand. Jesus clearly wanted to go beyond the law and express the matter itself, in other words, he wanted to emphasize that marriage was a gift and a promise.

§ 18 The Special and Obligatory Nature of the Apostolic Directives, pp. 168–179.

1. For the contributions made by exegetes to the question of the validity and the nature of the directives contained in the New Testament, see especially: W. Schrage, *Die konkreten Einzelgebote in der paulinischen Paränese*, Gütersloh 1961; H. Schlier, "Vom Wesen der apostolischen Ermahnungen

— nach Röm 12, 1–2," 1941, *Die Zeit der Kirche*, Freiburg 1968, 74–89; *id.*, "Die Eigenart der christlichen Mahnung nach dem Apostel Paulus," 1963, *Besinnung auf das Neue Testament*, Freiburg 1964, 340–357; J. Blank, "Zum Problem 'Ethischer Normen' im Neuen Testament," *Concilium* 5, (1967), 356–362; H. Schürmann, "Die Gemeinde des Neuen Bundes als der Quellort des sittlichen Erkennens nach Paulus," *Cath* 26 (1972), 15–37; *id.*, "'Das Gesetz des Christus' (Gal 6, 2). Jesu Verhalten und Wort als letztgültige sittliche Norm nach Paulus," *Jesu ureigener Tod. Exegetische Besinnungen und Ausblicke*, Freiburg 1974, 97–120; *id.*, "Haben die paulinischen Wertungen und Weisungen Modellcharakter? Beobachtungen und Anmerkungen zur Frage nach ihrer formalen Eigenart und Verbindlichkeit," *Gr* 56 (1975), 237–371; *id.*, "Die Frage nach der Verbindlichkeit der neutestamentlichen Wertungen und Weisungen," J. Ratzinger, ed., *Prinzipien christlicher Moral*, Einsiedeln 1975, 11–39.

2. The question of the validity of individual directives is not implied by the use of the word "model" here. What I have in mind is a model of ethics as a whole. By "model," I mean a pattern of Christian ethics understood as a function of the Church.

3. H. Schürmann, "Haben die paulinischen Wertungen und Weisungen Modellcharakter?" *op. cit.*, 267.

4. *Ibid.*, 267 ff.

5. For what follows in this section, see H. Schürmann, "'Das Gesetz des Christus' (Gal 6, 2)," *op. cit.*

6. *Ibid.*, 99.

7. *Ibid.*

8. H. Schürmann, "Haben die paulinischen Werungen und Weisungen Modellcharakter?" *op. cit.*, 261.

9. *Id.*, "'Das Gesetz des Christus' (Gal 6, 2)," *op. cit.*, 99.

10. *Id.*, "Die Frage nach der Verbindlichkeit," *op. cit.*, 23.

11. *Id.*, "'Das Gesetz des Christus' (Gal 6, 2)," *op. cit.*, 100.

12. *bid.*

13. R. Pesch, "Paulinische 'Kasuistik.' Zum Verständnis von 1 Kor 7, 10–11," *Publicado en "Homenage a Juan Prado," C.S.I.C.*, Madrid 1975, 433–442, 440.

14. According to R. Pesch, the reason why Paul did not regard reconciliation as the only solution and suggested it as the second possibility was that the husband who had previously been a pagan became "irreconcilable" because of the conversion of his wife to Christianity and could therefore not be compelled to accept human reconciliation (see *ibid.*, 441).

15. H. Schürmann, "'Das Gesetz des Christus' (Gal 6, 2)," 101.

16. Such demands, for example, as service of one's fellow-men (1 Cor. 9.19), humiliation of oneself (2 Cor. 11.7), love of one's neighbor (Gal. 5.14; Rom. 13.8 ff.), love of one's enemies (1 Cor. 4.12; 6.7; Rom. 12.14, 17, 21) and such admonitions as those against giving scandal (1 Cor. 8.12 f.) and judging or condemning others (Rom. 2.1; 14.4, 13, 21; 16.17). See H. Schürmann, *op. cit.*, 102.

17. H. Schürmann, "Die Frage nach der Verbindlichkeit," *op. cit.*, 19.

18. *Id.*, "'Das Gesetz des Christus' (Gal 6, 2)," *op. cit.*, 103 ff.; see Rom. 5.6 ff.; Gal. 2.20.

19. *Ibid.*, 105.

20. *Ibid.*, 110.

21. H. Schlier, *Der Brief an die Galater*, Göttingen 1962, 272; cited by H. Schürmann, "'Das Gesetz des Christus' (Gal 6, 2)," *op. cit.*, 110.

22. H. Schürmann, "'Das Gestez des Christus' (Gal 6, 2)," *op. cit.*, 111.

23. *Id.*, "Die Frage nach der Verbindlichkeit," *op. cit.*, 17.

24. H. Schlier, "Über die christliche Existenz," 1961, *Besinning auf das Neue Testament*, Freiburg 1964, 123–134, 132.

25. H. Halter, *Taufe und Ethos, op. cit.*, 280.

26. See H. Schürmann, "Haben die paulinischen Wertungen und Weisungen Modellcharakter?" *op. cit.*, 244 f.

27. *Ibid.*, 245.

28. *Ibid.*, 248.

29. H. Halter, *Taufe und Ethos, op. cit.*, 447.

30. See. F. J. Schierse, "Normen und Normfindung im Neuen Testament," *Religionsunterricht an höheren Schulen* 4 (1974), 176–83, 180: "Jesus personalized ethical norms to such an extent that man in the concrete, one's 'neighbor,' became the only criterion for all actions."

31. H. U. von Balthasar, "Gott begegnen in der heutigen Welt," J. B. Metz, *Weltverständnis im Glauben*, Mainz 1965, 11–23, 19.

32. See my detailed discussion of this problem below.

33. For *tupos didachēs*, see H. Schürmann, "Die Gemeinde des Neuen Bundes als Quellort des sittlichen Erkennens nach Paulus," *op. cit.*, 29 ff.

34. H. Halter, *Taufe und Ethos, op. cit.*, 454, with reference to H. Schlier, *Nun aber bleiben diese Drei. Grundriß des christlichen Lebensvollzugs, Kriterien* 25, Freiburg 1971, 15.

35. H. Halter, *Taufe und Ethos, op. cit.*, 469. For what follows in this chapter, see Halter's summary of the distinctive aspect of Christian existence and its ethos (440–477).

36. *Ibid.*, 470.

37. *Ibid.*, 469 f.

38. This form of list, catalogue or "household code" goes back above all to Stoicism. These catalogues contain, in a universally valid form, a summary of what was regarded as morally good or bad.

39. H. Halter, *Taufe und Ethos, op. cit.*, 472.

40. *Ibid.*, 473 ff.

41. *Ibid.*, 474. For asceticism, see K. Niederwimmer, *Askese und Mysterium, op. cit.*

42. For the wide-ranging debate on this question, see the books and articles listed under note 1 in this section.

43. See H. Schürmann, "Die Frage nach der Verbindlichkeit," *op. cit.*, 35 ff. What cannot be disputed is that universal validity is claimed not only by the theological or eschatological values and directives, but also by other categorial and partial values and directives which, "as ideal com-

mandments or counsels, express general spiritual admonitions or love of one's neighbor, again in a general sense" (H. Schürmann, "Haben die paulinischen Weisungen Modellcharakter?" *op. cit.*, 264 f.). We are exclusively concerned here with concrete material ethics.

44. *Id.*, "Haben die paulinischen Weisungen Modellcharakter?" *op. cit.*, 266.

45. *Ibid.*, 265.

46. *Ibid.*, 266. It would appear that opposition to certain ideas or tendencies in "autonomous morality" led Schürmann to criticize the way of speaking and thinking about the New Testament values and directives as paradigms or models from the exegetical point of view. If this criticism is directed against a too radical division between Christian faith and autonomous reason, then it is justified. Nonetheless, there is clear evidence in many biblical texts, provided in a paradigmatic way, of the effect of faith on reason when it is a question of devising a material ethos that does justice to the revealed reality of salvation.

47. H. Halter, *Taufe und Ethos, op. cit.*, 450.

§ 19 The Complexity of the Question, pp. 180–199.

1. A correct interpretation of Thomas Aquinas's questions about the *lex divina* (*Summa Theologiae* I-II, 98 ff.) and the *lex naturalis* would show quite clearly that he also taught within this tradition. See, for example, *Summa Theologiae* I-II, 108, 2 ad 1: "... *ea quae sunt fidei, sunt supra rationem humanam: unde in ea non possumus pervenire nisi per gratiam. Et ideo, abundantiori gratia superveniente, oportuit plura credenda explicari. Sed ad opera virtutum dirigimur per rationem naturalem, quae est regula quaedam operationis humanae. ... Et ideo in his non oportuit aliqua praecepta dari ultra moralia legis praecepta, quae sunt de dictamine rationis.*" The same also applies to the later scholastic theologians such as Dominic Soto and Francisco de Suarez, to the neoscholastic theologians working in the middle of the nineteenth century and even to those who taught after the First Vatican Council. Very clear evidence of the persistence of this view is provided by the work of the moral theologian Peter Joseph Weber, who was teaching at the end of the eighteenth century. In his *Dissertatio theologica inauguralis de genuina idea moralis christianae*, he stated: "*Nonne Matth. XXII. pro basi moralis christianae duo illa magna praecepta amoris, quae ipsissima et prima sunt iuris naturae principia sunt posita? vide S. Augustinus Enarrat. in Ps. 56 et S. Chrysostomus Expos. in Ps. 147, 110. Atque ex hac iuris naturae cum revelatione concordia fluit illud theologorum celebratissimum principium, nullam a servatore nostro legem rogatam esse, quae non sit iuris naturalis, exceptis his, quae pertinent ad fidem et Sacramenta*" (*ibid.* 19).

2. See F. Böckle, ed., *Das Naturrecht im Disput*, Düsseldorf 1966; *id.* and E.-W. Böckenförde, eds., *Naturrecht in der Kritik*, Mainz 1973.

3. Although the connection between *natura* and *nasci* is widely recognized, that between *phusis* and *phuein* is disputed. See N. Luyten, "Die Natur des Menschen: anthropologische Sicht," A. Müller *et al.*, eds., *Natur*

und Naturrecht, Freiburg 1972, 223–233, 223; the author appeals to D. Ross and R. G. Collingwood, *The Idea of Nature*, Oxford 1960.

4. This is Thomas Aquinas's *"Principium intrinsecum cuiuscumque motus"* (*Summa Theologiae* I, 29, 1). Kant regarded the purely formal meaning of nature as "the first inner principle of everything . . . that belongs to the being of a thing" (*Metaphysische Anfangsgründe der Naturwissenschaft, Werke*, W. Weischedel, ed., Darmstadt 1968, VIII, 11). He made a distinction between "nature" and "being." By "essential being," he meant "the first principle of everything that belongs to the possibility of a thing" (*ibid.*, 11, note).

5. W. Kern, "Zur theologischen Auslegung des Schöpfungsglaubens," *MS* II, 464–544, 536, with reference to Thomas's *"Creare autem est dare esse"* (1 Sent., 37, 1, 1). See also *Summa Theologiae* I, 8: *Utrum Deus sit in omnibus rebus?*: *". . . adest omnibus ut causa essendi"* (8, 3); *"Esse autem est id quod est magis intimum cuilibet et quod profundius omnibus inest: cum sit formale respectu omnium quae in re sunt"* (8, 1). See also *Summa Theologiae* I, 105, 5; *De anima* 9; *De vero* 8, 16 ad 12.

6. *Ibid.*, 537.

7. See I. Kant, *Metaphysische Anfangsgründe der Naturwissenschaft, op. cit.*, 11.

8. R. Spaemann, "Natur," *HPhG* IV, 956–969, 966. It has, for example, been established, within the sphere of nature (in the material sense) that can be observed, that the violent death of an antelope is the realization of the nature (in the formal sense) of the lion that kills it.

9. This is not meant in the sense of "objective" knowledge, but "insofar as the light of our understanding, whether this is the natural light or the light of grace, is nothing other than an impression of the first truth" (*Summa Theologiae* I, 88, 3 ad 1).

10. J. B. Metz, "Natur," *LThK* VII, 805–808, 807.

11. Unlike the sophists, Aristotle did not perceive any contradiction to nature or any unnatural suppression of nature in prevailing dispensation. Nature (*phusis*) and human society (*nomos*) were mutually complementary. See R. Spaemann, "Natur," *op. cit.*, 957.

12. According to M. Heidegger, *Sein und Zeit*, Tübingen 1963, 44 (§ 9), all explicatory statements that were the result of an analysis of being were derived from its existential structure. Heidegger called the aspects of existence that determined the specifically existential aspect of existence "existentialia" and made a clear distinction between these and "categories," which determined a being that was not in accordance with existence.

13. G. Muschalek, "Schöpfung und Bund als Natur-Gnade-Problem," *MS* II, 546–557, 555.

14. See *Summa Theologiae* I-II, 109, 4 ad 2.

15. The term "essential being" can be used in three ways in this context. In the first place, it is contrasted with the concrete appearance of a being and points to what necessarily belongs to that being — its distinctive and specific character. It can be applied to one being or to a class of beings.

The universal concept of essential being is based on this. Its essential content can be applied to each individual without pointing to any particular individual. In the second place, "essential being" can also mean the state of being so or *quidditas* ("whatness") and is, in this sense, contrasted with existence, as being there. Being so and being there are both related to the concrete, finite being. In the case of a concrete right or law, we are therefore able to speak of the content or existence of law. In the third place, "essential being" means simply *essentia* in contrast to being as *esse*. In its ontological difference from being (*esse*), the being, in accordance with its being (*essentia*) participates in the unlimited fullness of being.

16. It is here that we encounter the limits of phenomenology. The distinction between consciousness of the object and consciousness of self is justified, but this does not eliminate the problem of reflection. "The reduction of the theory of knowledge to an unprejudiced phenomenology of the being as a being brings us to its limits at the point where this reduction takes place and becomes a problem" (G. E. Gethmann, "Realität," *HPhG* IV, 1168–1187, 1177).

17. J. B. Metz, "Natur," *op. cit.*, 808.

18. Plato, *Phaidon*, 75 d.

19. K. Flasch, "Wesen," *HPhG* VI, 1687–1693, 1689. I would refer the reader to the discussion of the community of communication that constitutes language and is constituted by language for an understanding of the intersubjective claim of essential statements about being. See K.-O. Apel, *Einführung zu C. S. Peirce, Schriften, I*, Frankfurt 1967.

20. See R. Spaemann, "Natur," *op. cit.*, 963: "This can be traced clearly in the development of the concept of nature since the seventeenth century. Non-theological natural scientists have lost all interest in it."

21. In this case, nature loses its normative function. "What happens simply happens. Repression is as natural as the rejection of repression. This was first expressed in an extremely radical form by de Sade, who, in his thinking, took naturalistic emancipation to its ultimate conclusion" (*ibid.*, 963).

22. Spaemann pointed to Thomas Hobbes, Kant and Schiller in this context. For Marx, however, society was "the perfect essential unity of man with nature, the true resurrection of nature, the complete naturalism of man and the complete humanism of nature" (*Ökonomisch-philosophische Manuskripte, Werke*, H.-J. Lieber and P. Furth, eds., Darmstadt 1962, I, 596).

23. R. Spaemann, "Natur," *op. cit.*, 964.

24. *Ibid.*, 965.

25. *Ibid.*, 968.

26. According to H. Wenzel, *Wahrheit und Grenze des Naturrechts, Bonner Akademische Reden* 26, Bonn 1963, 7, "Natural law is the question asked by the law of the law, that is, of a factually existing social order. Whatever we may have meant by 'natural law,' the fact remains that it always contains the idea that law is not simply the same as the commandment of an exist-

ing power." The guarantee of legal positivism by the formal conditions that are indispensable for any formation of a consensus in a human community, that is, the formal conditions of a community of communication, cannot be regarded, however, as an element by which the natural law can be justified. This question is discussed more fully in § 19 B 1 (b).

27. H. Diels and W. Kranz, *Die Fragmente der Vorsokratiker*, Berlin 1951, I, 176; Heraclitus, Fragment 112. At this early stage of Greek thought, a unity was believed to exist between *nomos* and *phusis*. The human orders were incorporated into the limitations of man's being. See H. Welzel, *Naturrecht und materiale Gerechtigkeit*, Göttingen 1962, 9 ff.

28. Cleanthes extended the formula first used by Zeno, the founder of the Stoic movement, into *homologoumenōs tē phusei zēn*. Man's highest aim was to lead a natural life in accordance with his own nature and that of the universe. See H. Welzel, *Naturrecht und materiale Gerechtigkeit, op. cit.*, 37–47.

29. By neo-scholasticism, I mean the movement that aimed at the *restauratio christiana iuris naturalis* in the second half of the nineteenth century. For the problems confronting this movement, see L. Oeing-Hanhoff, "Thomas von Aquin und die Situation des Thomismus heute," *PhJ* 70 (1962–1963), 17–33; J.-M. Aubert, "Pour une herméneutique du droit naturel," *Recherches de science religieuse* 59 (1971), 449–492; A. Hollerbach, "Das christliche Naturrecht im Zusammenhang allgemeinen Naturrechtsdenkens," F. Böckle and E.-W. Böckenförde, eds., *Naturrecht in der Kritik, op. cit.*, 9–38, 27 ff.

30. H.-D. Schelauske, *Naturrechtsdiskussion in Deutschland. Ein Überblick über zwei Jahrzehnte: 1945–1965*, Cologne 1968, 114.

31. Aristotle, *Politicus* 1253 a; for the slave question, see 1254 a–1255 a; Plato, *Politeia* 433 b, d.

32. The Conference of German bishops has taken up a strong position toward the government of the country in various letters with regard to the reform of family law. On 30 January 1953, for example, a pastoral letter was published by all the bishops (see the *Kirchlicher Anzeiger* for the Archdiocese of Cologne, 1953, 92–101, 93). This letter stated explicitly that the hierarchical structure of marriage, in other words, the legally predominant position of the husband (although both sexes had fundamentally the same human dignity) was based on God's order of creation and on the natural characteristics of man and woman.

33. J. Ratzinger, "Theologie und Ethos," K. Ulmer, ed., *Die Verantwortung der Wissenschaft*, Bonn 1975, 46–61, 57.

34. G. Ellscheid, "Naturrecht," *HPhG* IV, 969–980, 974 ff.

35. H.-D. Schelauske, *Naturrechtsdiskussion, op. cit.*, 353.

36. J. Ritter, "*Naturrecht*" *bei Aristoteles*, Stuttgart 1961, 21.

37. See. J. Hirschberger, "Naturrecht oder Vernunftrecht bei Thomas von Aquin?" C. Fabro, ed., *Gegenwart und Tradition, Festschrift für B. Lakebrink*, Freiburg 1969, 53–74. "The fundamental appraoches to the *lex naturalis* are based not on the ontological aspect of the *rerum natura*, but on the human spirit," *ibid.*, 68. See also L. Oeing-Hanhoff, "Der Mensch:

Natur oder Geschichte? Die Grundlagen und Kriterien sittlicher Normen im Licht der philosophischen Tradition," *Naturgesetz und christliche Ethik*, Munich 1970, 11–47, 26 f.

38. *"et similia,"* I/II, 194, 2.

39. See F. de Suarez, *De Legibus*, Lib. II, cap. 6, n. 8: *"Ergo ratio naturalis quae indicat quid sit per se malum vel bonum homini, consequenter indicat esse secundum divinam voluntatem ut unum fiat, at aliud vitetur."*

40. *Ibid.*, Lib. II, cap. 5, n. 9: *". . . est vis quaedam illius naturae, quam habet ad discernendum inter operationes convenientes et disconvenientes illi naturae, quam rationem appellamus."*

41. See H. Welzel, *Naturrecht und materiale Gerechtigkeit, op. cit.*, 162 ff.

42. H.-D. Schelauske, *Naturrechtdiskussion, op. cit.*, 352.

43. See J. Messner, *Kulturethik mit Grundlegung von Prinzipienethik und Persönlichkeitsethik*, Innsbruck 1954, 225–267.

44. G. Ellscheid, "Naturrecht," *op. cit.*, 978 f.

45. *Ibid.*, 979. Ellscheid believes that a speculative philosophy of law could limit itself to "finding a basis for the structure of communication and drawing concrete conclusions from that structure for the positive law. This philosophy is still basing its reasoning on the natural law, insofar as it is looking for the source of law in a region that is already provided in a human principle, that is, in the logical structure of free communication between rational beings as such" (*ibid.*, 979).

46. *Ibid.*

47. R. Spaemann, "Die Aktualität des Naturrechts," F. Böckle and E.-W. Böckenförde, eds., *Naturrecht in der Kritik, op. cit.*, 262–276, 274.

48. *Ibid.*, 272.

49. A. Kaufmann, "Die ontologische Struktur des Rechts," *id.*, ed., *Die ontologische Begründung des Rechts*, Darmstadt 1965, 470–508, 482 f.

50. H. Welzel, *Wahrheit und Grenze des Naturrechts, op. cit.*, 7.

51. See E. Rorschacher, *Das Recht und die "Rechtssätze." Eine Kritik der traditionellen Naturrechtstheorie auf rechtsontologischer Grundlage*, Fribourg and Winterthur 1963.

52. H. Welzel, *Wahrheit und Grenze des Naturrechts, op. cit.*, 8 f.

§ 20 Presuppositions of Nature, pp. 199–207.

1. See G. Sala, "Die Begründung vernünftiger menschlicher Einsichten," *Concilium* 12 (1976), 634–640, 634.

2. If goods and values are not differentiated, but grouped together within the same concept, the fundamental values will be gradually lost and what is said about them will consequently become imprecise and meaningless. It cannot, however, be disputed that there is a great deal of feeling for justice and solidarity — both values of the first importance — especially among the younger generation. At the same time, however, there is also a good deal of uncertainty about how legal goods should be ordered. The contemporary longing for justice is also too vague. If the question of the ordering of goods is not openly discussed, all our complaints will be in vain.

3. I do this without reference to the debate about the relationship between value and being, as outlined above in connection with the "material value ethics" (see § 4 A 3).

4. It is important to point out in this context that the words "given as a task" do not mean that these goods form the basis of moral obligation. The goods are objects of responsible action.

5. See § 12 above. "You shall not kill; you shall not commit adultery; you shall not steal" (Ex. 20.13–15) had the aim of reminding the people of Israel of the fact that life, marriage and property were under the protection of Yahweh.

6. See, for example, the constitutional law of the Federal Republic of Germany, articles 1–19.

7. *Summa Theologiae* II-II, 58, 1. Thomas took over Ulpianus' definition as handed down in Justinian's Institutes (*Codex Iuris Civilis, Instit*. I, 1). He explicitly stressed the element of *habitus*, however, with regard to Aristotle (V *Eth*. c. 9): "*iustitia est habitus secundum quem . . .*"

8. According to the Godesberg program of the German Social Democratic Party, "freedom, justice and solidarity . . . are the fundamental values of socialism." These "common moral values" are also mentioned in the ten-year plan for 1975–1985. The fundamental political and social claims and objectives emerge clearly from the emphasis placed on these values. In this context, the meaning of "solidarity" is unambiguous. "Freedom" and "justice" might, on the other hand, be synonymous with "just order" or "free development for all men," in which case they would be goods, rather than ultimate aims in human activity which are objectively already given.

9. It would be impossible for me to discuss all the implications of ethology within the scope of this work on fundamental moral theology. I am certainly not competent to judge the controversial findings that have been made in the sphere of animal behavior. In addition to the authors whose work has been quoted in the text, the reader should consult N. Tinbergen, *Instinktlehre*, Berlin 1964; K. Lorenz, *Das sogenante Böse*, Vienna 1965; I. Eibl-Eibesfeldt, *Grundriß der vergleichenden Verhaltensforschung*, Munich 1967; F. Rauh, *Das sittliche Leben des Menschen im Lichte der vergleichenden Verhaltensforschung*, Kevelaer 1969.

10. See E. Fromm, *Anatomie der menschlichen Destruktivität*, Stuttgart 1974, 85; N. E. Miller *et al.*, "Die Frustrations-Aggressions-Hypothese," H. Thomae, ed., *Die Motivation menschlichen Handelns*, Cologne 1970; A. Mitscherlich, "Aggression und Anpassung," *Aggression und Anpassung in der Industriegesellschaft*, Frankfurt 1968.

11. See W. Wickler, *Antworten der Verhaltensforschung*, Munich 1970, especially 179–194.

12. J. Gründel, "Verhaltensforschung und theologische Ethik," St.-E. Szydzik, ed., *Christliches Gesellschaftsdenken im Umbruch*, Regensburg 1977, 65–71, 66. See also *ibid.*, "Naturgeschichtliche Voraussetzungen sittlichen Handelns," *Concilium* 12 (1976), 618–622.

13. W. Wickler, *Die Biologie der Zehn Gebote*, Munich 1971 (English trans.: *The Biology of the Ten Commandments*, New York 1972); id., "Ergebnisse der Verhaltensforschung — auch von Bedeutung für die Ethik?" St.-E. Szydzik, ed., *Christliches Gesellschaftsdenken, op. cit.*, 57–63.

14. W. Wickler, "Ergebnisse," *op. cit.*, 63.

15. *Ibid.*, 61.

16. *Ibid.*, 63.

17. See J. Gründel, "Verhaltensforschung und theologische Ethik," *op. cit.* 69.

18. J. Gründel, "Naturgechichtliche Voraussetzungen," *op. cit.*, 620.

19. *Ibid.*

20. E. Fromm, *Anatomie der menschlichen Destruktivität, op. cit.*

21. My argument here is based to some extent on the findings of H. Plessner, *Die Stufen des Organischen und der Mensch*, Berlin 1965; id., *Philosophische Anthropologie*, Frankfurt 1970; A. Gehlen, *Der Mensch. Seine Natur und seine Stellung in der Welt*, Frankfurt 1962; id., *Studien zur Anthropologie und Soziologie*, Neuwied 1963; A. Portmann, *Biologische Fragmente zu einer Lehre vom Menschen*, Basle 1951; id, *Biologie und Geist*, Freiburg 1963; T. Litt, *Mensch und Welt*, Heidelberg 1961; W. E. Mühlmann, *Kulturanthropologie*, Cologne and Berlin 1966. For a summary of the whole question, see R. Roček and O. Schatz, eds., *Philosophische Anthropologie heute*, Munich 1972.

22. See A. Plack, *Die Gesellschaft und das Böse*, Munich 1967, who has sharply criticized the prevailing morality, basing his arguments on a hypothesis of frustration and aggression. Clearly following Herbert Marcuse, *Triebstruktur und Gesellschaft*, Frankfurt 1965, he is of the opinion that the impulse that is not restricted by external compulsions should be able to impose its own norms on itself. The correct attitude in moral order is not subordination to compulsion, but incorporation into society.

23. See W. Korff, *Norm und Sittlichkeit, op. cit.*, 76–112.

§ 21 Experience and Reason, pp. 207–222.

1. See D. Sölle, *Die Hinreise*, Stuttgart 1976, 44.

2. H.-G. Gadamer, *Wahrheit und Methode*, Tübingen 1975, 329.

3. K. Lehmann, "Erfahrung," *SM* I, 1117–1123, 1117. For the concept of experience, see also: F. Kambartel, "Erfahrung," *HWP* II, 609–617; H. Rombach, "Erfahrung, Erfahrungswissenschaft," *Lexikon der Pädagogik* I, Freiburg 1970, 375–377; A. S. Kessler, A. Schöpf and C. Wild, "Erfahrung," *HPhG* II, 373–386; G. Siewerth, "Erfahrung," *LThK* III, 977 ff.

4. A. S. Kessler, A. Schöpf and C. Wild, "Erfahrung," *op. cit.*, 385.

5. *Ibid.*, 374; see also the concept of *empeiria* in Aristotle, who used it in the sense of being practised in or familiar with (see F. Kambartel, "Erfahrung," *op. cit.*, 609).

6. H. Rombach, "Erfahrung," *op. cit.*, 375; see also A. S. Kessler, A. Schöpf and C. Wild, *op. cit.*, 379 ff.: experience as a historical movement of theory (Hegel).

7. See J. von Kempski, "Der Aufbau der Erfahrung und das Handeln," *Archiv Für Philosophie* VI, 1956, 177–91.

8. See R. Egenter, *Erfahrung ist Leben. Über die Rolle der Erfahrung für das sittliche und religiöse Leben des Christen*, Munich 1974, 18.

9. *Ibid.*, 20.

10. *Ibid.*, 21, with reference to M. Heidegger, *Unterwegs zur Sprache*, Pfullingen 1959, 159: "Having an experience with something — a thing, a person, a God — means that this happens to us, affects us, comes over us, overthrows us and changes us."

11. *Ibid.*, 21 f.

12. D. Mieth, "Der Wissenschaftscharacter der Theologie," *FZPhTh* 23 (1976) 13–41, 30 f.

13. J. Messner, *Kulturethik, op. cit.*, 7.

14. See W. Korff, *Norm und Sittlichkeit*, Mainz 1973, 131 ff.

15. *Ibid.*, 139.

16. This outline of Aristotle's and Thomas Aquinas's understanding of experience is largely based on K.-W. Merks's dissertation, *Theologische Grundlegung der sittlichen Autonomie, op. cit.*

17. *Ibid.*, 80 f.

18. *Ibid.*, 81.

19. *Ibid.*, 83.

20. *Ibid.*, 84. with reference to the discussion of Thomas's concept of *consuetudo* in his treatise on *lex: Summa Theologiae* I-II, 97, 3 and *In EN* II, I, 1, n. 245 ff.

21. *Ibid.*, 87.

22. *Ibid.*, 322, with reference to *In EN* X, 1, 16, n. 2175 ff.

23. *Ibid.*, 320, with reference to I-II, 97, 2, c ad 2.

24. *Ibid.*, 320.

25. *Ibid.*, 321.

26. *Ibid.*, 322.

27. See the various contributions in F. Böckle and E.-W. Böckenförde, *Naturrecht in der Kritik, op. cit.*

28. E.-W. Böckenförde, "Kirchliches Naturrecht und politisches Handeln," F. Böckle and E.-W. Böckenförde, *op. cit.*, 96–125, 110.

29. *Ibid.*, 110. In this context, Böckenförde pointed to J. Messner, *Das Naturrecht*, Innsbruck, 1966, 101; "The principles are lived and experienced in the particular form in which they are determined by their content as the order of life of the family community. Later, their universal content is grasped by reason as it gradually develops and their universal validity is then understood."

30. F.-X. Kaufmann, "Wissenssoziologische Überlegungen zu Renaissance und Niedergang des katholischen Naturrechtsdenkens im 19. und 20. Jahrhundert," F. Böckle and E.-W. Böckenförde, *op. cit.*, 126–164, 147.

31. *Ibid.*, 147.

32. See D. Mieth, "Die Bedeutung der menschlichen Lebenserfahrung. Plädoyer für eine Theorie des ethischen Modells," *Concilium* 12, (1976),

623–633, especially 626–628. Mieth's article is quoted below as "Lebenserfahrung."

33. R. Egenter, *Erfahrung ist Leben, op. cit.*, 37.

34. See the section in § 15 above on the connection between action and consequence in the Wisdom literature. In the Wisdom books of the Old Testament, the process by means of which good and bad are distinguished on the basis of experience is revealed very clearly.

35. H.-G. Gadamer, *Wahrheit und Methode, op. cit.*, 338 f.

36. D. Mieth, "Praxis ohne Theorie?" *Diakonia* 2 (1971), 150–162, 159.

37. D. Mieth, "Lebenserfahrung," *op. cit.* 627.

38. *Ibid.*; Mieth pointed in this context to the moral development of the child.

39. See. H.-G. Gadamer, *Wahrheit und Methode, op. cit.*, 340 ff. This is the aspect that Hegel called negation. In his opinion, real experience began with the negation of the contrast. "The dialectical movement that the consciousness exercises on itself, both in its knowledge and in its object, insofar as the new and true object arises from it, is really what we call experience" (*Phänomenologie des Geistes*, J. Hoffmeister, ed., Hamburg, 1952, 73).

40. R. Egenter, *Erfahrung ist Leben, op. cit.*, 37, with reference to Hegel, *Enz.* § 7: "The principle of experience contains an infinitely important definition, namely that man himself must be present if the content is to be accepted and regarded as true and that he should find this content to be united with the certainty in himself."

41. See A. Schütz, *Der sinnhafte Aufbau der sozialen Welt*, Frankfurt 1974, especially 100 ff.

42. For the concepts "profile of norms" and "profile of significance," see R. Egenter, *op. cit.*, 32 f.

43. D. Mieth, "Lebenserfahrung," *op. cit.*, 627.

44. *Ibid.*

45. See B. Schüller, "Die Bedeutung der Erfahrung für die Rechtfertigung sittlicher Verhaltensregeln," K. Demmer and B. Schüller, *Christlich glauben und handeln. Fragen einer fundamentalen Moraltheologie in der Diskussion*, Düsseldorf 1977, 261–286, 277 ff. Schüller believes that the relevance of empirical insights for normative ethics can be summarized in the axiomatic statement that obligation presupposes ability (see *ibid.*, 284) and he recognizes in this relationship an essential basis for the "changeable nature of moral norms and even for the changeable nature of the natural law" (284).

46. R. Hofmann, "Was ist Sittlichkeit? Zur Klärung des Begriffs," J. Sauer, ed., *Normen in Konflikt*, Freiburg 1977, 102–124, 121.

47. *Ibid.*, 114 ff.; R. Egenter, *op. cit.*, 88 ff.

48. D. Meith, "Lebenserfahrung," *op. cit.*, 628.

49. *Ibid.*

50. See B. Schüller's analysis in "Die Bedeutung der Erfahrung," *op. cit.*, especially 267 ff.

51. For what follows, see D. Mieth, "Lebenserfahrung," *op. cit.*, 623 ff.

52. *Ibid.*, 623.

53. See R. Egenter, *Erfahrung ist Leben, op. cit.*, 29.

54. D. Mieth, "Lebenserfahrung," *op. cit.*, 624.

55. *Ibid.*

56. *Ibid.*

57. See R. Egenter, *Erfahrung ist Leben, op. cit.*, 30.

58. D. Mieth, "Narrative Ethik," *FZPhTh* 22 (1975), 297–326.

59. For the relationship between the ethics of the model and those of the norm, see *ibid.*, 318 ff.

60. See, for example, the relationship between the Torah and the new law in § 17 above. Jesus tried to make it possible for the real significance of the old law to be experienced as mediated through his own person.

61. D. Mieth, "Lebenserfahrung," *op. cit.*, 624 f.

62. G. Sala, "Die Entwicklung vernünftiger menschlicher Einsichten," *Concilium* 12 (1976), 634–640, 639.

63. See § 4 above.

64. K.-O. Apel, "Sprechakttheorie und transzendentale Sprachpragmatik zur Frage ethischer Normen," *op. cit.*, 126.

65. *Ibid.*, 129.

66. *Ibid.*, 134 ff. Unlike the empirical and analytical behavioral sciences, the critical and constructive social sciences are concerned with "a deepening of man's understanding of himself by means of a quasi-naturalistic phase of partial suspension of the relationship between the subject and the subject in communicative experience in favor of quasi-causal and quasi-functional explanations of compulsive behavioral processes and their institutional objectivizations" (*ibid.*, 143).

67. *Ibid.*, 134.

68. *Ibid.*, 129 f.

69. *Ibid.*, 135 ff. Apel refers to this fundamental knowledge in the later work of Wittgenstein and to H.-G. Gadamer's approach, according to which we understand structures of meaning "primarily from the context of a communication about things in which we always continue to be in the world" (*ibid.*, 136).

70. *Ibid.*, 136.

71. *Ibid.*

72. See, for example, the relationship between the social and the natural sciences.

73. *Ibid.*, 144.

74. It is, for example, no longer possible to regard human sexuality principally or exclusively as a means to the end of procreation, as was the case for centuries in the traditional sexual morality. What is now widely recognized is its independent value as an expression both of man's individuality and of his social nature. At the same time, however, it would be fundamentally wrong to regard sexuality exclusively as a means for the satisfaction of desires and this tendency together with the increasing conviction that everything that is attractive to the senses and emotions and

can be materially appropriated should be immediately available to the individual consumer must both be rejected. There is a clear and empirically established need for integration and the social consequences of impulsive behavior of both these kinds have been clearly demonstrated in many studies. A reduction of sexuality to a purely orgastic potential or to a mere activity of the genital organs is a new form of dualism that is not in any way less wrong than Manicheanism of the kind from which we have been set free only relatively late in our history. Simply to change our tradition will not bring us much further forward.

75. See G. Sala, "Die Entwicklung vernünftiger menschlicher Einsichten," *op. cit.* 638.

76. D. Mieth, "Lebenserfahrung," *op. cit.*, 630.

77. *Ibid.*, 631.

78. H. Marcuse, *Der eindimensionale Mensch*, Neuwied 1968, 245 ff.

79. B. Welte, *Determination oder Freiheit*, Frankfurt 1969, 94.

80. See G. Otte, "Über geschichtliche Wirkungen des christlichen Naturrechts," F. Böckle and E.-W. Böckenförde, *Naturrecht in der Kritik, op. cit.*, 61–79, especially 68 f.

81. *Ibid.*, 69.

82. *Ibid.*

§ 22 Knowledge of Faith, pp. 222–233.

1. R. Spaemann, "Christliche Religion und Ethik," *PhJ* 80 (1973), 282–291, 286.

2. Behind this question of the distinctive aspect of Christian ethics is the fundamental one: what is specifically Christian as such? See H. U. von Balthasar, "Merkmale des Christlichen," *Verbum caro*, Einsiedeln 1960, 172–194; J. Ratzinger, "Strukturen des Christlichen," *Einführung in das Christentum*, Munich 1977, 197–221; W. Kasper, "Was heißt eigentlich christlich?" J. Schreiner, ed., *Die Kirche im Wandel der Gesellschaft*, Würzburg 1970, 87–101; G. Adler, ed., *Christlich — was heißt das?* Düsseldorf 1972, containing contributions by J. Blank, H. Braun, K. H. Dreschner, E. Jüngel, W. Künneth, J. Milic-Lochmann, G. Mainberger, J. Ratzinger, G. Rendtorff, D. Sölle, H. Vorgrimler and others.

The theological discussion about ethics began with a conference at Lund in 1966 organized by the Societas Ethica. Among the papers read at Lund were those by K. E. Løgstrup, "Das Proprium des christlichen Ethos," and F. Böckle, "Was ist das Proprium einer christlichen Ethik?" *ZEE* 11 (1967), 135–147 and 148–159, respectively. For the specifically Christian aspect of ethics, see also K. Demmer, "Glaubensgehorsam als Verpflichtung zur Wirklichkeit," *Cath* 21 (1967), 138–157; W. van der Marck, *Grundzüge einer christlichen Ethik*, Düsseldorf 1967, especially 17 ff.; R. A. McCormick, "Human Significance and Christian Significance," G. Outka and P. Ramsey, eds., *Norm and Context in Christian Ethics*, New York 1968, 233–261; B. Schüller, "Beansprucht die Botschaft Christi eine Zuständigkeit in Fragen gesellschaftlichen Lebens und seiner Entwicklung?" *Fragen des sozialen*

Lebens: Möglichkeit und Grenzen einer katholischen Soziallehre. Bericht über das symposion der Katholischen Sozialakademie Österreichs vom 8.–10. November 1968, Vienna, n.d., 16–29; A. Manaranche, *Y a-t-il une éthique sociale chrétienne?* Paris 1969; J. Fuchs, "Gibt es eine spezifisch christliche Moral?" *StZ* 95 (1970), 99–112; R. Simon, "Spécificité de l'éthique chrétienne: L'Ethique chrétienne à la recherche de son identité," *Le Supplément* (VS) 23, No. 92 (1970), 74–104; J. Gründel, "Ethik ohne Normen? Zur Begründung und Struktur christlicher Ethik," J. Gründel and H. van Oyen, *Ethik ohne Normen? Zu den Weisungen des Evangeliums, Ökumenische Forschungen, Kleine ökumenische Schriften* 4, Freiburg 1970, 9–88; L. E. Curran, "Y a-t-il une éthique sociale spécifiquement chrétienne?" *Le Supplément* (VS) 24 (1971), 39–58; A. Auer, *Autonome Moral und christlicher Glaube*, Düsseldorf 1971; B. Schüller, "Die Bedeutung des natürlichen Sittengesetzes für den Christen," G. Teichtweier and W. Dreier, eds., *Herausforderung und Kritik der Moraltheologie*, Würzburg 1971, 105–130; F. Compagnoni, "La specificità della morale cristiana," *Studi e ricerche* 17, Bologna 1972; F. Furger, *Anspruch Christi und Handeln des Menschen. Elemente christlicher Welt- und Lebensgestaltung*, Freiburg 1972, especially 189 ff.; K. Demmer, "Moralische Norm und theologische Anthropologie," *Gr* 54 (1973), 263–306; P. Delhaye, "La mise en cause de la spécificité de la morale chrétienne. Etude de quelques prises de position récentes et réflexions critiques," *RThL* 4 (1973), 308–339; W. Korff, *Norm und Sittlichkeit. Untersuchungen zur Logik der normativen Vernùnft. Tübinger Theologische Studien* I, Mainz 1973, especially 42 ff., 110 ff., 128; H. Rotter, "Die Eigenart der christlichen Ethik," *StZ* 98 (1973), 407–416.

3. R. Spaemann, in "Christliche Religion," *op. cit.*, 286, has pointed out that "Christianity has not the same problems of adapting its teachings to the universal ethics of our modern technological civilization as other religions often have. It is able to discover in that civilization the spirit of its own Spirit. . . . The commandment to love one's neighbor is not tied to a specific form of self-expression on the part of man. . . . Divisions are broken down in Christianity — a clear example of this Christian process is the overcoming of the division between gentile and Jew in the early Church. If it is intolerant, then it is only intolerant of intolerance itself. The only demand made by Christianity is that all that stands in the way of the restoration of a universal consensus should be removed."

4. We do not include among our list of moral norms (*mores*) in the narrower sense of the word instructions prescribing that certain religious actions should be carried out. Examples of such instructions are the obligations to have one's children baptized, to attend Sunday Mass and to confess all mortal sins. The concept *mores* has a much wider application in the Christian tradition. In this sense, the instructions mentioned above are *traditiones . . . ad mores pertinentes* (DS 1501). They may even perhaps have been intended only to be applied in the sense of the twofold formula *tum ad fidem, tum ad mores* that was used by the Council of Trent. (See J. Murphy, *The Notion of Tradition*, Milwaukee 1959, Appendix III: "'Faith and Morals' at Trent," 292–300.) The term "faith and morals" (*fides et mores*)

was, however, used in a much wider sense by canon lawyers and theologians in the twelfth and thirteenth centuries. (See Y. Congar, *Die Tradition und die Traditionen* I, Mainz 1965, 194) After the Council of Trent too, there was another change in the meaning of the term. (See M. Bévenot, "'Faith and Morals' in the Councils of Trent and Vatican I," *The Heythrop Journal* 3 (1962), 15–30, especially 16 ff.

5. See above, § 19, note 1.

6. See K. Rahner and H. Vorgrimler, *Concise Theological Dictionary*, London, 1965, 17: "In the Catholic sense, it (= the *analogia fidei*) means that every affirmation of revelation or faith must be understood in the light of the Church's objective faith as a whole. The *analogia fidei* also requires that it be quite clear that the terms used in any dogmatic formula bear a merely analogous meaning. This principle is recognized by the magisterium (DS 1943, 2146, 2315)."

7. See K. Rahner, "Zum Begriff der Unfehlbarkeit in der katholischen Theologie," *Zum Problem Unfehlbarkeit*, QD 54, Freiburg 1971, 25. Rahner has seen in this distinction "an important and indeed fundamental question of the (logical) 'classes' of statements about faith." Research into this question would, however, show that "the difference between apparently positively and concretely verifiable moral theological statements on the one hand and other so-called metaphysical statements on the other is not so great or so unambiguous as we might at first sight be inclined to think." Rahner also insists that "such moral theological statements must also be statements about faith," since they are "only themselves when their relationship with the absolute mystery is fully realized." This means that the moral and therefore unconditional obligation and the relationship between that obligation and salvation involved in any action, the content of which is determined by the normative principle, are derived from the transcendental reference of man's expression of his freedom as such. This question is discussed later. No light, however, is thrown on the specific aspect of normative statements by this shared factor in dogmatic and moral theological statements. This specific aspect is to be found in the regulative function of those statements with regard to categorial action. What is required here is an unambiguous clarity.

8. M. Seckler, "Kommt der christliche Glaube ohne Gott aus?" H. J. Schulz, ed., *Wer ist das eigentlich-Gott? op. cit.*, 189 ff.

9. *Ibid.*, 190.

10. H. U. von Balthasar, "Merkmale des Christlichen," *Verbum Caro. Skizzen zur Theologie* I, Einsiedeln 1960, 179. Balthasar contrasts Christian life with natural life and says that the latter "can only be a life of needs and the satisfaction of needs, in the sense of Plato's eros. Natural life is incessantly and insatiably aiming at fullness."

11. R. Schnackenburg, "Biblische Ethik II," *SM* I, 1967, 547.

12. J. Fuchs, "Gibt es eine spezifisch christliche Moral?" *StZ* 185 (1970), 99–112, 102. See also *id.*, "Moraltheologie und Dogmatik," *Gr* 50 (1969), 689–716. In connection with the dogmatic theology of transcendental morality, Fuchs correctly stressed that when moral theology is concerned

"more or less exclusively" with the "specifically categorial character" of the individual act, there is always a danger of overlooking the fact that "the person expresses himself when he performs that individual act and that this self-expression is a supernatural and a Christian one. These two elements form the deepest reality of Christian morality" (698 ff.).

13. J. Fuchs, "Gibt es eine spezifisch christliche Moral?" *op. cit.*, 103.

14. In one sense, it is correct to say that the content of Christian ethics is human and not distinctively Christian. (See, for example, A. Auer, *Autonome Moral und christlicher Glaube*, Düsseldorf 1971, 161, who interprets some of the statements made by J. Fuchs in "Gibt es eine spezifisch christliche Moral?" *op. cit.*, 100–105.) It would, however, be more correct to say that the content of Christian ethics is both human and, without neglecting "what can be understood in the light of human knowledge" (see J. Fuchs, "Gibt es eine spezifisch christliche Moral?" *op. cit.*, 103), also distinctively Christian. I am completely in agreement with Auer in that a distinctive aspect of ethically normative statements and of categorial moral values in a thematically reflective form is that they should be intelligible and therefore also fundamentally orientated toward universally human understanding (see A. Auer, *op. cit.*, 176). The question with which I am concerned, however, goes further than this statement — which, I believe, ultimately expresses the underlying intention not only of J. Fuchs, but also of B. Schüller, W. Kerber and other authors — to the extent that only one aspect of the whole problem as to how what is "distinctively Christian" can be defined is discussed by Auer. For the rest, I differ from Auer more over the concept "distinctively (or specifically) Christian" than over the matter itself, since what is, in Auer's opinion, critically adapted in the secular morality by a specifically Christian insight into faith results in a morality which is "specific to the group" — even though it may not be intelligible only to Christians — and which is quite clearly characterized as far as its content is concerned.

15. See B. Schüller, "Zur Problematik," *op. cit.*, 8.

16. In sociology, a distinction is made between transcendent and immanent human dignity. In the case of the first, man is the "representative of existing humanity" or the "representative of the community of all existing social systems" (see W. Siebel, *Soziologie der Abtreibung*, Stuttgart 1971, 230).

17. It is almost impossible to solve the problem as to whether this understanding can be traced back to the history of the effects of the gospel on man. H. U. von Balthasar has said laconically: "it is not possible to justify the statement that the individual may have an eternal and irreplaceable value, either by reference to pre-Christian philosophy or in post-Christian idealistic terms and certainly not by appealing to materialism or the philosophy of biological evolutionism" ("Gott begegnen in der heutigen Welt," *Spiritus Creator*, Einsiedeln 1967, 274).

18. See W. Siebel, *op. cit.*, who is of the opinion that the dignity of membership that is based on transcendent human dignity does "not have any official status today. To admit that this is possible would be to take up

a religious position" (230; see also note 12, in which the author explicitly emphasizes, with reference to N. Luhmann, R. Marcic, W. Maihofer and H. D. Schelauske, that "human dignity cannot be derived exclusively from man's state as a person on the basis of the natural law").

§ 23 Two Types of Justification, pp. 233–247.

1. The concepts "morally good" and "morally bad" or "morally right" and "morally wrong" are not used uniformly in moral theology. I prefer to use these terms in the following way: on the basis of disposition, that is, equating love with benevolence, I use "morally good" (because of benevolence) or "morally bad" (because of self-seeking). On the basis of the act itself, I use "right" or "wrong." Whenever love expresses itself in actions (when, in other words, it does works), it is confronted with the choice, measured against an order of goods, of acting either rightly or wrongly, that is, of performing a "morally right" or a "morally wrong" action.

2. In connection with our insight into values, reason is our natural spiritual ability to understand reality. In the consideration of goods that is discussed in this section, it has the character of positively practical reason. The objection that is occasionally raised, namely that moral theologians take an abbreviated or empirically concrete concept of reason as their point of departure, is, in my opinion, without foundation, at least insofar as the different use to which the concept is put with regard to different questions is taken into account.

3. See B. Schüller, "Zur Problematik allgemein verbindlicher ethischer Grundsätze," *ThPh* 45 (1970), 1–23; *id.*, "Typen ethischer Argumentation in der katholischen Moraltheologie," *ibid.*, 526–550; *id.*, "Zur Rede von der radikalen sittlichen Forderung," *ThPh* 46 (1971), 321–341; *id.*, *Die Begründung sittlicher Urteile*, Düsseldorf 1973; *id.*, "Neuere Beiträge zum Thema 'Begründung sittlicher Normen,'" J. Pfammatter and F. Furger, eds., *Theologische Berichte* IV, Einsiedeln 1974, 109–181; *id.*, "Empfängnisverhütung im Lichte einer ethischen Theorie teleologischen Typs," R. Olechowski, ed., *Religion, Wissenschaft, Kultur, Jahrbuch der Wiener Akademie* 25 (1976–1977), I, 57–63; *id.*, "Typen der Begründung sittlicher Normen," *Concilium* 12 (1976), 648–654.

4. J. Fuchs, "Der Absolutheitscharakter sittlicher Handlungsnormen," H. Wolter, ed., *Testimonium veritati, Frankfurter Theologische Studien* 7, Frankfurt 1971, 211–249; F. Böckle, "Theonomie und Autonomie der Vernunft," W. Oelmüller, ed., *Fortschritt wohin?, op. cit.*, 63–86, 81 f.; J. Ratzinger, *Prinzipien christlicher Moral*, Einsiedeln 1976; F. Scholz, *Wege, Umwege und Auswege der Moraltheologie*, Munich 1976; D. Mieth, "Autonome Moral im christlichen Kontext," *Orientierung* 40 (1976), 31–34; B. Schüller, "Zur Diskussion über das Proprium einer christlichen Ethik," *ThPh* 51 (1976), 321–343; see also the articles in the number of *Concilium* — 12 (1976) — that was devoted exclusively to this theme and several of the articles in K. Demmer and B. Schüller, eds., *Christlich glauben und handeln*, Düsseldorf 1977.

5. See C. D. Broad, *Five Types of Ethical Theory*, London 1967; H. J. McCloskey, *Meta-Ethics and Normative Ethics*, The Hague 1969; W. Frankena, *Ethics*, Englewood Cliffs 1963; D. H. Hodgson, *Consequences of Utilitarianism*, Oxford 1967; D. Lyons, *Forms and Limits of Utilitarianism*, Oxford 1970; G. E. Moore, *Principia Ethica*, Cambridge 1903, 1966; W. D. Ross, *The Right and the Good*, Oxford 1930, 1967; *id.*, *Foundations of Ethics*, Oxford 1939, 1968; G. J. Warnock, *The Object of Morality*, London 1971.

6. The concept "teleological" is used here in the sense in which C. D. Broad, *Five Types of Ethical Theory*, *op. cit.*, employed it, in his distinction between the "teleological" and the "deontological" types of theories of the justification of ethical norms. (The word "deontological" is derived from the Greek *deon*.) According to Broad, the rightness or wrongness of an action is "always determined by its tendency to produce certain consequences which are intrinsically good or bad" in the teleological theory (*ibid.*, 206 ff.), whereas, in the deontological theory, "such and such a kind of action would always be right (or wrong) in such and such circumstances, no matter what its consequences might be" (*ibid.*, 206). A typically teleological ethical theory is utilitarianism — unlike institutionism (*ibid.*, 206). It should, incidentally, be pointed out that a distinction is made by these English philosophers between a utilitarianism of action and a utilitarianism of rule. The second is a restricted form of utilitarianism, insofar as the predictable consequences are regarded less as norms of action and certain more or less fixed rules are more accepted as norms, because it is generally assumed that they produce the best consequences. See J. R. Connery, "Morality of Consequences: A Critical Appraisal," *ThPh* 34 (1973), 396–414.

7. It should be stressed that it is only in the interpersonal sphere that moral norms can be justified on the basis of the predictable consequences of man's actions. Demands that are concerned with man's fundamental relationship with God (faith, hope and love) are determined by the absolute good and cannot be considered within this category. (See A. Auer's distinction between the "ethos of the world" and the "ethos of salvation," which points to the same datum; *Autonome Moral und christlicher Glaube*, Düsseldorf 1971.)

8. Examples can very easily be reduced to analytical judgments, since the aspect that is contrary to morality is often taken into account in forming a judgment. Such examples are tormenting another person for selfish reasons or committing adultery — illegally associating with someone else's partner. But is sexual intercourse on the part of the divorced and remarried partner under all circumstances adultery? That is surely the question. The conditioned nature of moral judgments has always been recognized in the Church's traditional moral theology. Most actions were listed in the manuals under the category of *moralitas conditionata*. Only two interpersonal actions — lying and the sexual act that is closed to procreation — were treated as exceptions and called acts of *moralitas absoluta* or *malitia intrinseca absoluta*. (See J. Mausbach and G. Ermecke, *Katholische Moraltheologie* I,

Münster 1959, 240; O. Schilling, *Handbuch der Moraltheologie* I, Stuttgart 1952, 178.)

9. The practical consequences are not difficult to recognize. If we insist on the *moralitas absoluta*, we can only regard a different judgment — as the commentaries on the encyclical and various decisions and resolutions on the part of synods would seem to think possible — as a *conscientia erronea*. As B. Schüller has pointed out, "A teleological justification admits that a *conscientia recta* is possible, since the norm appears to be that the use of contraceptive means cannot be permissible, unless the avoidance of contraception is morally justified and continence on the part of the partners is harmful to their well-being" ("Zur Problematik," *op. cit.*, 4 f.). If the conditions have changed now to such an extent that the prevention of conception is morally justified, not simply exceptionally, but regularly, then we do not need to change our moral judgment, but it is necessary to clarify normatively the regularity which has changed. This may perhaps be done by declaring openly that the prevention of conception is bound to be justified in every case by corresponding reasons and that the method used depends on the health and the personal dignity of the partners. The bishops have in various recent synods shown that they are moving in this direction.

10. See G. Grisez, *Abortion: The Myths, the Realities and the Arguments*, Washington 1970.

11. See R. McCormick, "Das Prinzip der Doppelwirkung einer Handlung," *Concilium* 12 (1976), 662–670, 666.

12. The concept of the double effect of an action refers to a text in Thomas Aquinas (*ST* II-II, 64, 7): "*Nihil prohibet unius actus esse duos effectus, quorum alter solum sit in intentione, alius vero sit praeter intentionem. Morales autem actus recipiunt speciem secundum id quod intenditur, non autem ab eo quod est praeter intentionem . . . Potest tamen aliquis actus ex bona intentione proveniens illicitus reddi si non sit proportionatus fini.*" As F. Scholz has recently shown in a very convincing way, this passage in the *Summa* has frequently been totally misinterpreted. (See F. Scholz, *Wege, Umwege und Auswege der Moraltheologie. Ein Plädoyer für begründete Ausnahmen*, Munich 1976, 112–120.)

13. For the formulation of these conditions, see R. McCormick, "Das Prinzip der Doppelwirkung einer Handlung," *op. cit.*, 662; F. Scholz, *Wege, op. cit.*, 79; A. Vermeersch, *Theologia Moralis, Principia — Responsa — Consilia* I, Rome 1947, 105 ff.

14. By "means" we are, like Aristotle, referring to the datum toward which we are not striving as an aim for its own sake, but which we want to bring about intentionally for the sake of another aim that we want to reach. See Aristotle, *Nicomachean Ethics* I, 1 (1094 a 1–25) and I, 6 (1097 a 25–34).

15. F. Scholz, *Wege, op. cit.*, 125.

16. P. Knauer, "La détermination du bien et du mal moral par le principe du double effet," *Nouvelle Revue Théologique* 87 (1965), 356–376; *id.*,

"The Hermeneutic Function of the Principle of Double Effect," *Natural Law Forum* 12 (1967), 132–162; *id.*, "Überlegungen zur moraltheologischen Prinzipienlehre der Enzyklika 'Humanae vitae,'" *ThPh* 45 (1970), 60–74.

17. P. Knauer, "The Hermeneutic Function," *op. cit.*, 141.

18. "The action is proportionate to its reason" (P. Knauer, "La détermination du bien et du mal moral," *op. cit.*, 369.

19. "There is a proportionate reason when the act itself is proportionate to the value that it follows" (P. Knauer, "La détermination du bien et du mal moral," *op. cit.*, 368 f.).

20. This implies the sharp distinction between physical evil and what is morally bad that has in the past been given insufficient attention. As F. Scholz, *Wege, op. cit.*, 123, has pointed out, "A morally bad action is implied in this concept if physical evil is caused by man's action or omission, even if that evil cannot be realized." It is in this (new) sense that Knauer has retained the distinction between direct and indirect in the traditional argument: "the permission or causing of physical evil can be either direct or indirect, according to whether a corresponding reason is present or not." If there is a reason, "it occupies the same place as what is directly intended and determines the whole moral content of an action" ("The Hermeneutic Function of the Principle," *op. cit.*, 141).

21. L. Janssens, "Ontic Evil and Moral Evil," *Louvain Studies* 4 (1972), 115–156.

22. "*voluntas fertur in finem ut est ratio volendi ea quae sunt ad finem*" (*Summa Theologiae* I-II, 8, 3).

23. *Summa Theologiae* I-II, 12, 4 ad 3; see also 12, 1 ad 4.

24. "*Manifestum est ergo quod unus et idem motus voluntatis est quo fertur in finem, secundum quod est ratio volendi ea quae sunt ad finem, et in ipsa quae sunt ad finem*" (*Summa Theologiae* I-II, 8, 3).

25. "*Finis autem comparatur ad id quod ordinatur ad finem, sicut forma ad materiam*" (*Summa Theologiae* I-II, 4, 4).

26. "*Finis enim dat speciem in moralibus*" (*Summa Theologiae* II-II, 43, 3; cf. I-II, 1, 3).

27. L. Janssens, "Ontic Evil and Moral Evil," *op. cit.*, 141.

28. *Ibid.*, 140.

29. The distinction between direct and indirect that is involved here means, in fact, an identification of these concepts with the adequate reason.

30. B. Schüller, "Direkt Tötung — indirekte Tötung," *ThPh* 47 (1972), 341–357.

31. See above, note 20.

32. See F. Scholz, *Wege, op. cit.*, 125.

33. See B. Schlegelberger, *Vor- und außerehelicher Geschlechtsverkehr. Die Stellung der katholischen Moraltheologen seit Alphons von Liguori*, Remscheid 1970. In very much the same way, there is clear evidence of the continued validity of the order of law as it exists in the concrete for the indissolubility of marriage. (See R. Gall, *Fragwürdige Unauflöslichkeit der Ehe?* Zürich 1970.)

34. See B. Schüller, *Die Begründung sittlicher Urteile, op. cit.*, 180 ff.

35. Lying is a much deeper contradiction of the rational order. Truthfulness as a fundamental form of truth is so closely connected with it that it so to speak forms its *a priori*. In this case, the very principle of rationality is endangered by the contradiction itself (*Summa Theologiae* I-II, 18, 5; 94, 2). Moral activity is primarily rational activity that cannot be carried out in contradiction and realizes and fulfills human nature. (See F. Böckle and E. W. Böckenförde, eds., *Naturrecht in der Kritik, op. cit.*, 179–183.)

36. See above § 19.

37. See F. Suarez, *De legibus*, Lib. II, cap. 16, n. 6: "*lex autem secundum se spectata non praecepit actum nisi ut illum bonum esse supponit, nec prohibet nisi prout supponit intrinsece malum, et ideo ad intelligendum verum sensum naturalis praecepti, necesse est inquirere conditiones et circumstantias cum quibus actus ille secundum se malus est vel bonus, et haec vocatur interpretatio praecepti naturalis quoad verum sensum eius.*"

38. See A. Vermeersch, *De castitate et de vitiis contrariis*, Rome, 1921, note 305. This text is quoted by B. Schlegelberger, *Vor- undauß erehelicher Geschlechtsverkehr, op. cit.*, 129.

39. See K. Rahner, "Bemerkungen über das Naturgesetz und seine Erkennbarkeit," *Orientierung* 19 (1955), 239–243.

40. J. Ratzinger, "Theologie und Ethos," K. Ulmer, ed., *Die Verantwortung, op. cit.*, 57.

41. *Ibid.*

§ 24 The Church and Moral Norms, pp. 248–256.

1. K. Demmer, "Die Weisungskompetenz des kirchlichen Lehramts im Licht der spezifischen Perspektivierung neutestamentlicher Sittlichkeit," K. Demmer and B. Schüller, *Christlich glauben, op. cit.*, 143.

2. The frequently used concepts "authentic" and "infallible" belong to quite different spheres of thought. "Authentic" was originally a legal term and indicates an official proclamation of the Church as distinct from a private proclamation. The two concepts "fallible" and "infallible" describe a process in which judgment is involved. They are, in other words, not concerned with a knowledge of truth, but with the judgment as to whether this knowledge forms part of the deposit of faith or not.

3. A. Müller, *Das Problem von Befehl und Gehorsam im Leben der Kirche*, Einsiedeln 1964, 100.

4. In the enquiry that preceded the joint synod of the bishops of the Federal Republic of West Germany and formed part of the preparation for the synod, the most striking divergence of opinions was found in the sphere of sexuality and marriage. With regard to the prevention of conception, 61 per cent of West German Catholics thought differently from the official teaching of the Church, while, according to the survey at least, as many as 35 per cent had difficulties in this area. With regard to sexuality in general, 43 per cent had different views from those traditionally held, and even on the question of the indissolubility of marriage 39 per cent differed

from the Church's official teaching. See J. Gründel, "Kirche und moderne Wertsysteme," K. Forster, ed., *Befragte Katholiken*, Freiburg 1973, 64–72.

5. J. Mayer, "Die Notwendigkeit einer Autorität in religiös-sittlìchen Fragen," J. Mausbach, ed., *Moralprobleme*, Freiburg 1911, 248.

6. J. Fuchs, *Theologia moralis generalis*, Rome 1960, 71; A. Lanza and P. Palazzini, *Theologia moralis* I, Turin 1949, 13; J. Mausbach and G. Ermecke, *Katholische Moraltheologie* I, Münster 1954, 48.

7. O. Schilling, *Handbuch der Moral* I, Stuttgart 1952, 17.

8. J. Mausbach and G. Ermecke, *Katholische Moraltheologie* I, *op. cit.*, 48.

9. F. Hürth, *Notae ad praelect. theol. mor.* I, 38; J. Fuchs, *Theol. mor. gen.*, *op. cit.*, 71.

10. J. Mausbach and G. Ermecke, *Katholische Moraltheologie* I, *op. cit.*, 116; K. Hörmann, *Handbuch der christlichen Moral*, Innsbruck 1958, 84–86.

11. J. Mausbach and G. Ermecke, *Katholische Moraltheologie* I, *op. cit.*, 32.

12. F. Hürth, *Notae, op. cit.*, 8.

13. T. Bouquillon, *Instit. theol. mor. fundamentalis*, Bruges 1903, 214; see also R. Hofmann, *Moraltheologische Erkenntnis- und Methodenlehre*, Munich 1963, 147.

14. "*Ecclesiam posse etiam authentice et infallibiliter interpretari legem naturalem*": J. Aerdnys and C. Damen, *Theol. moralis* I, Turin 1956, 95, see also 122; see also H. Noldin, A. Tanquerey, Varceno and others.

15. J. Mausbach, *Katholische Moraltheologie* I, Münster 1922, 12; J. Mausbach and G. Ermecke, I, 44 f. See also K. Hörmann, *Lexikon der christlichen Moral*, Innsbruck 1969, 876, who expresses a similar view.

16. Among the examples that are given are adultery, infanticide and abortion as mortal sins. This, however, presupposes a very general concept and possible exceptions are not even considered. See L. van Peteghem, "Zekerheidsgraden in moraaltheologie," *Coll Gand* 28 (1945), 173–175.

17. See J. D. B. Hawkins, *Christian Morality*, London 1963, 63. Hawkins believed that a long list of solemn definitions of a moral kind could not be found alongside the dogmatic definitions of the Church, because Christianity did not offer a new moral code, but rather made it possible for the commandments to be known rationally and to be defended by reason, with the result that there was no need for any pronouncement on the part of the Church about those commandments in the form of articles of faith. On the other hand, Hawkins insisted that the Church had never ceased to admonish men morally at a less solemn level.

18. The address given by Pope Pius XII on 2 November 1954, quoted by K. Hörmann, "Die Zuständigkeit der Kirche für das Naturrecht nach der Lehre Pius' XII," J. Höffner *et al.*, eds., *Naturordnung. Festschrift für J. Messner*, Innsbruck 1961, 143.

19. "There is essentially no real difference between the *tamquam divinitus revelata credenda* of the Constitution *Dei Filius* of Vatican I and the *tamquam definitive tenenda* of the Constitution *Lumen Gentium* of Vatican II, since, as in the definition of papal infallibility (*doctrinam de fide vel moribus*

ab universa Ecclesia tenendam definit; DS 3074), the definitive tenere refers to the faith of the Church itself." (E. Klinger, "Die Unfehlbarkeit des ordentlichen Lehramts," K. Rahner, ed., *Zum Problem Unfehlbarkeit, QD* 54, Freiburg 1971, 277 f.)

20. See K. Rahner, "Kommentar zu Art. 25 der Dogmatischen Konstitution über die Kirche," *LThK* Vat. I: "In this way (*sancte custodiendum*), certain truths are included within the object of the Church's teaching authority which serve to protect the real deposit of revelation even if they have not formally been (either explicitly or implicitly) revealed themselves" (No. 236). Insofar as such truths and a corresponding faith of the Church are at all possible — and their existence is disputed by scholars — we are bound to ask whether rational moral insights can be an unconditioned presupposition for the preservation of the deposit of revelation (and if so, which insights satisfy this condition). To answer this question, we must know precisely what this revealed *depositum in re morali* is. This problem cannot be settled with a simple reference to the material presence of a moral demand in Scripture or tradition. (That should be obvious to anyone with a knowledge of the simplest rules of hermeneutics.) The concrete moral demands of the Bible are intimately connected with a historical and social process. This process has continued and is still continuing. The real problem is to be found in the mutual interrelationship of faith and progress.

21. Universal moral principles are not included in this category. Their unconditioned validity is the result of their tautological and explicative nature.

22. The commandment against divorce and remarriage in the present law of the Church is a good example of this. Marriage is indissoluble when three conditions are satisfied — the marriage must be validly solemnized, it must be a sacramental union between two Christians and it must be consummated. If one of these conditions is not satisfied, the marriage can be either declared null and void or dissolved. This normative rule has, like the decisions of the Council of Trent, two aspects. It expresses an indispensable demand made by the gospel and it also subjects that demand to contingent presuppositions. "Church praxis is not simply the teaching of the gospel, nor is it simply not contrary to the teaching of the gospel. It is rather alongside and in the line of the gospel, including it and making it concrete" (J. Ratzinger, "Zur Frage nach der Unauflöslichkeit der Ehe," *Ehe und Ehescheidung, Münchener Akademie-Schriften* 59, 1972, 49 f.).

Index

and grace, 185f.
and history, 187–188
human, 183–187
and liberation, 187
and man, 187
meanings of, 182
and need, 187
non-arbitrary, of social order, 206
order of, 190, 245–246
and praxis, 187f.
pure (natura pura), 185
and reason, 192f.
and rectitudo naturalis, 193f.
and science, 183
and theology of creation, 182f.
Needs, 31, 39f., 220f.
and instinct, 103
structure of, 183
Niederwimmer, K., 277, 278, 279, 285, 287, 292
Nielsen, E., 280, 282
Nomos, 167f.
Norms
concept of, 20–22
and custom, 21
and deontology, 243–247
and fashion, 21–22
"from below," 250f.
and insight, 224–227
and models of behavior, 178–179
and revealed moral demands, 225–227
and teleology, 236–243
unambiguity of, 225
and universal moral principles, 20f.

Obligation
ground of, 19–21, 30f., 198–200, 233
hypothetical, 20
justification of, 20f.
Oelmüller, W., 276, 277
Otte, G., 303

Parsons, T., 262
Participation, 61f., 192
Perfection, 164–167
Performance, 156, 174
Person
and body, 26–28, 106f., 109f., 120–121
and decision making, 110f., 166, 228
finitude of, 57f., 105
and interpersonal relationships, 184
and nature, 106f.
and soul, 26–28
Pesch, O.H., 276
Pesch, R., 278, 290, 291
Peukert, H., 267
Plack, A., 103
Plato, 187, 190
Pohlmann, R., 264
Promise
fulfillment of, 157–158
in New Testament, 98, 161f., 167f., 174–175
in Old Testament, 98, 135, 144
Property, Old Testament law of, 139ff.
Prophet
office of, 141–142
significance of, 141f.

Rad, G. von, 275, 281, 283, 284, 285
Radicalism, Christian, 84, 161f., 174, 231–233
Rahner, K., 263, 269, 276, 277, 305, 311, 313
Ratzinger, S., 290, 296, 311, 313
Reality of action, 16, 22
classification of, 22f.
Reason, 6
and critical reflection, 215–222
and judgment, 177f.
ordo rationis, 60, 191f.
Reich, W., 103
Responsibility, 85
and guilt, 73–75, 81
social, 104